T0247913

Democracy Unmoored

Democracy Unmoored

Populism and the Corruption of Popular Sovereignty

SAMUEL ISSACHAROFF

OXFORD
UNIVERSITY PRESS

OXFORD
UNIVERSITY PRESS

Oxford University Press is a department of the University of Oxford. It furthers
the University's objective of excellence in research, scholarship, and education
by publishing worldwide. Oxford is a registered trade mark of Oxford University
Press in the UK and certain other countries.

Published in the United States of America by Oxford University Press
198 Madison Avenue, New York, NY 10016, United States of America.

© Oxford University Press 2023

CIP data is on file at the Library of Congress

ISBN 978–0–19–767475–8

DOI: 10.1093/oso/9780197674758.001.0001

1 3 5 7 9 8 6 4 2

Printed by Sheridan Books, Inc., United States of America

For Julian, and the hope for better tomorrows.

CONTENTS

Introduction: The Populist Challenge

About a decade ago, I found myself alone for dinner one evening in Buenos Aires, the city of my birth. I had a lecture to give the next day, and I had reserved the time alone to prepare over dinner in a typical neighborhood restaurant. Such a "boliche," in the local *porteño* slang, was a comfortable setting to have a meal. I sat down to enjoy typical Argentine fare and the inescapable good wine and turned to my lecture materials. I soon found myself distracted by an excellent soccer match shown on a large-screen TV that had been brought in for the occasion. A couple of glasses of *tinto*, the reds of Mendoza province, and a close football game, and I accepted that lecture preparation was concluded.

This was no doubt the best of Argentina. Steak, wine, and football. I sat and allowed my thoughts to run to what might have been. What if I had not emigrated to the United States as a young boy? Would I have survived the dirty war of military repression that landed so heavily on my generation? Would I have achieved what became possible in emigration amid the constant economic and political disruptions? But also, would I appreciate the aspects of life in Buenos Aires that are still so alluring to the outside visitor?

Periodically, I would be drawn from the comfortable domain of steak, wine, and football to return to another reality of Argentina, one that well illustrates the central framework of this book. Every few minutes, an announcer would garishly proclaim that the football match was part of La Copa Kirchner. La Copa Kirchner? I had been engrossed in match play and was suddenly thrust back into the reality of Argentine politics. The national championship had been renamed in 2011 for Néstor Kirchner, the former president of Argentina, who had died the year before.

In itself, there is nothing striking about a country honoring a deceased head of state. In the U.S., we think nothing of naming cities, airports, bridges, sporting events, holidays, even clearance sales after our former presidents or other significant figures in our history. But the Argentine story was more complicated. Back in 2007, Néstor decided to forego a run for re-election. But the claim to a legacy continued; instead, he was succeeded as candidate to the presidency by his wife, Cristina Fernández de Kirchner. Cristina, known widely as CFK, proved a strong candidate and became president. Again, not remarkable. In the U.S., we have had the families of the Adams, Harrisons, Roosevelts, and Bushes follow in electoral success. What was distinct was that I was watching the Copa Kirchner in the run up to the presidential election of 2012, in which CFK was running for re-election.

Joy over a perfect Argentine evening quickly turned to deeper concern during the match's halftime. Instead of the usual sports commentary, the entire halftime show was a tribute to the wise and courageous leadership of Néstor Kirchner, a sign of the ongoing Argentine trauma of Peronism. To the untrained eye of a foreigner stumbling upon this spectacle, the tribute might have appeared as bordering on election propaganda for the incumbent president as successor to the Kirchner legacy. To the more discerning eye, there could be no ambiguity. The government had hijacked the most important domestic sports event to brand it as its own. It was as if a sitting president in the U.S. renamed the Super Bowl as a family tribute.

La Copa Kirchner was hardly an isolated event in the process of government ingratiation with its base. In 2009, the Argentine government under Cristina Kirchner had nationalized the cable television stations that broadcast football matches in Argentina, the Fútbol Para Todos (Soccer for All) program, with the indisputable claim that soccer was the birthright of all Argentines. So by the time of the first broadcast of the Copa Kirchner, there was no doubt of the mass audience for the halftime tribute to Kirchner's legacy as president. A leading Argentine newspaper, *La Nación*, prompted a scandal by estimating that the Fútbol Para Todos program amounted to hundreds of millions of dollars of free publicity for the incumbent Peronist ticket of Cristina Fernández de Kirchner. Undeterred, the government then decreed that poorer Argentines may have need for new digital televisions to take advantage of the largesse, and then—only months before the 2012 presidential elections—decreed a new TVs for All program for subsidized purchases of new model televisions.

Government largesse in an election year knew no bounds. It turned out that football was not the only legacy that the Kirchner administration could bestow on all Argentines. For the poor, suddenly there were the Beef for All subsidies inaugurated during the election year. And that was followed by the Dairy Products for All campaign. And to top it off, the program that in translation captures it all—the Pork for All initiative.

Putting aside my reflections of the evening, as scheduled I continued the next day to give a lecture to the Argentine Society of International Law on the use of drones and the legal dimensions of war against nonstate actors. That was the consuming issue of the day for the U.S. and the Obama administration, and one that engaged much of my thinking.

But the image of the halftime political tribute in the midst of an election campaign tugged at me. What are the limits of the use of executive power in a democracy? How can democracy ensure electoral accountability in the increasing world of executive domination? What happens when the executive dominates the legislature through partisan alignment, as argued in the American context by my colleagues Daryl Levinson and Richard Pildes,[1] or simply through the accretion of unilateral administrative authority?

Upon further reflection, I realized that this was not a new question for me. Encountering the use of great executive power to tilt the playing field of what remained formally an electoral democracy was an ongoing feature of the 21st century. I had dramatically encountered a similar set of issues only a few years earlier.

In 2006, on the eve of Hugo Chávez's re-election as president of Venezuela, I found myself sneaking into a hotel room in Caracas for a meeting with the heads of the major opposition newspapers and television stations. I was in Venezuela to give some lectures on freedom of the press at the invitation of the State Department, a challenging tour given the virulent anti-Americanism of the regime. By the time I got to this hotel room, a newspaper site I was supposed to speak at had been blown up the night before, and things had been thrown in my face while lecturing at the University of Caracas.

But that hotel meeting allowed me to understand the new world of incipient authoritarianism. Would-be autocrats around the world no longer relied on the detention camps, the tanks in the street, the machine guns in the hands of soldiers on the street corner. What Venezuela rolled out, the "Chávez playbook," was a new form of repression within the law, substituting intralegal abuse for the crude human rights abuses of yesteryear.

The independent media of Venezuela described a world that today seems almost routine. Vilification of the press, accusations of faking the news, and claims of being foreign agents were the first layer of an increasingly charged information environment. Pro-government publishers found themselves with privileged access to state information and interviews. Government public service advertisements doled out on a strictly partisan basis provided a blatant subsidy for Chávez-friendly newspaper views. Demands for government access for prime-time presidential discourses (*la hora del comandante*) cut into important advertising time for the networks, threatening their financial viability. For the pro-government media, lavish state buys were ready substitutes. For the less servile, the bottom-line consequences were severe.

Most unexpected, however, was the answer to my question of the most immediate threat to journalistic independence. For the newspaper editor directly next to me, the answer came quickly. He recounted dozens of defamation suits brought directly or indirectly by the government as a result of his newspaper's articles and editorials. Even more surprising was the burst of laughter from the other fifteen people in the room. I was stunned. I protested that they must understand the tremendous resources of time, money, and will that would be necessary to defend one's integrity against repeated legal processes. They then made clear that I had no idea why they were laughing.

In turn, they each recounted the defamation suits filed against them. The first to speak had almost one hundred. Then the numbers piled up with each successive speaker. By the time the director of the leading all-news station spoke, the numbers were astronomical. This one brave journalistic leader reported over 5,000 defamation actions against him. They had laughed at the first speaker not because this was not a huge attempt to silence dissent but because of the relatively modest number of lawsuits that the first journalist had encountered thus far.

While the confrontation with the growing illiberalism of the Chávez regime was arresting, I could not help but be aware we were meeting up in the hills of East Caracas, the wealthier precincts of that divided city, near the Caracas Country Club, long the bastion of Venezuelan privilege. The attempt to silence critics through the instrumentalities of law and the state captured the disregard for democracy of the Chávez regime, but it could not explain the regime's solid base of support. The leafy neighborhoods of East Caracas, as well as the institutions of culture and free expression that were nurtured there, coexisted with wrenching poverty and one of the worst inequalities of wealth among any nation on earth.[2]

By the end of the 20th century, Venezuela was the richest nation in all of Latin America,[3] a resounding success story not only economically but also based on its status as a strong, uninterrupted democracy, which stood out compared to its neighbors.[4] Unfortunately, as is the fate that befalls countries relying on extractive industries, a subsequent drop in oil prices doomed Venezuela. Moisés Naím, Venezuela's minister of trade and industry from 1989 to 1999, observed in 2001:

> The disappearance of the party system that dominated Venezuelan politics for more than four decades was not a sudden, Soviet-style collapse resulting from an excessive concentration of power in the hands of a small clique of politicians; in fact, Chávez's ascendancy owes more to the long-term dilution of the political power once held by Acción Democrática (AD) and COPEI, Venezuela's two main political parties.[5]

Indeed, from Naím's vantage, the policy package that exacerbated inequality in the mid-1990s represented two factors. First, entrenched political actors becoming detached from local forces like labor unions, and, second, a full-scale capitulation to "anti-elite" sentiment:

> During this period, the two political parties that were the building blocks of Venezuelan democracy for more than five decades lost almost all of their influence, as did the country's business, labor, and intellectual elites. A new set of hitherto unknown political actors emerged, along with new rules of the game. Elections and referenda proliferated, with voters going to the polls five times in 18 months during 1999 and 2000.[6]

The following day rounded out the picture of the popular support that would lead to Chávez's re-election. I was flying back to the U.S., but a tropical downpour and a mudslide had taken out the modern highway bridge that connected downtown to the airport. Instead, I had to cross over the old road in the hills above the city, a poorly paved two-lane road that ran through the precarious villages and shantytowns that invariably surround Latin American capitals. Amid the poverty and the signs of gang domination stood out one feature that I had not seen before. In just about every hamlet, there was a spotless, brown hexagonal building in the main square or intersection in perfect repair and freshly painted.

Each of those small but distinctive buildings was a health clinic provided for and staffed by the Cuban government. Exporting medical services was no doubt a propaganda effort by Cuba intended to shore up an ally in Latin America. But, who cares? This was medical services for people living in pretty desperate conditions. If access to health services cemented support for Chávez among the laboring poor, it was hard to see this as other than an indictment of the elites who had so long ruled in Venezuela and used the accumulated oil wealth in ways that left so much of the population at risk. Political gain for the regime? No doubt. But, no one can claim that the U.S. creation of Medicare and Medicaid, or the extension of prescription drug coverage, or the insurance protection of pre-existing medical conditions did not redound to the political benefit of each president who brought new health protections to the voters.

Health services in poor regions are only the beginning of the story. In order to cement their electoral base, populist leaders redirected important resources to the poorest parts of the population. For Venezuela, the source was oil revenue. For other populist leaders in the region, such as President Rafael Correa of Ecuador or the Kirchners in Argentina, the gains from the commodity boom of the 2000s permitted genuine redistribution and attention to the neglected sectors of the society. As expressed by advisers to the current Argentine regime, "We're putting meat on the grill for those who put us in power. . . . The debt can wait."[7] But the cost was a massive expansion of the state sector and the consolidation of economic power in the service of a personalist political agenda. When the oil market became glutted or the seemingly insatiable Chinese demand for soy and other commodities slackened, then suddenly these populist regimes stood exposed amid scandal and insolvency.

Latin America went through this cycle first, but now the same question of how democracy operates in the face of immediate demands of populism confronts the entire democratic world.

* * *

These personal observations set the foundation for this book. The inquiry begins with the simple observation that democracy today is under siege, but from a source that could hardly have been imagined in the world before the fall of the Berlin Wall. For much of the 20th century, the existential threat to democracy was authoritarian rule. The modern language of human rights was born to thwart the usage of state authority in bending the population to the will of the rulers. Human rights defined the inalienability of an irreducible core of human dignity. The rights holder was the individual at risk. In turn, this rights discourse became the lingua franca of the empowered judiciary that took hold in Europe after World War II and then across so much of the world in the post-1989 third wave of democratization.[8]

The 20th century closed with a certain vision of market-based liberal democracy triumphant against its ideological rivals of fascism and communism. The imprecise contours of ascendant democracy included generally robust markets, welfarist protections for citizens, a broad commitment to secularism (even in countries with an established church), and liberal tolerance of dissent and rival political organizations. All this was packaged in robust constitutional protections of civil liberties and the integrity of the political order. And, characteristic of the era, all was under the supervision of increasingly commanding constitutional courts or other apex tribunals.

These features were sufficiently widespread that a great deal of imprecision could be accepted in the exact pedigree of this new world order. It was the ascendency of both democracy and of constitutionalism. It represented the triumph of liberalism and the realization of the Enlightenment project. It was both the vindication of capitalism and the realization of the state of social welfare. Precisely because it seemed to be all at once, the conflict between majoritarian politics and constitutional restraint, between the creative destruction of markets and social guarantees, between liberty and security, all could be pushed aside.

The fall of the Soviet empire was the crowning achievement of the postwar democratic order. Yet, the triumphant era of what Samuel Huntington termed the third wave of democracy would not last much into the new millennium.[9] The democratic euphoria following the fall of the Berlin Wall barely ran its course before it confronted a new virulent reaction to the new modern imperium. In short order, Islamic-inspired terror introduced a malevolent new international actor. The Arab Spring collapsed into familiar patterns of tyranny or, as in Syria, violent communal strife. By the early 2000s, a number of newly minted democracies were retreating to customary forms of autocratic rule.

But the biggest shocks came not from the periphery but from within the established democratic order. These shocks were not the product of military conflict or attempts at violent overthrow but were instead largely prompted by economic insecurity and the changing demographics of a globalized world. Populist upsurges from right and left revealed the disrepair of the post–World War II general consensus of politics in the democratic world. From France to India, the historic parties such as Congress, the socialists, and the Gaullists were discredited and effectively pushed outside the political order. Brexit prevailed over strenuous opposition from within both the Tories and Labour. The American presidential election of 2016 featured a determined Democratic run by Bernie Sanders, not even a member of that party, and the eventual victory by President Trump, a candidate with only fleeting relations to the Republican Party. The new political challenge saw democracy not as the culmination of the postwar era but as a failed elite endeavor that had left the laboring classes vulnerable. Populist leaders, from left and right, learned to bypass institutionalized forms of politics in favor of direct and frequent communications with the population, from Hugo Chávez's frequent multi-hour television appearances to Donald Trump's infatuation with Twitter.

Even before the dramatic assault on the U.S. Capitol in the waning hours of the Trump presidency, ascendant populism had made clear its rejection of the foundations of modern democratic governance. The secret to democratic stability is repeat play, which requires an extended time horizon. Time allows the losers of today the prospect of reorganizing and emerging as the winners of tomorrow. An election may yield a bad result, the tenor of the era may prompt poor legislation, but what remains critical is the capacity to recover. The American experiment in democratic self-rule was consolidated in the election of 1800, which represented the first time a head of state had been removed through electoral means. In his wide-eyed review of American democracy, de Tocqueville thought that the key to non-aristocratic rule was the capacity to make what he termed retrievable mistakes.[10] At the time, he assumed that the challenge to successful democratic governance would be military intercession, as with the disastrous War of 1812, that would shorten the time horizon needed for republican prospects.

The constricting force today is not external but internal, notwithstanding the continuing threats of terrorism and the reorganization of international relations in light of Chinese ascendancy. Populist impulses shorten the time frame of relevant political consequences and turn everything into a bimodal choice, a political life defined by existential issues. Us or them, success or perfidy, the people or the oligarchs, our nation or foreigners. There can be no spirit of partial victory, of legitimate disagreement, or even of mutual gain through engagement. The effects of compressed time horizons can be seen in the willingness to discard long-standing institutional rules that protect the minority, such as the Senate filibuster in the U.S., in favor of immediate political gain. Efforts to alter election rules or the powers held by elected governments, as shown in the American context in North Carolina or Wisconsin, are perhaps the most combustible manifestation of the current challenge to the necessary long horizon of stable democratic governance. The stable democracies pass from being a challenge among adversaries to an unyielding battle against enemies, to borrow from Michael Ignatieff.[11]

Democratic politics under the sway of populism loses the sense of collective enterprise among all political actors. Not only does the commitment to repeat play drop out, but so does the limitation on what the victors can expect to do. Modern democracies govern through institutional arrangements that run the gamut from separation of powers at the formal level of the state to the private associations that provide stability and continuity over time, most notably the political parties that undergird a stable political order. Populism, noted Isaiah Berlin a half century ago,

> is not principally interested in political institutions, although it is prepared to use the state as an instrument for the purpose of producing its ends. But a state organization is not its aim and the state is not its ideal human association. It believes in society rather than in the state. . . . All these movements believe in some kind of moral regeneration. . . . There must have been a spiritual fall somewhere. Either the fall is in the past or it is threatening—one of the two. Either innocence has been lost and some kind of perversion of men's nature has occurred, or enemies are breeding within or attacking from without.[12]

This book will largely follow Berlin's diagnosis of populism as being grounded in political mobilization in disregard of the institutions of governance. Much has been written on the economic preconditions for the current populist surge,[13] and the role of failing economic fortunes in prompting a backlash in politics,[14] particularly in the face of immigration.[15] Others have focused on the role of social media in allowing mass incitement outside the boundaries of established political institutions.[16] Many ground the investigation in the particulars of a single country.[17] Others, most notably Jan-Werner Müller, look to the clientelism and demagogy that are characteristic of populist leaders.[18]

Each of these approaches captures an important strain of the nature of populism and its threat to democratic governance. For present purposes, however, the striking feature is the anti-institutionalism of populism both as a political movement and as a governance strategy. The attack on Congress's ceremonial function of counting the electoral votes for president is both symbol and substance of the war on inherited forms of governance. In the assault of the immediate, democratic institutional arrangements are particularly vulnerable.

Populist elections claim a mandate from the people that goes beyond choosing officeholders. Elections over mandates risk the same repudiation of institutional accommodation of divisions as do plebiscites. It is not that populism is plebiscitary as such; rather, neither is well suited to institutionalized politics that presume deliberation, procedural order, and compromise. For both plebiscites and populism, the immediate election defines the agenda. Both populism and plebiscites look to the maximal leader rather than the legislature as the source of deliverance. In turn, the ensuing *caudillo* politics yields a web of cronyism, corruption, and clientelism all turning on relations to the commander.

Previously my attention was devoted to the distinct frailties of new democracies as they emerge from conflict or an autocratic past.[19] One of the defining characteristics is that the complete package of democratic institutions rarely mature together, or quickly. Democracy proves to be a complicated interaction among popular sovereignty, political competition, stable institutions of state, vibrant organs of civil society, meaningful political intermediaries, and a commitment to the idea that the losers of today have a credible chance to reorganize and perhaps emerge as the winners of tomorrow. Few if any of these criteria are likely to be satisfied amid the birth pangs of a new democratic order.

What is striking in the current era is that the mature democracies encounter the same forms of institutional failure as the necessarily weak nascent democracies, even if the clock seems to be running in reverse. In virtually all democracies, the populist onslaught is accompanied by the increased command of a hypertrophic executive. There are the odd exceptions as in Poland, where power is effectively wielded from outside the formal command structure of the state, but populist governance yields strongman rule, regardless of the national setting. As a result, any explanation of the weakness of democratic politics in the face of populism cannot rest on the merely conjunctural. The weak recovery from the financial crisis of 2008 certainly provides fuel to the fire. But the seemingly overnight rise of populist challenges and the failures of conventional postwar political institutions to channel the political upsurge requires greater explanation.

It is also possible to root particular populist impulses in domestic national settings. No doubt reforms in American laws governing political parties and campaign finance have weakened the parties as institutions. Similarly, persistent weak government in Britain under an unstable coalition contributed to the Brexit upheaval. And Italy had Berlusconi, Spain had the housing bust, France had untenably high unemployment, and so on. But the persistence of this pattern across stable democracies prompts an inquiry beyond the national level. Unlike the populist wave that swept Latin America in the early 2000s, populism in the U.S. and Europe is not aspirational in terms of national policy but angry at a sense of loss and betrayal. As expressed by Cas Mudde and Cristóbal Rovira Kaltwasser:

> Whereas in Latin America the emphasis is on *establishing* the conditions for a good life for "the people," in Europe populists primarily focus on *protecting* these conditions, which they consider increasingly threatened by outside forces (notably immigrants). Hence, their prime focus is on the exclusion of the outgroups rather than on the inclusion of (parts of) the ingroup.[20]

The sense of loss provides the combustible material for a charismatic leader organizing on the basis of rejection of customary politics and the institutional order. True, Jarosław Kaczyński does not command charismatically, and Brexit caught on without a dominant individual at the head of the movement. Nonetheless, the standard mix is familiar across the democratic world. Cas Mudde elaborates:

> The populist heartland becomes active only when there are special circumstances: most notably, the combination of persisting political resentment, a (perceived) serious challenge to "our way of life," and the presence of an attractive populist leader. However, what sets the populist heartland apart from other protest-prone groups is their *reactiveness*; they generally have to be mobilized by a populist actor, rather than taking the initiative themselves.[21]

Behind the momentary events in any particular country stands the perception of democratic rule serving as cover for the failure of elites to address the security and prosperity of citizens of the advanced democratic societies. Much as the topic at hand opens the door to all sorts of failings of modern democracy, the immediate task must remain narrower. To return to the opening theme, the challenge to democracy is not primarily state repression but institutional failure. The language of human rights poorly captures the tension when the electoral choice of the voting public is impulsive, demagogic, unconstrained by the language or norms of governance, and oftentimes publicly committed to unwinding the very institutional arrangements that allowed populist electoral success in the first place. The mark of the authoritarian regimes of the 20th century was the ready recourse to *extralegal* means of oppression to reinforce brute power. By contrast, the current populist leaders rely heavily on their electoral mandate and choose the means of *intralegal* mechanisms to wear their opponents down. Rather than tyranny wielded by a state-enabled minority, populism risks the tyranny of the majority threatening to break through institutional constraints.

In turn, the altered nature of the threat to democratic integrity requires a different metric for legal intervention, one separated from the customary protection of individual autonomy that characterizes the primary human rights domain. It is important to emphasize, as do Levitsky and Way, these regimes are dependent on electoral approbation as the foundation of political legitimacy, and the combination of "meaningful democratic institutions and authoritarian incumbents creates distinctive opportunities and constraints."[22] Following their definition, these are "civilian regimes in which formal democratic institutions exist and are widely viewed as the primary means of gaining political power, but they are not democratic because the playing field is heavily skewed in favor of incumbents. Competition is thus real but unfair."[23] To the extent that opponents of current populist demagogues engage in facile comparisons of such elected authoritarians to Nazis or fascists or communists, they are wide of the mark. Whatever the autocratic inclinations of the rulers,[24] these are not the authoritarian regimes of yesteryear.

The question then becomes whether there are forms of legal intervention that may preserve democratic accountability by frustrating the populist claim to permanence. In what follows, I address three primary issues. First is the sources of populist ascendency against the established democratic order of the post–World War II period. Second, I turn to the institutional dimensions of populist governance. And third (and with the most difficulty), I address the reforms that might restore some sense of order in the house of democracy. Each of the three parts of the book focuses on the relation between populism and how a democratic society is governed. The thesis that will emerge is that the populist insurgency following the 2008 financial debacle found democracies with weak and poorly performing governance institutions. In turn, populist politics took aim at these institutional buffers, what Levitsky and Ziblatt usefully term the "guardrails" provided by state institutional practices.[25] The toxic combination of weak governance and the populist assault contributed to a world of increasingly autocratic elected leaders. Finally, the institutional inquiry frames the hardest part of the enterprise: considering what ameliorative steps might be on the agenda.

PART I

THE WORLD
THE POPULISTS FOUND

The Frayed Social Fabric
of Democracy

It is difficult to recapture the optimism that filled the democratic world only a quarter century ago. It was not just that the 20th century saw the defeat of the great ideological challenges of fascism and communism. It was also the sense that, unbound from authoritarianism, the forces of democratization and markets would unleash a world of freedom and prosperity unmatched in human history. Certainly there was merit to the claim. In short order, more humans were able to select their rulers in reasonably free elections, state repression waned, and expressive liberties reached the far corners of the globe. Perhaps more impressive, the period between the fall of the Berlin Wall and the financial crash of 2008 saw more people lifted from poverty than at any other time in human history—indeed, more than most would have thought possible. It seemed that the proponents of democratic governance and liberal freedoms were poised for a well-merited victory lap.

On this victory lap, democratic enthusiasts could observe that, over the past two centuries, democracies had outfought, out-innovated, and out-produced their rivals. With singular capacity, democracies raised the living standards of the broad masses of their populations, raised education levels to permit citizen engagement, and at the same time were able to trust powerful militaries to protect them from foreign assault without themselves succumbing to military rule. History is obviously much more complicated, and this is a somewhat tendentious reading, but it captures the ideological consensus that prevailed after the collapse of the Soviet empire and the brief era of apparent democratic universalism.

For many observers, myself included, the question of the day was how quickly these newly liberated parts of the world would achieve the levels of prosperity and liberty associated with the advanced democratic countries. And indeed, many countries went on to hold elections for heads of state and legislatures. But rotation in office and toleration of the opposition and of rival political parties developed slowly or not at all. By 2006, the democratic tide was receding and the number of countries classified as democratic began to decline.[1] Certainly, the retrocession took place in some of the former Soviet Republics of central Asia and southeastern Europe, regions that seemed foreboding terrain for democracy under any circumstances. In hindsight, elections and the appearance of democratic choice were the product of a temporary disruption of strongman rule, unlikely to survive the first reconsolidation of state authority.[2]

Yet lurking behind democratic triumphalism were signs that the foundations of democracy inherited from the 19th century were eroding. It was these foundations of citizen engagement and elite commitment to electoral accountability that had allowed these democracies to prevail across what Philip Bobbitt terms the "long war" of the 20th century.[3] When World War II dispatched the forces of fascism, the history of the second half of the 20th century became the battle of democracy against the communist empire of the Soviet Union and its client states, at least until the independent rise of China. Unlike the decisive defeat of the Axis powers in World War II, there never was a decisive military confrontation with the Soviet Union. Instead, there were brutal but confined conflicts in Korea and Vietnam, hosts of proxy wars from Indonesia and the Philippines to Central America, and even confrontations whose Cold War underpinnings may now be obscured. To give just one example, the United States backed the apartheid National Party of South Africa while the Soviet Union funneled resources to the African National Congress. The decades long struggle against South African racialism quickly came to a close after the fall of the Berlin Wall.

In hindsight, the ultimate battlefield of the Cold War was economic. To be sure, there was a military component to the economic contest. The maintenance of the Soviet bloc and the arms race with the U.S. took a tremendous economic toll, especially with the escalation of the latter by the Reagan administration. But the struggle for the hearts and minds of the world, as well as the loyalty of the West's working classes to the capitalist order, was waged in terms of what a market economy versus central planning could deliver.

Looking ahead to the 21st century, the critical challenge to democracy would emerge when that market order largely ceased to deliver—or at least was no longer perceived to tilt upward—to greater generalized prosperity. No account of the rise of populism in the 21st century can ignore the erosion of working-class incomes in the advanced industrial countries over the last decades of the 20th century. Whatever sentiments of nationalism, xenophobia, and outright racism might infect the current populist surge, any fair rendering begins with the sense of economic insecurity among the laboring classes.

Consequently, the account of democratic decline must begin in the economic domain.

I. Freedom from Want

On January 6, 1941, Franklin Roosevelt delivered a transcendent State of the Union Address, preparing the nation for the likelihood of war and taking the first steps with the Lend Lease Program, thereby offering a lifeline to the United Kingdom, and setting the nation on the path to direct confrontation.[4] The speech is remembered for its proclamation of Four Freedoms, including "freedom from want—which, translated into world terms, means economic understandings which will secure to every nation a healthy peacetime life for its inhabitants— everywhere in the world." Together with freedom of expression, freedom of worship, and freedom from fear, the address introduced a guarantee of material well-being into the arsenal of democracy.

The inclusions of material security as one of the essential freedoms provided the ideological linchpin for the New Deal and its radical expansion of the wel- farist state. At the same time, the speech redefined international relations by in- viting competition over the ability to provide enhanced social welfare for the citizenry. The Four Freedoms transformed the claims for the superiority of de- mocracy against other social orders. Roosevelt's speech served as "the moral backbone behind the establishment of the United Nations, and it informed the creation of both the European Union and NATO. If the New Deal was . . . a pro- ject comparable only to the French Revolution in its enduring political signifi- cance, then the Four Freedoms address was its Declaration of the Rights of Man and Citizen."[5]

That economic commitment provoked immediate dissent from market apostles such as Friedrich Hayek and backers in the banking class still harkening for the Gilded Age before the Great Depression. For them, "what was promised to us as the Road to Freedom was in fact the High Road to Servitude."[6] As Hayek was to sum up several decades later, Roosevelt's claim that democratic freedom encompassed not just liberty but also economic returns to ordinary citizens mandated state responsibility inconsistent with a classic liberal commitment to laissez-faire. Such promises, the argument ran, "could not be made universal within a system of rules of just conduct based on the conception of individual responsibility, and so require that the whole society be converted into a single organization, that is, made totalitarian in the fullest sense of the word."[7]

Following the Depression, the world war, the reconstruction of Europe under the Marshall plan, and the emergence of social democratic commitments in the postwar period, the arguments about democracy as limited to the preservation of autonomous individual liberties ceased to define the era. In the U.S., once the Four Freedoms became enshrined in the iconic paintings of Norman Rockwell (Figure 1.1), the ability to deliver prosperity to the masses became not only a centerpiece of the claimed superiority of democracy and markets but also the keystone of the American century.

Figure 1.1   Norman Rockwell, *Freedom from Want* (1943).

For my parents who watched the Hollywood movies of the postwar era in Argentina, the splendor of America seemed overwhelming. An actor unable to sleep would wander to the kitchen to open what seemed to be a massive refrigerator door and grab a leftover chicken drumstick to snack on. Seen from a country where refrigerators were only then coming within the reach of consumers and where chicken was a luxury item (oddly, beef was a staple), the combined image of a home refrigerator and excess chicken was beyond reach, if not simply inconceivable.

Fast forward to the height of the Cold War period and the "cultural exchange" between the U.S. and Russia in the late 1950s. At that point, the freedom from want championed by Roosevelt was no longer simply the broad justification of New Deal intervention into economic affairs to restore security following the Great Depression. Rather, freedom from want, and indeed growing affluence, became the challenge of the American century to non-democratic states as incapable of delivering prosperity to their citizens.

An illustrative high point was the construction of exhibit halls by Russia in New York City and by the U.S. in Moscow. When the Moscow exhibit opened in 1959, Vice President Nixon escorted Premier Khrushchev through a model American home filled with devices unknown in the Soviet Union, such as color television sets. But it was in the model kitchen, of the sort that so impressed my parents in Argentina, that Khrushchev famously blew up at Nixon and proclaimed, "We have powerful weapons, too, and ours are better than yours if you want to compete."[8] The tension between the two was building throughout the engagement, but it begs noticing that the final trigger appeared to be the labor-saving devices and small kitchen luxuries available to ordinary Americans everyday. Khrushchev's outburst began with the promise—never realized—that the Soviet Union would overtake the U.S. in providing material comforts for its working population.

A similar story may be told about Europe in the postwar period. The 1972 Munich Olympics will forever be associated with the massacre of Israeli athletes and, quite secondarily, with the introduction of systematic doping by the East German delegation. But 1972 also played an important role in destabilizing the Soviet bloc. East Germany had only recently been afforded member status in the Olympic community, and the regime wanted to show off Soviet-era athletic prowess (before the doping came to light) as evidence of superiority over the West. As a result, East Germany allowed for live broadcasting of the Munich Olympics to a population that had been fed a steady diet of regime propaganda about the imminent collapse of the capitalist world. What captivated East Germans were the live television images of the magnificent West German roadways around Munich, the elegance of the street life, and the size and quality of the automobiles.[9] For a population barely recovered from the wartime devastation of the country a quarter-century earlier, the images starkly undermined all the claims about East German superiority, particularly with regard to the living standards of the mass of working people.

Material well-being sustained a complicated faith of working people in Western democracy. Over the postwar period, support for the Western communist parties steadily fell, and the social democratic left, deeply rooted in the trade union movement, emerged as a dominant political actor in country after country. Working-class loyalty to unions and center-left political parties provided stability for democracies, even across the cultural upheavals of the 1960s. The political dynamics were defined by the national setting, and some social democrats found themselves in coalition governments with increasingly domesticated Communist Parties. Others, including the American Democratic Party, remained staunchly anticommunist, while following a similar trajectory of generous labor rights and state welfarist policies.

A similar story could be told across the aisle for centrist democratic politics. Christian Democrats in Europe, the Tories in the UK, and the Republicans in the U.S. all offered a similar solicitude to the material aspirations of small businesses, farmers, and other vulnerable entrepreneurs who a generation or two previously might have been seduced by fascists or the nativist right. Here, too, the steady economic uplift of the postwar period, together with farm subsidies and small-business loans, secured the loyalty of this broad and potentially politically volatile sector to the welfarist state of a booming economic period.

So long as the postwar economic expansion held, and so long as working-class aspirations were tied institutionally to stable domestic governance, the stage was set for the triumphalism that greeted the ultimate collapse of the Soviet bloc. But that state of affairs did not hold. The reasons are varied and complex, turning on some measures of decreased productivity gains in the economy,[10] globalized production and distribution networks, growing immigration, and other trends that disrupted prosperous but once-protected economies in the developed world. This volume will focus not on the causes but on the consequences of the disruption that ensued. One can accept that the postwar economies were being unsettled by the time the Soviet Union collapsed without necessarily agreeing on the relative contribution of the many factors that led to that state of affairs.

Democratic decline and the rise of populist anger are not simply products of economic stagnation and retrocession. Still, continuing economic expansion and rising incomes foster a sociological mood of rising expectations, as well as an optimism that might be essential for the collective enterprise of democracy. That is a topic for later discussion.

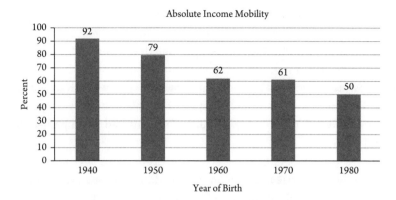

Figure 1.2   *Source:* YASCHA MOUNK, THE PEOPLE VS. DEMOCRACY: WHY OUR FREEDOM
IS IN DANGER AND HOW TO SAVE IT 155 (2018).

Figure 1.2 illustrates the demise of rising expectations. Perhaps more telling in terms of immediate political consequences is the present-day sense of vulnerability and fear of falling further behind that stem from the same broad-scale economic transformations. If democracy relies on a collective sense of upward possibility, then the sense of how a young generation will succeed relative to the parental generation is a domestic shorthand for hope. For the generation born during World War II and the baby boom thereafter, there was a period of seemingly endless expectations relative to the privations of war and the Depression. But the time line also introduces evidence of failed expectations and the lack of hope that is increasingly present throughout the country, particularly in those areas that were once the industrial hearth of a burgeoning economy. In place of rising optimism of the American century of the postwar period comes a world of drug addiction, widescale depression and despair, and—shockingly— a lowering of life expectancy for non-college-educated whites, once the stable foundation of the American economy.[11]

II. Falling Behind

While the roots of the modern populist era are many, none is as explosively decisive as the 2008 financial meltdown.[12] In the years preceding the meltdown, the U.S. economy redirected more activity into the financial sector than it ever had before. "At its peak in 2006, the financial services sector contributed 8.3 percent to US GDP, compared to 4.9 percent in 1980 and 2.8 percent in 1950."[13] Capital assets, even home ownership, became the target of securitization in the ensuing redirection of energy and creativity. Financial expansion not only put the holdings of ordinary people at risk, but it also crowded out real economic development in industry, particularly the research and development that are normally considered "engines for growth."[14] And so more than any other event, the economic downturn triggered a strong sense that the system of advancement was rigged, that state resources would always be available to protect the privileged, and that massive, destructive fraud could go unpunished when perpetrated by the top 1 percent.

However great the political and economic dislocations after the 2008 meltdown, these did not arise in a vacuum. Even within the economic domain itself, the financial crash came at the end of a protracted cycle of eroding real wages among the same working- and middle-class sectors that had been the backbone of democratic stability. The "elephant curve" produced by the World Bank, reproduced in Figure 1.3, depicts the global redistribution of wealth and income growth over the twenty-year period leading into the financial meltdown, perhaps as significant as any ever recorded.[15] On the horizontal axis, the entire population of the world is arrayed from the poorest to the richest in 5 percent increments; the vertical axis tracks each segment's income gains or losses from 1988 to 2008. The graph shows a stunning rise in the real incomes of the great majority of the world's population, with huge numbers rising from poverty—primarily, though not exclusively, the result of the Chinese economic transformation.

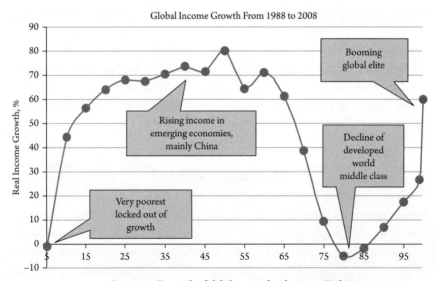

Figure 1.3   *Source:* Branko Milanovic, *Global Income Inequality by the Numbers: In History and Now—An Overview* 7–8 (World Bank Dev. Research Grp., Working Paper No. 6259, 2012), http://documents1.worldbank.org/curated/en/959251468176687085/pdf/wps6259.pdf, http://perma.cc/Q3U3-5EL8.

With the exception of the very poorest of the poor, over the past thirty years, lives around the world have transformed from extreme poverty to levels of income, health, material possessions, and life prospects that begin to challenge those of the advanced industrial democracies. While this pattern has halted under the pandemic strains of COVID-19, it is nonetheless impossible to overstate the dramatic change in prospects for the well-being of the human race overall. As Figure 1.4 demonstrates, there has never been such a dramatic change in the circumstances of the world's poor in such a short period of time.

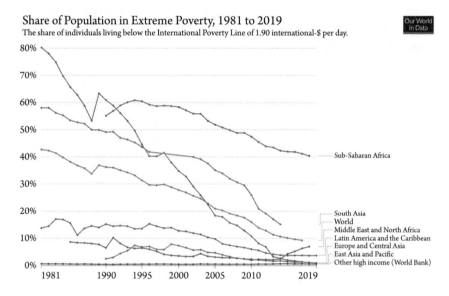

Share of Population in Extreme Poverty, 1981 to 2019
The share of individuals living below the International Poverty Line of 1.90 international-$ per day.

Figure 1.4   *Source:* Max Roser & and Esteban Ortiz-Ospina, *Global Extreme Poverty*, OUR WORLD IN DATA (2013), https://ourworldindata.org/extreme-poverty.

The trend lines in Figure 1.4 show marked declines in poverty around the world. The results are most dramatic in East Asia, which reflects the growth of the Pacific Rim economies of South Korea and Taiwan. But mostly this is the story of the transformation of the Chinese economy into an export-oriented behemoth, and the trailing economic emergence of Vietnam, Bangladesh, and the other industrializing nations.

Unfortunately the elephant curve in Figure 1.3 introduces the economic disruptions that followed. The upper-right quadrant reflects the rise of finance and the dominance of the top 1 percent, a subject of democratic challenge for some form of equitable redistribution. But the most important part of this chart is the downward curve: real levels of income variously increased at significantly lower rates than before, stagnated, or even decreased over the same twenty-year period.[16] This is the two deciles of the world's population found at roughly the 65th to 85th percentiles of world income distribution. That group is roughly the working and lower middle classes of the advanced industrial countries that form the longest-standing core of democratic societies.

As a normative matter, redistribution from wealthier nations to poorer ones in a period of rising wealth must be applauded. The economic dislocations in the advanced industrial countries lift hundreds and hundreds of millions of people from truly destitute conditions. But the global processes that have done much to alleviate human suffering do not dampen the consequences of the advanced societies' inability to cushion the domestic effects of international migration, stay the fallout from global economic integration, or redistribute wealth internally from the winners to the losers of globalization.

The democratic sense of common mission comes under siege as the laboring backbones of the advanced industrial countries find themselves challenged by rapidly changing demographics that make their country difficulty to recognize. It also comes as the rest of the world is exerting downward pressures on their living standards and as wealth shifts markedly to other parts of the world. As voters, these threatened groups in advanced societies were the backbone of the major parties of 20th-century democracy—the labor and social democratic parties on the left, and the Christian democratic and center parties on the right.

Once economies were integrated internationally, domestic national activity followed comparative strengths. Emerging service economies centered in the developed world, and labor-intensive industry grew in the developing economies that were the prime beneficiaries of the global shuffle leading up to the financial collapse of 2008. As Paul Collier well describes from his perch as a distinguished Oxford professor—and as one very conscious of his roots in the decaying industrial midlands of England—the world increasingly divided between those able to prosper in the cosmopolitan world of global demands and those who perceived themselves left behind in a world that deemed them superannuated where they felt increasingly isolated. That divide played out in what he terms the "salient identity." It delineates between those for whom the broader world of work is a source of reward and those for whom there is the sense of being left behind in a national setting that no longer offers protection:

> That final serving of esteem, the one generated by having chosen the same salient identity as many others, starts to diverge. Those who choose to make their job the salient identity, get more from their membership of the same-salience group. Conversely, those sticking with nationality as salient lose esteem. This divergence itself induces

people to switch their choice of salience from nation to job. Where does it end?

It might seem that everyone ends up switching their choice of salience, and this is possible. But a more likely alternative is that those in less-skilled jobs continue to make their nationality salient. When we compare this ending to where society started, the skilled have peeled off from their nationality.[17]

The sense of isolation was both economic and cultural, in part reflecting the rise of immigration in many of the countries now experiencing populist upheavals—and in some where the perception of immigration could be stoked well beyond the reality of actual demographic shifts. While immigration will be taken up subsequently, the sense of being subject to forces beyond traditional conceptions of nationhood contributed not only to political unrest but also to the repudiation of traditional political outlets of the postwar democratic order.

Across the major democratic countries, the labor and the center-right parties were traditionally cautious to speak out against immigration and cross-border trade.[18] While their policies differed, each saw a central part of its political role as protecting the always vulnerable working and small entrepreneurial classes, including the highly subsidized agricultural classes in countries like France, from economic dislocation. Both immigrants and the entry of cheaper goods from abroad threatened the less dynamic sectors of the advanced world economies. This is especially true for the working classes. Private-sector labor unions saw immigration as a source of downward pressure on wages and resisted it as such. By contrast, public-sector unions, which today constitute most of union membership, tend to be neither protectionist on trade nor cautious on immigration. Unions dominant in the public sector cannot be relied upon to resist downward pressures on private sector wages. Rather than serving as an important source of civil society resistance to the marginalization of working people, public-sector unions became an integral part of the state apparatus.

When we look to the upper Midwest voting for President Trump, the decayed industrial north of England voting for Brexit, or the frayed industrial towns of northern France voting for the National Front, the message of governmental failure to provide for basic social security rings loudly. And, when that failure is coupled with the sense of the traditional institutions being disengaged from working-class concerns, the field is left open to populist anger, whether from the right or left.

Indeed, the message resonates in those communities feeling left behind. One simple measure in the U.S. is to break down the vote by county, the basic unit of local governance. Trump won roughly five times as many counties as Hillary Clinton, but the counties that Clinton won included almost all the largest and most dynamic urban areas of the country—indeed, although a numerical minority, the counties won by Clinton generated 64 percent of the national gross domestic product.[19] In Britain, the same pattern obtained in the Brexit vote (see Figure 1.5).

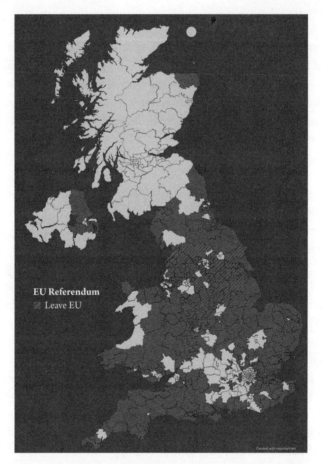

EU Referendum
Leave EU

Figure 1.5   *Source*: Chris Hanretty, *Replication Data for Areal interpolation and the UK's referendum membership*, Harv. Dataverse (2001), https://doi.org/10.7910/DVN/S4DLWJ.

Leaving aside Scotland and the eastern precincts of Northern Ireland (where voters were probably more inclined to leave the UK than the European Union), the Brexit vote matched the economic prospects of the local populations. Brexit lost in London and the relatively prosperous South, while it carried in most of the rest of the country, save for a few areas of economic resurrection in Manchester and Liverpool.[20]

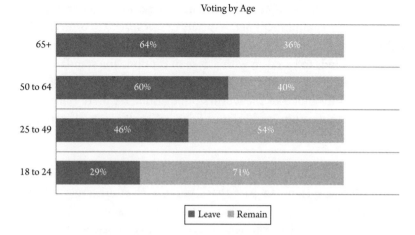

Figure 1.6 *Source:* Peter Moore, *How Britain Voted at the EU Referendum*, YouGov (2016), https://yougov.co.uk/topics/politics/articles-reports/2016/06/27/how-britain-voted.

Put another way, Brexit was the dominant choice of those over fifty, the generations that had felt declining wage prospects, but not the generations under fifty (Figure 1.6). Comparable distributions could be found in the French presidential elections, as well.[21]

The groups threatened by declining economic prospects, a sense of isolation in their own countries, and the combined effects of foreign threat delivered Brexit in the UK and Trump's victories in the upper Midwest, only mildly offset in the narrow Joe Biden victories in the Rust Belt. Now feeling vulnerable, these voters are increasingly deserting their former political affiliations in favor of angry populist reactions, frequently led by demagogic appeals to isolation and the sense of lost horizons. From Brexit to Italy's Five Star Movement to Trump to the National Front to Spain's Podemos, the trends are dramatic. The historic array of postwar political parties offered neither economic security nor a sense of political protection from outsiders and were displaced by those much closer to the sense of populist dismay.

In particular, the financial crisis of 2008 appears to have been the defining blow that exposed the frailty of democracies. The sudden economic dislocation stressed the already weak political institutions of governance and the ability of traditional political parties to offer prospects of remediation.[22] For the laboring classes of the advanced democracies, the decades leading to 2008 had often offered a steady decline in relative real-wage growth, so their confidence in any remnant of the political status quo to cushion the further postcrisis economic decline was exceedingly low.[23] Without functioning politics, democracies are ill prepared to offer security, redistribution, or optimism about life prospects for their citizens. That large populations in democratic countries no longer trusted in the solidaristic commitment of the society or its capacity to protect them fueled the current populist backlash.

All of this needs to be taken with a dose of caution. The standard of living of the working classes of the advanced countries remains an object of distant aspiration for much of the world's population. Yet there remains a difference between absolute and relative financial health, as well captured by Yascha Mounk:

> It isn't necessarily the poorest members of society who turn against the political system; in part that's because they are most reliant on the benefits it provides them. Nor is it necessarily the people who have personally experienced economic calamity. Rather, it is the groups with the most to fear: those that are still living in material comfort but are deeply afraid that the future will be unkind to them.[24]

The status anxiety associated with real or threatened downward mobility echoes strongly in political expression. Michael Sandel captures the tie between economic and cultural transformations, as well as the sense that a known world has slipped away from the promise of security. Populism offers an invitation for "reassertions of national sovereignty, identity, and pride." At bottom, it was a rejection of

> meritocratic elites, experts, and professional classes, who had celebrated market-driven globalization, reaped the benefits, consigned working people to the discipline of foreign competition, and who seemed to identify more with global elites than with their fellow citizens. . . .
>
> The populist backlash was provoked, at least in part, by the galling sense that those who stood astride the hierarchy of merit looked down with disdain on those they considered less accomplished than themselves.[25]

Across many of the national political battlefields, certain factors seem to conspire to increase populist appeal. Dominant are the effects of globalization, the consequent decline in earnings for those that cannot compete in the international arena, and the growth of austerity in the wake of the financial crisis.[26] Not every country falls under this rubric. Poland is the most notable exception. It did not experience a downturn after 2008, it benefited from

European integration, and it is relatively untouched by formal immigration, not the immediate consequence of the Ukraine war. Yet the pattern is there in too many countries to ignore. If the expansion of markets threatens the well-being of a broad swath of the voting population, then voting for the promise of immediate returns looks to be the antidote. As Slovenian political scientist Alen Toplišek argues, democracy is finally striking back after decades of control over economic policy being in the hands of the markets rather than those of the state.[27]

III. At Sea at Home

Compounding the dislocation in the economic domain is the sense of cultural estrangement from one's own country. Beginning with the 1960s, cultural symbols began to challenge the traditional order, including changed gender roles, increased racial and ethnic pluralism, and urbanization.[28] Of these, none is as immediately salient as the pressure of immigration and the sense of being a stranger in one's own country—real or perceived.[29] For Stanford's Larry Diamond, the result is a divide between those who inhabit the world of privileged integration into a dynamic order and those who fear being left behind. Focusing on Britain in particular, the divide is between conservative, uneducated white citizens, and cosmopolitan, young urbanites[30]—although that same pattern could be applied to many of the advanced industrialized democracies.

Before turning to the changing demographics themselves, we need to address a broader (and perhaps uncomfortable) word about what is at issue in the lost sense of solidarity that accompanies rapid change. Our era of diversity may applaud the benefits of broad democratic aspirations, but citizens of Burundi or Bosnia-Herzegovina or Iraq would well understand the frailties of democracy and formal elections without a solidaristic commitment to a collective future. It is only recently that the theme of democracy could be separated from that of an identifiable people, generally defined by language, culture, religion, and race.

Certainly, the role of communitarian solidarity suffers from the traumas of the 20th century, from Nazism to the ethnic slaughter in the Balkans. One reads back with horror at Carl Schmitt proclaiming that "democracy requires . . . first homogeneity and second . . . elimination or eradication of heterogeneity."[31] The unmistakable message is that "a democracy demonstrates its political power by knowing how to refuse or keep at bay something foreign and unequal that threatens its homogeneity."[32]

Yet, a look back at our democratic inheritance shows how central earlier generations thought the sense of shared identity. The ties between social cohesion and self-government are not an invention of 20th-century reaction. In the background of the founding documents of constitutionalism in the U.S. is the claim, no doubt jarring from a slave society, that the American blessing of liberty could be traced to the conception of homogeneity of the population, a claim that hauntingly echoes in Schmitt. In the words of John Jay, in *Federalist* no. 2:

> Providence has been pleased to give this one connected country, to one
> united people, a people descended from the same ancestors, speaking
> the same language, professing the same religion, attached to the same
> principles of government, very similar in their manners and customs,
> and who, by their joint counsels, arms and efforts, fighting side by side
> throughout a long and bloody war, have nobly established their general
> Liberty and Independence.[33]

Jay may today be the least celebrated of the authors of *The Federalist Papers*, but the sentiment was widely shared. John Stuart Mill later extended the argument to make it not simply an observation about America but also a prerequisite for democracy: "Free institutions are next to impossible in a country made up of different nationalities. Among a people without fellow-feeling, especially if they read and speak different languages, the united public opinion necessary to the working of representative government can not exist."[34]

Liberal theorists, notably including John Rawls, continued that tradition into the 20th century. Rawls contended that claims for the just treatment of citizens turn, at least in part, on a shared sense of "political traditions and institutions of law, property, and class structure, with their sustaining religious and moral beliefs and underlying culture. It is these things that shape a society's political will."[35] The arguments do not sound the need for consanguinity so much as they stress the continued importance of a sense of collective identity in order to sustain citizen self-government. Democratic politics has long provided a critical forum in which solidarity could blossom. Across democratic societies, political parties provided the organizational framework for sports leagues, adult education projects, and newspapers—all of which served as intermediaries between citizens and the broader society.[36] These agencies of civil society are weakened and leave citizens increasingly disengaged from political life, as reflected in declining voter participation rates across the democratic world. The risk of democratic alienation is stronger when decision-making is removed from direct electoral accountability to the concerns of local populations. In Europe, for example, decisions over population migrations are taken by the European Union and implemented through the bureaucratic apparatus known unflatteringly as "Brussels." This compounds the difficulty of constructing a democracy without a *demos* and fosters an estrangement between local concerns and where decisions are actually implemented.

Among the contemporary challenges in advanced democratic societies are significant erosions in the sense of collective solidarity that provided the historic glue for the common project of democratic governance. For immediate purposes, I focus on two: the challenge of declining work prospects for the broad mass of the population, discussed above, and the challenge of immigration. There are many manifestations of contemporary social dissolution. But the combination of economic insecurity and the presence of perceived outsiders seems invariably to lead to fear of the other's rising political power and blame on the other for a corresponding loss in social standing and wealth. The point here is not the normative claim that this sense is or is not justified, or even the positive claim of a causal relation between immigration and economic malaise. Rather, the issue is the democratic challenge posed by the widespread plebeian sentiments that their class is under siege. There is not a populist movement in a Western democracy at present that does not play to both xenophobia and economic insecurity. The immediate question is why these strains have such force at present, and why they seem to operate in tandem.

There is a compounding effect between economic insecurity and the fear of being overwhelmed in one's own country. When examined in isolation, both the economic and the immigration factors seem a sufficient strain on democratic society to prompt the populist response. When analyzed separately, there are many countries in which the political prompts "were right-wing ideology and anti-immigrant sentiment" rather than economic disaffection.[37] Portugal, on the periphery of EU economic life, has seen limited far-right populism, while economically healthy societies like Switzerland, Denmark, and Sweden have strong movements to contend with. While populism has gained traction in Portugal recently, with the Chega Party winning twelve seats in the last parliamentary elections, the electoral gains were fueled by issues of migration rather than economic dislocation.[38]

While the answers are no doubt complex, they must begin with an assessment of the empirical realities of modern democratic societies still reeling from the financial meltdown of 2008. The brute fact is that there is a loss of cohesion that accompanies high periods of immigration until the new immigrants are integrated into the national consensus.[39] What Americans celebrate as the melting pot is undoubtedly a process of change and is a recreation of the national identity that, when successful, provides for mechanisms that integrate waves of immigrant populations. Even in the best of circumstances, the process of integration and the corresponding accommodation of prior governing values will take time. What hopefully ends up a richer cultural environment (oftentimes with side improvements from food to music) invariably begins as a project of social and linguistic strain.

Taking the U.S. as the key example, there is no escaping the fact that immigration has risen dramatically in the past quarter century and that the level of foreign-born Americans is at its highest in a century—precisely the time of the last great burst of nativist populism in the U.S. (See Figure 1.7.)

Number of Immigrants and Their Share of the Total U.S. Population, 1850–2019

Figure 1.7   *Source: U.S. Immigrant Population and Share over Time, 1850–Present,* MIGRATION POL'Y INST., https://www.migrationpolicy.org/programs/data-hub/charts/ immigrant-population-over-time?width=1000&height=850&iframe=true.

What is striking here, apart from any concerns about the distribution of immigrant labor skill levels or even the number of legal versus illegal immigrants, is just the sheer number. The last immigration-fueled nativist turn transformed American politics for a generation, including closed-border constraints on immigration, isolationist politics, and even Prohibition directed at the drinking habits of recent immigrants. By any measure, the U.S. is now approaching a level of foreign-born residents not seen in the past century.

The same phenomenon may be observed in Europe. As shown in Figure 1.8, the percentage of migrants in the established countries of Western Europe has risen exponentially in recent decades.

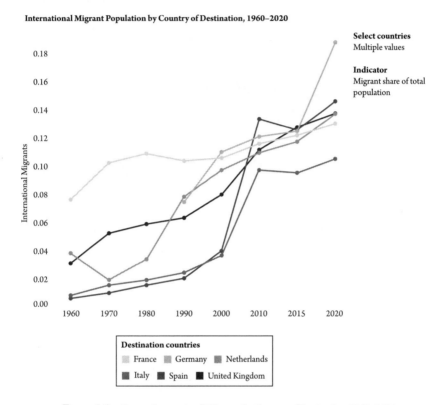

International Migrant Population by Country of Destination, 1960–2020

Figure 1.8   *Source: International Migrants by Country of Destination, 1960–2020,*
MIGRATION POL'Y INST., https://www.migrationpolicy.org/programs/data-hub/
charts/international-migrants-country-destination-1960-2020.

Some of the politically salient effects followed from the Syrian civil war and the German decision to allow over a million asylum seekers to enter in a short period of time in 2015–2016. The immediate political dislocations were staunched in 2016 in a deal that paid Turkey billions of euros to stop the flow of refugees into Europe and to keep several million in Turkey at the EU's expense. But the migratory pressure is far broader than the immediate repercussions of the Syrian humanitarian crisis, as shown by the comparative demographics of the African and European continents in Figures 1.9 and 1.10.

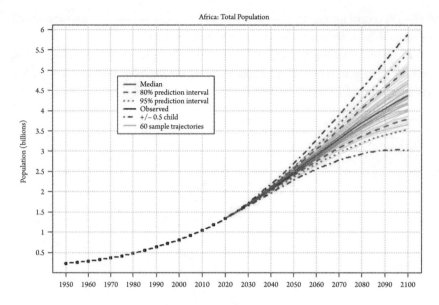

Figure 1.9   *Source:* U.N. DEP'T OF ECON. & SOC. AFF., POPULATION DIVISION,
WORLD POPULATION PROSPECTS: THE 2019 REVISION, AFRICA: TOTAL POPULATION,
https://population.un.org/wpp/Graphs/Probabilistic/POP/TOT/903.

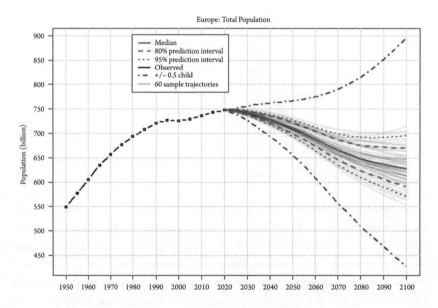

Figure 1.10   *Source:* U.N. DEP'T OF ECON. & SOC. AFF., POPULATION DIVISION,
WORLD POPULATION PROSPECTS: THE 2019 REVISION, EUROPE: TOTAL POPULATION,
https://population.un.org/wpp/Graphs/Probabilistic/POP/TOT/908.

In 1950, there were about half as many Africans as the roughly 550 million Europeans. By 2020, the European population had grown marginally to about 700 million, while Africa had quintupled its population to about 1.2 billion people. Current demographic trends would have the population of Europe roughly stagnant for the rest of the 21st century, while Africa's population should easily reach billions more.

The population growth of Africa is a ceaseless migratory pressure on Europe. Most African countries do not have the state capacity to manage such populations, a governmental failure compounded by the effects of wars, disease, and the escalating effects of global warming. The depletion of historic ground-water sources has left much of North Africa without sustainable agriculture and grazing.[40] One summary of pressures for migration concludes that under current trends

> more than 100 million Africans are likely to cross the Mediterranean Sea over the next two generations. As a result, like many European families who had an "American uncle" in the first half of the twentieth century, many African families will have a nephew or niece in Europe in the second half of the twenty-first century.[41]

For now, Europe has tried to create a corridor across the Mediterranean, paying Libyan militias to hold off migrants in a more odious version of the deal struck with Turkey.[42]

The data on immigration trends and the pressures from globalized aspirations in poorer countries provide the fuel for the surge in populist anger. But a simple causal claim based on objective indicators misses the political dimension of the populist moment. The image of culturally or ethnically distinct migrants is more powerful politically than the reality of migration to Poland or Hungary. The entry of Ukrainian refugees into Poland at the outset of the Russian invasion provoked no nationalist backlash—quite the contrary. The image of being overwhelmed requires political mobilization rather than mere antipathy toward outsiders. Larry Bartels notes, paradoxically, that "the attitudes fueling right-wing populism have been remarkably stable since at least 2002" though "political entrepreneurs may be getting better at exploiting those attitudes."[43] On this view, "populist attitudes lie dormant among the public, and through framing can be activated given the right contextual conditions."[44]

Recent studies have suggested that populist voting might be better explained as a reaction to mainstream political elites' systematic failure to respond to certain policies demanded by their constituents. On this view, well captured in a recent paper by Professors Brady, Ferejohn, and Paparo, "the populist vote is mostly driven by people dissatisfied with the menu of choices offered by the

traditional parties."[45] Populism responds to the perception that traditional politics has failed, not the power of ideology: "The populist vote is, in fact, mostly
accounted for by cultural or economic issues rather than populist ideas. Populist
voters in every country tend to be especially opposed to immigration policies
pursued by the traditional political parties. In Europe populist voters also manifest hostility to European institutions, partly because those institutions are
thought to force immigrants into their own country."[46]

The conclusion across the U.S. and fourteen countries in Europe, including
both old and new democracies, is that established political channels do not confront the sense of isolation and insecurity felt by the working classes that had
once been the mainstay of modern democracy. The conclusion points directly
to political failures of democracy: "Populist voters seem mostly concerned with
specific issues that the mainstream political parties are ignoring. . . . They vote
populist because populists promise to address their concerns."[47] In turn, those
failures implicate the effectiveness of both politics and governance, once the
strength of democratic rule.

2

The Capacity to Govern

Over the past two centuries, democracies have outfought, out-innovated, and outproduced their rivals. With singular capacity, democracies lifted the living standards of the broad masses of their populations, raised education levels to permit citizen engagement, and at the same time were able to trust powerful militaries to protect them from foreign assault without succumbing to military rule. History is obviously much more complicated, and this is a somewhat tendentious reading, but it captures the ideological consensus that prevailed after the collapse of the Soviet empire and the brief era of presumed democratic universalism.

However, as shown in the elephant curve chart of income distribution presented in Chapter 1's Figure 1.3, the optimistic story is under serious challenge. The China/Singapore models of autocratic rule coupled with high state competence highlight an emerging disability of democracies:[1] the presence of multiple veto points blocking the creation of public goods and equitable policies. Mature democracies include mechanisms of transparency, due process, and participation that provide an entry point for private interests to challenge and oftentimes forestall undesired governmental action.[2]

The same mechanisms that secure democratic accountability may have the paradoxical effect of constricting the ability of governments to respond to the needs of public order. Allowing citizen comment on proposed legislative or administrative initiatives, or requiring environmental impact statements prior to construction, should in theory allow for more transparent and informed state decision-making, as well as providing enhanced means of citizen input beyond retrospective voting on the performance of those in office. In practice, however, the participating citizens will frequently turn out to be interest groups able to leverage insider knowledge of such procedural requirements into outsized control over policy results.

Under such circumstances, it is easier to block than to build, raising the costs of public endeavors dramatically. Francis Fukuyama terms this the rise of "vetocracy," defined as "a situation in which special interests can veto measures harmful to themselves, while collective action for the common good becomes exceedingly difficult to achieve." Fukuyama concludes that "vetocracy isn't fatal to American democracy, but it does produce poor governance."[3] Easy confirmation can be found in the congressional Republicans' wobbly efforts after the election of President Trump in 2016 to pass from a party of opposition to a party of governance on their signature demand to repeal the Affordable Care Act.[4] After seven years of campaigning on a promise to repeal Obamacare, a clear Republican majority in the House of Representatives had trouble even proposing legislation to be submitted to a congressional vote,[5] and President Trump left office with Obamacare still on the books.

For champions of what is termed an "epistemic" defense of democracy, results legitimize democracy. "Democratically produced laws are legitimate and authoritative because they are produced by a procedure with a tendency to make correct decisions."[6] The central claim to the superior competence of democracies is not the process of governance but the outputs that result. As discussed in the first chapter, for much of the 20th century the banner of democracy was imbued with the sense of what West Germany could offer its citizens relative to East Germany, the United States relative to the Soviet Union, and on across the zones of ideological competition.

All such claims must reduce to some empirical support, and the claim that democracies are more likely to make correct decisions is highly contestable. Certainly the response to COVID-19 was imperfect around the world, but one need not look further than the United States' inability to muster an accepted public health mandate for vaccination to realize this issue. Somehow the United States was able to blaze extraordinary new trails in the "Operation Warp Speed" development of the antiviral vaccines, yet unable to secure a high enough vaccination rate to thwart repeated waves of infection, disease, and death.

Of necessity, deliberation must be slower and more complicated than decree. If democracies are indeed superior at generating welfare-enhancing outcomes, there must be some consistently better policies that offset the time lag in state action. What democracies sacrifice in rapid response must be remedied and overcome by the likelihood that public accountability and public reason tend to direct toward superior outcomes.

At some point, however, deliberation is not a process of citizen inputs but a public-choice nightmare in which vested sectional interests can marshal resources to overwhelm the passive majority. The result is a failure of public policy leadership and a collapse into rewards for privileged access to the strongest forces in government, which almost invariably are the executive. As I described the process elsewhere, "the 'three C's' of consolidated power take hold: clientelism, cronyism, and corruption."[7] The result is "weak democracies with autocratically minded leaders, who govern through informal, patronage networks . . . . Clientelism binds many citizens to ruling elites through cooptation and coercion."[8] Such failing democracies lack the organizational superiority of more decisive regimes, and, indeed, the presence of numerous veto points to action may actually make democracies less capable.

Consider an example from major new airport construction, a massively complex undertaking that has not even been attempted in the United States since the opening of the Denver airport in 1995. An international traveler upon arrival to Beijing cannot help but be awed by the majestic beauty of Terminal 3 (Figure 2.1). Built for the opening of the Beijing Olympics, and designed by English architect Norman Foster, its dramatic arches evoke both the red lacquer motifs of Imperial China and the bird's nest design of the Olympic stadium. The new terminal was constructed, from design to completion, in four years, a massive effort that included three work crews a day, laboring on rotating eight-hour shifts.[9]

Figure 2.1   Beijing Capital International Airport in Beijing, China

Next, compare Terminal 3 with London Heathrow's Terminal 5 (Figure 2.2). Like Terminal 3 in Beijing, Heathrow's Terminal 5 is designed by Norman Foster. Yet it is at best functional, a desperately needed additional space for an overcrowded airport. It has no grandeur, no inspiration, no sense of tribute to a rising power—and it took twenty years to complete. Amazingly, Beijing's

Terminal 3 is not only 50 percent larger than Terminal 5, but it is also larger than all the Heathrow terminals combined. And in 2019, China opened a second new international terminal, itself larger than any British rival.

Figure 2.2   London Heathrow Airport in London, England

When pressed about the time to airport completion in a BBC interview, Foster acknowledged the gains in completion time in China from more efficient labor use, lower regulatory demands, ease of siting, and a host of other factors. But even on Foster's account, there were years of delay that could not be accounted for. Instead what emerges is the capacity of Chinese authorities to simply get the job done: "You've taken out the democratic process, you've taken out the plan, so that comes down to decision making, it comes down to having a very, very clear idea of objectives and getting on with it."[10] At the end of the day, the capacity to produce turned on the difficulties of democracy, an observation that challenges democratic claims of superior capacity. Thus, Foster contrasts the British perspective—"Oh well, it took a long time but we are a democratic society"—with the societal "hung[er] for change and . . . for progress" driving rapid production in China.[11]

Of course, my home airport in New York is LaGuardia, which for much of its existence would have made Terminal 5 look like paradise. After years of debate, it became clear that repairs could no longer be postponed. The planned renovation finally got underway but somehow failed to anticipate how passengers would get to the terminals in the interim, yielding chaos as travelers had to hike the last section from the highway (Figure 2.3).

Figure 2.3   La Guardia Airport in New York, United States

One of the few benefits of COVID-19 was that the collapse of air travel allowed the repairs to proceed in somewhat orderly fashion. At long last, New York has a quality airport, but it is still not serviced by mass transportation and leads onto a decayed road system.

Among New York's signature contributions to democratic dysfunction is the much ballyhooed opening of the Second Avenue subway extension in 2017, a mere eighty-eight years after it was initially proposed. Even more striking than the delay were the extravagant costs, a self-imposed problem of poor governance (see Figure 2.4). Digging a subway in a dense urban environment necessitates disrupting delivery of gas, water, telecommunications, and so forth. Doing so efficiently in turn requires coordination so that service disruptions and alternative sources can be adjusted. The builder of the subway found coordination among the various utilities and regulatory agencies that covered each service so daunting that it decided the only solution was to dig deep into the bedrock of Manhattan to avoid having contact with any other utilities or administrators.[12] The result is that more than eighty years after first proposed, the Second Avenue subway finally opened in 2017, encompassing a total of four subway stops, running a grand total of about three kilometers, and pricing in at a whopping figure of almost $2 billion per kilometer.[13]

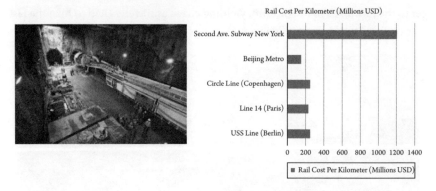

Figure 2.4   *Source:* https://www.nytimes.com/2016/10/24/nyregion/new-york-today-
how-to-build-a-subway-tunnel-boring-machines-second-avenue-subway.html

The capacity to cushion the dislocations of the modern global economy and the press of immigration is another measure of state competence. Germany's ability to integrate the former East Germany confirms the difficulty of the enterprise, even among people who already shared a language and a clear national identity. It is here that all the themes of democratic stress come together. The inability of institutional political actors to debate policy, to appeal to collective interest, and to assure that costs are carefully considered through competent leadership all drain from the democratic project. Populist anger is stoked by state incompetence and increased clientelism for those with privileged access to the executive. Weakened forms of participation and deliberation, in turn, compound the sense of democratic failure.

I. Diminished Legislatures

Democracies are conceived around legislative power, from Magna Carta's parliamentary check on the Crown, to the expansive role of Congress defined by Article I of the Constitution, to the revolutionary emergence of parliamentary power throughout the 19th century. Colloquially, Americans once spoke of the Senate as the "world's greatest deliberative body."[14] It is no overstatement to say that this is the world's ennobling democratic inheritance. Or, put another way, the hallmark moments of 20th-century authoritarian rule are intertwined with the rejection of parliamentary deliberation and with the rejection of a legislature's capacity for long-term bargained compromise in favor of the plebiscitary triumphs of a Hitler or Mussolini.[15]

The legislative arena, at least in theory, is the clearest institutionalized setting for democratic deliberation. In its classic rendition, it is the arena in which "participants of deliberation, before counting votes, are open to transform their preferences in the light of well-articulated and persuasive arguments."[16] On this view, the process of deliberation transforms democratic politics because it "requires the participants to display the reasons why they support a particular stand. It comprehends an exercise of mutual justification that allows a thorough type of dialogue before a collective decision is taken."[17]

Yet, in the modern era, the words "Congress" and "dysfunction" seem to go together like a horse and carriage, with some apology to Frank Sinatra. Consider that the total enacted legislation annually by the U.S. Congress has declined considerably from the 1970s, falling from a figure of 804 bills passed to more recent totals of 329 bills passed (see Figure 2.5).[18] The 114th Congress, the last Congress before the Trump ascendency, is just the most recent example of government divided between a Democratic president and a Republican-led Senate. Yet the pattern of inaction persisted even when the presidency passed to Republican Donald Trump. Writing in the *New Yorker*, Jane Meyer echoed the assessment that, under the leadership of Senator Mitch McConnell, the chamber that calls itself the world's greatest deliberative body has become, "by almost every measure," the "least deliberative in the modern era."

> In 2019, it voted on legislation only a hundred and eight times. In 1999, by contrast, the Senate had three hundred and fifty such votes, and helped pass a hundred and seventy new laws. At the end of 2019, more than two hundred and seventy-five bills, passed by the House of Representatives with bipartisan support, were sitting dormant on McConnell's desk.[19]

Consider just one partial indicator of the trend over time in the United States. Since President Franklin Roosevelt's fabled first hundred days in office, which ushered in the transformative New Deal, presidents have routinely devoted themselves to hitting the ground running, using the initial period of pride among the partisans and disorganization among the vanquished to show muscular leadership. The effort to blaze through the first hundred days has not changed, but the form has. The number of legislative initiatives of the first hundred days has dropped steadily, from seventy-six new statutes under Roosevelt, to seven and fourteen under Presidents George W. Bush and Barack Obama, respectively.[20] Under President Trump, twenty-eight bills were passed in the first hundred days, though none was considered a "major legislative accomplishment,"[21] and most took the form of fast-track administrative repeals. Similarly, President Biden signed eleven bills during his first hundred days, though one of note was the $1.9 trillion coronavirus-relief package dubbed the "American Rescue Plan" (see Figure 2.6).[22]

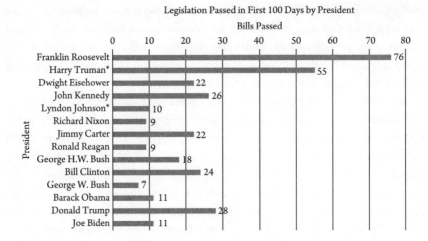

Figure 2.5   *Sources:* Julia Azari, *A President's First 100 Days Really Do Matter*, FIVETHIRTYEIGHT (Jan. 17, 2017), http://perma.cc/852T-G5DF. Jordan Fabian, *Trump 'Disappointed' in Congressional GOP*, THE HILL (Apr. 28, 2017, 3:18 PM), https://thehill.com/homenews/administration/331 140-trump-disappointed-in-congressional-gop. James Crump, *Biden's First 100 Days in Numbers, from Executive Orders to Vaccines*, GUARDIAN (Apr. 27, 2021, 5:02 PM), https://www.independent.co.uk/news/world/americas/us-politics/biden-100-days-bills-executive-orders-b1838313.html.

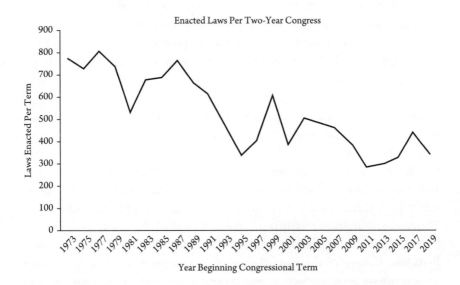

Figure 2.6   *Source:* Chart data from *Statistics and Historical Comparison: Bills by Final Status*, Govtrack, https://www.govtrack.us/congress/bills/statistics (last visited Oct. 5, 2021).

Even though, of course, presidents do not pass legislation, and even though they might often confront a Congress or a chamber with an opposition majority, the drop-off does not mean presidential inaction. While legislation has dropped, executive decrees have increased throughout the modern period. Consistent with this trend, President Trump had no significant legislative activity at all during his first hundred days in office and the number of substantial legislative initiatives amounted to zero.[23] President Biden, by contrast, well-seasoned in legislative politics and riding a precarious partisan balance in the Congress, managed to pass his $1.9 trillion stimulus package less than two months into his first term. The American Rescue Plan represents the sole major piece of legislation early in an administration in many years.[24] Biden's coronavirus-relief bill, one of the largest federal aid packages since the Great Depression, provided direct payments to Americans, extended federal unemployment benefits, and earmarked billions of dollars for vaccine distribution and relief for state and local governments.[25]

Even with President Biden's efforts to stimulate economic recovery with large-scale legislation, the long-term trend is unmistakable.

II. Deliberation and Decision

Claims about the superiority of democratic decision-making inevitably fall back on the process of democratic deliberation to find the common good in its discursive elements and to reach beyond mere sectional claims on spoils. For proponents of the more classic deliberative tradition, the domain of discourse is in public participation and direct engagement. The advantage of deliberative, collective decision-making, according to philosopher Joshua Cohen, comes "with its explicit attention to considerations of the common advantage and in the ways that that attention helps to form the aims of the participants."[26] Even for those beginning from radically different assumptions, public deliberation is critical to realizing the benefits of democratic governance. Thus, the economist Joseph Schumpeter argues that "the democratic method is that institutional arrangement for arriving at political decisions which realizes the common good by making the people itself decide issues through the election of individuals who are to assemble in order to carry out its will."[27]

Rarely would Professor Joshua Cohen and Joseph Schumpeter be lumped together in theories of democratic legitimacy. Yet they both look to a discursive element to raise democratic governance's capacity to reach the common good and to reach beyond mere sectional claims on spoils. For Cohen and the more classic deliberative tradition, the domain of discourse is in public participation and direct engagement.[28] For Schumpeter and those in his tradition, myself included, elite competition in the electoral arena provides the foundations for citizen engagement and education, and the ensuing retrospective accountability for the exercise of governmental power.[29]

Under either view, democratic political theory justly emphasizes the educational gains of deliberation in an engaged citizenry.[30] Even when citizens in modern democracies govern through representatives rather than as a collective body, periodic elections guarantee that citizens encounter political arguments that may be removed from their everyday lives.[31] Elections compel deliberation among the citizenry as candidates and parties attempt to sway and educate. That deliberation then translates into the legislative arena as elected officials seek to translate campaign promises into governing policies. "The act of choosing a party is the act of choosing whom we trust to transform our values into precise policy judgments."[32]

When parties operate effectively, they can ensure that general abstract preferences are balanced and implemented in government without having the individual decide the appropriate income tax percentage or the number of troops stationed in Germany. This necessarily requires a significant amount of compromise, which had been the historical norm in the United States and other mature democracies: "Parties help to overcome the inherent fragmentation of interests in a diverse country by forging alliances among constituent groups; this gives the parties legitimacy in claiming to govern for the common good."[33]

The haunting question for the future of democracy is how to perpetuate the historic virtues of popular sovereignty if its central organizational form, political parties, is no longer able to play the critical roles of coordination and moderation. Nor is this simply an American story prompted by the Trumpian capture of the Republican Party. Focusing on the United States alone misses the scope of the issue: the fate of political parties across the democratic world—a topic explored more fully in the next chapter.

What is inescapable is that, across a number of markers, the legislative branches of mature democracies have declined as centers of policy debate and formation. Regardless of the exact mix of parliamentarism and presidentialism, democracies are centered on the parties. "Without parties, any politics that government pursued would necessarily be based on present needs."[34] Parties institutionalize politics, and their longer term horizon allows policy and planning over the horizon. Like corporations in the economic domain, parties are endowed with the capacity for life beyond that of its founders. "Legacies matter, so parties that expect to stick around have an incentive to work for long-term benefits, even if they impose short-term costs."[35] Even in the absence of genuine democratic competition, the ability to deliver into the future distinguishes party politics from populist immediacy.

As one account of the economic takeoff in East Asia describes, the "high-performing Asian economies were governed by dominant parties that enjoyed long time horizons, had the power to maneuver around potential veto points, could shield the bureaucracy from special interests, and could effectively oversee policy implementation."[36] By contrast, the diminished political parties of the Philippines "contributed to a chronic undersupply of collective goods and comprehensive national policies, which by all accounts has stunted growth prospects."[37]

In theory, any legislative body is plagued by the risk of indecision. There are so many competing interests, and trade-offs among them introduce many potential political outcomes with no guarantee of consistency. Controlling the agenda, deciding what is debated, and in what form it is presented can alter the final legislative decision. And, any deliberative formula yields the risk of complete incoherence in the legislative process.[38] The cycling-of-preferences problem, the great insight of Professor Kenneth Arrow and the ensuing study of public-choice theory, threatens to collapse the capacity of any legislative body charged with policy leadership.[39] The need for coordination is apparent, with the Supreme Court long ago observing that parties emerged "so as to coordinate efforts to secure needed legislation and oppose that deemed undesirable."[40]

Parties break through this logjam. In turn, candidates then run as part of a slate, and the demand for a larger share of seats in parliament is what offers the prospect of national stewardship. Subsequently, the candidates stand for election based on how their party has delivered in office, or how it proposes to act if elected to power. There is an interlocked dependence. A candidate's need for a shorthand identity, which is provided by party affiliation, reinforces the party's need for a long-term identity that justifies its role in the national political arena.

Politics, like nature, abhors a vacuum. Legislatures are no longer the focus of the sort of deliberation and planning presented in idealized accounts of democratic governance. In place of legislative initiative, executives around the world have adopted more muscular policymaking roles, with parliaments serving only to check the level of partisan support for the president or prime minister. The result of parliamentary dysfunction is correspondingly rising executive unilateralism,[41] the increased dependence on administrative law to set policy, and the central checking role of the courts as restraints on presidentialism—even in formally parliamentary systems.

Doctrinally in the United States, the absence of congressional action not only removes the central democratic branch from the reins of government but also makes even judicial constraint more difficult. Following Justice Robert Jackson's famous *Steel Seizure* typology, the power of the executive is at its "lowest ebb" when the president seeks to countermand the actions of Congress.[42] The unstated flip side of Jackson's observation is that the pathway for judicial repudiation of executive action is correspondingly easier when Congress has blazed the trail. When Congress fails to act, the mechanisms of democratic constraint are compromised.

For Jackson, congressional inaction posed the most difficult issues for demo-cratic governance and, by extension, for the judiciary. As he framed the problem:

> When the President acts in absence of either a congressional grant or denial of authority, he can only rely upon his own independent powers, but there is a zone of twilight in which he and Congress may have concurrent authority, or in which its distribution is uncertain. Therefore, congressional inertia, indifference or quiescence may some-times, at least as a practical matter, enable, if not invite, measures on independent presidential responsibility. In this area, any actual test of power is likely to depend on the imperatives of events and contempo-rary imponderables rather than on abstract theories of law.[43]

In the absence of legislative initiative, executive power naturally rushes to fill the void, whether through governance by direct decree or by indirect administrative command. Without the legislative branch offsetting the powers of the executive, the job of defining the boundaries of prerogative power and regulatory authority falls to the judiciary. As Jackson cautioned, the lines of judicial engagement are least clear—the "zone of twilight"[44]—when there is institutional failure in the legislature, and the "least dangerous branch" finds itself at risk of open conflict with the executive.[45]

There is nothing distinctly American about hypertrophic executive power in the modern era. Even before the UK Supreme Court had to engage the au-thority of the prime minister to implement Brexit, a topic to which I shall return, the British government confronted the military consequences of executive uni-lateralism in the disastrous Iraqi campaign.[46] One proposal, from the House of Lords Select Committee on the Constitution, would have implemented limita-tions similar to those of the American War Powers Act,[47] obligating parliamen-tary approval for any long-term military engagement.[48] As future Prime Minister Gordon Brown observed at the time, "Now that there has been a vote on these issues so clearly and in such controversial circumstances, I think it is unlikely that except in the most exceptional circumstances a government would choose not to have a vote in Parliament [before deploying troops]."[49] The lack of ac-countability and the absence of parliamentary engagement were confirmed by the 2016 Chilcot Report, whose many condemnations of Prime Minister Tony Blair included criticism of unilateral decision-making by the executive.[50]

Nor has widespread legislative paralysis, as well as the subsequent failure to check the executive, gone unnoticed in the extensive discussions of national democracies. A review of the literature shows a persistent theme among both ac-ademic commentators and pundits—the collapse of responsible government at the parliamentary level.[51] The causes for that collapse identified in the academic literature include concerns about thresholds of representation, party fragmentation, increasing presidentialism and semipresidentialism, and the displacement of parliamentary authority by international accords, or, in the case of Europe, the overreach of Brussels.[52] Pundits are more inclined to point to the venality or corruption of parliamentary officials, though in some countries, such as Brazil, the two come together.[53]

Parliamentary democracies are centered on the parties. Candidates run as part of a slate, and the demand for a larger share of seats in parliament is what offers the prospect of national stewardship. The collapse of parliaments compounds the consequences of the collapse of parties, and the two are both the cause and effect of each other. Invariably, the locus of political activity shifts to the executive, and the defining feature of democratic politics turns to the triumphalist claims of the victorious head of state. Consider this account of contemporary European politics:

> What we are seeing in the presidential campaigns . . . is that the more chance the candidates have of winning—or the more chance they think they have of winning—the more they are prepared to play the game that I call "national presidentialism." They go in for speeches that amount to saying: "If I'm elected, then everything . . . is going to be different because I'm the only one able to lead this country." . . . All that matters is how the candidate is going to be able to restore [the nation's] image once he or she has been given supreme power.[54]

This account of contemporary politics would ring true in many democracies around the world, the United States clearly included. In my native Argentina, such "caudillo politics" has generally been the mark of the demise of democracy rather than its fulfillment.[55] That this particular statement happens to be about France and that the speaker is Daniel Cohn-Bendit, the leader of the 1968 student uprising, only makes it a bit more piquant.[56]

III. Getting It Done

The impulse toward executive authority is certainly buttressed by state incapacity in democratic countries. The ability to "get it done" is an underappreciated measure of governmental legitimacy in any state. In its most obvious manifestation, state capacity defines the ability to survive in times of military conflict. Failure in war frequently leads to outright state collapse either from external occupation or internal insurrection. While the inability to build airports, or even appropriately manage a pandemic, may not give rise to the sudden collapse associated with wartime defeat, there is nonetheless the sense of defeat that arises from an inability to deliver any of the core state functions of peace, prosperity, and security.

Historically, low state capacity has been thought incompatible with the prospects for democratic governance. For example, political scientists have estimated minimum levels of economic development that serve as rough estimates of the preconditions for democracy to exist.[57] At the same time, the "petro-curse" of countries dependent on natural-resource extraction allows quick wealth (and corruption) to emerge without the full range of government institutions, including public education and health.[58] Under conditions of state underdevelopment, the public surpluses needed for civic engagement and the development of successful democracies' strong civil society institutions do not have a chance to mature. Whether this is due to poverty or the distortions of a one-product economy does not matter. The result is the same problem of state inability to deliver.

As with so much of the current period of democratic decline, what was characteristic of fragile democracies trying to take root in difficult terrain has now come full circle to more stable democracies, including those in the wealthiest countries on earth, first and foremost the United States. The core problem is that institutional frailty quickly slips over into governmental incapacity. If the legislative branch is assumed to be the generator of social policy and the primary overseer of its implementation by administrative agencies, it is entirely predictable that the fading legislative role will translate into weakness of the state. The failure of policy inputs from Congress compounds the risk that the administrative pathways will ossify around established pathways, seemingly impervious to demands for reform.[59] In turn, as Justice Kagan wrote in her days as an academic lawyer, "Presidents have tried to control the bureaucracy only to discover the difficulty of the endeavor."[60]

If the problem is diagnosed as congressional dysfunction and bureaucratic inertia, the readiest answer might be to unleash executive power with fewer obstacles either from administrative law or even separation of powers. The temptation to bypass obstacles is clear. As former presidential advisor Paul Begala once noted, "Stroke of the pen, law of the land. Kind of cool."[61] In blunt form, and starting with the U.S., "modern administration is presidential administration."[62]

Once down this path, however, especially when examined from just the question of state capability, the attractive alternative seems to emerge from countries in which a dominant executive justifies command based on the delivery of superior results, to wit, China and Singapore. The rise of what Richard Pildes and I term "executive unilateralism"[63] is a persistent source of concern for those who accept the separation of powers rationale for maintaining accountability, what Madison famously invoked as "ambition made to counteract ambition."[64]

The combination of legislative dysfunction and the ensuing diminished capacity of government to act invites an impatient desire to dispense with the edifice of democratic deliberation and reward simple capability. Simply in terms of observed manifestations, it is not hard to argue that "presidential administration has become the central reality of the contemporary national government."[65]

To a certain degree, the commanding role of the executive may be checked by internal accountability and oversight mechanisms that can serve to slow down the exercise of command. Going back to the New Deal one can find that "the architects of executive control over the administrative state embraced separation of powers, especially internal to the executive branch."[66] Among the sophisticated accounts of internal checks on the executive in the contemporary American context are those that find independent sources of authority within subdivisions of agencies, such as the Office of Legal Counsel of the Department of Justice,[67] or even within the intelligence services and the national security administration.[68] No matter how institutionalized, however, these intra-executive forms of separation suffer from a lack of democratic legitimacy that can never reproduce the fact that the legislative branches are composed of elected officials who clearly presented alternatives to the voters.

But the departure from both the presumption of legislative primacy and the formal textual rendering of constitutional commands demands something more. The departure can be toned down by claims that the executive always had broader authority in the American constitutional design, as examined by Sai Prakash.[69] But if this is the fate of democracies in the modern era, it is not to posit that separation of powers can be reproduced to some extent within the executive branch.[70] At some point there must be a claim that this new form of executive command fits some conception of democracy.

Here the strongest normative claim for this form of presidential supremacy is put forward by Elena Kagan, all turning on the immediacy of the direct presentation of the national executive for selection by the electorate: "Presidential leadership establishes an electoral link between the public and the bureaucracy, increasing the latter's responsiveness to the former." Further, "because the President has a national constituency, he is likely to consider, in setting the direction of administrative policy on an ongoing basis, the preferences of the general public, rather than merely parochial interests."[71] Subsequently, the Supreme Court narrowly rejected this view. The Court could not accept an expansive reading of presidential authority based upon "direct[] accountab[ility] to the people through regular elections."[72]

The trade-off between state competence and the risk to democratic accountability inheres in finding the right mix of executive powers. Nor is this a new debate in democratic societies. In the United States, greater executive authority and the expansion of administrative control had been a hallmark of the Progressive

Era. This debate continues under pressure of ascendant populism. And, it does so in terms that would have resonated for a 20th-century audience confronting the calamity of depression on the one hand and the rise of demagogic author-itarianism on the other hand. Indeed, the debate dates to the founding strokes of democracy, long before its modern manifestations in the U.S. and Western Europe.

Finding a workable compromise between popular engagement and effective governance is a struggle that goes back as far as the Athenian democracy, which confronted the conflict between plebiscitary and representative institutions. The Assembly, which encouraged participation by all free male citizens of Athens, was a form of plebiscitary democracy within the circumscribed defini-tion of citizenship. Yet the domain over which the Assembly exercised its powers was significantly circumscribed. The tasks of governance were performed by a governing cohort consisting of magistrates, often selected by lot for fixed, non-renewable periods of time.[73] The Athenian response, by drawing the leaders di-rectly from the people (narrowly defined), minimized the risk of elected officials departing from the will of the people, what today would be referred to as agency costs. Indeed, in classic democratic thought, as with Aristotle, the frequent ro-tation between being ruled and becoming a ruler was the defining characteristic of a democracy.[74]

As the complexity of managing an expanding society grows, a division of labor suggests itself as inevitable. While the vast majority devote their time to economic and domestic affairs, others are tasked with carefully attending to the public weal. Yet the relationship between these two groups has always been a problem. The people remain the fount of political legitimacy as the indispensable *demos* of democracy. Ultimately, however, attention to political decision-making is limited; watching football is a more engaging way of passing the weekend than spending time in meetings to decide the right gauge of sewer pipes. Add the other demands on time and energy from family and economic activity, and life forces constant choices between public and private pursuits.

Expanded executive authority addresses one part of the divide between ac-countability and competence, and thereby requires some foundation in demo-cratic principles. The fact that the national executive stands more directly before the entire citizenry hearkens back to the defense of the referendum or plebiscite as an alternative to representative institutions. Though, such suggestions are long removed from the frequent replenishment from below that characterized classical Athens. In the modern era, there is the cautionary historic use of referendums to bypass or eviscerate democratic institutions altogether. Quoting former Labour Prime Minister Clement Attlee, Margaret Thatcher in a speech to Parliament famously dubbed the referendums of the twentieth century "a device of dictators and demagogues."[75] Both Mussolini and Hitler had used referendums to rouse their supporters and disband constitutional limitations on power. Constitutional structures necessarily fractionate political power and compel bargaining over desired political aims. When operating properly representative institutions reinforce compromises generated by repeat interactions. Votes of approbation through a plebiscite, by contrast, reduce all decisions to a yes/no threshold that does not force repeat play.

The problem in the 20th century was not simply the role of the plebiscite in providing the forms of governmental selection, but the unleashing of the executive power that followed. Even in the debates leading to the New Deal, the slide of corporatist efforts into fascism in Italy and then Germany "suggested a risk to executive-centered government that Progressive reformers had not considered: concentrating too much power in the executive could make even a democratic government fascistic."[76] By contrast, the defense of representative government focuses not so much on the potential misuse of the referendum but on its inherent governance limitations. Representative institutions emerge as the compromise between governance and democratic accountability.[77]

What if the true source of populist anger is increased state incapacity in fractious democracies? For political scientists William Howell and Terry Moe, certainly among the most sophisticated analysts of the presidency in the U.S., it is precisely the "ineffectiveness of American government" that both fuels populism and propelled Donald Trump to the presidency.[78] For them, the chief culprit is the way fixation on separation of powers yields "a byzantine structure of government, designed for a bygone era, that is disastrously ill-equipped to handle the problems of modern society."[79] The solution is not only expanded administrative authority but also a greater presidential role in the legislative process, as with the authority of the president to propose legislation that would command the congressional agenda.

Were the problem facing democracies simply a matter of competence and were there some guarantee that the beneficiaries of greater executive authority would govern more like Singapore and less like Brazil under Bolsonaro or the U.S. under Trump, then freeing up executive authority as proposed by Howell and Moe has an unmistakable logic. But if the problem lies deeper at the heart of modern democracy, in the U.S. and abroad, then I find myself joining other critics who see the momentary remedy as further compromising the health of an ill patient.[80]

The Political Institutions
of Democracy

The decline of the legislative branch is a virtual constant across the democratic world. Certainly, there are conjunctural events that push power toward the executive, such as the risks of terrorism or the sudden emergence of the COVID-19 pandemic. Each demands a certain form of swift, oftentimes nontransparent, decision-making that plays to executive commands. Some countries, such as Taiwan, managed to retain the primary role of parliament and legislative initiatives even in the face of the coronavirus, but that is the rare exception. The decline in legislative authority is so widespread, so persistent, that it must be explained in terms that are not merely the accretion of discrete emergencies.

To ground the inquiry, let me offer a personal observation from having participated in the 2008 and 2012 election efforts of President Obama. In 2008, then-Senator Obama was a decided outsider who became the party's nominee only in June of that year. In the quick run-up to the election, Obama for America put together a national field operation, including campaign attorneys, across the country, with particular focus on the battleground states for that November. I served as one of the senior legal advisors to the campaign and worked extensively with the legal representatives in states around the country. I was not surprised that an outsider candidate would not have a working command of the state party structures and would instead quickly organize a national operation based on the presidential campaign and its resources. For all practical purposes, the Obama campaign felt like a top-down presidential effort that intersected only sporadically with any pre-existing party operation.

What did surprise me, however, was the 2012 campaign, where I again served as a senior legal advisor to Obama for America. With the benefits of Obama's incumbency and what was essentially a four-year run-up to the re-election effort, I had expected that the 2012 campaign would be largely organized around the state political parties, in conjunction with state and local election efforts.

Notably, and with few exceptions, that was not the case. There were certainly more points of contact with state officials that helped smooth the voting process on Election Day, and more time to litigate contested issues before Election Day. But in terms of organizational structure, the campaign was run through the presidential effort and not through the state parties.

Nor was this a quirk of the Democratic Party or the particulars of Obama for America. I am told that the same pattern held in the campaign of Governor Romney in 2012, even as he emerged from extended front-runner status in the Republican Party. By 2016, the weakness of the parties was on full display when, on one side of the aisle, Donald Trump managed to swamp all the institutional candidacies of the Republican Party and walk off with the nomination, while, on the other side, Bernie Sanders, not even formally a member of the Democratic Party, nearly toppled the presidential nomination of the consummate party insider, Hillary Clinton.

Neither party appeared to have a mechanism of internal correction. Neither could muster the wise elders to steer a more conventional course. Neither could use its congressional leadership to regain control of the party through its powers of governance. Neither could lay claim to financial resources that would compel a measure of candidate loyalty. Neither could even exert influence through party endorsements.

The parties proved hollow vehicles that offered little organizational resistance to capture by outsiders. And what was captured appeared little more than a brand, certainly not the vibrant organizations that are heralded as the indispensable glue of democratic politics. If indeed the "political parties created democracy and . . . modern democracy is unthinkable save in terms of the parties,"[1] then something seemed deeply remiss. Even President Biden's remarkable rise from near oblivion in the 2020 primaries was not an instance of a party selecting its standard-bearer. Rather, it was an encapsulation of the electoral base's deep fear of a repeat of the Trump administration.

What accounts for the weakness of the national political parties at present? The presidential campaigns may serve as an initial focal point, but the problem exists across institutional domains. The distance of the parties from the operation of the presidential campaigns is also evident in the greater distance of the party leadership from the organization of legislative efforts. The exasperation over the dysfunctionality of Congress returns time and again to the absence of a leadership structure able to corral hot-headed members of the legislative caucus to just get things done—even on matters where there is reasonably broad agreement on the general contours of needed legislation. This is the process well captured by Richard Pildes in focusing not so much on polarization among political activists or even elected officials but on political "fragmentation," defined as "the external diffusion of political power away from the political parties as a whole and the internal diffusion of power away from the party leadership to individual party members and officeholders."[2]

There is a legal dimension to the uncertainty over the role of political parties. One indicator of the age of the American Constitution is the absence of any formal recognition for political parties. By contrast, Article 21 of the German Constitution, adopted after World War II, places parties front and center in the organization of democratic politics, and it commands that "parties participate in the formation of the political will of the people."[3] The German Constitution reflects a historical evolution that, only in the 20th century, came to grant political parties constitutional recognition as part of the fabric of democratic politics. Indeed, the first 19th-century constitution that addressed the status of political parties was that of Colombia in 1886, and it did so in order to ban parties.[4] In the period of ascendancy of democratic constitutions in the 20th century, political parties enjoyed privileged constitutional status as the galvanizing force of democratic politics.[5]

By contrast, the framers of the U.S. Constitution equated parties with factions and aimed for a form of democratic politics that would rise above sectional concerns, immediate gratification of wants, and the risk of succumbing to the passions of greed and envy. But as early as the first contested presidential election in 1796, the founding generation discovered the need to coordinate national candidacies in furtherance of a political program. They quickly formed the very factions they had sought to avoid, now organized as incipient political parties. Even in the founding era, partisan actors learned that they could not mobilize the rather inert mass of the population into a national campaign without coordination of resources, messages, and programmatic commitments for governing. Each of these undertakings required not only the right of citizens to participate electorally in self-governance but also the creation of intermediary institutions that could mobilize citizens into partisans.

As experience in electoral self-government grew, democrats throughout the world learned that parties provide a forum for the integration of the different interests that must coalesce for successful policymaking, more so in first-past-the-post elections than in proportional representation systems. Where there is a single winner in an election (as in congressional elections in the U.S.), successful campaigns require an ability to mobilize an electoral coalition broader than the immediate demands of any particular constituency. Even in proportionally based parliamentary systems, in which minor parties can achieve representation on much more sectional platforms, some form of aggregation is necessary to draw sufficient attention to the party platform and to make the party a desirable suitor in forming a governing coalition. Regardless of the form of representation, parties emerged as the institutional mechanism for translating interests and ideology into governance. Politics is the art of the possible, even if what is possible and necessary at any particular moment fails to inspire. Without parties, responsible and productive governance rested on the happenstance of enlightened leaders rather than an institutionalized mechanism for making hard decisions, cutting deals, accepting short-term costs for long-term gain, and all the mechanisms that define wise stewardship.

In the United States, parties also served as the political expression of the spirit of voluntary associations critical to the young Republic. As Alexis de Tocqueville noted, "Americans of all ages, all conditions, and all dispositions, constantly form associations.... Wherever, at the head of some new undertaking, you see the government in France, or a man of rank in England, in the United States you will be sure to find an association."[6] By the time Tocqueville came to America, political parties were emerging as among the most salient of these associations. As they matured through the 19th and early 20th centuries, parties provided the organizational resources for political campaigns, selected candidates, coordinated platforms, and disseminated information about politics.[7] In exchange, parties dispensed patronage and access to power, the glue that held the activist wings of the party in check and allowed a coordinating discipline to be imposed on the party's elected representatives.[8]

The organizational fabric of parties came undone in the United States in the late 20th century, partially as a result of legal reforms that left significant aspects of party governance outside the control of party leaders, and partially through external factors, such as the rise of low-cost social media and mechanisms of direct access to funding and the party constituency.[9] To recognize the change in the organizational form of politics is not necessarily to posit the loss of a halcyon age when all was right with politics. American party politics were dominated by backroom deals, well-lubricated with funds of sketchy provenance, and reinforced by handing out patronage of oftentimes scant public interest. This crude account of Boss Tweed or the Huey Long machine in Louisiana or Chicago under Richard Daley is hardly a normatively compelling account of a healthy democracy. There was much to party politics of the 19th and 20th centuries that does not conform to contemporary sensibilities: "For most of the nineteenth century, parties operated without any legal recognition or restriction. Party organizations, the descendants of local, elite clubs, chose their own nominating procedures and established their own bodies for internal governance."[10]

We live in more democratically transparent times, and the image of the political parties as they emerged from the 19th century may seem aberrant, even shocking. But politics is dynamic, and as the party organization falters, other actors emerge, from the lone-wolf candidate-entrepreneur to the rival special interest groups and private financiers of super PACs and related domains. To some extent, the diminished role of political parties is the product of reform efforts with unintended consequences. As Bruce Cain has well cautioned, eager political reformers too often ignore the institutional settings of politics at considerable peril to their desired aims.[11]

Yet the parallels across the democratic world are too great to attribute excessive significance to institutional reforms gone awry in any particular country. Examined globally, the American experience of tottering political parties appears emblematic rather than exceptional. The result in country after country is the dissolution of the discipline of political parties in favor of a politics of free agency formed largely around the personae of individuals or momentary issues, devoid of a sustaining institutional presence. Indeed the breaking up of central institutions extends far beyond the domain of politics—the economic conglomerates of yesteryear, such as ITT and Gulf & Western, were long since dismantled in favor of independent specialized units.[12]

In the political domain, fragmentation is a fact of life in all democratic countries, meaning that attempts to find the causal roots at the national level will necessarily be incomplete. The process of what is termed "fissuring" in labor economics reflects the broad destabilization of large integrated organizations in the face of technological change, ease of communication, globalization, and other pressures on previous advantages of scale.[13] Whether across supply markets or in the domain of politics, ease of communication and transportation puts pressure on broad horizontal organizations whose prime advantage was access to markets, economic or political. In the language of the Nobel Prize–winning economist Ronald Coase, to which we shall return, in multiple domains it became less administratively burdensome to buy off-the-shelf services rather than make an entire product, and political actors, like their economic counterparts, could become a purer form of their particularized specialization rather than coordinated enterprises.

In the political domain, parties failed to the extent to which access to voters and donors is no longer coordinated through the large umbrella of a single organization. Populists eschew political parties, and social media allows direct appeals for both money and support.[14] Part of the ability of populists to bypass established party structures is no doubt the failure of the political parties to adapt to the modern era. But the cumulative result is the decline of the parties as the locus of democratic politics and the rise of the individual-centered definition of politics. As parties fragment, a spiral ensues. Targeting specific groups of voters, activists, and donors requires more focused and generally more extreme messages. Broad-tent parties become an impediment to a new form of politics that channels passion rather than rewarding the necessarily limited returns from governance.

More broadly, the disengagement from the parties leads to what Professor Emanuel Towfigh and his colleagues term the "party paradox," in which parties, though necessary to democratic functioning, become a contributing source of disenchantment with the political process: "This paradox of representation may reduce the acceptance of political decisions by the electorate and contribute to the overall disillusion with democracy."[15] The result, well captured by Professor Peter Mair in his work on "hollowed out" European democracies, is that politics "has become part of an external world which people view from outside," as opposed to the old world in which they participated.[16]

Weakened political parties do not have the institutional fortitude to withstand the impassioned campaigns of charismatic leaders fueled by an independent donor base and a harnessed social media that reaches voters directly. Candidate-driven elections are increasingly the norm in Europe as parties that emerged from the capacity to gain parliamentary representation are no longer needed as an electoral platform.[17] Even the desultory elections for the European Parliament witnessed an effort to attract personalities to the candidate roster in a vain attempt to boost voter turnout.[18] Direct candidate appeal to voters goes hand in hand with the documented fragmentation of political parties in, among other places, Bolivia, Bulgaria, Denmark, Ecuador, Finland, France, Guatemala, India, Israel, Italy, the Netherlands, and Thailand.[19] Mair summarizes this well:

> Parties are failing . . . as a result of a process of mutual withdrawal or abandonment, whereby citizens retreat into private life or into more specialized and often ad hoc forms of representation, while the party leaderships retreat into the institutions, drawing their terms of reference ever more readily from their roles as governors or public-office holders.[20]

Put less delicately, Nigel Farage, the leader of the UK Independence Party (UKIP), touted the Brexit vote as the story of the British people telling the political elite to stick it: "It is, after all, rather extraordinary that more than half the voting population defied a large majority of its own elected parliament, all of the traditional political parties, and virtually every important institution in the country—from the Central Bank to the leaders of industry to the trade unions."[21] The ultimate referendum vote on Brexit had the quality of a "Hail Mary," a desperation play for a team failing within the confines of customary behavior. The parties could no longer resolve the perceived critical issue facing the British electorate and threw it up to the voters in the hope of relieving political pressure.

Nor did the Brexit fiasco prevent embattled Italian Prime Minister Matteo Renzi from turning to a constitutional referendum to shore up his government in 2016, with the same disastrous results.[22] The immediate need to seek political ballast through a plebiscite may reflect the momentary political crises in Britain or Italy. But the allure of referenda reflects the disenchantment with political parties, and the desperate effort to restore governing authority simply confirms the weakness of parliaments as authoritative institutions. Rather than offering a lifeline to government, these referenda are a desperate gambit reflecting the problems that gave rise to Brexit in the first place: "Tensions have grown in most Western nations between the existing processes of representative democracy and calls by reformists for a more participatory style of democratic government."[23]

If Brexit highlights the perceived weakness of political parties as coordinators of democratic politics, it raises the question of the root cause of that weakness.

In substantial part, the weakness follows from the simple fact that the parties cannot claim to speak for much of a constituency. In other words, they have significantly lost their participatory quality. To give but one example, in 1950, 20 percent of Britons were members of political parties; as of 2014, that figure was about 1 percent.[24] In the United States, according to the Pew Research Center's yearly studies of American political behavior, party identification is at an observed all-time low. Heading into the 2016 presidential election, 39 percent of Americans identified as independents, 32 percent as Democrats, and 23 percent as Republicans: "This is the highest percentage of independents in more than 75 years of public opinion polling."[25]

Snapshots of party identification in the UK, as well as declines in voter share of major political parties in France, Germany, and India present the picture across the democratic world as shown in Figures 3.1 and 3.2:

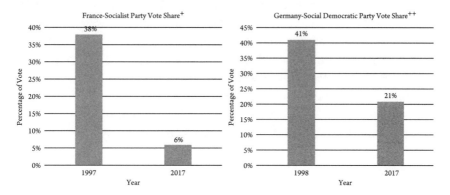

Figure 3.1   Chart data from *Statistics and Historical Comparison: Bills by Final Status,* Govtrack, https://www.govtrack.us/congress/bills/statistics (last visited Oct. 5, 2021).

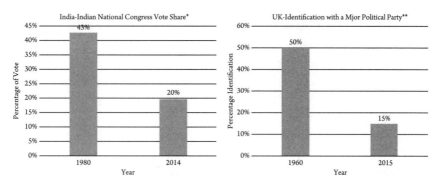

Figure 3.2   *Praveen Rai & Sanjay Kumar, *The Decline of the Congress Party in Indian Politics,* Econ. Pol. Wkly. (Mar. 29, 2017), https://www.epw.in/journal/2017/12/web-exclusives/decline-congress-party-indian-politics.html?0=ip_login_no_cache%3Dbb66f7574bd263f36810413c16433343

** Bobby Duffy et al., The Policy Institute, King's College London, Divided Britain? Polarisation and Fragmentation Trends in the UK 50 (2019), https://www.kcl.ac.uk/policy-institute/assets/divided-britain.pdf (last visited Sept. 13, 2021).

Party failures are intrinsically connected to the demise of the institutional supports of those parties. Throughout the 20th century, parties relied heavily on other forms of organization to provide their active constituency. For the Democratic Party in the United States, for the Labour Party in Britain, and for the social democratic parties of Western Europe, that organizational backing came heavily from the labor unions.[26] For the Republicans in the United States and the Tories in Britain, and the Christian democrats and conservative parties in Europe, the organizational ties were to the chambers of commerce or other locally based representatives of small businesses and agricultural interests.[27]

One statistic gives a snapshot of the speed of removal from traditional bases of support. In 1990, before the rise of Tony Blair and New Labour as a political mobilization independent of the Trade Unions Congress, about a third of Labour members of Parliament came from working-class backgrounds. This is already down from the 70 percent figure when Labour first reached significant political representation in the 1920s, but it remains a strong connection to the historic roots of the party. By 2018, the percentage of Labour MPs from working-class backgrounds stood at only 8 percent.[28] This low figure represents not only the Labour Party's estrangement from its historic base but also the diminution of the organized foundation of the party.

Taking the United States as an example, the erosion of underlying institutions is as precipitous as the decline of parties. Union density today is at an all-time low since the New Deal created federally mandated rights of collective bargaining. Union decline captures only a part of the picture. Significant as well is the shift in composition of the unionized workforce reflected in the domination of unionization in the public sector. About 11 percent of the American workforce is unionized, but the figure for the private sector has fallen below 7 percent, while public sector unionization remains at about 35 percent.[29] Not only have unions declined outright, but also, perhaps more significantly, they have ceased to be an independent source of support for political parties outside the state realm. To the extent that unions centrally become the expression of public employees, they no longer organize a constituency independent of the political realm. Instead, labor unions are largely an expression of the political party to which they are affiliated and become another political actor whose fortunes are tied to that party's electoral capabilities.[30] Not surprisingly, efforts to consolidate Republican political power at the state level, as brought to the fore in the administration of Governor Scott Walker in Wisconsin,[31] seek to undermine the power of public-sector unions as a proxy for the Democratic Party. These are not battles reflective of participatory engagement by diverse sectors of the society, but power struggles within the state itself.

On the other side of the ledger, we find a corresponding erosion of broad-scale institutional engagement with the parties of the center-right. In the United

States, the Chamber of Commerce presents the best example, evolving from the organizational representative of local enterprise to the exponent of the interests of concentrated capital: "Mention the Chamber of Commerce, and most people think of a benign organization comprised mostly of small business owners who meet for networking and mutual support in local chapters across the U.S. But today's Chamber is anything but that."[32] The Chamber's interests are now highly focused around a small number of industries and interests, including "tobacco, banking, and fossil fuels."[33] According to one article, sixty-four donors were responsible for more than 50 percent of all donations to the Chamber, while 94 percent of its donations came from a pool of just 1,500 top donors.[34]

Across the political spectrum, parties become tied not to broad-based constituency organizations but to much narrower sectional interests, already well entrenched in the corridors of power. The claim of parties as a special arena of participatory engagement in the democratic project wanes accordingly. The parties emerge hollowed out, just as do their organizational bases of support.

I. Make or Buy

To understand what is lost with the erosion of the political parties that have buttressed democracies over the past two centuries, it is first necessary to understand what parties actually do in democratic politics. Parties are not disembodied compilations of political positions. Rather they are organizations that operate in a complex environment defined by voter preferences, the needs of governing, and the maintenance of party officials to carry the work forward. If we understand voters to be the ultimate consumers, the task of governance to be the productive activity of the party, and the party officials to be the management cohort, the party begins to resemble an economic firm such as a corporation that similarly must navigate the need to produce something that the market will value. The correspondence between political parties and economic actors may not be perfect, but it provides an initial framework for understanding how and why parties were central to democracy.

Parties like economic actors survive and prevail when they deliver value better than can other rivals. To play out the analogy initially, it is best to turn to the core argument in Ronald Coase's seminal work *The Nature of the Firm*, published in 1937.[35] The signature contribution of Coase's work, for which he was awarded a Nobel Prize, was to model economic behavior as conditioned by the transactions costs of operating in the real world. To the prevalent neoclassical model of marginal costs and benefits driving economic decision-making, Coase introduced a separate inquiry into how the transaction costs of bargaining, supervising, negotiating, searching, and other such day-to-day necessities powerfully shaped the decision of economic firms to expand production, contract out for production or services, or even to stay in business.[36]

Firms must always decide not just what to produce but also whether to produce. The decision to engage in any of the economic activities of a firm, from subparts production to bookkeeping to janitorial services, follows from a decision to undertake the task internally rather than to contract out that necessity to another business actor. Firms ultimately prosper by selling a product on the market. But the process of production involves a series of decisions about how best to realize the final goods that might return a profit to the firm. Each firm must decide whether to specialize narrowly or to assume broad responsibility for its market ventures. Colloquially, this is the make or buy decision.

In principle, the market should set the price for goods and services and, in the absence of transaction costs, such as monitoring of quality, the ability to buy or make should be fairly interchangeable. This is clearly not the case, as firms seek to control internally that which is within their core competencies and leave to market actors secondary activities, such as providing coffee and lunch. As Coase explained, "Within a firm, these market transactions are eliminated and in place of the complicated market structure with exchange transactions is substituted the entrepreneur-coordinator, who directs production. It is clear that these are alternative methods of coordinating production."[37] Accordingly, "the main reason why it is profitable to establish a firm would seem to be that there is a cost of using the price mechanism."[38] Responding to these transactional advantages means that "a firm becomes larger as additional transactions . . . are organized by the entrepreneur and becomes smaller as he abandons the organization of such transactions."[39]

Firms are constantly revisiting the decision to make or buy based on the costs of substitution of one function for another. Relying exclusively on price to control production may be counterproductive if price alone is an imperfect monitor of the quality of production.[40] If a manufacturer depends heavily on product quality, the consequences of a drop in subpart quality will be borne only indirectly by those further down the supply chain. Such circumstances compel the decision to make rather than buy, even though that decision requires expenditure of firm capital and the need to monitor production internally. On the flip side of the equation, shifting costs may result in functions that were once internalized being outsourced. Put simply, an increase in the transaction costs of internalizing production may increase the attractiveness of finding other institutional arrangements, as with the outsourcing of production to overseas suppliers, for example.

II. The Party as a Firm

Roughly contemporaneous with Coase's groundbreaking writing on the nature of the firm came the first sustained inquiry in political science into the nature of the political party as an organization and of the divergent forces harnessed in the modern political party. In 1942, V. O. Key published his landmark work on the inherent conflict between the contending factions within political parties, *Politics, Parties, and Pressure Groups*.[41] Nathaniel Persily and Bruce Cain framed Key's great insight as the need to "disaggregate[] the simple description of 'party' into three components: the party-in-the-government, professional political workers, and the party-in-the-electorate."[42]

As its name implies, the party-in-the-government may include elected politicians and executive party heads.[43] Key describes a popular conception of "a group which could be held accountable for the conduct of the government," but he also describes smaller groups, such as "Democratic Representatives" and "Republican Senators."[44] Key's "professional political workers" constitute the group that staffs the political organization.[45] The party-in-the-electorate is formed of voters at large who identify as party members as reflected in their voting patterns.[46]

Starting from Key's framework, the modern political party can be seen as an uneasy amalgam of electoral engagement, popular ideology, and governance. Like an economic firm, parties can prosper if they reach an optimal measure of coordination of these inputs and deliver a final product that the market values. And yet, politics is a more demanding taskmaster than economics. A model of political parties becomes much more complicated than one of corporations, whose primary and unambiguous goal is to maximize profits.[47] To a very large extent, the market is a sufficient check on economic actors that always face the prospect of "creative destruction" if they fail to keep up with the times.[48] The outside societal interest in corporate structuring is a generalized public interest in the efficient use of firm resources, an aim largely internalized into the wealth maximization focus of the business firm.

By contrast, proper party functioning is critical to the central public good of democratic self-governance. The public good dominates any particular consideration purely internal to the political party. As a result, no simple metric, such as efficiency, can fully integrate the internal momentary objectives to the overall public aims. Facing competing goals, parties must at times weigh difficult sacrifices. For example, achieving legislative or governance objectives may require exposing swing-district candidates to unpopular votes. This in turn requires considerations derived not so much from the Coasean concern for minimizing transaction costs, but from the need to ensure loyalty and voice rather than exit from the parties.[49]

The public face of any political party is its candidates for office, particularly its successful candidates who hold office, and it is this portion of the party that is most vulnerable to organizational failure. This group foremost looks to winning elections, generally by hewing close enough to the center of the political distribution of voters, which is presented in the political science literature as the median voter theory of politics.[50] In any given unit of election, the voters will spread across a series of positions and interests. As a general matter, candidates who can best capture the interests of the middle of the electoral distribution ("the median voter") will prevail. Accordingly, candidates are rewarded for running to the interests of their voters. Depending on the particular constituency and the ultimate ambitions of the candidate, a wide variety of positions could ensue, even from nominal members of the same party. A candidate running in a swing district and one running in a gerrymandered district with little to fear from the other party would be pushed closer or further away from the national center of politics, respectively. Absent some organizational reason for cohesion, candidates would likely drift from a coherent set of policies or priorities. Left to the interests of local constituents, ethanol might dominate elections in Iowa while marriage rights might center politics in San Francisco.

The same lack of cohesion afflicts the party-in-the-electorate. Key conceived voter loyalty and partisanship as "a set of concentric circles," with declining levels of enthusiasm at further distances from the core of highly engaged activists.[51] Most surveys of overall voter preferences reveal generally bell-shaped normal distributions of views, resulting in the unsurprising truism that the center is, well, centrist.[52] Even in our current polarized era where the centers of the two main parties have pulled apart, the ideological distance between the parties tends to be less than in the more fractured preferences of parties operating in proportional representations systems, for example.[53] But the electorate has no way of presenting itself in the political system except on Election Day, and so the candidate positions and the party platform tend to be shaped by activists and donors, who represent a far more polarizing constituency than the bulk of the electorate.[54]

Key incorporates his observations on the conflicts among professional political workers with a larger discussion of party organization. Though parties are commonly conceived as an ordered hierarchy, Key describes the successively broader geographical party units—"layers of organization"—as seized with independent electoral interests; cooperation cannot be coerced.[55] The role of national committee chairmen in setting policy can provoke conflict with other components of the party, including congressional leadership, that is, the party-in-the-government.[56] Unsurprisingly, Key observed that strong electoral prospects for candidates drive greater organizational discipline and cohesion whereas weakness can lead to muted support or outright defection within the party organization, anticipating the concept of organizational exit as used today.[57] Even writing in the mid-20th century, Key observed significant upheaval and conflict in party organizations, as machine systems came under pressure from candidate- and personality-driven factions.[58]

Lack of cohesion also threatens the effectiveness of elected representatives, Key's party-in-the-government. Just as candidates may move across a range of issues and positions depending on their personal ambitions and the particular needs of their constituencies, so too do those candidates once in office bring with them competing agendas. In theory, there are so many competing interests and such inconsistency in potential political outcomes, which depend on agenda setting (what is presented in what form), that there is a risk of complete incoherence to the legislative process, where the rubber hits the road for actually governing. The various rules and power structures that control Congress can serve to amplify majority party power and compel compromises.[59] The problem of cycling of preferences, the great insight of Kenneth Arrow and the ensuing study of public choice theory,[60] threatens to collapse the capacity of any legislative body charged with policy leadership. The need for coordination is apparent, with the Supreme Court long ago observing that parties emerged "so as to coordinate efforts to secure needed legislation and oppose that deemed undesirable."[61]

Despite the great academic search for examples of cycling, it never seemed to happen very much in Congress.[62] In theory every amendment could trigger a shift in preferences, meaning that, whereas A is preferable to B, the consideration of C makes B preferable, even if C is the losing option.[63] And so it is when D is offered up as yet another option, and on and on. The simplest reason is that the party hierarchy serves to coordinate messages and preferences for the party-in-the-government, just as it does among the candidates. With strong committee structures and rewards in the form of pet projects for constituencies or earmarks, not just any measure can get to the floor. Just as planets do not spin out of orbit, so too the gravitational force of the party organization reins in the fractional tendencies. In politics as in physics, energy is required to conquer entropy.

To give a concrete example, consider the fate of Senate Bill 1 in every Texas legislative session. By Senate rules, every bill must be taken up in order unless the order is altered by the presiding lieutenant governor or by a five-ninths vote of the Senate, a slight change from the historic practice of two-thirds being needed for an out-of-order bill.[64] Senate Bill 1 is the first bill introduced at each legislative session, but it has no content. It is merely a parliamentary blocking device that in practice means that nothing will come to the Senate without an affirmative act of the lieutenant governor, who historically has been the most powerful political official in that state. There is no cycling of preferences because the agenda is set by one individual wielding the collective power of the dominant party.[65]

On this view, the party provides coherence to politics, disciplines candidates not to stray too far from the party message, offers a mechanism for the ineffectual center to be protected from the extremes within each party, and maintains the ability to govern effectively. Key attributes the moderating influence of parties to their diversity of constituent interests; electoral success on the national stage requires not deviating too far from the party's center of gravity toward any particular interest, even if catering to particular interests is advantageous at a local level.[66] This is quite an undertaking. While the mass of the electorate would have great difficulty organizing itself, the same cannot be said of candidates, officeholders, and the party activists. Each one of these groups necessarily bristles at the restraints imposed by the party and threatens to go it alone or withdraw its support. Yet somehow the party has persevered, through organizational assistance, financial support, and rewards to the faithful—in other words, by wielding its organizational energy so it remains the center of authority. And in every democratic country, it has done so primarily in the service of the capacity to govern through elected officials.[67]

III. The Logic of Supply and Demand

Viewing political parties through the logic of a firm identifies why party leadership would have a historic advantage in the battle for control of democratic politics. The mass of the party-in-the-electorate is disabled by a collective-action problem in organizing for its interests—usually center leaning.[68] The candidates would historically have been disabled without the endorsement and organizational resources of the party. And the party-in-the-government could not govern effectively, and deliver on its campaign promises, without the party providing coherence to the legislative agenda. The transactional costs of overseeing disparate entities would be too great for any individual politician to stray too far from the party. Instead of agreeing with the party whip on support for one piece of legislation in order to achieve a private concern, each congressman would have to reach out to enough other congressmen to get the requisite 218 members to support the bill in the House of Representatives. As well captured by Seth Masket:

> Quite simply, a partyless legislature is a collective action nightmare. Having to cobble together a winning coalition on every bill one cares about is nearly impossible, ensuring that incumbents will fail to enact

much of the agenda on which they ran for office and will fail to deliver redistributive benefits to their district.[69]

The transaction costs of repeating this across all legislation, as well as the credible threat by the party to retaliate for defection from the core legislative agenda, disciplined the members to the party historically. Similarly, the ability of the party to reward its activists with both access and positions in government keeps centrifugal forces at bay. And finally, the party's authority regarding who gets to speak as a candidate of the party disciplines the message in the electoral arena.

It has always been possible for independent entrepreneurs, whether candidates themselves or outside interest groups, to engage politics outside the framework of the political party. Independents from Teddy Roosevelt to Ross Perot have engaged at the presidential level and likely turned the outcome from one major party candidate to another. But only the unitary organization within the party could historically translate political activism into election results and the prospect of actually governing.

Recent events have shown, however, that party politics are a dynamic process. There are endless sources of discontent within a political party, and everyone from voters to activists to candidates to incumbent officeholders are always evaluating whether they are better off setting off on their own, crossing the aisle, or just withdrawing altogether from politics. For those committed to the political enterprise, the question is whether putting up with the inevitable frustration within the party is worth it, or whether independence or an alternative institutional arrangement might be superior. In other words, the various constituencies within the party are searching for an optimal equilibrium between making or buying.

The equilibrium that kept parties in place can be altered. For example, candidates might conclude that the party franchise is too weak or too unenforceable and may decide to set off on their own contrary to the party elders. Alternatively, it may be that entire categories of erstwhile party activities may be performed more effectively outside the party. The best example of this is when constraints on party fundraising make super PACs a better vehicle for channeling campaign finances.

Turning again to an economic analogy, the role of parties can be challenged on both the supply and demand side of the ledger. On the supply side, the parties have less to offer solo venturer candidates who can both run and finance outside the party structure. And on the demand side, these candidates do not benefit from submitting to the discipline of the party. Using the United States as an example, it is possible to identify a host of factors, including rules governing how parties may function, as altering the critical domains of party access to funds, party control over government jobs, and party control over candidate nominations. These factors increase the supply of viable, populist candidates, reducing the demand for political parties and their coordinating influence.

A. Party Money

In the post-Watergate period, there has been an effort to squeeze the financing of electoral politics so as to reduce the amount (and presumably the influence) of money in politics. For example, when the Federal Elections Campaign Act of 1974 codified the post-Watergate reforms, it provided federal funding for presidential campaigns. But the amount of money it provided was equal to two-thirds of what George McGovern had spent in 1972—in the most lopsided loss in American history at the time. Few aspirants to high office enter the process with a desire to replicate a spectacularly losing effort.[70]

Artificially limiting political funding exposed the hydraulic quality of money in politics: like water, money will seek its own level and restrictions on its flow in one direction will soon generate other outlets.[71] The inquiry here is not on the effectiveness of such reforms—all evidence is that campaigns continue to gobble up cash—but the impact on politics.

The United States may represent one end of the spectrum in the use of private money rather than public funds for its political campaigns. But in all electoral systems, candidates have to tap into a source of funds to make their campaign viable, whether the funding is to the candidate alone or through a party slate. To the extent that parties control access to funds, either because state funding is based on a party-denominated formula or because the party provides access to potential individual donors, the financing of campaigns compels candidate fidelity to the central planks of the party.

By implication, the more the candidates can credibly raise funds independent of the parties, the more they are likely to tailor the message to funding sources rather than to party coherence. Because of the centrality of private funding in the United States, the American experience provides an object lesson on how changing in funding may further undermine party stability. This cannot be the sole explanatory variable because the same party weakness is seen in democracies very far from the private funding model in the United States.

Nonetheless, the ability of candidates to reach a donor base without the party as intermediary changes the political valence of fundraising. The American experience has shown that, as a general matter, campaign donors tend to be more ideologically polarized than the electorate at large.[72] At the same time, a party-centered finance system tends to blunt the polarizing effect of ideological donors and candidates because parties have "the potential to dampen the tendency to elect highly ideological candidates who will not necessarily receive financial support from the political party."[73]

But the trend in American campaign finance reform has been not to channel money to the parties, but to try to limit the amount of money available and, by extension, the role of money altogether.[74] With unfortunate similarity to the drunk searching for the lost car keys under the streetlight, reform attention turns to those domains most readily subject to restrictive regulation, most notably both parties and candidates.

The failure to recognize the tempering effect of parties is reflected in the campaign finance jurisprudence. In a series of cases emerging from the 1986 Senate campaigns in Colorado, the Supreme Court found that a political party was to be treated as just another electoral actor, no different in kind from any other supplicant seeking to curry favor with an actual or potential officeholder.[75] Further, the Court held that where a party acts in concert with its candidates, its expenditures may be treated as de facto contributions from the party to the candidate, no different from the contributions of any other private actor, and subject to the same restrictions to avoid the risk of a pass-through to the candidate.[76]

Lost in the rush to restrict money in politics was the fact that the integration of access to voters, candidates, and officeholders allowed parties a privileged position as political actors. Once the party was no longer able to raise money to support its candidates on any basis distinct from any other contributor and once the interaction between party and candidate was limited by a principle of non-coordination, the logic of internalizing the candidate's campaign within the political party dissipated. In Coasean terms, there was no longer a manifest advantage to making as opposed to buying from outside vendors.

Oddly, in the 1990s, the weaker restrictions on campaign contributions to state parties allowed the parties a brief respite. First the Democrats and then the Republicans figured out how to channel national funding activities through state parties, who would in turn transmit the money raised to the national parties[77]—a contrived transformation of non-federal funds into clean federal dollars, a practice remarkably similar to money laundering. Even the going terms of a 15 percent charge by the state parties looked like standard rates for money laundering.[78] And so were born the White House sleepovers, the rides on Air Force One, the golfing weekends with Republican House leaders[79] (alas, there were no presidential perquisites for the party out of power).

No doubt, the perception of access for sale could not have been worse.[80] But amid the stench, the soft money period of the 1990s restored a unifying role to the national parties and lent coherence to the party messages. Again, this was not an unalloyed good. It drove to the government shutdown of 1995[81] and then to the essentially straight-line party voting on the impeachment of President Clinton.[82] Nonetheless, channeling money through the parties meant that parties emerged as the centerpieces of politics[83] and, as with the Contract with America,[84] gave a national coherence to electoral politics—warts and all.[85]

This landscape changed with the passage in 2002 of the Bipartisan Campaign Reform Act (BCRA), known after its sponsors as the McCain-Feingold Act.[86] The Act targeted soft money accumulation by the parties and effectively shut down the flow of campaign funds through the state political parties. But, as anticipated by the hydraulics account, new outlets emerged for political donations outside the candidates and parties. Between 2000 and 2008, independent expenditures in the federal domain increased by at least 1,258%.[87] The losers were the political parties, most notably the state parties.[88] The winners were what Joey Fishkin and Heather Gerken call the shadow parties, ranging from the independent expenditure outfits to the self-sustaining campaigns of individual candidates.[89]

While the rise of spending by super PACs and other evasive campaign organizations has been well chronicled,[90] less attention has been given to another systemic shock from 2008: the decision of President Obama to forgo public funding altogether. As a result of both intensive and innovative fundraising, the Obama campaign had roughly three times the resources in the general election as the McCain campaign.[91] Roughly one-quarter of the Obama fundraising came from small donors, totaling about $200 million— about the same amount of money available to McCain in the general election under public funding.[92] The Obama for America strategy revealed that a presidential campaign could raise large amounts of money outside the party structure. Even more significant, the small contributions showed that technology had lowered the transaction costs of dealing directly with the party-in-the-electorate without intermediation by the party apparatus. Not surprisingly, small donor appeals were the hallmark of the two major party outsider candidates in 2016: Sanders and Trump,[93] and they continue to define politics in 2020 and beyond.[94]

Certainly the rise of new technologies cannot be attributed to legal intervention. But the combined effects of recent reforms have hampered the ability of parties to raise money. In place of party-centric campaigns are efforts to push hard dollars to the candidates independently through small donor appeals or to direct major funding of politics outside the regulated domain altogether. The new campaign finance regime "puts individuals and relatively small coalitions on a fairly equal footing with political parties."[95] Neither the funders nor the candidates risked going it alone so long as the party-controlled campaign resources could maintain the discipline of the party apparatus and could control candidate access to the nomination process. Removing party organization of campaign resources was a significant step in eroding this entire organizational framework.

Without the integrative power of the party and the efficiency of political integration that party politics could deliver, the different components of the party could look to contract for the apparatus they needed or seek the nomination outside the customary party structures. Indeed, as was seen with the Koch brothers in 2016, outsiders could even hold beauty pageants to shop for suitable candidates.[96] Even in the absence of these external forces, however, the party infrastructure cannot necessarily block a candidate who bypasses the party and appeals directly to the electorate for support, to wit, President Trump. Further, an outsider capturing the party-in-the-electorate then has tremendous leverage to compel the party-in-government to knuckle under—a complete inversion of the internal party relations of a bygone era.[97]

B. Patronage

Historically, the prospect of public employment was the glue that held together the party apparatus, particularly at the local level. Patronage was "the response of government to the demands of an interest group—the party machine—that desires a particular policy in the distribution of public jobs."[98] Patronage was the carrot that induced active work on behalf of the party, and the stick to maintain loyalty for those who might diverge from the party's platform. American political parties leveraged patronage to ensure that the ideological fringe of their parties remained within the parties,[99] or even to forge alliances with third parties where local law favored their existence.[100] Particularly in times of political ferment, patronage loyalists "will impose fewer constraints on the party's flexibility in terms of policy and organizational innovation" compared to activists who are motivated by ideological or social goals.[101] However morally complicated the use of public contracting to grease the skids of political parties might be, patronage nonetheless represents the "necessary transaction costs for a decentralized and dispersed political system," critical building blocks for both compromise and coalitions.[102]

Moreover, patronage allowed the integration of an expanding electorate and new immigrants into democratic politics,[103] such that in operation "the spoils system was the triumph of democracy."[104] The party apparatus served to educate the expanded electorate and enable it to meaningfully exercise its voice in policymaking. Patronage, in turn, served as the necessary means to fund this party apparatus, supplementing limited party funds. Permitting this type of de facto public funding of political parties prevented politicking from becoming the exclusive prerogative of the rich, who without funding assistance would be the only ones able to engage in such an endeavor full time.[105]

The big-city patronage machines spawned a distinct type of politics based on a huge apparatus.[106] One account of George Washington Plunkitt, the consummate Tammany Hall ward boss, well captures real-life political parties a century ago:

Everybody in the district knows him. Everybody knows where to find him, and nearly everybody goes to him for assistance of one sort or another, especially the poor of the tenements. He is always obliging. He will go to the police courts to put in a good word for the "drugs and disorderlies" or pay their fines, if a good word is not effective. He will attend christenings, weddings, and funerals. He will feed the hungry and help bury the dead. A philanthropist? Not at all. He is playing politics all the time. Brought up in Tammany Hall, he has learned how to reach the hearts of the great mass of voters. He does not bother about reaching their heads. It is his belief that arguments and campaign literature have never gained votes.[107]

Patronage provided the structural support necessary to maintain the hierarchy of the machine.[108] The party boss used patronage as an inducement to his ward committeemen to garner their loyalty and to incentivize performance.[109] As one Chicago ward leader exhorted his field captains seeking promotion, "carry your precinct or you not only won't get it, but you'll lose your job altogether."[110] And the stakes were substantial; there were more than 450 patronage jobs per congressional district available in Chicago.[111]

Whatever the benefits, patronage could not shake the association with graft, as Chicago well exemplifies. Defending patronage on the basis of the benefits it provided to the parties risked justifying political parties' appropriation of government resources for its own benefit. Not surprisingly, patronage is most commonly perceived as a form of political corruption. In the United States, and across the advanced industrial world, patronage was tamed by the civil service reforms of the 19th and early 20th centuries.

In the United States, beginning with the civil service reforms of the Progressive Era, and continuing through the Hatch Act of 1939, political currents turned decisively against the patronage machines. The Pendleton Act of 1883[112] required that positions that fell within the scope of the federal "classified service" be filled by competitive examination and established the United States Civil Service Commission to oversee the Act.[113] The Act also impaired the ability of parties to house politically active members in the bureaucracy by prohibiting civil service members to "coerce the political action of any person or to interfere with any election."[114] An amendment in 1907 gave that prohibition more bite by forbidding civil service employees from taking "active part in political management or in political campaigns."[115] The Hatch Act of 1939 extended these prohibitions on political involvement, previously applicable only to members of the classified service, to all executive branch and agency employees with the exception of certain high-level officials.[116]

The Supreme Court then got in the act in 1976 with *Elrod v. Burns*.[117] The case arose from Cook County, effectively ground zero of patronage in America, and concerned a group of Republican patronage appointees who were either fired or were about to be fired when political control shifted to the Democrats. Per Justice Brennan, the Court found that firing public employees for their political affiliation violated the First Amendment, notwithstanding the political provenance of their initial patronage appointments. As against the potential impact on political parties, the Court held:

> We are not persuaded that the elimination of patronage practice or, as is specifically involved here, the interdiction of patronage dismissals, will bring about the demise of party politics. Political parties existed in the absence of active patronage practice prior to the administration of Andrew Jackson, and they have survived substantial reduction in their patronage power through the establishment of merit systems.[118]

In a subsequent dissent, Justice Scalia challenged that the Court's "categorical pronouncement reflects a naive vision of politics and an inadequate appreciation of the systemic effects of patronage in promoting political stability and facilitating the social and political integration of previously powerless groups."[119] For Justice Scalia,

> The statement that "political parties have already survived" has a positively whistling-in-the-graveyard character to it. Parties have assuredly survived—but as what? As the forges upon which the essential compromises of American political life are hammered out? Or merely as convenient vehicles for the conducting of national Presidential elections?[120]

In Justice Scalia's view, this decline of the party could be combatted by the patronage system:

> What the patronage system ordinarily demands of the party worker is loyalty to, and activity on behalf of, the organization itself rather than a set of political beliefs. He is generally free to urge *within the organization* the adoption of any political position; but if that position is rejected he must vote and work for the party nonetheless.[121]

C. Selecting the Candidates

Just as control over public employment and other benefits provided the operational drive of the parties, the main disciplining device enjoyed by political parties has been the capacity to ensure that any candidate for office be committed to its core political agenda. In turn, "he who can make the nominations is the owner of the party."[122] But that power has been increasingly pulled from the party hierarchy in the democratizing spirit of the day. When Boris Johnson was selected to fill the vacancy as prime minister through a poll of the Tory Party membership[123]—and the membership alone—this seemed almost anachronistic, a throwback to the days when the parties commanded the choice that would be put to the voters. It does not matter that the prime minister is formally the head of government of the prevailing parliamentary coalition. Formalities aside, the prime minister is the dominant figure of the British government and was in effect picked by a rump election among the 140,000 Tory Party members.[124] And the process was repeated to select Liz Truss once Johnson's government was compromised by his penchant for indiscretions.

The UK clearly stands as an outlier in maintaining the distinction between closed party processes and democratic participation in elections. Beginning with the reforms of the Progressive movement, the U.S. became the trailblazer in the opposite direction. Increasingly in the U.S., and around the democratic world,[125] the power to designate a party's electoral standard-bearer has passed from the party hierarchies to the mass of the electorate. The Supreme Court placed the causal responsibility for replacing "the caucuses of self-appointed legislators or other interested individuals" on "dissatisfaction with the manipulation of conventions."[126] But the result of a primary-based system was to "allow candidates to appeal over the heads of voters. They have become a prime device for weakening party discipline."[127]

Nor is this result happenstance. The rise of the primaries for candidate selection was part and parcel of late 19th-century efforts to thwart the power of political parties: "Party reforms sought to deprive local bosses of control over elections, and thereby diminish bosses' ability to leverage their influence over electoral outcomes to secure post-election indebtedness and loyalty."[128] Reforms proceeded as "state legislatures across the country adopted 'Australian' (i.e., state-printed, secret) ballot and party primary laws to regulate general elections, party nominating procedures, and the internal governance structure of parties."[129] Between the 1890s and World War I, more than half the states had enacted laws requiring direct primary nomination of candidates for office.[130]

There was little legal resistance to the rise of the primary requirement. These reforms predate the Brandeis and Holmes dissents that auger the modern law of political liberties.[131] The challenges to the mandatory primary were brought in state court, and the decisional law of the time saw parties not as rights-bearing entities capable of claiming liberty of association or expression, but as "agents of the state, whose functions were intimately tied up to the machinery of the state."[132] Further, "the election law jurisprudence of the time was fueled by profound distrust of party leaders, viewed to be corrupters of the electorate's will."[133]

In short order, the primary system spread across the country, though typically as part of a mixed system of selection:

> By the end of 1915, the direct primary had become the most widely employed nominating system in the United States. All but three states (Connecticut, New Mexico, and Rhode Island) used it for selecting candidates to at least some elective offices. Most of these forty-five states nominated virtually all offices in this way—78 percent of states in the east and 95 percent of western states did so.[134]

The direct primary set in motion a system pointing to the demise of the inherited model of the parties. Primary reform, along with many other reforms such as the Australian secret ballot, "ended the parties' firm-like control over ballot access and effectively created a 'market' for candidate entry."[135] The result was "neutered" political parties:

> Without direct control over nominations, parties could no longer determine the identity, loyalty, or quality of candidates appearing on the ballots under their name. As such, they could no longer effectively offer insurance to losing candidates as the number of party controlled positions rapidly diminished throughout the country. The cartel-like system of nominations was transformed into a political market, where individual, strategic politicians had to now make their own determination as to whether seeking a particular elective office was a worthwhile venture.[136]

Entrepreneurialism changed the incentive structures for candidates and even for incumbent officeholders. A new dynamic emerged in which "the loss of the party insurance mechanism increased the cost of candidate entry as the candidates themselves had to bear the full risk of running (i.e., they are now insuring themselves). Nevertheless, individuals now controlled their own electoral destiny."[137]

Even so, party leaders continued to maintain considerable power over the vetting of candidates and over likely primary nominations by a variety of means, most notably through the ongoing role of the convention in selecting the party's presidential nominee.[138] That too proved unstable. The events of 1968 set off changes relatively quickly, as "the disastrous Democratic Convention of that year . . . set in train a series of events that led, eventually, to a report that recommended reform of rules governing the selection of delegates."[139] After 1972, party control of even the presidential nomination process diminished drastically. The reforms following this period occurred in both parties, resulting in today's familiar system where: "A frontrunner emerges after the early primaries and all rivals then fall by the wayside; since 1972, there has always been one candidate in each party who has a clear majority of delegates committed to him by the start of the National Convention."[140]

Paradoxically, the post-1968 reforms failed in their major objective of shifting the nomination power from the party apparatus to the party-in-the-electorate. Primaries, and even party caucuses, draw scant voter participation. Typically, less than 20 percent of eligible voters participate, and, at times, that number is shockingly fewer.[141] As a result, "primary races now tend to be dominated by highly motivated extremists and interest groups, with the perverse result of leaving moderates and broader, less well-organized constituencies underrepresented."[142] By conferring decisional responsibility directly to the citizens, populist reformers create additional openings for media and interest groups to influence policy and electoral outcomes.[143] Not only is the party apparatus weakened but also incumbent politicians—once virtually untouchable in primary elections—are vulnerable to money and activism only loosely tethered to the party. A key moment came in 2014, when an unknown party insurgent defeated the House minority whip in the Republican Party. In bottom-line terms, "everyone worries about being the next Eric Cantor."[144]

Invariably, the loosening up of party controls over nomination weakens the hold of the party on not just candidates but also on elected officials: "Without direct control over nominations, . . . the cartel-like system of party control in place during much of the nineteenth century gradually began to give way to a political marketplace that is more common in today's largely candidate-centered electoral environment."[145]

IV. Conclusion

The demise of the political party is a common refrain in American political history. Many of the reforms of the Progressive Era were designed to kill off what Robert LaFollette termed the "impersonal, irresponsible, extra-legal" political machine.[146] At each stage, parties proved resilient and adapted to the changed legal environment. In LaFollette's own Wisconsin, the centerpiece of the reform effort was the open primary movement, finally approved by citizen referendum in 1904. Within a decade, however, the parties had reasserted themselves through stronger command of the patronage system and other levers of power, with LaFollette himself proving to be a master of the darker political arts.[147]

Critical to the party's reassertion at each stage has been the identity between the party and a program of governance. That identity, forged in negotiation with the interest groups that define the base of the party, in turn represents the party's platform vis-à-vis the external world. In the American context in which the parties draft a formal platform for the presidential nominating convention, "platform deliberations are a venue for activist groups to try and flex their muscles—to demonstrate their sway within the party and influence on the presidential nominee."[148] The bargain over platform is a visible give and take between the prospective party in government and the necessary constituents who will predictably lose sway after the election. The most powerful interest groups are often able to use their influence within the party to write their policy objectives directly into the platform. For example, each plank of the Tea Party's Contract from America was represented within the 2012 Republican national platform.[149]

Reducing to writing a party's theory of governance frames the core constituent boundaries of the political parties. At the same time, because party platforms are aspirational, not operational, and because they mostly go unread by the public, presidential candidates often view the platform-drafting process as an opportunity to engage in the indispensable process of placating various activists and interest groups.[150] The 2016 Democratic platform provides an instructive example: the Clinton campaign was willing to make several policy concessions to activists aligned with Senator Bernie Sanders, a form of appeasement after a bruising primary, while avoiding any explicit commitment itself to their policy demands.[151]

For populist leaders, a formal party platform operates as a constraint, even if just a declaration of programmatic intent. The limitation is not unlike a *caudillo* head's formal role within an organization hierarchy that included a potentially ambitious number two. Juan Perón and Peronism in Argentina present a useful example. Peronism continues to this day, but it was never a party. It is perpetually a "movement" or, today, a set of alliances.[152] As a result, Perón never operated within a structure in which either the organization or the ideology could displace the maximal leader.

Under Donald Trump, the Republican Party, once forged in the political commitments of Abraham Lincoln, abandoned any claim to party coherence. For the first time in its history, the Republican Party did not issue a national platform in 2020.[153] In place of the fifty-eight-page 2016 platform,[154] the party substituted a pro forma endorsement of the same platform and a short resolution proclaiming "that the Republican Party has and will continue to enthusiastically support the President's America-first agenda."[155]

Perhaps the apparent weakness of contemporary political parties is a phase that will pass, as has been true in the past. Perhaps. But parties are complex institutional actors that play an essential coordinating role in politics. Absent such a coordinating role, there is no particular reason for activists or funders or candidates or elected officials to harness themselves to the inevitable constraints of the party. There are many advantages to the scale of the modern political party, returning to the basic idea of the party as a political firm, but historically control over funds, government employment, and the ability to stand for office were the levers of party power. All have been compromised by legal reforms and, perhaps, we are witnessing the unraveling of the institutional form of American politics for the past two centuries.

At stake is far more than the candidacies of Trump or Sanders; Barry Goldwater and George McGovern were hardly inspired nominations at earlier times. Rather the unraveling of the integrative function of the parties means not only that the nomination process can spin out of control but also the coordination function of the unified firm is lost across the dimensions of party activity, most notably in governance. Looked at prescriptively, parties "might be the most effective vehicle for enabling the compromises and deals necessary to enable more effective governance despite the partisan divide."[156] Where parties fail, others fill the gap as "pressure groups thrive on the weaknesses of the parties."[157]

The dysfunctionality of Congress today is in no small measure the product of weak political institutions unable to cohere the disparate actors of the political arena into the ultimate aim of democratic governance. The structure of modern primaries and campaign finance reform efforts have stifled the ability of parties to effectively coordinate and direct production from within. At the same time, social media and direct fundraising lower transactions costs for candidates seeking to connect with voters, thus creating incentives to bypass what was largely feasible only through the moderating forces of the party machine. The result, in Coasean terms, is that our political entrepreneurs now find it better to buy, not make.

PART II

POLITICS UNDER POPULISM

4

Populism and the Here and Now

If the key to democratic stability is the strength of the core institutions both inside and outside government, then institutional weakness is an invitation to a new form of politics. The decline of the legislative branch is a virtual constant across the democratic world. Unlike the 20th-century confrontations between democracy and various forms of authoritarian or even totalitarian rule, the organizing principle of today is elections. The issue of power is resolved ultimately at the ballot box, and the elections are meaningful assessments of popular approbation, even if frequently held under circumstances far from laboratory purity.[1] Any assessment of the current state of democracy must start from the premise that the leaders most problematic for democratic legitimacy also are elected to office, oftentimes with tremendous popular support. The consolidation of power by Orbán in Hungary or Modi in India or Erdoğan in Turkey or even Putin in Russia begins with an electoral mandate, and in some cases a strong base of popular support.[2]

The fact of elections alone marks the triumph of some form of popular sovereignty. Using a relatively austere metric of whether the head of state and legislature are elected, Freedom House captures the dramatic transformations at the end of the 20th century. In 1987, there were only sixty-six countries that were considered electoral democracies. By 2003, there were 121 electoral democracies, a number that has remained more or less stable, and by 2017 there were 123 countries that could claim a head of state and legislature elected through substantially free and fair elections.[3]

At the same time, the circumstances of new rulers coming to office through the electoral process should not obscure the fundamental departure from democratic norms. Unfortunately, the formal processes of governmental selection tell only part of the story. While the number of electoral democracies has nominally remained high, the number of countries that afford relatively free political rights to opposition groups, rival political parties, minorities, and others seeking to dislodge the incumbent regime is much smaller. Only eighty-three countries are now deemed "free" by Freedom House, meaning they afford at least a minimum of the political rights associated with democracy and ensure acceptable levels of transparency and non-corruption in government.

The Freedom House data demarcate the dual requirements for democracy. The first is a simplified matter of form: elected heads of state come to office and are retained through popular selection. The second is a matter of substance in terms of the institutional attributes of democratic governance. Coupling the two features to include political freedoms and transparency of government hearkens back to a sense of democracy as not only the selection of who rules but also a mechanism of meaningful review by the electorate of the performance of those in office. This account of democracy presents elections not merely as a present choice of who should rule but as a system of retrospective accountability by which an informed populace can remove from office those who have lost the confidence of the voters. As presented most famously by Joseph Schumpeter, the ability of voters to grade their rulers for past performance, especially to find them wanting, is what keeps political elites in check.[4] The measure of political freedom in regimes that have elections provides a real sense whether it is possible to mobilize around opposition to how governmental power has been exercised. In turn, these political freedoms offer an important point of demarcation for liberal democracy from illiberal regimes in which opposition electoral prospects are compromised, if not totally illusory.

Presented as a conflict between electoral choice and illiberal restrictions on political activity directs the inquiry back to populism. Much has been written on the nature of populism, and it is befuddled by a central paradox. Populism in its modern incarnation is an electoral phenomenon that claims to represent the will of the people. The asserted right to speak for the people is validated by winning elections, seemingly the fulfillment of democracy. Claiming to speak for the people is a rhetorical trope of a demagogue like Donald Trump, but it was also the hallmark of Franklin Roosevelt. It is best to dig a little deeper into how the claim for popular approbation cashes out.

There is an authoritarian streak to both left- and right-wing populist movements that, with alarming frequency, threatens some of the preconditions of democratic governance. Populists tend not to tolerate opposition parties. They are at their core anti-pluralist. The list of departures from idealized democracy goes on. Populists tend to use police and prosecutorial power against adversaries; they tend toward suppression of dissident speech, either through curtailment of access to the media or through legal retaliation; and they tend to push the boundaries of executive unilateral authority.[5] Certainly, questions of intensity and degree may take the Venezuela of Nicolás Maduro or the Hungary of Viktor Orbán outside the boundaries of democracy. But elements of aggressive use of incumbent power are seen in many regimes that still function as democracies, even if beleaguered ones at times. Standing alone, this illiberalism is not sufficient to define populism.

Rather, returning to the observation from Isaiah Berlin a half century ago, the defining feature for present purposes is the hostility to established institutional pathways.[6] The norms of governing are not perceived as matters of statecraft to be learned. Such norms are obstacles to the politics of immediacy. Here, Eric Posner captures the essence simply as populism centered on "a political attitude that distrusts established institutions on the assumption that they thwart popular will."[7] Populism challenges stable democratic governance that, at its heart, must ensure that the majority is ultimately able to prevail, while at the same time making sure that the majority does not win too much. Put another way, populism sets aim at the ability of established democratic governance to "tam[e] political power through a constitutional framework."[8] To return to Schumpeter, one of the preconditions for successful democratic governance must be an "effective range of political decision."[9] No electoral system can long survive if each election poses anew the continued existence of the fundamentals of governance. In much the same way, no baseball game would ever come to resolution if each side could forever contest the fundamentals of the game, such as how many balls and strikes resolve each at bat.

Much attention is paid to the rhetorical style of populism and its anger at unresponsive elites on high and menacing outsiders from below.[10] But demagogic rhetoric and sheer anger do not capture the complexity of populist grievances: "Populism is keenly attuned to the distribution not only of resources and opportunities but of honor, respect, and recognition, which may be seen as unjustly withheld from 'ordinary' people and unjustly accorded to the unworthy and undeserving."[11] The concern for dignity echoes the "status anxiety" that historian Richard Hofstadter chronicled as integral to a paranoid tradition in American politics.[12] But the emotive quality of the political appeals alone cannot capture the fundamental tension between populist immediacy and the institutionally restrained core of stable democracy.

A well-functioning democratic state should offer citizens a sense of individual dignity emanating from control over their political fate and a sense of collective gain from an accountable state delivering material improvements over time. In its place, populism offers a sense of shared indignation and nurtures a demand for immediate personal returns. As David Runciman well captures the dynamic, in "place of personal dignity plus collective benefits," populist leaders "promise personal benefits plus collective dignity."[13] This in turn fuels the "axis of resentment" unifying the nationalist agenda from Europe to Asia.[14]

For purposes of this book, "populism" is defined primarily as a form of democratic governance with weak institutions. Democracy without institutional foundations becomes unmoored, unable to plan or deliver long-term benefits, unable to mediate social conflict, and unable to invoke the longer time horizon necessary for commitment to repeat engagement by political rivals. For many, such as political theorist Nancy Rosenblum, the commitment to repeat play starts with the building blocks of democratic politics, the political parties. Invoking Edmund Burke's idea of a regulated rivalry,[15] the longer time horizon of politics allows government to deliver beyond the immediate demand of satisfaction of desires.

Populism asserts the right to majoritarian command, what Ming-Sung Kuo well captures as a claim to "unmediated politics."[16] Such unmediated politics mistakes the electoral form of democratic selection for the manner in which democracies are governed. Populists bring a blend of anti-elitism and anti-institutionalism that is in turn validated by a view of elections as plebiscitary processes that must command through an ultra-majoritarian ethos.[17] On this view, winning is everything that matters, and each election is a validation of the assertion of majority power.

By contrast, democracies function by having elections determine who is in charge but leave relatively unaddressed the question of, "In charge of what?" Democratic governance operates through institutional arrangements that have a presumptive claim to endurance for having served across momentary considerations. These institutional arrangements, particularly the political institutions of governance, become targets for populism precisely because they "place effective constraints on the executive."[18]

Modern constitutional governance draws from the unwritten English constitutional tradition, which in turn has long recognized that there are "legally unenforceable customs that regulate and restrain the formal powers granted to governmental actors."[19] Such conventions derive from past practice, from the fact that officials believe themselves bound by the rule, and that the rule appears reasonable as time goes on.[20] Under this view, "customs and conventions arise from what people do, not from what they agree or promise."[21] In the constitutional tradition exemplified by Edmund Burke, the foundations of constitutional government

> evolved slowly and incrementally over hundreds of years . . . because the existing institutional arrangements reflect the accumulated wisdom of centuries of political decisions; each incremental step is the product either of rational deliberation or natural development and has been tested by the experience of many years. The cumulative product reflects a reason far superior to that of any individual or generation.[22]

As understood, the aim of British constitutionalism "was to ensure that these legal powers, formally in the hands of the Crown, were in practice exercised by

Ministers in accordance with the principles of responsible and representative government."[23] A. V. Dicey, the most recognized expositor of the English constitutional tradition, concluded that the role of constitutional law, regardless of whether enforceable by judicial decree, was the preservation of democratic governance: "Our modern code of constitutional morality secures, though in a roundabout way, what is called abroad the 'sovereignty of the people.' "[24] Even in the conservative exposition by Edmund Burke, the constitution compels that the "constituent parts of a state are obliged to hold their public faith with each other."[25]

This veneration of established traditions and limitations on popular demands fares poorly in our more democratic age. The conflict is well captured by Bulgarian political scientist Ivan Krastev, who finds in the post–Cold War period a rise of individual engagements that have deepened the democratic experience, but they also made democratic societies less governable.[26] Writing of the populist wave in Europe, Krastev argues that the "current crisis is rooted in the fact that European societies are more open and democratic than ever before. But it is precisely this openness that leads to the ineffectiveness and lack of trust in democratic institutions."[27] In effect, the electoral mechanism proved available as a lever to push back against the ways liberal democracies govern themselves, particularly their mix of social welfare and market freedoms.[28] In a deep sense, after decades of post-1989 reforms leaving more and more to the market to decide, rather than the state, democracy is finally striking back not only in the newly created fragile democracies but also across the established democratic order.[29]

The burgeoning literature on populism defines its core in terms of its demagogic style of politics, its claim for democratic immediacy in terms of policy demands, its fear of outsiders and elites, its sense of a victimhood born of cultural assault, and its disregard of core values of democratic contestation. All this comes together in a mix of xenophobia and agitation that yields deep contempt for the liberal norms of modern democracies. For present purposes, the issue is not to separate out this taxonomy nor to rank the relative importance of each attribute. What matters is how the populist moment leads to a confrontation with the forms of democratic governance.

"Caudillo" politics requires the leader to speak to "the people" directly without legislative or administrative channels, sidelining the easily denounced institutional media and the customary filters of office. And so, the first Twitter presidential campaign in the United States became the nation's first Twitter presidency. From Roosevelt's fireside chats on, presidents have capitalized on the new channels provided by the technologies of communication. But for Trump, Twitter was not simply a means of communication. It offered him the ability to deliver messages without official process. He touted accomplishments and boosted allies; demeaned anyone who provoked his ire; and spread rumors, falsehoods, and conspiracy theories. He even used Twitter to announce policies, often without establishing legality or political support.

For Trump, Twitter was a technological upgrade. What Hugo Chávez pioneered with his thousands of hours of nightly "Alo Comandante" television gabfests, Trump imported as a constant cycle of Tweets directed to millions of supporters. When Trump used the pandemic daily briefings for hours of unmediated self-promotion, Chávez's ghost smiled knowingly.

Chávez and Trump also shared the propensity for self-absorption that often descended into absurdity. Gaffes are inevitable, but all the more so when all wisdom putatively springs from a compromised leader. Institutional capabilities are cast aside in favor of boasts, unfounded claims, exaggerations, and dissembling, all put to the crude partisan test of are you with me or against me. This crude discard of anyone not deep in the camp—including other nations and the U.S. citizenry—has insidious consequences when lives depend on the veracity of the president's words.[30] Trump consistently exaggerated throughout his tenure. He compounded the issue with implausible projections about the path of the virus that causes COVID-19 and the promotion of drugs of highly questionable efficacy against the disease, such as hydroxychloroquine. In Brazil, Bolsonaro matched these fabrications step for step. As Jan-Werner Müller summarizes, populists "will persist with their representative claim no matter what; because their claim is of a moral and symbolic—not an empirical—nature, it cannot be disproven. When in opposition, populists are bound to cast doubt on the institutions that produce the 'morally wrong' outcomes."[31]

To focus the discussion, it is important to identify the key mechanisms by which the hyper-democratic claims of legitimacy of populist rules conflict with the premises of democratic governance.

I. The Temporal Dimension of Democracy

At the heart of any conception of democracy is the simple ability "to throw the bums out." Whether termed "rotation in office," as advanced by Adam Pzreworski and his collaborators,[32] or as a renewal of consent, as framed by Bernard Manin,[33] there is a requirement of repeat play necessary for democratic governance. Indeed the central challenge in any new democracy is the ability to convince the losers of today that they might indeed be the winners of tomorrow, made critical by the fact that in any new democracy there will by definition have been no evidence of a successful electoral surrender of power to future challengers. It is well worth recalling the lack of historical precedents for the American election of 1800, the first time an incumbent head of state was removed electorally by a challenger.[34]

Stable democracies require an internalization of politics as repeat play. Populist elections claim a mandate from the people beyond choosing officeholders. The mandate does not hearken back to the successes in office of past partisan affiliates but to an indictment of a system that is claimed to be rigged or captured by enemies of the people. Elections over mandates risk the same repudiation of institutional accommodation of divisions as do plebiscites. Stable democracies require the institutionalization of a politics that presumes deliberation, procedural order, and accommodation. For both plebiscites and populism, the election defines the agenda. Period.

In each case, there is an up/down choice as to policy outcomes, without intermediation of legislative trade-offs, measures of the intensity of preferences, negotiated accommodation, and all the mechanisms that elicit cooperation from those in dissent and moderation from those in power. Recognition of the temporal dimension of democratic governance draws back at least as far as Tocqueville's famous account of pre–Civil War America. Among his many observations, Tocqueville focused on the prospect of deep mistakes in elections that could promote men of unknown capacities or proven temperament.[35] The famous warning about the "tyranny of the majority" was penned in observations about America under President Andrew Jackson, a wealthy and rapacious real estate speculator who was elected on the crest of popular hatred of the "elites" represented by John Quincy Adams and the established politics after the Revolution.[36] For Tocqueville, a central question in the survival of the republican experiment was the chance to make what he termed "retrievable mistakes," the capacity to allow time to correct missteps.[37]

The concept of intertemporal trade-offs is key to the design of many democratic institutions. One theory for the acceptance of judicial review is precisely the desire of all parties to hedge their bets in the face of uncertainty about future electoral prospects. In new democracies with strong constitutional courts, this is the process that I have termed "democratic hedging"[38] and that Tom Ginsburg addresses as an "insurance" theory of limits on the exercise of political power.[39] Many of the institutional features of healthy democracies incorporate structures that serve as a check on the majority, ranging from the shadow cabinet in Britain to the use of the American filibuster to force supermajority legislation on issues of deep contestation.[40] When functioning properly, each of these mechanisms allows the opposition to check majoritarian excesses by offering alternative policy claims within the framework of a shared governance enterprise. Of course, if a shadow cabinet became simply a platform for denunciation or if the minority party in the U.S. Senate were to attempt to filibuster every piece of legislation or executive appointment, then these deliberative mechanisms would become their opposite. The institutional line between participatory inclusion and sheer obstruction of governance is at all times precarious in the fraught world of partisan politics.

Impetuous populism rejects temporal restraints in the name of the will of the people. As a result there is an urgency to overcoming all such restraints to maximize the power of angry incumbency. The forms vary, but the need to unleash the power of the moment persists. This pattern is repeated with shocking regularity. Elections persist even in Putin's Russia and provide a useful modern source of legitimacy for increasingly old-fashioned despotism.[41] If the Venezuelan Congress is an impediment to the increasingly tyrannical rule of President Nicolás Maduro, then the captive Supreme Court can declare the Congress disbanded and a new constituent assembly created.[42] At the other end of the spectrum, if North Carolina Republicans lose the governorship, they too can rewrite the rules of government by neutering gubernatorial power and curtailing voter access to the polls.[43] In each case, the institutions that cool off politics prove vulnerable to a one-time power grab.

II. Fractionated Power

In an earlier work, *Fragile Democracies*, I devote considerable attention to the distinct frailties of new democracies as they emerge from conflict or an autocratic past. One of the defining characteristics is that the complete package of democratic institutions rarely mature together or quickly. In circumstances of duress and uncertainty, power gravitates to the first organized entity to consolidate. Almost invariably that will be the executive, and with it comes the pathologies associated with unilateral executive rule: corruption, cronyism, and clientelism. A hypertrophied executive in turn resists efforts to limit its authority and has every incentive not to allow other sources of constitutional authority to realize their mandate.

Populism runs this account in reverse. Populism takes issue with obstacles to immediate returns to electoral success, in which case all separation of powers fails a legitimacy test before the mandate of the national leader. What James Madison hailed as the virtues of "filtration" of popular sentiment through institutional intermediation becomes understood as the frustration of the will of the people.[44] The hostility to cross-institutional constraints flows from the same impulse as the narrowing of the timeframe for political rewards. For Jan-Werner Müller, the new populism begins with hostility to pluralism.[45] There is a claim to speak for a unified people, fighting against elites whose perceived illegitimacy is a source of great anger. The impulse toward what Nancy Rosenblum terms "holism" challenges the concept of institutional accommodation that underlies constitutional democracy.[46] A monist commitment to an abiding truth that captures the interests of all the people (save the unredeemable outliers) cannot commit to separation of powers any more than it can to rotation in office.

Part of this phenomenon is kicking in an open door; the dysfunctionality of parliamentary authority is a plague upon almost all the houses of democracy. The premise of modern constitutional democracies is the primacy of the legislative branch, denominated by the Article I powers in the U.S. setting. Legislative weakness furthers the trend. Regulatory control grows as a reflection of expanded executive authority. No one rises to the level of chief executive without a desire to act, and legislative inaction invites executive circumvention. But congressional inaction can result from the sheer dysfunction of the legislature, a political disagreement with the agenda of the executive, or the inability to cohere on a policy initiative in the face of internal political disagreement.[47] An executive riding a populist wave would not distinguish among the sources of legislative inaction and would instead see each as a rejection of his or her electoral mandate.

Around the world, populist regimes attempt to curtail any challenge to executive authority, not simply parliamentary opposition. In Poland the ruling party mobilized around attacks on judicial independence; in Hungary it even includes the attempt to expel the entire Central European University; and in South Africa it included President Zuma's efforts to hand-pick government officials ranging from ministers to chief justice of the Constitutional Court, to anticorruption enforcers.[48] In each case, the overweening executive appeals to the plebiscitary authority of his own election.

Particularly vulnerable to populist attack is the judiciary. In the face of legislative lack of capacity to govern, a strong executive increasingly finds the judiciary to be a major obstacle to its immediate designs. Part of this is structural, especially in recent democracies that followed the German example of creating a powerful constitutional court. Such apex courts stand apart from the ordinary judiciary in being tasked with restraint of antidemocratic excesses of the state. That lands courts in the uncomfortable position of invoking authority under the generally underspecified principles of a democratic charter against the democratically elected governments. As a result, the courts frequently find themselves in pitched battles with consolidating political power. But part of the tension is a different by-product of the personality driven populist style of governance. Judicial appointment typically marches to a different beat than political election. Judicial terms do not dovetail with legislative or executive elections and thus serve to retard the immediate realization of the popular will—by design. But that means that judges are rarely the executive's people and are perceived as an impediment.

Not surprisingly then, the courts are a frequent irritant to the populist agenda, precisely because they may assume the role of "safeguarding the integrity of the legislative process," protecting against "legislative capture" and "correcting [for] external effects" of seemingly ordinary exercises of executive authority.[49] Once courts assume the mantle of protectors against democratic backsliding, there is a push toward an expansive view of the judiciary's mandate as protecting the minimum core requirements necessary for competitive democracy.[50]

No less surprising, the courts then become the targets for political attack, most clearly in countries such as Poland and Hungary where curtailing the power of the courts is a central plank of the populist agenda. But in numerous other countries, such as Israel and South Africa and Argentina, to name but a few, a plebiscitary executive tries to use his or her political wave of support to overwhelm the judiciary. When Donald Trump railed against "so-called judges" or the "Mexican judge," he joined a well-orchestrated chorus of attacks on judicial independence as a division of power that thwarts the demand for immediacy of the populist surge.

The institutional capacity for judicial resistance is limited. Depending on the form of judicial appointment, the executive is restrained for varying time periods in dismantling judicial frustration of a populist agenda. In Israel, for example, the self-selection of Supreme Court justices was overcome by nomination reforms.[51] In Argentina, the Kirchner government repeatedly sought to make any federal judge removable by a majority vote in the Congress, a threat that ended only with the defeat of the Peronists in national elections.[52] In Poland, the government limited the ability of the Constitutional Tribunal to publish opinions and imposed lowered retirement age limits to remove many from office—a tactic borrowed from the Orbán assaults on the Hungarian Constitutional Court.[53] And in the United States, the primary legislative success of the Trump administration was the rapid appointment of young, ideologically tinged judges who will alter the political valence of the federal judiciary for a generation to come.[54]

III. Intermediary Organizations

In separate works, David Cole and Jack Goldsmith argue that the risk of executive unilateralism is held in check, even in an era of legislative dysfunction, by the soft power of civil society institutions.[55] These take many forms, from the formal organizations of trade unions or churches, to the volunteer missions of groups like the American Civil Liberties Union, to the systemic review offered by an independent media. By and large, modern populism eschews the hard edge of state repression as such. While there are some regimes, Turkey's Recep Tayyip Erdoğan comes immediately to mind, that have used the police power to jail journalists and selected political opponents, that is more the exception than the rule.[56] While these intermediary institutions play an invaluable checking function against anti-governance excess, they are also perceived to be the rearguard fighters for the established order against which the populist wave rebels.

The easiest example is the press. The parcelization of information is an increasing feature of the high-tech era. The loss of a common core of observed facts in the face of social media networks facilitates polarized politics and fuels the paranoid streak that invariably accompanies populism. The desire to retrench amid the familiar is a commonplace reaction to social and economic insecurity, something that new information sources can nurture and insulate from challenge. Thus is born the charge of "fake news" as part of the rallying cry against the established order. And just as Hollywood sets the cultural norms for the arts, Washington has inspired every tyrant in the making to accede to the fake news claim, invariably to obscure misdeeds from corruption to human rights violations.

But the issue cuts deeper. Embedded within the populist impulse is, in Müller's words, the desire "to cut out the middleman . . . and to rely as little as possible on complex party organizations as intermediaries between citizens and politicians."[57] The classic intermediary institutions of modern democracy are the political parties. Indeed, as famously formulated by E. E. Schattschneider, "political parties created democracy and modern democracy is unthinkable save in terms of the parties."[58] But as democratic governance is hollowed out by the failing legislative branch, the parties and the party leaders become perceived as part of what Robert Dahl in 1965 already identified as the "new democratic Leviathan," a self-perpetuating form of governance that is "welfare-oriented, centralized, bureaucratic, tamed and controlled by competition among highly organized elites, and, in the perspectives of the ordinary citizen, somewhat remote, distant and impersonal."[59]

The hollowing out of customary democratic politics, to borrow Peter Mair's formulation, is most vivid in Europe. It results in part from the expansion of European-level bureaucratic command in which "there is little scope for input-oriented legitimacy and decision-makers can only rarely be mandated by voters."[60] In exaggerated form, this means that Belgium and Spain can withstand many months without a national government and yet continue most functions relatively unimpeded.[61] The traditional political parties become not so much organized forms of policy debate, but rival administrators of the same bureaucratic enterprise that largely exists outside the sphere of democratic accountability. Nor is this simply a European disorder. Substitute Beltway for Brussels and the demand for starving the beast for Brexit and the same phenomenon is observable in the U.S. as well.

Being subject to commands imposed from without affronts the dignity of democracy as self-government by the demos and compounds the sense of community being taken over by those from outside. As Ivan Krastev and

Stephen Holmes capture the post-1989 insult felt in Eastern European terms, the "countries ostensibly being democratized were compelled, in order to meet the conditions for EU membership, to enact policies formulated by unelected bureaucrats from Brussels and international lending organizations."[62] National-level elections increasingly had less to do with governance and more to do with expressive politics venting deep cultural and social grievance. "Voters regularly threw the incumbents out, it is true, but the policies—formulated in Brussels—didn't substantially change."[63] Democratic elections require a fine balance between meaningful choice and systemic stability. "If nothing is at stake, if policies remain the same regardless of who wins, people observe that they voted in election after election, governments changed, and their lives remained the same."[64] But that is only half the balance: "The mirror danger occurs when too much is at stake, when having been on the losing side is highly costly to some groups and their prospects to be on the winning side in the future are dim, so that they see their losses as permanent or at least long-standing."[65]

Without intermediary institutions capable of transmitting interests into governance, and without institutions able to do so within an accepted democratic governance framework, the executive strongman appears as the only hope for the ill-defined populist agenda. Intermediary institutions cease serving as the glue that ties the population to the project of self-governance. Instead, like the press and political parties, their utility is only in fidelity to executive commands. The advent of social media and targeted broadcasting allows direct engagement to bypass the organizational structures formerly necessary for populism. Even a comparison of Donald Trump and Silvio Berlusconi shows the difference in impulse. Whereas Berlusconi carefully built a party apparatus of Forza Italia, with local committees adjacent to every parish in Italy, Trump used Twitter and other forms of direct outreach to communicate directly to disengaged partisans.[66]

IV. Transparent Governance

With few exceptions, where the full range of institutions of democratic governance fail to take hold, what emerges is executive rule. It is far easier to elect the national savior than it is to forge political parties and legislative competence. Such rulers have a propensity to identify themselves with the struggle of the people. Sometimes, perhaps often, this is justified in the new days of a democratic regime. The first rulers are often those that led the struggle for a democratic opening, with Nelson Mandela a prime example. But once in office, these leaders—and here Mandela is the exception not the norm—frequently and unfortunately come to identify their continued rule with the fruition of the popular will. Not for nothing, take the cynical British account of postcolonial rule: "one man, one vote, one time."[67] The longer in office, the more likely that an engorged executive stands as the key to any claim to government benefits, contracts, or favors. In turn, much of economic life becomes impossible without increased engagement with state regulatory authority, further collapsing the prospect of democratic contestation.

In newly minted democracies, the risk is that the first party in office will use the soft forms of power to cement rule. Concentrated state authority means that prospects for employment and government contracts depend on contacts to the ruling elite, oftentimes the ruler himself. From the post-revolutionary PRI in Mexico to the legacy of Robert Mugabe in Zimbabwe, unfractionated power in the hands of a dominant leader or party translates to a kleptocratic network that reinforces the pivotal role of the central leader.

South Africa's painful descent into corruption is an object lesson here. The South African Constitution makes the president the head of state and head of government, and selection of the president is by the National Assembly, meaning that there is no separation of powers anywhere in the federal government except for the independent Constitutional Court.[68] No opposition party has matured in South Africa, and there is no experience of rotation in office outside the African National Congress in post-apartheid South Africa. The dominance of the ANC beyond the political realm is captured in the derisive term of "tenderpreneurs," the name given to wealthy so-called business venturers whose primary capital is lucrative government contracts.[69] Control of the state apparatus allows the older structure of political parties to be pushed aside in favor of political movements organized around the personality of the leader and a mass following based on loyalty to that leader.[70] Sujit Choudhry notes that "dominant political parties [often] politicize public resources over which government has a monopoly and deploy them for partisan purposes, which gives them an electoral advantage which opposition parties lack, precisely because they do not wield government authority."[71]

As with the problem of fractionated power, the experience of new democracies illustrates the risk for the established ones. Populism tends to unwind internal norms of compliance that help keep self-interest within tolerable bounds. In some ideal fashion, government decision-making should be transparent, the rules should be well established ex ante, there should be independent ombudsmen to check temptations to graft, and there should exist a host of institutional practices that smooth transitions in governance. The problem is that no democracy ever satisfies all these conditions all the time. Incumbents are always eager to do more than they should before ceding office. Partisans are always rewarded with an extra dollop of government jobs or contracts. There is always a temptation to alter the rules so as to stymie the prospects of the opposition. Even as a formal matter, rules may be bent; Britain and Canada still allow the government the power to call elections when it perceives it most suitable to its prospects for re-election.

What sets apart the populist regimes is the systematic assault on all these structures of governance. One result is a propensity to exercise state authority through one-off arrangements, a form of governing through a series of dependent attachments on the formal or informal discretion of the chief executive. This is the core of the clientelism that plagues despotic regimes. An obvious rhetorical example is Trump who championed himself as mastering the art of the deal. Trump began his tenure as president with a rejection of seemingly all institutional forms of doing business, with examples from NAFTA to every multilateral treaty in the international domain. This translated into attacks on the State Department, the intelligence services, and any institutional byway that did not turn on idiosyncratic personal assessments.

All new presidents resent the constraining role of the administrative state. Settled bureaucracies frequently show all the dexterity of an overloaded cruise ship in changing direction. But that bureaucratic constraint allows government to function predictably across changes in administration and helps order the lives of the dependent citizenry. In populist times, however, those ordinary workings become an impediment to immediate returns.

Consider the tax bill that was the one actual legislative initiative of the Trump administration prior to the COVID-19 stimulus. The tax bill is not so much instructive for its paradoxical redistribution toward corporate earnings but for the process of its implementation. There were no committee hearings, no attempt to reconcile the likely impact on the deficit with the scoring of the fiscal impact of the congressional budget estimates, and no attempt to cohere a policy that justified disparate treatment of similarly situated taxpayers. The previous institutional checks on budget impacts and the requirement of scoring spending and tax bills through the Congressional Budget Office and the Joint Committee on Taxation were jettisoned.[72] Indeed, when the Congressional Budget Office issued a caustic report on the proposed Trump repeal of Obamacare, the Republican response was a proposed dismantling of the office.[73] Similarly, any mechanism of public debate was removed from adoption of the tax bill by the Senate, the so-called world's greatest deliberative body. Power not policy is the leitmotif of populist governance, even if few of the benefits are likely to provide actual benefit to the populist electorate.

The dismantling of independent checks on command-center politics bears special attention. Again South Africa provides a cautionary note. As President Zuma consolidated power and plunged the country into the deeper and deeper recesses of cronyist corruption, there was little if any opposition from within government itself. The exceptional checking function came from the National Prosecuting Authority and its Directorate of Special Operations, an independent anticorruption watchdog agency. In 2009, at the instigation of President Zuma, the Congress abolished these organizations and placed their power within the national police, which was in turn accountable to the Security Ministry and, by extension, to President Zuma himself. Only the intervention of the South African Constitutional Court in *Glenister v. President of the Republic of South Africa* saved this last bastion of independent accountability.[74]

Using the history of fragile democracies as a warning for mature ones suggests a discomforting parallel in the U.S. The corruption scandals that swirled around the Trump candidacy and presidency also sparked investigations by independent authorities. The response from the administration was the firing of a non-subservient FBI director, vitriolic attacks on the independent prosecutor Robert Mueller, and the systematic dismantling of the Inspector General system for overseeing the functioning of the executive branch. The U.S. is not South Africa, but the warning signs are there.

V. Norms of Governance

A constitutional democracy is defined by more than the formal allocations of power, the parchment barriers of last resort. As Steven Levitsky and Daniel Ziblatt note, "Democracies work best—and survive longer—when constitutions are reinforced by norms of mutual toleration and restraint in the exercise of power."[75] English constitutionalism provides the great lesson in how institutional accommodations never reduced to writing can nonetheless provide a blueprint for democratic governance.[76] Whether in the unwritten British model or in the practices that give life to the spare American text, constitutional governance requires fidelity to norms that are understood to constrain the exercise of power, even if never reduced to formal commands.

Constitutionalism has never been exclusively reduced to the written text either in terms of its commands or its interpretation. The American framers drew deeply from the lessons of British constitutional structure, despite the absence of any textual articulation of its constitutional law. Instead, Britain relies on a series of statutes, practices, and under-specified understandings to frame a constitutional order that, in turn, depends heavily, in the words of William Gladstone, on "the good faith of those who work it."[77] For Schumpeter the ensuing acceptance of "democratic self-control" allows moderation, and "this involves a lot of voluntary subordination."[78]

American constitutional law tends to overvalue Supreme Court decisions, particularly on matters of contested definitions of individual rights, at the expense of the less celebrated and less litigated experience-based forms of governance. Only rarely do such institutional matters present themselves for litigated resolution. And even then, as often as not, they are treated as political questions not proper for judicial resolution. Lived experiences and the institutional arrangements they have generated have been critical components of the actual practice of government since the early years of the Republic. As the Supreme Court put it recently, although the judiciary has the responsibility " 'to say what the law is,' . . . it is equally true that the longstanding 'practice of the government' can inform our determination of 'what the law is.' "[79] This is especially true when it comes to the distribution of authority among the branches of the federal government. Indeed, the idea that historical practice might inform that distribution is "neither new nor controversial."[80] Two hundred years ago, James Madison recalled that it "was foreseen at the birth of the Constitution" that "difficulties and differences of opinion might occasionally arise in expounding terms & phrases necessarily used in such a charter . . . and that it might require a regular course of practice to liquidate & settle the meaning of some of them."[81]

All established political orders incorporate the institutional memory embodied in "long-term accretions of practice."[82] Government, like any complex organization, must be able to function efficiently. Allowing practices to settle allows coordination across diverse fronts.[83] Enforceable law must reach beyond the formal text to the "network of tacit understandings and unwritten conventions, rooted in the soil of social interaction."[84] The idea of constitutional governance as a means of effectively coordinating societal needs derives at least from David Hume and the insight that "the goods of human society stem largely from doing as others do, in certain limited but crucial matters, so that each person's purposes in all other matters will mutually further others' purposes instead of crossing them."[85] The process of institutional settlement is then the integration of accepted mutually beneficial arrangements into the conduct of governmental affairs.

Populism disrupts the presumption of legitimacy attaching to time-honored institutional arrangements that come to define the settled expectations of citizens in the society. Two examples illustrate this point. The first grows out of the role of the political opposition in a system that accepts rotation in office as a historic norm. Invariably, the shift in power means that one side has control of the police power that includes the power to prosecute.

Successful democracies avoid criminalizing the opposition, or, put another way, democracies that use the criminal law to retaliate politically do not long remain democracies. Despite arguable violations of law during Bush's war on terror, the Obama administration wisely resisted calls for initiating criminal prosecutions of the prior Administration. Similarly, despite the power of Congress to initiate impeachment proceedings against an opposition party president, such examples are rare in American history. The four historic examples highlight the importance of restraint. The impeachment of Andrew Johnson came after determined Republican congressional efforts to more aggressively prosecute the Civil War and reflected deep political divisions in the Republican coalition. Yet the particulars for which Johnson was impeached involved political choices of the executive. Johnson was ultimately absolved by the Senate.[86] In contrast, Richard Nixon was charged with offense against his office and was forced to resign. But the impeachment of Bill Clinton bore neither the historic decisiveness of the Civil War nor the clear criminality of the Nixon obstruction of justice. Rather, it signaled a descent from principle into the demonization of the opposition and tarnished American politics as a result. The first impeachment of Donald Trump may prove to have been a mistaken exercise in partisan engagement, despite the charged offenses being grounded in the use of official power than in personal political agenda or personal failings. A freighted partisan environment does not readily distinguish between the missteps of a Richard Nixon, on the one hand, and that of an Andrew Johnson or Bill Clinton, on the other hand. The election of Donald Trump came at a period of polarization that takes so many of the customary presumptions of a working democracy off the table.[87] Under conditions of polarization, the impeachment power had to be wielded surgically to signal only the clearest and most wanton departures from institutional propriety. The American Republic has been strengthened by the reluctance of the Congress to start a potential death spiral of war of the legislature against the executive when each rests in different partisan hands.

While impeachment is a power that should be held in reserve, there are some powers that history cautions should simply not be used. No greater departure from the presumption of democratic legitimacy of the opposition can be found than the fixation of the Trump administration with "crooked Hillary." The crowd incitement to "lock her up" was unheard of in American history. History looks well upon the pardon of Richard Nixon by Gerald Ford, preferring the political repudiation of official misconduct to the criminal justice system. But populist impatience allows none of these niceties. To the campaign chorus of locking up Clinton was added the persistent berating of the Department of Justice for not turning on Trump's political opponents. There is no express constitutional prohibition against the prosecution of the nominee of one major political party by her victorious opponent, assuming the norms of indictment and trial are followed. Nor is there any textual restraint on a president's efforts to direct the investigative powers of federal law enforcement authorities. But constitutional culture is to the contrary. Quite simply, there has never been anything like this in American history.

As with many parts of the populist assault on democratic governance, the same themes echo internationally. Bolsonaro described the country's armed forces—the agents of twenty years of military dictatorship—as the ultimate arbiters of democracy. "Democracy and liberty only exist when your armed forces want them to," he professed at a naval event.[88] Modi routinely attacked the independent press and championed attacks on dissent.[89] A similar theme is found in Orbán's championing of order[90] and his efforts to use the fight against COVID-19 to further consolidate unilateral rule, as well as extend that rule by constitutional amendment under the pretext of Russia's 2022 invasion of Ukraine.[91] For Duterte in the Philippines, the same demand for complete authority emerged from the war on drugs—a different claimed crisis but to the same effect.[92]

Similarly under attack is the presumed legitimacy of the civil service. As will be discussed in the concluding chapter of this Part, the post–New Deal U.S. has functioned with a narrow strata of political appointees overseeing a large and cumbersome career bureaucracy, a pattern followed in every mature democracy. The sheer size of the federal government and its pervasive role in American society require no less. In fact, mature democratic governance relies on a civil service that "must be in a position to evolve principles of its own and sufficiently independent to assert them. It must be a power in its own right."[93]

Yet there is no constitutional mandate for the civil service that operates under a series of statutory restrictions on appointment and political engagements. Indeed, the Supreme Court has had to read into the First Amendment a constitutional protection of incumbent nonpolitical civil servants against politically motivated removal and replacement.

Many is the president frustrated by an administrative sector with a life of its own. But none has acted to rid the federal government of the personnel needed to function as under the populist fury of the Trump years. And this leads to an assessment of the effect of populism in the decidedly most mature of constitutional democracies, the United States.

Caudillos in Command

Many have tried their hand at capturing the essence of the new elected autocrats. Certainly, there is a command imperative to politics under a central leader. The claim to a single authoritative representative is reminiscent of Carl Schmitt's arguments a century ago about the German head of state's inherent authority as the only true agent of the "entire German people."[1] But, as set out in earlier chapters, that tendency toward executive authority has been building for quite some time, independent of the current populist surge. As well, there are fascistic elements in the demagogy and demand for fealty to the maximal leader. But these are elected regimes, and the fact of being elected is a source of both claimed legitimacy and vulnerability. Incumbent President Andrzej Duda, the candidate of the ruling Polish Law and Justice Party (PiS), narrowly eked out a victory in the 2020 Polish presidential elections; such electoral challenges are inconceivable in North Korea. The illiberal populists of today are neither military despots nor ideological authoritarians. They remain dependent on popular support and their ability to draw legitimacy from elections, even if those elections are more than occasionally imperfectly conducted.

Instead, the distinctive feature, especially in countries with more established and capable governments, is the dismantling and deprecation of the structures of governance. This is the essence of what may be termed "*caudillo* command," in the idiom of Latin American strongmen. Evoking the cowboy image of the cavalry leader, the term refers to personalist control, without party or political institutions, dependent on individual charismatic authority both with the populace and the military.

Populism targets "intermediary opinion making bodies, such as parties; established media; and institutionalized systems for monitoring and controlling political power."[2] By deinstitutionalizing government, these new autocrats create not a totalitarian state apparatus but a dizzying array of deals and favors. Rather than the absolutism of the state in totalitarian regimes, populism offers the centrality of one individual. Masha Gessen terms this the "mafia state" that is defined as a "specific, clan-like system in which one distributes money and power to all other members."[3] Along the same lines, one of President Trump's first victims in office, former FBI Director James Comey, compared the demand for loyalty in the Trump administration to the hours of Mafia tapes he overheard in his days as a line prosecutor.[4]

Oddly, electoral democracy provides the perfect medium for populist agitation that "places the leader and his party (or movement) in a daily electoral campaign."[5] As well summarized by Ivan Krastev and Stephen Holmes, the aim of elections for these autocrats is not to promote a contest of governing policies or philosophies and certainly not to promote the messianic visions of the 20th-century enemies of democracy. Rather, "the goal was to create a political regime where the legitimacy of those in power came less from the rulers' ability to represent the people and deliver palpable results than from the impossibility of imagining any alternative to the current political leadership."[6] Populists dangle not a comprehensive view of society but a series of short-term demands that promise immediate gratification for the perceived insults suffered by their audience. Indeed, this "short-termism is the most consistent expression of this project."[7] Once in office, the sense of inevitability takes on its own political force. "Having chosen to vote for them because of the short-term rewards, however, [voters] are then unable to quit, because of the populists' capture of institutions."[8] Once the institutions become the discretionary sandbox for the maximal leader, the electoral base of the legislative branch withers and the capacity for policy initiative diminishes.[9]

In the first set of post-1989 elections in the newly christened third-wave democracies, the initial holders of consolidated executive power sought to entrench themselves through open electoral manipulation and constitutional amendment. These were the structural alterations that have the effect of "mak[ing] it harder to dislodge the incumbent leader or party, and to weaken checks on their exercise of power."[10] In turn, emboldened courts fashioned doctrines of resistance. These judicial assertions defined a core of democratic functions that, with surprising sweep, could buttress repeat assertions of constitutional supremacy against the immediate changes sought by incumbent political officials. The judicial resistance deemed the political alterations to be unconstitutional constitutional amendments—in the terminology excavated by Rosalind Dixon, David Landau, and Yaniv Roznai.[11]

While populist autocrats may still attempt and even succeed in altering the constitution, as in Hungary, that phase is no longer central. The more difficult challenge is what Alvin Cheung terms the intralegal abuse of the opposition and the rewarding of the faithful.[12] Inescapably, "political actors intent on entrenching their preferred parties or policies need not resort to manipulating the formal rules of the Constitution, elections, or legislation."[13] Rather, the imprecision and discretion of the ordinary law may provide ample fuel for entrenching political power without resort to constitutional amendment or even major legal overhauls.[14]

I. Abuse by Law

What emerges today in illiberal populist regimes is less an emphasis on constitutional amendment and the formal expansion of centralized governmental power; instead, there is more reliance on the use of ordinary legal mechanisms to wear down the opposition and consolidate the power of the state. "A new political force with a strong ideological agenda can work an existing system to entirely rework a nation; so much can be subverted by keeping so much intact."[15] Under this approach, businesses can be kept in check through a combination of overregulation and selective exemptions from regulation that depend on connections to the state. Media can be bridled by a combination of taxes on newsprint, costly labor regulations, and interruptions of remunerative prime-time broadcasting for emergency government broadcasts—but always set off by either direct state subsidies or lucrative state advertising for the docile wing of the media.

The use of ordinary law and the formal process of legislation to debilitate the opposition is not a tactic of the police state of the Latin American militaries of the 1970s nor the totalitarian states of Stalinism or Nazism. It is not the attempt to amend the constitution to centralize unilateral executive power at the expense of checks and balances. It is highly *intralegal* as opposed to the *extralegal* repression that is typically deployed by more openly repressive regimes. And the defining feature is how ordinary the mechanisms of attack appear to be. As set out in Wojciech Sadurski's meticulous dissection of the PiS regime in Poland,[16] the de facto rule of Jarosław Kaczyński has coexisted with the inability to alter substantially the Polish Constitution. The increased concentration of power by the ruling party in Poland does not depend on either a formal break with constitutional separation of powers or an express rewriting of the authority of rival institutions, such as the judiciary.

Tarunabh Khaitan's recent account of the Modi government in India furthers this point.[17] India's autocratic turn comes not from the domain of constitutional politics primarily, but from the quotidian mix of statutory, regulatory, and decretal authority. When Modi refuses to recognize the legal role of the head of the opposition, or marginalizes members of the Cabinet, or attacks governors from other parties, these are in their whole efforts to erode one pillar of executive accountability. Yet they are familiar legal/political maneuverers that may exist in a democracy, except in their composite effect. As well summarized by

Tom Ginsburg and Aziz Huq: "The key to understanding democratic erosion is to see how discrete measures, which either in isolation or in the abstract might be justified as consistent with democratic norms, can nevertheless be deployed as mechanisms to unravel liberal constitutional democracy."[18] What emerges is not fascism or totalitarian command, but rather a process of "authoritarian retrogression" in which the forms of governance appear to be maintained but the tolerant core is voided.[19]

This process of "intralegal" suppression takes two primary forms. The first is the use of common legal rules to oppress the political opposition, such as by commanding the public arena. I previously referred to this as the "Chávez playbook," because the populist set of intralegal abuses of the opposition seems to have been honed in Venezuela. With Chávez's famous "La Hora del Comandante" came the frequent claims of airtime for public service broadcasting by the regime, which would frequently stretch for several hours of prime-time transmission each night. "Thus, Hugo Chávez spent more than 1,500 hours denouncing capitalism as well as domestic and foreign enemies on Alo Presidente, his own TV show; Silvio Berlusconi was for many years a daily presence on both his private television states and Italian state television; and Donald Trump was on Twitter day and night."[20]

This is then combined with low-grade harassment of the opposition to stymie the effective use of the more limited political resources of those not backed by government largesse. Among the myriad techniques include the following: constant defamation lawsuits, both civil and criminal, against opponents; the targeted use of state advertising to subsidize and subordinate the domesticated media; the selective withdrawal of eligibility for state contracts or employment for regime opponents; the denial of business licenses for opponents; the particularized grant of one-time exceptions from impossibly high regulatory burdens; and the list goes on. This is much the same list that Eric Posner terms the demagogue's playbook in assessing President Trump in the American framework.[21]

Each of these demagogue's mechanisms has a formal foundation in law; only the discretionary application reveals its use as a political cudgel.[22] As *The Economist* writes about Latin America: "The region's states are marked by heavy-handed regulatory overkill mixed, in practice, with wide discretionary power for officials."[23] The key is the toxic mix of choking levels of regulatory exactions with large margins for discretionary application or exemption. This becomes the entry point for political consolidation through the punishment of those who run afoul of that consolidated power.

Formal legal resistance to this form of political retaliation is difficult. There are no entitlements to government contracts or employment, to specific licenses, or to even be free from defamation actions. In countries with poorly realized norms of bureaucratic regularity, many state benefits tend to be dispensed on a one-off basis, depriving those who are shut out from raising process-based arguments to challenge retaliation. The American Administrative Procedures Act does not generalize, nor do the norms of the German civil service; Max Weber, it turns out, had limited reach. And an earlier era's customary languages of individual rights poorly capture the discretionary power of ordinary governmental authority's ill-defined boundaries to reward and punish, and thereby compel proximity to the incumbent regime.

The risk is that the process of democratic selection will be overwhelmed and yield to "the deformed version known as *presidencialismo*, which is characterized precisely by that exaggerated predominance and by the tendency to exceed the maximum time allowed for the exercise of presidential power in order to maintain the *caudillo* and his political project in power."[24] The Constitutional Court of Colombia's denial of a constitutional amendment that would have allowed President Álvaro Uribe to run for a third term exemplifies this point.

The second mechanism is even more difficult to engage as a matter of law. Populists necessarily divide the world into us versus them. There is a constant sense that the true people are victimized both by the elites above and by others below. Each make illegitimate claims on the society, and each threatens the true people with perdition. Presented across this cataclysmic divide, elections are not programmatic but existential. In turn, the xenophobia and racism that infect populism are not incidental by-products of complicated social orders, but a ready lever that can be pulled to fuel the demands for immediacy. The perceived threat from the outsiders is as present as the economic demands. Each serves to secure the legitimacy of the elected leader as a guardian of the communitarian claims of the people.

Populism invariably plays to the sense that real people have been burdened by the outsiders, either elites or foreigners or some combination thereof. The troubling issue becomes the use of governmental powers to realize electoral gain, especially when the dispensation of state largesse is consistent with the demands of the regime's populist base. I began the book with an example from Argentina, but that is neither unique nor exceptional. The same story could be told of rice subsidies by the last Thaksin Shinawatra Red Shirt government in the run up to elections in Thailand, some of the social welfare pledges of the Bolsonaro regime in Brazil, and many others. In Poland, the PiS government used public handouts reaped from its predecessor's austerity reforms to bolster a thin electoral mandate, as with the "500+" program of subsidies for every child after the first.[25]

At some level, these are all social welfare programs with a claim to public approbation. At the same time, there are real-world boundaries to raiding the fisc to underwrite electoral support, as the economic collapse in Venezuela demonstrates. But the temptation to use economic discretion to cement political power is always present, even in healthy democracies. Here again, there is the nagging truth that this account of populism reveals an exaggerated permanent feature of democratic politics. Many of the greatest American leaders, certainly including Lincoln and Franklin Roosevelt, invoked the name of the people to forge claims upon the state. It is hard to overcome the paradox, as captured by Francis Fukuyama, "that interest groups are corrupting democracy and harming economic growth, and that they are necessary conditions for a healthy democracy."[26]

Nor is there any legal barrier that says that politicians cannot be attentive to their constituencies in setting a political agenda or using proper political forms for redistribution of resources. FDR no doubt drew political support from providing social security benefits to a first generation of protected retirees—that pattern continued through the expansion of prescription drug benefits under George W. Bush, and the expansion of health insurance under Barack Obama. The massive expansion of economic assistance and stimulus under President Biden, or the proposed discharge of student debt, surely has political implications for the groups most likely to benefit. Nor is this unexpected in a healthy democracy. Under a now classic view of democracy as premised on interest group competition, all successful politicians must be attentive to the desires of their constituencies or face electoral defeat.

What may serve to distinguish the populist use of state resources could be the lack of generalizable programs, the failure to embed reforms within state institutions, and the play to the most short-term interests of a voting constituency. What is troubling in other words is that populism offers a means to corrupt the polity, promising the sugar high of one-off gifts without any sustaining economic foundation. Even seemingly "kept promises," such as the PiS continuing to dole out government stipends after their immediate election, have stemmed from short-sighted government budgeting that causes unsustainable side effects such as rising prices and an increased cost of living.[27] Such undermining of governance structures is neither criminal nor antidemocratic in the sense of violating the primacy of electoral commands. Give-away politics creates a dependency of the electorate that cements incumbent rule in much the same fashion as does the use of state employment or contracts to reward electoral loyalty.

A cycle of short-term offerings is the predictable result, while the command of governmental structures falls to populist control. "Voters may rationally choose to become 'addicted' to populist politicians, electing them despite the subsequent institutional capture."[28] However, populists often secure their continued electoral success not through successful realization of policy objectives, but through thoroughgoing control of democratic institutions and the accompanying spigot of patronage and clientelism. Voters have no way out. Because of the short-time horizon, these populist initiatives may be distinguished from the substantive commitments to reallocation of societal wealth under European social democracy or under the New Deal or Great Society programs in the United States. As well captured in an early assessment by Jeffrey Sachs, the populists came to power "promising the 'immediate psychic and material gratification of the needs of society's underdogs'" and consequently relied on "distributive policies rather than redistributive policies."[29]

The question remains whether there are constraints on the populist use of the perquisites of state authority to cement political rule. The issue necessarily is different from efforts by outsiders, including foreigners, to bribe government officials to get illicit favors. A growing regime of transnational bribery enforcement is directed to that more transgressive form of corruption.[30] Instead, the problem of populist efforts to induce ongoing support through targeted, short-term dispensations concerns the use of government resources to prop up incumbent political power.

How then is this addressed from within? An early intuition from the comparative constitutional scholarship is that constitutional amendment presents a decisive galvanizing event that may prompt legal challenge. Constitutional amendment will almost invariably prompt debate, and it invites a highly visible confrontation. For example, the fear of entrenchment of political dependence on the multiterm executive was central to the Colombian Constitutional Court's invalidation of the proposed third term for President Uribe. As the Court noted: "The advantage of having served as president for eight years" allows "the progressive increment in presidential periods [that] can allow a leader to perpetuate himself in power and potentially create a vicious cycle permitting the consolidating of only one person in power."[31] The Colombian Court captured the problem of consolidated power exactly, but the terms of court intervention arose in Colombia because of the dramatic legal setting of a constitutional amendment that would expressly alter the powers of the executive.

Such direct confrontations with expansions of presidential power by thwarting a proposed constitutional amendment are necessarily rare. Much as the scholarly literature touts the Colombian Court's successful stand against Uribe, it is hardly generalizable. The Colombian intervention stands alone in Latin America as a successful effort to curb the expansion of presidential constitutional authority.[32] Courts have trouble enough facing up to a direct presidential attempt to command greater formal constitutional command.

Much more common, and more difficult to confront than the high-profile process of constitutional amendment, is the incremental expansion of authority through the quotidian manipulative exercise of governmental power. To return to the Argentine example, among the manifestations of populist state expansion is the sheer number of people who rely on the state for the essentials of life. In the period of the two Cristina Kirchner governments, the percentage of the population dependent on state employment or transfer payments in whole or major part rose from roughly 20 percent to over 40 percent. This is an extraordinary stratification of the economy, and one that was unsustainable as an economic matter, particularly once the short-term infusion from the commodity boom of the early 2000s began to fade.[33] At the same time, this expansion created a dependency relationship between huge sectors of the population and the munificence of the incumbent government, something that would make electoral overhaul difficult and would render post-Kirchner economic reforms exceedingly volatile.

Many of the resulting economic distortions are beyond legal constraint when enacted through the populist-infused mechanisms of ordinary politics. It is important to be clear on this point. Populism taps into a genuine sense of the society having been left behind key sectors of the population. The demand for redistribution and for benefits for the forgotten is a legitimate form of democratic politics. The difficulty comes with programs that are not rooted in the institutions or fiscal realities of the society. Deficits soar under Chávez, or Modi, or Trump. These may be irresponsible policies, and they may be an abuse of political powers, but they are not criminal.

But maybe not all are quite so neatly beyond legal oversight. As I have noted elsewhere, the concentration of executive command fuels the emergence of the "three C's" of cronyism, clientelism, and outright corruption. When I began turning my academic interests to the question of democratic fragility, my primary focus was the multiple layers of institutional arrangements necessary for democratic governance, both inside government and through the layers of civil society. I now believe that corruption turns out to play a larger role in this story than previously appreciated. In a recurring pattern, the fight over independent authority to investigate and prosecute corruption turns out to be a flashpoint in stemming the consolidation of executive rule.

II. The Politics of the Short Term

Corruption provides an unanticipated entry point for addressing the distortions of majoritarian populism. Others have identified the perceptions of elite corruption as galvanizing support for populism initially,[34] but the focus here is on the question of targeting corruption as an avenue for re-establishing functioning legal institutions.

Populist governments show a propensity to fall prey to corruption scandals, as in South Korea and South Africa. As will be discussed in subsequent chapters, examples of corruption of the electoral process, including the Taiwanese confrontation with the KMT trying to hold itself in office or the North Carolina Republicans, represent efforts to compromise electoral accountability. Corruption offers a different set of legal transgressions and the potential for well-established grounds for legal intervention.

When judges face incumbents seeking to manipulate electoral rules, the intervention is systemic against the temptation to preserve power in the face of electoral defeat. Populism does not necessarily seek to alter the rules of elections. The broad strokes of populism fit poorly into a simple approach that looks to preexisting norms of electoral accountability to check populist excesses. Similarly, populist distortions are not centrally ones of state repression that might be addressed through rights jurisprudence. Nor does a populist majority bloc present the defiance of electoral accountability that shows when minorities about to be voted out of office try to shield themselves from electoral challenge.

Put another way, much of the discussion about the emergence of strong courts starts from one of two premises. The first is that constitutional courts have served primarily as guardians of rights interests against governmental threat. This may be further refined along the axes of negative and positive liberties to account for the more venturesome spread of social rights jurisprudence in the hands of apex courts. As a matter of historical account, the primacy of rights jurisprudence no doubt best captures the means by which constitutional jurisprudence, including at the hands of the European Court of Human Rights, has commanded post–World War II democracies. Rights claims generally do not necessarily force a direct confrontation with political institutions and thus allow for an expanding domain of court responsibility.

Alternatively, a minority claim, to which I am partial, is to find in the courts a necessary brake on the propensity of fragile democracies toward institutional failure, something that is often termed a structural account of the role of constitutional courts. Especially in the formative period after the fall of the Soviet Union, new democracies embarked upon an experiment with popular sovereignty without consolidated political parties, with weak civil society institutions, and with a pronounced risk of executive action that would thwart future electoral accountability. The point of departure here is the role of election competition and rotation in office among political contenders in constraining state authority. On this view, review of claims of electoral access, minority party protection, party financing, and other institutional details of democratic politics form a critical foundation of the role of modern constitutional courts. Even proponents of this view understand the difficulty of courts invoking higher notions of democratic legitimacy as against the elected political branches.

The challenge of populism is that, in its current manifestation, it is not defined by either overwhelming human rights violations or threats to undo elections as such. Certainly, there are the inflammatory appeals of the need to rise against outsiders or other enemies that are accompanied by the loose rhetoric of violence, and on occasion by actual instigations of violence. But, by and large, the opposition is able to air its claims and meaningfully contest for office in an organized fashion in regimes such as Hungary and Poland; even Turkey manages contested elections. Opposition parties win the mayoralty in Budapest and Istanbul and sweep the Delhi state offices in India. These are legitimately contested elections, despite the distortions introduced by being able to dole out benefits in support of incumbent re-election. No such electoral challenge would have been conceivable in Nazi Germany or in North Korea today.

But the emergence of elected autocrats challenges inherited legal categories. The world no longer turns on easy binaries such as democratic or not, particularly if the only operational definition of democracy is having elected heads of state. Europe perfectly illustrates the disutility in defining a tolerable constitutional order solely through elections. For years, the European Union could ably define eligibility for membership through what were termed its "Copenhagen criteria" for ascension. With regard to the political order, these criteria required "stability of institutions guaranteeing democracy, the rule of law, human rights, respect for and protection of minorities."[35] In practice, the institutional guarantee of democracy could be boiled down to an elected head of government and an elected legislative branch. That was sufficient to distinguish France, or Italy, or West Germany from Nazism, or the Soviet bloc, or the military despots of Portugal and Greece. After the expansion of the EU following the collapse of the Soviet Union, the Copenhagen criteria remained the same, but there was little attention to the deeper institutional commitments in the political domain. Thus, the EU has largely failed to address the constriction of democracy under elected autocrats in Poland or Hungary.

Neither the jurisprudence of rights nor democratic reinforcement quite captures the aggrandizement of discretionary state authority and the increased integration of incumbent political power into economic privilege. This provides a bridge between political retrenchment from democracy and the likelihood of corruption under a freewheeling executive. If the question of corruption is not epiphenomenal but rather systemic under such regimes, the question becomes whether corruption might provide an important element for challenging populist excess. Moreover, protections against corruption generally infuse both the criminal and administrative law, allowing rather ordinary legal mechanisms to be utilized against populist claims on economic power.

Focusing on corruption begins with a crucial observation about populism in office. There appears to be something in the genetics of populist governance that invites corruption. Whether or not the animating aim of populism in seeking office, and whether or not a matter of formal program, corruption does seem to sprout. What if this relationship were not a matter of individual greed or frailty? What if the breakdown of institutional buffers that animates populism provides the fertile breeding ground for many pathologies, corruption included? What if undermining the functioning of state institutions predictably leads to corruption?

There is no escaping the effort to dismantle the protective institutional walls of governance. The first step is diminishing the role of intermediary institutions that serve as watchdogs over government functioning. As well captured in the rise of Italy's Five Star movement:

In *Siamo in Guerra* ("We are at War"), Roberto Casaleggio and Beppe Grillo . . . claim that there is a war going on between the "old world" and the "new world." The old world stands for party democracy, partisan politics and political representation; the new one stands for citizens free from ideologies and connected horizontally through the Net, without intermediary organizations and without any division between "inside' and outside." Hence the projection: "*The Net does not want middleman*," and political parties and traditional media are doomed to disappear as structured establishment that *obstructs* democracy.[36]

The transactional relations with constituents provide the next step: "Clientelism often evolves into pure corruption because politicians have the power to distribute public resources as they wish; money that could go to clients often ends up in their own pockets."[37] For all the problems with a highly bureaucratized state, procedures and oversight do restrain political self-aggrandizement, no matter how imperfectly. As with all claims about distortion under populism, the background norms may not be without fault. Certainly pre-populist governments in Italy were not without major corruption scandals. Rather, the claim that follows is that the anti-institutionalism of populist rule breaks down the governmental structures that should brake corruption as democratic societies mature. As Figure 5.1 shows, there is a predicted decline in corruption as governing institutions mature and as the society becomes wealthier.

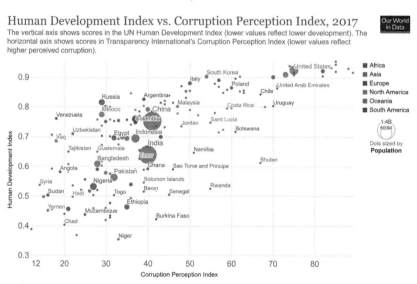

Human Development Index vs. Corruption Perception Index, 2017

The vertical axis shows scores in the UN Human Development Index (lower values reflect lower development). The horizontal axis shows scores in Transparency International's Corruption Perception Index (lower values reflect higher perceived corruption).

Source: United Nations Development Programme, Human Development Report 2020, Transparency International (2018)
OurWorldInData.org/corruption/ • CC BY

Figure 5.1   *Source: Human Development Index vs. Corruption Perception Index, 2017,*
OUR WORLD IN DATA (2018), https://ourworldindata.org/grapher/human-development-index-vs-corruption-perception-index.

My contention is that there is a link between several features of populist rule that may pave the way to outright corruption. These features include the anti-institutionalism of populist governance, the propensity for cronyist relations to the regime as a way around stifling bureaucratic legalism, and the short-term seductions of clientelism. If the Argentine or Polish or Thai governments offer blandishments to the voters on the eve of an election, and the voters respond positively, there is little that law can do to thwart this persistent vulnerability of democracy. Hobbes warned that citizens in a democracy would be vulnerable "to evil counsel, and to be seduced by orators."[38] So too did Thucydides in his account of the ultimate fall of Athens in the Peloponnesian Wars.[39] The very nature of democracy is to mobilize self-interest in the aim of societal advancement, a process that cannot escape the appeal to what voters want. So long as the blandishments honor the political requirements of transparency and presentation of program to the voters, there is little the criminal law can or should say about it—no matter how ill-advised the policy outcomes. The question is more complicated when the line is crossed dividing the political from the personal.

III. Corruption

Defining the parameters of corruption is difficult. In the U.S., the introduction of the concern for corruption in campaign finance law unleashed two generations of debate over what exactly constitutes such corruption. As played out in the case law, the constitutional efforts at regulation of campaign expenditures may even turn not on proof of actual corruption but on the more nebulous perceived risk of corruption. Inspired by divisions on the Supreme Court, corruption can be as narrow as a furtive quid pro quo exchange between a state patron and an incumbent official, or as broad as the inequality of income in a market society, or as functional as the "dependence corruption" of politicians pursuing money for election.[40] Public perceptions of corruption are no less contested. A study of American politics found that campaign finance rules had little impact on perceived corruption of the political process and that support for a losing candidate was among the best predictors of a perception that corruption had infected the process.[41] If corruption becomes a euphemism for political loss, then corruption is a definitional attribute of electoral choice.

Certainly, the mere offer of material rewards as a condition for electoral support cannot be a sufficient definition of corruption. At a certain level of abstraction, electoral politics is often about promising returns to political supporters. Rome had its bread and circuses. George McGovern promised to give every American $1,000. Ronald Reagan ran on a promise of dramatic tax relief, something that once victorious translated into an immediate economic benefit to over 80 percent of Reagan voters.[42] If one of the attributes of the modern state is to redistribute wealth from the most advantaged to the most vulnerable, then democratic politics will have predictable redistributive elements, which alone cannot condemn electoral choice and certainly cannot invite the claim of criminality of elected politicians.

The U.S. Supreme Court addressed this issue in rejecting an attempt to prosecute a victorious candidate under the Kentucky Corrupt Practices Act, which prohibited candidates from making an "expenditure, loan, promise, agreement, or contract as to action when elected, in consideration for votes."[43] The candidate under indictment had openly pledged performance once in office that would reward materially the voters he was courting. As the Court ruled, "so long as the hoped-for personal benefit is to be achieved through the normal processes of government, and not through some private arrangement, it has always been, and remains, a reputable basis upon which to cast one's ballot."[44] Clearly elements of generalizability, publicity, and diffusion of benefits provide some safe harbor in electoral politics, even if a candidate appeals to voter self-interest, no matter how crassly defined.

A continuum suggests itself. At one extreme is the pocketing of state money or ownership of state-affiliated enterprises by the powers that be. That comes closest to theft. At the other extreme is a generalized program of redistribution, whether as tax relief, agricultural subsidies, or any of the myriad ways revenues raised through taxation support one or another political claim to state support. More difficult is the use of state resources for immediate political gain, as with the Argentine example of extraordinary one-time expenditures on the eve of an election. Such expenditures can be distinguished from a generalized state program that has clear redistributive effects, including the expansion of health and prescription benefits under Presidents Obama and Bush, or the Reagan tax cuts, or the Biden stimulus package. The ongoing and generalized quality of these programs place them within the continuum of being legitimate, if contestable, public policy aims of either the right or left in a system of democratic choice.

What may distinguish populist regimes is the propensity for power over policy and particularized grievances over broader commitments. In the American context, for example, although the tax code is replete with special interest benefits, the Trump tax cuts singled out parts of the country that voted against the president and actually increased the tax burden on citizens of those states.[45] By removing the deduction for state and local taxes, the Trump tax package raised the effective tax rate in states with higher levels of public programs—read Democratic states. The design of these tax reforms to punish parts of the country deemed politically antagonistic to the administration in office has the feel of a change in the form of government action.

The Trump tax reforms point to an underlying empirical claim that the use of particularized economic benefits and punishment is endemic to populist regimes. This follows from populist regimes cultivating a competitive political nature of "enemies" rather than adversaries and from their claim to represent the authentic people against the illegitimate other. If this normative claim can be accepted as accurate, the style of government may explain the propensity of populist regimes to act as gatekeepers for the selective conferral of benefits and imposition of punishments. Needless to add, corruption is not the exclusive domain of populist regimes. It may exist in authoritarian regimes and under well-functioning democracies, but the claim is that the antagonism of populist regimes toward institutionalized norms fosters the use of state resources to reward and punish in more direct and notorious forms than seen in normal politics.

From this follows the likelihood of descent into outright corruption, the propensity for gatekeepers to become toll collectors. Those that confer favors from state coffers are sorely tempted to dole out rewards to themselves, and they frequently succumb to such temptations. The concept of corruption, as in the lead definition from the *Oxford English Dictionary*, conveys the sense of degradation. That which exists as part of a normal or healthy ordering becomes corrupted when the core functions are compromised, even if the appearance remains recognizable. Any definition that follows this approach risks just pushing the inquiry up one level. Thus, Dennis Thompson notes, "in the tradition of political theory, corruption is a disease of the body politic."[46] But Deborah Hellman rightly responds, "if corruption is a disease of the body politic, it depends on an antecedent idea of the healthy state of the political system."[47] Alternatively, Laura Underkuffler pushes the metaphysical boundary by looking to the core of corruption at the individual level as "the capture, by evil, of one's soul."[48] Using disease as a metaphor is emotionally alluring but begs operational clarity.

Some definitions are easy, as when an elected government cements its power and wealth by redirecting benefits to itself and its cronies through bribes, illicit contributions, or compelled ownership of profitable enterprises. The combination of surreptitious arrangements and extralegal accords must be deemed to be on the corrupt side of the ledger. As Sarah Chayes set out, these kleptocratic regimes tend to sit atop an upward flowing form of corruption.[49] Even the traffic police secure positions from bribes paid to higher-ups, which in turn continue to flow up to the very top of the regime. Thus, in Uzbekistan, to take but one example, "the purchase of office is a key vehicle for the transfer of money from subordinate to superior."[50] The subordinate is beholden to the superior, must continue to pay tribute, and must in turn extract the money from those below, be they lower government officials or the populace. As one works down the chain of authority, at some point there is no one left to exploit but ordinary citizens. In turn, citizen engagement with state officials is largely a matter of exploitation by government officials, either in the form of demands for payment for bureaucratic favors or bribes at the point of enforcement. As a result, the Uzbek populace's "most frequent contact with their kleptocracy is through everyday shakedowns, especially at the hands of the police."[51]

The concern for corruption offered here is not a categorically distinct species of politics, but one that is a consequence of a politics disconnected from the broader assumption of the need to be public regarding. An elected government that pledges and carries through redistribution policies that benefit its supporters is not corrupt. Political virtue cannot require that the "private-regarding" demands of ordinary concerns be replaced by "public-regarding citizens and thus members of a people."[52]

Rather, it is the elements of surreptitious bargains and non-generalizability of benefits that inform the definition of a politics that has run askew. A review of recent Hungarian elections shows the centrality of "electoral clientelism" defined by "outright vote buying, intimidation and threats to withdraw social benefits or jobs."[53] The propensity of populist regimes to reject established institutional forms of governance, as well as the prevalence of populist executives claiming unilateral authority to speak for the people by personalizing political discretion, provides a political environment rife with the prospects for corruption. This corruption includes both the classic quid pro quo, in which public officials obtain benefits in exchange for public grace, and the distortion of public policy as a consequence of the influence of wealth.[54]

The anti-institutionalism of populism is likely to yield greater levels of corruption than is found in ordinary democratic politics. As a general matter, social science examinations find that political accountability—or more precisely political competition—is central "in generating good governance practices and, particularly, in reducing corruption."[55] Simply put, electoral vulnerability keeps incumbents in check.[56] But if populism does tend toward corruption, the answer cannot be simply the relative level of political competition. Britain suspended wartime elections with Churchill as prime minister, and FDR won sweeping elections in the U.S. in the same period. Neither stood at the head of a government particularly known for its corruption scandals.

Rather, it is the anti-institutionalism of populist politics that provides the link. Established political parties represent long-term commitments to policy objectives that "allow them to recruit new members and place those members into office, even as existing members of the coalition may exit political life due to, say, an electoral loss, term-limits or death."[57] These long-lived parties aspire to perpetual life, as with corporations, and must temper the short-termed demands of incumbent officials to simply vacuum up the immediate perquisites of office. As a result, the intergenerational demands will force attention "to time periods beyond the present and the immediate future precisely because members who would otherwise care very little about the future are forced to bargain with their cadres who do care about the future since they have reasonable expectations of being politically active for many years to come."[58] In turn, the demand for a time orientation beyond the present creates vigilance against outright theft by leaders for their own gain, the future be damned.[59]

By contrast, populist leaders tend to operate outside the formal structure of a political party. They present themselves as head of a movement, one that does not have subordinate officials or other claims to programmatic command. Strikingly, the Republican Party in 2020 abandoned the American tradition of debate and horse-trading over a party platform.[60] In fact, Republican Senate leader Mitch McConnell stressed that, even when out of power, the Senate GOP would not release a party platform, "saying the party only needs to reveal its plans for running Congress 'when we take it back.' "[61] They eschewed a formal declaration of principle for voters and an empowerment of various constituencies within their broad-tent organization. Instead, the party adopted a platform consisting exclusively of blanket support for President Trump, shorn of any commitment that might provide for institutional constraints or internal contestation.

Reducing political commitment to the immediate triumph of a maximal political leader has direct consequences for the time horizon of policy. Immediacy commands consumption. The tragedy of the commons is that if there is no credible commitment to cooperative behavior, each will compromise the public domain by seizing what can be seized. Commitments not to overfish a lake, or not to cut too much of a forest canopy, or not to overgraze the meadows are the product of a coordinated vision of a common future. Hobbes posited that there would be no "incentive to industry" absent a commitment to legal expectations and order.[62] The coordination needed to make joint commitments possible ultimately falls to the state. Without such state commitments to future welfare, societal commitments fail.

Long-term commitments, even intergenerational sightlines, are not necessarily unique to democracy, nor even most characteristic of democratic governance. Tom Ginsburg attributes to David Hume the insight that a hereditary monarchy might well have an extended time horizon; the monarch wishes to preserve the prerogatives of the Crown's sires for when they assume power.[63] Hume's specific concern was the propensity for internally beneficent republics to turn tyrannical in the exploit of their conquered subjects, a classic version of satisfying immediate demands.[64] By contrast, monarchies not dependent on immediate popular approbation might extend the time horizon to seek to integrate new subjects on a more equitable basis.

Applying Hume's insight to the context of modern elected regimes, the corruption scandals that swirl about populist leaders always come back to the view of the public fisc as a treasure trove for immediate gain or consumption. The longer time horizon in a democracy belongs not to a hereditary monarch but to institutional actors that have a horizon beyond immediate election, to wit, political parties. "Legacies matter, so parties that expect to stick around have an incentive to work for long-term benefits while imposing short-term costs."[65] The institutional presence of political parties promotes not only responsive politics but also a sense of stewardship over the affairs of state that the politics of immediacy reject.

Studies of economic development find that, even in the absence of genuine democratic contestation, an institutional commitment to the future dampens immediate demands for consumption. Thus, for example, "high-performing Asian economies were governed by dominant parties that enjoyed long time horizons, had the power to maneuver around potential veto points, could shield the bureaucracy from special interests, and could effectively oversee policy implementation."[66] The trick is to combine the capacity for economic stewardship with democratic politics, something notoriously missing in the take-off periods in East Asia. But here again, the institutionalization of politics may provide the key:

> Strong parties establish a relationship of accountability between party leaders and party members, encourage long time horizons, and enhance the party's capacity to solve coordination problems. These features enhance the probability that politicians engage in responsible economic management, provide public goods, and help to ensure political stability. This behavior, in turn, triggers investments and other productivity-enhancing actions by economic actors that enhance economic growth in the short and long term.[67]

The compressed time frame of populist governance exacerbates what may be thought of as the "last period" problem in democratic accountability. In the formal models of game theory, the imperfect yet critical solution to the inescapable prisoner's dilemma is repeat play. Two one-time confederates in crime will quickly betray each other under separate police interrogation for fear that the other will confess in exchange for a better deal. But make the partners in crime a part of a broader criminal enterprise rooted in their community of origin, the willingness to maintain silence is enhanced under threat of reputational loss or more direct retaliation against relatives. If you stretch the time horizon and the repeat consequences, then cooperation is possible, even if the aims are not necessarily praiseworthy.

All robust theories of democracy return in one form or another to the role of elections in keeping the governors responsive to the needs of the governed. At bottom, the ability to "throw the rascals out" is the hallmark of popular sovereignty.[68] Presumably, elected politicians should not stray too far from the will of the people or risk voting retaliation. But for any politician at the end of her tenure, or facing term limits, the last stage problem remains. Lame ducks face no personal electoral retribution unless their time horizon extends beyond themselves. Leadership with a short-time horizon mobilizes its partisans with the claim that to lose electorally is the end of their control over the levers of power. In the throes of all or nothing contests, populist leaders "intensely politicize all areas of organized collective existence" and stoke the sectional divisions they rode to power.[69] In turn, "the 'short-term protection' feature of populist policies correlates very well with the commonly emphasized anti-elite rhetoric":

> If a non-populist politician counters a populist proposal . . . with statements about future costs, future debt accumulation or banking crises, the rational response by the populist challenger is to claim that all such statements of concern for the future consequences of the protection policies are instead driven by the self-interest of the elites.[70]

When the only aim is immediate election, the bounties of the state can be claimed to reward the faithful. Populist movements defined by commitment only to the leader blunt elections' supposed checks on opportunistic abuses of office by those in power. When democratic politics is organized around political parties, the party assumes a life beyond the careers of the individual politicians of today. The party is like a corporation endowed with indefinite life and must engage in constant tradeoffs between immediate returns and future prospects. But reduce democratic politics to one individual and the need is for the here and now. This is nothing more than common wisdom. No one will save the seed corn for future harvests if there is no commitment to planting next spring. Or, more colloquially, no one takes a rental car to a car wash. One-time play by definition has no future consequences that need to be anticipated.

On this account, populist governance compromises accountability in two ways. First, populism narrows the time horizon to the present and offers its constituents a political program of immediate gratification. Corruption becomes a particularly powerful mechanism to tilt the immediate electoral balance in favor of incumbent rule. Second, populism tends to be deeply anti-institutionalist and resists submerging the leader into a political party that will develop longer term institutional aims. Notably, elected populists such as Perón in Argentina or Fujimori in Peru formed and quickly disbanded electoral alliances repeatedly in order to maintain the primacy of the *caudillo* at the top, rather than any political organization that might make independent demands.

The absence of a long-horizon institutional form and the existence of a unilateral authority in a populist leader come together to create a fertile environment for increasingly discretionary uses of governmental power. In turn, the central argument is that the combination of short termism and freewheeling governance is a powerful breeding arena for outright corruption. If so, ordinary mechanisms of law may provide a check on the ability of unilateral rule to compromise democratic integrity in much the same fashion that constitutional law may protect against the compromise of electoral accountability.

For this approach, three different forms of corruption must be distinguished. The first is the corruption of the electoral system itself. Here the use of corruption captures the degradation of the electoral mandate that ensues. Congressional scholar Norman Ornstein well captures this sense of corruption of an institution. He assessed that Senate majority leader Mitch McConnell's acquiescence to the demands of President Trump means that "McConnell will go down in history as one of the most significant people in destroying the fundamentals of our constitutional democracy. . . . There's nobody as corrupt, in terms of violating the norms of government."[71]

Second is the most conventional form of corruption and addresses the private capture of public resources, either by bribes and direct payments, or by letting government contracts in exchange for political contributions or benefits to family members of the commanding powers.

The third, and most difficult, concerns the problem of corrupting the body politic, inducing vitriol toward others and short-term benefits for the faithful. In the discussion that follows, the first two show themselves amenable to legal constraint, while the latter is the most difficult for a democratic polity to address through law.

Judicial Intercession

Populism rejects the core premises of democracy: first, the idea of repeat play by political actors demonstrated through the capacity for rotation in office; second, the premise of institutional constraints on the governors of the moment. Each rejection invites a distinct form of corruption of democratic governance. The first, the subject of this chapter, is a corruption of electoral accountability and processes of governance. The second, addressed in the next chapter, is the more familiar corruption that takes the form of graft and misdirection of state resources for private gain.

Both implicate confrontations with legality and invite established responses in law. Challenges to electoral accountability test the constitutional commitment to democratic processes and prompt the controversies that may engage constitutional courts. Corruption by public officials may be the province of special prosecutors and procedures, including impeachment in the United States, but the concerns are far more quotidian. Concepts of theft and illicit dealing typically implicate rather ordinary questions of morality and illegality than would a question of political accountability. What these concerns share is a foundation in law established outside the immediate problem of populism. Indeed, the legal response draws from wellsprings that exist independently of the current populist challenge.

While the prior chapters have addressed primarily the conditions for the rise of populism and the forms under which populists govern, the focus now is on the legal consequences of populism in office. A robust democracy requires fixed rules for the conduct of elections and limitations on the exercise of state authority, lest each election risk becoming the ultimate showdown for survival.[1] This chapter's focus is primarily on constitutional law as a means to preserve limitations on power and the prospect of repeat electoral accountability. The concept of intercession is the act of intervening on behalf of others, including through intercessory prayer, the act of seeking divine aid for another. In effect, the question is the role of constitutional law and its judicial enforcement in allowing democracies the chance for self-repair. Intercession can be an effective delaying device, but it is not a long-term solution to stave off populist impulses. The next chapter will address the sub-constitutional workings of ordinary law to address the abuse of office that frequently accompanies strongman rule.

I. Changing the Rules of the Game

A number of democracy's current defects stress the separate spheres of power that frame constitutional democracies. The fractures of governance can be seen in dominant party democracies, in illiberal regimes that increasingly rely on concentrated executive power, in mature democracies in which legislative dysfunction hampers governmental effectiveness, or in direct populist assaults on institutional boundaries that frustrate immediate political gain. In each, the pressure on formal divisions of governmental authority defines the modern political era. In many such instances, courts may play a checking function if for no other reason than the fact that courts tend to be non-synchronic with election cycles and may lag in efforts to cohere unilateral power. This means that courts may not be overwhelmed by a strong executive quite so quickly as other institutions. In the long run, of course, we are all dead, as John Maynard Keynes famously posited. In time, as David Landau and Rosalind Dixon show, courts may well succumb to power and become active agents of executive consolidation, as in Nicaragua and Ecuador.[2] Nonetheless there remains the possibility for court intervention to restrain the impulse to circumvent institutional constraints on consolidated power.

It is difficult to catalogue the myriad ways incumbent authority can compromise electoral choice. Changes in voter eligibility by restrictive voter registration schemes (as in the U.S.)[3] or sudden expansions of the franchise to include sixteen-year-olds or resident aliens (as in Argentina)[4] can serve to manipulate likely electorate preferences. Districting configurations can be gerrymandered. Times and mechanisms of voting can be altered. Opponents can be harassed through legal and extralegal tactics. The list is long, and I loosely join these as a form of corruption of the democratic enterprise, defining corruption here as a structural compromise of the workings of a complex system.[5] These examples point to the long-term need for independence of election administration and intermediary institutions to buffer political expediency. Taken together, the ability to manipulate rules of the game to the benefit of incumbent power compromises the regenerative capacity of democracy. As well expressed by Tom Ginsburg, "enduring commitment facilitates democracy because it reduces the stakes of electoral loss."[6]

Instead of attempting a collection of the many ways incumbent power might be exploited electorally, I will focus here only on one key area that is emblematic of the power of incumbent authority. There is no greater threat to democratic selection of rulers than changes that limit electoral accountability altogether or that remove power from electoral contestation altogether. Thus, for example, in a recent paper, Mila Versteeg and coauthors chronicle how about one-third of electoral regimes across all countries categorized as democratic attempted to evade limits on re-election of heads of state, using formal constitutional amendment in about two-thirds of the cases.[7] Repeat re-election allows the marshaling of incumbent power either to eliminate electoral challenge altogether or to create a condition of dependence on the established government that raises the barrier to challenge to foreboding heights. The key is not just entrenchment by which political change is made more difficult as a result of the powers of incumbency,[8] but also that which occurs when politics is fought at the level of irreversibility. In turn, this "implies not just the absence of political change but some kind of special *constraint* on the usual processes of political change."[9]

Perhaps the simplest form of judicial intervention is to defend the primacy of rotation in office as the key to democratic governance.[10] There are categories of constitutional change that are so fundamental as to be "incompatible with the existing framework of the constitution and instead seek[] to unmake one of its constitutive parts."[11] Such "dismemberments . . . aim to unmake a constitution without breaking legal continuity."[12] In the U.S., for example, an increasingly radicalized Republican Party has deemed governance by Democrats illegitimate and has responded by altering the customary functioning of the offices to which Democrats are elected. In North Carolina and Wisconsin, the loss of the governorship to the Democrats led the outgoing Republicans to attempt to neuter the power of the executive. This is a classic one-and-done strategy (a term from American college basketball) in which all that matters is the immediate. The alterations included limiting the staffing of the governor, limiting the number of executive appointments, and a variety of technical changes that all shifted power from the executive to the legislature—which in turn was controlled by Republican gerrymanders, at least for the next two years at the time of the change.[13]

Again, this is hardly a novel maneuver in current times. When supporters of Hugo Chávez lost the mayoralty of Caracas in 2008, for example, the government simply rewrote the rule of political authority for the capital, effectively denying the Chávez opponents the political authority that had traditionally accompanied the officeholding.[14] The Chávez playbook once again. Later, President Maduro faced a recalcitrant Venezuelan Congress. He turned to a stacked Constitutional Court to bypass the entire legislative branch first through court rulings and subsequently by the creation of a parallel constituent assembly to attempt to

supplant legislative power altogether. In effect, this was but the latest manipulation of governmental authority to curtail accountability.[15] As Wojciech Sadurski
meticulously examines in the Polish context, the manipulation of rules of retirement for judges, administrative assignments for dissident public officials,
jurisdictional reassignments among levels of government, and even the ability
to publish unfavorable court rulings can be exploited to punish the opposition
and reward the loyal without seemingly dramatic legal overhaul. At bottom,
"Jarosław Kaczyński and his closest allies, who are deeply distrustful of any independent social powers, be they the judiciary, media, local self-government,
non-governmental organizations (NGOs), non-partisan military, or a neutral
civil service (but not yet the clergy, though that time may come), and who present the democratic mandate given to their party through the electoral choice of
2015 as a basis for extending personal control over all social powers."[16]

The extreme form, and the one that has proved most conducive to judicial
intervention, is the use of legislative majorities to push through "abusive" constitutional amendments aimed at eroding electoral accountability.[17] These are the
structural alterations that have the effect of "mak[ing] it harder to dislodge the
incumbent leader or party, and to weaken checks on their exercise of power."[18]
In response, national constitutional courts have on important occasions fashioned new doctrines to thwart even procedurally proper forms of constitutional amendment; in effect, to draw a line around core democratic features that
cannot be transgressed. The postwar constitutions of Europe, particularly the
post-Nazi consolidation of democracy in West Germany, categorially placed certain matters outside the ambit of democratic choice, including even by constitutional amendment. In effect, there could be no return to Nazi rule. Some national
courts emerging from states formerly under Soviet rule similarly constructed a
non-voidable commitment to democracy out of post-authoritarian governance.
But some courts, as in India, did so in terms of an overriding constitutional commitment to democracy, independent of any historic legacy of authoritarianism.
In so doing, these courts have written unamendability conditions through judicial interpretation that carry forth the inviolability provisions of postwar West
German constitutionalism[19] into national constitutions where such eternity
clauses were textually absent.[20]

No court played a more significant role in defining the judicial role in defending
democratic principles than the Indian Supreme Court. In a series of cases, that
Court gave robust content to the "basic structures" of democratic governance
such that the core principles of electoral accountability would be protected, even
from constitutional amendment. These cases took hold in response to the declaration of emergency powers by Prime Minister Indira Gandhi. Beginning in
1973 in the landmark case of *Kesavananda Bharati v. Kerala*,[21] the Indian court
introduced the world to the concept of judicial protection of basic structures.

Under this approach, the role of judicial review was to determine as a practical matter, "whether or not [the challenged act] destroys the basic structure"[22] of democratic governance, and for these purposes, "the form of an amendment is not relevant, its consequence would be [the] determinative factor."[23]

The activist modern era of judicial pushback in favor of democratic contestation may be dated from the *Elections Case*[24] in which the Indian Court applied the basic structures doctrine to strike down efforts to make election law reforms non-reviewable in the courts. The Indian Supreme Court used the doctrines to invalidate amendments giving Parliament, rather than an independent electoral commission and the courts, the power to regulate and void elections.[25] The attempt to place the election code in what is termed the Ninth Schedule of the Indian Constitution would have precluded any judicial oversight. Instead, the Court found that election administration was too central to the core functioning of democracy to allow unreviewable incumbent political authorities a free hand in this domain. The practical result was that the Court retained authority over the first elections after the end of emergency rule in 1977, an election that resulted in, for the first time in India's history, a non–Congress Party government.[26]

The same judicial commitment to democratic governance principles may be found in constitutional pronouncements by newly constituted apex courts in the second half of the 20th century. As framed by the Italian Constitutional Court, a constitutional commitment to democracy "contains some supreme principles that cannot be subverted or modified in their essential content either by laws of constitutional amendment or other constitutional laws . . . [that form] part of the supreme values on which the Italian Constitution is based."[27] Courts have used this power of protecting core "supreme values" to strike down even procedurally proper amendments with astonishing frequency in recent years.[28] At bottom, these decisions invoke a democratic commitment so fundamental as not reducible to simple textual commands. In the words of the Czech Constitutional Court commenting on the post-1989 political structure, "our new constitution is not established on neutrality of values, it is not merely a definition of institutions and processes, but incorporates in its text certain regulatory ideas, expressing the basic untouchable values of a democratic society."[29] The catalogue of such decisions is by now quite extensive, but two brief examples will have to suffice to set out the breadth of the basic structures doctrines that have emerged.

Among the growing canon of democracy-reinforcing constitutional interventions, no case is as widely heralded as the decision of the Colombian Constitutional Court in 2010 that denied popular incumbent President Álvaro Uribe a third term in office,[30] a decision whose careful analysis has previously been discussed here. But the facts require more attention as they highlight the judiciary's potential to break a consolidation of power by the executive.

Colombia, like many Latin American countries, vested great power in the office of the president, but in turn limited presidents to a single term in office. Uribe became president amid the chaos of armed insurrection against the state and large areas of the country being under the effective control of narcotraffickers. Uribe succeeded in reimposing order against the persistent guerrilla insurgency and his popularity soared throughout his term.[31] Congress then initiated the process of amending the constitution to allow a second term, something accepted by the Court as a necessary accommodation to the practical realities of popular approbation for Uribe's triumphs in office.[32]

Although there were some warning signs of increasing corruption and brutality in the anti-insurgent military campaigns, Uribe remained popular throughout his second term. The logical result was the simple question: If two terms, why not three terms? Once again, the Uribe-dominated Congress initiated a basically proper process of constitutional amendment to permit Uribe to run a third time. Enter the Constitutional Court and the question of whether the judiciary could invoke a principle even higher in authority than the constitutionally ordained processes of amendment.

In the tradition of the Indian Supreme Court, the Constitutional Court did just that. Surprisingly, in light of its acquiescence to the earlier amendment permitting a second turn in office, the Court ruled that even a procedurally proper constitutional amendment would violate the core democratic spirit of the 1991 Constitution. A third term would disrupt the electoral accountability of the president, according to the Court, and would also compromise separation of powers by allowing a prolonged stretch of executive appointments by a single head of state.[33] In order to enjoin a procedurally proper constitutional amendment from going into effect, the Court had to rely on broader democratic principles that both preserved the centrality of competitive elections and sought to limit the de facto power of a long incumbent president.[34] Stunningly, President Uribe deferred to the Court's decree, allowing competitive elections to go forward and thrusting the Constitutional Court into a central position as the guarantor of constitutional democracy.[35]

Clearly the idea of a court ensuring democracy against the concerted will of the political branches cannot be the norm, nor is it likely to be sustained in isolation. The Colombian ruling denying President Uribe a chance to run a third time remains the only example in all of Latin America of a court thwarting an attempt to extend executive tenure.[36] And, further, that trajectory is now called into question by the decision in 2020 to order the house arrest of Mr. Uribe on charges emerging from the battles against insurgent forces and narcotraffickers. Unfortunately, the history of democracies that survive the prosecution of former heads of state is precarious at best.

Less dramatic than a claim to continue in office indefinitely is the use of incumbent political power to forestall anticipated shifts in electoral preferences. Taiwan provides a useful example with the 1999 constitutional revisions that sought to entrench the dominant party, Kuomintang (KMT), in two main ways. Democracy itself was frail in Taiwan, and the KMT had ruled since it fled the mainland in 1949 following defeat by Mao Tse-Tung and the Chinese Communist Party. As the 20th century drew to a close, the once untouchable KMT chokehold on Taiwanese politics started to come undone. The 1999 reforms were an effort to buttress the flailing dominance of the KMT by holding in permanence aspects of the party's commanding position. First, all elections for the National Assembly, the constitutional chamber of the bicameral legislature, beginning in 2000 were to be delayed for two years.[37] Second, the seats in the National Assembly were to be guaranteed to the parties with representation in the lower chamber (the Legislative Yuan), without any direct election.[38] The combined effect would have been to perpetuate KMT hegemony in the upper chamber regardless of changing voter preferences. Compounding the insult to democratic principles, the legislators voted on these constitutional changes anonymously, thereby removing even rudimentary political accountability.[39]

Constitutional law is frequently intertwined with constitutional politics. The KMT had dominated Taiwan since its expulsion from the Chinese mainland in 1949, but it was losing ground electorally—hence the attempts to lock in the prior distribution of power. The breakthrough election of Democratic Progressive Party (DPP) President Chen Shui-bian in 2000 ushered in an era of genuine political competition in which state institutions could emerge from the suffocating control of the KMT. Among the emergent institutions was the Taiwanese Constitutional Court. The Court moved out of its historic dormancy to issue *Interpretation No. 499*, striking down the proposed constitutional revisions.[40] The bottom-line holding was that "delegates must be directly elected by the people to exercise the powers and duties of the National Assembly," and absent such election, "the amended provisions on the installation of National Assembly delegates violate the constitutional order of democracy."[41] While the formulation is abstract, the court grounded its decision by reference to international norms of democratic accountability, a necessary substitute for the lack of any robust constitutional precedents in Taiwan.[42]

Judicial assertions of authority do not typically emerge from a vacuum. The existence of political competition is usually a prerequisite for any form of judicial intervention, as in Taiwan. But, on occasion, courts have struck first to preserve the terrain for political challenge. A recent, striking example is the emergence of judicial authority in sub-Saharan Africa, a decidedly inhospitable setting. In 2020, the Supreme Court of Appeal of Malawi upheld a lower court order finding fraud in a closely contested election purportedly won by the incumbent. Claiming the central commitment to a "constitutional democracy," the Court declared not only its authority but that "a case challenging an election cannot be an ordinary venture. More so, a case challenging the election of a President. It challenges the very core of any representative democratic system."[43] This was only the second time in African history that a court had dared overturn the results of a presidential election, the first having been in Kenya only in 2017.[44] For a court in a country with such weak institutions as Malawi to engage presidential power is nothing short of astonishing.

Examples of courts assuming the mantle of democracy's protectors are widespread but should not be exaggerated.[45] For example, *Interpretation No. 499* is the only time Taiwan's Constitutional Court has invalidated a constitutional amendment.[46] Nothing inherent in the role of courts protects rulings against being rejected by the political branches, and the scope of judicial authority is in delicate interplay with the political realities of each country.[47] The critical examples of successful judicial challenges to one-party rule is not the predicate for allowing competitive democracies, but generally follows the fracturing of the ruling party's lock-hold on power, whether in Taiwan or, another example, Malaysia.[48] In Malaysia, the Federal Court (the constitutional high court) even ventured into the fraught area of religious authority. The Court declared that judicial review and constitutional interpretation are "pivotal constituents of the civil courts' judicial power" and that "as part of the basic structure of the constitution, it cannot be abrogated from the civil courts or conferred upon the Syariah Courts, whether by constitutional amendments, Act of Parliament or state legislation."[49] As with the initial formulation of the basic structures doctrine in India, and as repeated in many invocations around the world, the Malaysian Federal Court proclaimed its basic structure to invalidate a constitutional amendment that would have stripped the judiciary of the power to review and invalidate certain categories of legislation.[50]

As compelling as these cases are for using constitutional authority to repel threats to democratic accountability, there are limits, both practical and more broadly theoretical. The practical limitation is that, for all the heralding of the Colombian Constitutional Court, it stands as the only judicial decision in Latin America that was able to challenge term expansions of the executive. In fact, by one analysis, the 2010 decision in the Uribe case is the *only* example of a court successfully thwarting an executive claim to extended tenure.[51] More fundamental is that unleashing the power of constitutional courts unfortunately invites efforts to compromise these institutions and to subvert them into instruments of "abusive judicial review."[52]

The most notable example comes from Bolivia, where President Evo Morales lost a referendum that would have amended the Constitution to allow him to run for a fourth term as president. Here it was the voters and not a court that denied an attempt to install a permanence of officeholding. Supporters of Morales then crafted a higher level democratic claim that any constitutional limits on the terms that a president might serve would violate the fundamental right of the voters to decide, purportedly established by some vague international human rights commitments.[53]

President Morales showed that empowering courts may mean upholding higher democratic principles, but maybe not. By the time the issue came to the Court, four of the seven justices had already served as cabinet officials in the Morales governments and dutifully endorsed the claimed right of the people to have Morales run again in 2019.[54] A supine constitutional court declared that the fundamentals of democracy demanded not rotation in office but unfettered electoral choice. Under this reading of higher principle, the inability of voters to elect Morales over and over was a frustration of democratic will. Having obtained a ruling from a compromised constitutional court that such a referendum was permissible, Morales placed the issue before the voters and—to his obvious surprise and dismay—proceeded to lose the election.

Bolivia exposes a deep paradox in looking to constitutional courts as a hopeful bastion of protection for political accountability. The capacity of courts to perform the function of ensuring against,[55] or hedging against,[56] may in turn depend on the pre-existence of political competition. Absent such competition, the constitutional courts can be captured through appointments by the executive or simply overwhelmed by the realities of centralized political power. As Sergio Verdugo well captured the problem, the attempt to vest the power to safeguard democracy in putatively independent institutions runs the risk that a hegemonic regime will invariably "captur[e] the institutions that are supposed to check or balance their power, especially if those countries have an hyper-presidential regime."[57]

II. The Soft Power of Democracy

The institutional pathways of democratic governance serve to slow demands for immediate satisfaction of the momentary majority. Unlike plebiscitary governance, which may permit radical swings in programmatic commitments, institutionalized democratic governance provides what James Madison hailed as the virtues of "filtration" of popular sentiment through institutional intermediation.[58] Committee structures, bicameralism, staggered election cycles, federalism, separation of powers—all are instruments that delay the implementation of momentary popular preferences until they command sufficient support, measured in terms of both the intensity of the majority commitment and its endurance over time. In the perhaps apocryphal exchange between George Washington and

Thomas Jefferson, Washington likened the need for a second legislative chamber to Jefferson's custom of pouring hot coffee from cup to saucer: after passage by the popularly accountable House, explained Washington, "we pour our legislation into the Senatorial saucer to cool it."[59]

Such delayed gratification frustrates populist insurgents for whom institutional constraints are seen as an impediment to the realization of the will of the people, as reflected in the most recent election. To the tempering effect of long-standing political parties come the independent, charismatic candidates increasingly untethered to any governmental experience. To the labored processes of administrative procedure come the demands for draining the swamp.[60] To the separation of prosecutorial power from direct political commands comes the chant of lock her up.[61] And, to the difficulty of working the legislative byways comes the recourse to executive decrees. In large measure, these are the frustrations of political immediacy that bedevil every new administration in every democracy. The ship of state is cumbersome and alters course hesitatingly.

Legislative weakness compounds the problem. The inability to govern through representative organs invites capture of government authority by the executive, a tendency for policy to be initiated through regulation or decree rather than legislation. These executive-dominated governments look to elections as a mandate rather than as the normal process of parliamentary ups and downs.[62] Increasingly, the dominance of the executive diminishes the significance of presidential versus parliamentary regimes. Both come to be governed by administrative decrees, and neither offers legislative resistance outside of narrow partisan affiliations.

Populist executives see the legislature not as their partners in policy initiatives but as obstacles to moving ahead with executive prerogatives. A legislature that does not deliver risks being overwhelmed by the executive branch. It does not matter that legislative inaction may result from fractured political parties incapable of negotiating for the public good, from the sheer dysfunction of the legislature, from a political disagreement with the agenda of the executive, or from the inability to cohere on a policy initiative in the face of internal political disagreement. An executive riding a populist wave would not distinguish among the sources of legislative inaction and would instead see each sign of legislative reprobation as an unwarranted threat to the executive's electoral mandate.

Without the primacy of legislative authority, the legitimacy and support of democratic governance erodes. The ensuing period of "democratic decline" allows a populist leader to launch "a concerted and sustained attack on institutions whose job it is to check his actions or on rules that hold him to account."[63] Such a populist leader, as formulated by Kim Lane Scheppele, "does so in the name of his democratic mandate. Loosening the bonds of constitutional constraint on executive power through legal reform is the first sign of the autocratic legalist."[64] Renáta Uitz further explains that executive power grows when legislatures fail to exercise a cooling function and undertake to resolve difficult questions:

> The powers of the executive branch to execute the laws . . . are neither self-standing, nor self-explanatory. Rather they are part of a complex web of legislative and executive powers, mended by the judiciary and extended by the political branches based on practical needs, fears, and personal ambitions. Complexity leads to complication and complications are left unresolved under the banner of being (too) complex. This becomes the convenient source of unstoppable executive overreach.[65]

While extreme, the examples from Taiwan or Eastern Europe or India have a resonance even in the established democratic countries. There are temptations for incumbent authorities to either bypass the formal accountability structures that limit their immediate power (George Washington's "cooling" function) or to thwart the electoral mechanisms that, having brought them to office, might well lead to their removal. Richard Pildes and I have referred to the problem of "lockups" on power by incumbents as a major justification for judicial intervention, as well as a guiding principle for distinguishing democracy reinforcement from mere policy imposition by the judiciary.[66]

When the U.S. Supreme Court ventured into the "political thicket" in the Reapportionment Cases of the 1960s, it was the failure of electoral accountability that provided the key doctrinal justification,[67] as it later proved to be around the world, including unexpected examples such as Taiwan. The core fact of the political question cases of the 1960s was that the American political establishment refused to reapportion political power from 1910 on. As the population grew, urbanized, and welcomed new generations of immigrants, reapportionment would invariably have shifted political power from rural America to the numerical strongholds of an urbanizing, integrating nation. Even Congress, despite an express constitutional duty to reapportion after every decennial census, refused to do so after the 1920 census,[68] which confirmed that legislative control would pass to the rising urban, industrial North under a proper apportionment.[69] Absolute power loves power, absolutely.

As the 20th century progressed, the refusal to reapportion at the state level meant that some counties had representation sixty times as great, indeed even one hundred times as great, as other counties on a per person basis.[70] Even though one person, one vote was not yet enshrined as constitutional doctrine, there was no question that the intuitive principle of equal shares among voters was in grave disrepair. For decades, American courts refused to intercede on the grounds that such political questions, as the constitutional doctrine was termed, placed these matters outside the judiciary's purview. Ultimately what foundered the political question doctrine was the sheer futility of seeking political redress for a political power grab. In the seminal case of *Baker v. Carr,* the concurring opinion of Justice Tom Clark perfectly captured the absurdity of a legislative solution:

> Although I find the Tennessee apportionment statute offends the Equal Protection Clause, I would not consider intervention by this Court into so delicate a field if there were any other relief available to the people of Tennessee. . . . I find none other than through the federal courts. The majority of the voters have been caught up in a legislative strait jacket. Tennessee has an "informed, civically militant electorate" and "an aroused popular conscience," but it does not sear "the conscience of the people's representatives." This is because the legislative policy has riveted the present seats in the Assembly to their respective constituencies, and by the votes of their incumbents a re-apportionment of any kind is prevented. . . . We therefore must conclude that the people of Tennessee are stymied and without judicial intervention will be saddled with the present discrimination in the affairs of their state government.[71]

Most often, the cases that command attention are judicial interventions when the legislature has acted perniciously, as with the Taiwanese power grab or the declaration of emergency powers in India. More complicated than a power grab through legislative action is legislative refusal to act and a corresponding lack of political accountability before the electorate. One of the obstacles to entering the political thicket to confront the refusal to reapportion was the generalized legal difficulty with acts of omission versus acts of commission. Yet legislative passivity in the face of consolidating power may also be the occasion for critical judicial intervention.

III. Brexit

Brexit provides an important illustration of what may happen when institutional practices break down and courts are forced into the breach. Prime Minister David Cameron had formed a Tory government in 2015, having first ruled as head of a weak coalition government beginning in 2010. Cameron sought to defuse pressure from anti-EU activists and, not incidentally, to consolidate his new government's mandate by putting the question of EU membership to a referendum vote. The political calculus was no doubt abetted by the fact that all the institutional parties in Britain were in the "remain" camp.

The referendum was held in 2016, and British voters sent shock waves through British politics with a demand to leave, as forceful as it was abstract. As Britain reeled under an ill-specified mandate from a popular referendum, a surprisingly critical actor became the UK Supreme Court, among the most recent additions to the world of constitutional courts. This role for the Court is a serious alteration of the British constitutional tradition that has long posited that there are "legally unenforceable customs that regulate and restrain the formal powers granted to governmental actors."[72] Such conventions derive from past practice, from the fact that officials believe themselves bound by the rule, and from the understanding that the rule appears reasonable as time goes on.[73] Under this view, "customs and conventions arise from what people do, not from what they agree or promise."[74] In the constitutional tradition exemplified by Edmund Burke, the foundations of constitutional government

> evolved slowly and incrementally over hundreds of years . . . because the existing institutional arrangements reflect accumulated wisdom of centuries of political decisions; each incremental step is the product either of rational deliberation or natural development and has been tested by the experience of many years. The cumulative product reflects a reason far superior to that of any individual or generation.[75]

Unlike the heavily court-centered constitutionalism in the U.S. and in 20th-century democracies, the aim of British constitutionalism "was to ensure that these legal powers, formally in the hands of the Crown, were in practice exercised by Ministers in accordance with the principles of responsible and representative government."[76] As explained by A. V. Dicey, the most recognized expositor of the English constitutional tradition, the role of constitutional law was the preservation of democratic governance: "Our modern code of constitutional morality secures, though in a roundabout way, what is called abroad the 'sovereignty of the people.'"[77] Even Edmund Burke's conservative exposition acknowledges that the constitution compels the "constituent parts of a state . . . to hold their public faith with each other."[78] Unlike in the U.S., the courts did not serve as the constitutional glue that interpreted and refined public obligations. Rather, British constitutionalism presumed ultimate parliamentary sovereignty, including matters of constitutional interpretation. Even the location of the British judiciary confirmed the role of Parliament as sovereign. Until the creation of the Supreme Court in 2009, the highest court in Britain had been the Appellate Committee of the House of Lords, formally a part of the legislative branch of government, and officed within the House of Lords itself.

At the same time, the very existence of a referendum is a significant departure from the commanding role of Parliament under British democracy. The question of whether a referendum can bind Parliament is constitutionally suspect in the UK, and—perhaps for this reason—there had been only one nationwide referendum in Britain in the 20th century. Brexit represented only the second in the 21st century, the other being an inconsequential referendum on voting procedures in parliamentary elections. "The emergence of referendum politics in the late twentieth century can be seen as a shift away from parliamentary sovereignty," presents Erin Delaney, in favor of direct elections that are "expedient, haphazard, and untheorized."[79] In effect, a referendum under British traditions represents a potential challenge to the dominant role of Parliament, a recognition that the institutionalized political process could not resolve a particularly contentious issue.

Recourse to a referendum raises the specter of institutional failure in British governance. British politics worked best when the dominant parties divided along the major political cleavages of the polity. Parliamentary elections had broad legitimacy in setting the basic agenda between the welfarist agenda of Labour and the market orientation of the Tories. The resulting election would mandate the broad policy goals of government, to be implemented by the expertise held at the Cabinet and administrative levels.

However, holding the prospect of a referendum in reserve helped protect against the one-off issues that did not centrally define national politics and that did not map onto the main divide of the political parties. But the risk is ever present that, where the parties could not internalize the broad social divisions, parliamentary norms would collapse, and Britain could be forced to turn to the imprecise mechanisms of the plebiscite as a stopgap. On this view, holding in reserve the prospect of an extraordinary ballot initiative could perhaps serve as a backstop for parliamentary conduct—what Dicey called a "people's veto" over vexatious legislation imposed by a parliamentary majority—or as a corrective to the failure of Parliament to take up the pressing matters of the day.[80] But a referendum is not legislation and cannot serve as the defining resolution of difficult political issues that stand at the core of domestic politics.

The demand for Britain to leave the European Union altered this understanding of parliamentary democracy. Specifically, with Labour and the Conservatives each internally divided over Brexit, Britain struggled without a government capable of claiming a mandate for any course of conduct. As explained by Lord King, the former governor of the Bank of England, this disrupted the customary role of elections:

> In normal circumstances, a general election is the mechanism by which
> one party obtains both a public mandate and a majority of seats in the

Commons. Over many years the system worked pretty well. On most big questions the two parties had different views which could be put before the electorate. And elections ensured some rotation of the party in power and gave voters the opportunity to throw out governments that were seen to have failed.[81]

Or, most simply, "Brexit split not only the nation but also both the Conservative and Labour parties."[82]

With each of the major parties deeply divided on the question of European integration, immigration, EU regulatory authority, and a number of subsidiary issues, British politics were at a standstill.[83] The repeated cataclysms over Brexit well illustrate the problem of politics without an institutional framework. The 2016 plebiscitary referendum to leave provided little direction on how to structure innumerable trade, tax, transportation, and migration laws and agreements. As several years and several prime ministers have revealed, however, the consequences of leaving complex directives merely implicit in a plebiscitary decision are quite severe, even if the government has vowed to respect the ill-formed sentiment of referendum voters. The path from a leave vote to Britain's structured exit from the EU became an ongoing source of governmental instability even across historic fault lines, such as Northern Ireland.

At bottom, the difficulty stems from the failure of a parliamentary mandate over Brexit. Neither major party had staked a position on the central issues of European relations that had been presented to the voters, and neither could provide a political consensus, regardless of outcome. In turn, three successive prime ministers tried to circumvent Parliament by one mechanism or another. The first attempt, and the one that prompted the still unresolved saga, was the initial ill-considered referendum offered up by Prime Minister David Cameron, himself at the head of a government without any parliamentary backing for any course of conduct on the critical domestic issue of the day. In effect, this was a desperate gambit by a weak prime minister to compensate for the lack of any parliamentary mandate to take charge of an explosive political issue.

The avoidance strategy was to stage a direct appeal to the population. Prime Minister Cameron, like many failing politicians, misjudged the times and was repudiated by the voters. To the surprise of most London-centric commentators, leave became the rallying cry for the areas of the country that time had forsaken and for whom immigration and European integration seemed to offer the least hope. With the exception of Scotland and the Catholic counties of Northern Ireland—for whom departure from England was viewed more favorably than separation from the EU—support for Brexit stood in almost perfect relation to distance from London.

Following the stunning victory of Brexit, Cameron quickly departed the scene and a chastened and ultimately unstable Tory government formed under Prime Minister Theresa May. Unable or unwilling to resist the wave of populist anger, the government of Prime Minister May announced its intention to implement the Brexit vote as the voice of the people. The result was an attempt to disentangle Britain from the EU by executive fiat. The prime minister and her cabinet substituted claimed prerogatives over foreign affairs for the power of deliberation and resolution customarily lodged in Parliament. This provoked a major legal challenge in the UK Supreme Court, itself something that would have been an unlikely legal challenge when the judiciary remained a part of the House of Lords. The ensuing first *Miller* case prompted a remarkable discussion on the nature of British democratic governance and the importance of institutional order. In effect the question was understood as whether executive action through the ministries could supplant a dysfunctional Parliament. The inquiry was thus:

> [The] Act envisages domestic law, and therefore rights of UK citizens, changing as EU law varies, but it does not envisage those rights changing as a result of ministers unilaterally deciding that the United Kingdom should withdraw from the EU Treaties.[84]

That a weak government had appealed directly over the head of Parliament to enraged voters did not alter the institutional commitments to the democratic supremacy of Parliament. Nor could the prime minister invoke plebiscitary approval as a substitute for proper institutional process:

> The question is whether that domestic starting point, introduced by Parliament, can be set aside, or could have been intended to be set aside, by a decision of the UK executive without express Parliamentary authorisation. We cannot accept that a major change to UK constitutional arrangements can be achieved by ministers alone; it must be effected in the only way that the UK constitution recognises, namely by Parliamentary legislation. This conclusion appears to us to follow from the ordinary application of basic concepts of constitutional law to the present issue.[85]

In substance, the British Court had to choose between two fundamental constitutional principles—if it chose to enter these waters at all. Parliamentary sovereignty is no doubt the heart of English constitutionalism, but so too is the capacity of the government to exercise the royal prerogative on behalf of the Crown. As expressed by Dicey, this is "the residue of discretionary power left at any moment in the hands of the Crown" that may be exercised by government ministers.[86] One such prerogative is foreign engagements, including even the ability to deploy British forces, a power that the government traditionally exercised without securing prior parliamentary approval.[87] The presumption of sovereign prerogative in the conduct of foreign affairs was already weakened by the debacle of the Iraq War and Prime Minister Gordon Brown's agreement to structure a consultative vote by Parliament as a prelude to foreign military engagement.[88]

When the system worked properly, the political process could force Parliament and the government to share decision-making responsibility. The question was what would happen when Parliament was incapable of implementing its electoral mandate to address fundamental questions of policy.

Undoubtedly there would ultimately have been political retribution for the entire Brexit imbroglio, including for Prime Minister May. Perhaps in the absence of judicial intervention, the parliamentary leadership would have paid the price for any ensuing dislocations and its failure to discharge the leadership responsibilities under Britain's parliamentary constitution. But in the immediate political moment, the Supreme Court forced a political accounting. The Court's intervention did not predetermine either the ultimate decision on Brexit or substitute for the political accountability of Parliament. Instead, in a fashion that borders on the soft power of institutional arrangements in a functioning democracy, the Court's limited intervention aimed to reinforce the constitutional constraints necessary for democratic governance.

In an ill-fated gambit, reminiscent of Cameron's decision to call the referendum in the first place, May called snap elections in 2017 hoping to increase her parliamentary leverage. That gambit failed, and she proceeded first to lose seats in Parliament and then to lose three successive votes on her Brexit Leave strategy, including a final vote by a margin of 432 to 202 in early 2019, the single greatest defeat for a sitting government in British parliamentary history.[89] Once again in the 2017 elections, the political parties failed to align around clear positions on leave, with the result that Parliament was unable to function as the center for governance on the critical issue of the day.

Ultimately, parliamentary paralysis led May to resign, followed by the still governing Tories' selection of Boris Johnson as prime minister. Significantly, Johnson had been a supporter of Brexit since the original referendum and campaigned within the Conservative Party as a champion of unilateral exit. Thus, for the first time, at least one of the major political parties became defined by its position on Brexit. At the same time, however, Johnson stood for election on Brexit only within the Conservative Party as the replacement for Theresa May. Unlike in a presidential system, May's forced resignation as prime minister did not prompt new national elections, only the selection by the ruling

Tories of a new head of the party and, in turn, head of government. That meant that roughly 140,000 party members selected the new prime minister in an internal caucus process that shut out the broad mass of the British population. There was still no Parliament elected on the basis of contested positions for and against Brexit, and the Tory members of Parliament had not campaigned or been elected on the basis of their position on Brexit.

Johnson fared no better than his predecessors on trying to force his Brexit plan upon a dysfunctional Parliament. For a while, the most visible member of the British government seemed to be John Bercow, the witheringly droll speaker of the House of Commons, who tried to impose order on a rudderless ship. After two failed efforts to gain parliamentary approval for Johnson's unilateral Leave policy, Bercow shut down debate on a third effort and forced the government into crisis. Only Anthony Trollope[90] could capture the ensuing parliamentary wrangling that ultimately ended with a call for a new election in December 2019. In that election, the Tories ran decisively as the party of exit, while Labour floundered amid internal strife, centrally but not exclusively focused on Brexit. Of immediate concern, however, is not the parliamentary elections, the decisive Tory win, or the ultimate political realignment around the Leave strategy.

Instead, the concern here is with Johnson's efforts to prorogue Parliament in August 2019. This was a move to harness the power of the Crown by placing Parliament in a state of suspended animation and concentrating power exclusively in the hands of a prime minister, to wit, a prime minister acting without legislative oversight. In restoring a practice essentially unknown since the 17th century and the Glorious Revolution, Johnson claimed the authority of the Crown as sovereign to place Parliament out of session and, in effect, bypass parliamentary sovereignty more convincingly than even Theresa May had attempted. Once again, this introduced the role of the emergent Supreme Court in the breathtaking *Miller II* decision.

Following the track laid down in *Miller I*, the Supreme Court once again assumed the role of protector of the constitutional order.[91] The Court insisted that "the issue in these appeals is not when and on what terms the United Kingdom is to leave the European Union."[92] The bold statement that the Court would serve as the guarantor of constitutional guardrails on the separation of powers then allowed the critical conclusion:

> A decision to prorogue Parliament (or to advise the monarch to prorogue Parliament) will be unlawful if the prorogation has the effect of frustrating or preventing, without reasonable justification, the ability of Parliament to carry out its constitutional functions as a legislature and as the body responsible for the supervision of the executive.[93]

Once framed as a question not of the power of prorogation, but whether prorogation would frustrate parliamentary governance, the answer, per the Court,
"is that of course it did. This was not a normal prorogation in the run-up to a
Queen's Speech. It prevented Parliament from carrying out its constitutional role
for five out of a possible eight weeks between the summer recess and exit day."[94]
The bold relief of the Court's opinion could not be tempered by the mundane
description of the intervention: "It is important to emphasise that the issue in
these appeals is not when and on what terms the United Kingdom is to leave the
European Union. The issue is whether the advice given by the Prime Minister
[to prorogue Parliament] was lawful."[95]

Even more stunning is the unembroidered directness of the Court's judgment, a remarkable statement of judicial confidence by Lady Hale, the first fe-
male chief magistrate. Per the Court,

> [It] will be unlawful if the prorogation has the effect of frustrating or
> preventing, without reasonable justification, the ability of Parliament
> to carry out its constitutional functions as a legislature and as the body
> responsible for the supervision of the executive. In such a situation, the
> court will intervene if the effect is sufficiently serious to justify such an
> exceptional course.[96]

Unmistakably, the Supreme Court opined that the Queen's prerogative power
had been exercised unconstitutionally. Stunning.

There could also be no mistaking the powerful insertion of a new constitutional actor. John Finnis, for example, argued that the Court in *Miller II* made a
"historic mistake" by disrupting the British Constitution's careful division between legal rules and political conventions.[97] By muddying this dichotomy, he
contends, the decision was of a "radical or even revolutionary character."[98] But
is that right?

The argument here is not dependent on the pros or cons of Brexit. Were I a
British subject in similar circumstances to my university role in the U.S., I do not
doubt my sympathies would lie firmly with the remain camp. But the question
here is not the substance of the ruling pro or contra on Brexit, but the effect of
the Court's two *Miller* decisions on forcing the central axis of British democracy to turn decisively on Parliament. Taken as a constitutional intervention
in forcing Parliament to play its proper democratic role, the judicial function
appears not so menacing as Professor Finnis would have it. As Lord Sumption
described *Miller II*: "The decision undoubtedly was that it was unlawful, and
that was a decision that was radical in its reasoning but very conservative in its
result."[99]

Like its judicial predecessor, *Miller II* forced the government's hand. With a rebellious and recalcitrant Parliament seemingly objecting to any Brexit scenario, Prime Minister Johnson had no choice but to call elections at the end of 2019. This time, however, at least the Tories aligned as the party committed to an exit strategy and won a sweeping electoral victory to endorse Johnson's "oven-ready" Brexit plan. The new Parliament had eighty new Tory MPs, and that Parliament then legislated the exit from the EU for January 2020—which then triggered a new set of legal calamities surrounding the COVID-19 shutdown and some questionable personal judgments of Prime Minister Johnson. Fortunately, those lie beyond the scope of the present inquiry.

Judicial intercession is all the more important to face down what even *The Economist* nervously labelled "the executive unchained."[100] Britain has few structural limitations on what a majority Parliament may do, save for fidelity to tradition and ministerial good faith. In practice, the risk of parliamentary unilateralism was kept in check since its 1973 accession to the EU. Apart from the economic dislocations that may follow from Brexit comes the risk that a political tradition of caution may have grown flaccid in a period in which restraint was exercised from without. The politically volatile commands from Brussels and Strasburg, that is, from the bureaucracy and the human rights commands of European law, may no longer rein in populist fervor.

The lesson is not the valor of Brexit or the still undetermined relationship between Britain and the European Union. Nor is it that Boris Johnson would emerge from the new elections as a powerful if complicated political leader. Rather, the unexpected intervention of the British Supreme Court forced politics back into the democratic arena of Parliament. As Tarunabh Khaitan observes, modern autocracy kills democracy "by a thousand cuts." Discrete assaults on "accountability-seeking mechanisms" seem small, but taken as a whole, the systemic damage can be great.[101] At least in this one domain, judicial intercession appears to have ameliorated an ailing body politic.

7

Corruption Simpliciter

Three propositions then come together. The first is that the lack of institutional constraints in populist governance will create the sort of clientelist politics evidenced in the run-up to the 2012 presidential elections in Argentina. The second is that this form of populist governance will yield a distinct form of personalized decision-making. The third is the likelihood that this will result in outright corruption because of weakened institutional constraints. If these propositions are true, combatting corruption may provide a legal check on populist excess and may provide a means of reaching this conduct through the ordinary mechanisms of administrative and criminal law rather than the human rights or broader democracy agendas. I return here to older concerns on corruption that focus not on how candidates get elected—the input side of the ledger—but on the discharge of public office: "The inquiry on officeholding asks whether the electoral system leads the political class to offer private gain from public action to distinct, tightly organized constituencies, which in turn may be mobilized to keep compliant public officials in office."[1]

There is relatively little experience with legal constraints on the directed use of public resources to buttress electoral support, whether as in the Argentine example at the opening of this book or in any other electoral democracy. On the eve of the 2020 U.S. election, President Trump ordered that $200 discount cards be sent to all senior Americans to defray the cost of prescription drugs. No doubt this was an electoral stunt designed to appeal crassly to a decisive electoral constituency. It followed from no comparable program directed at healthcare during the prior three years of the Trump administration (unsurprisingly the Trump administration backed off from its promise just days before Inauguration Day when the gambit seemed to offer no electoral returns). While the propriety of such a move may be questioned under ordinary mechanisms of administrative law as beyond the scope of presidential authority, this cannot be a matter for criminal law. The executive gambit was transparent and was not directed at the personal enrichment of the president's entourage. Necessarily this was a matter reserved to the political process, leaving aside the administrative steps through which it was enacted.

By contrast, there is ample experience with legal responses to corruption of public officials, at least as a formal realm of conduct prohibited under the criminal laws of democratic states. The question then becomes whether the ordinary law against corruption may serve as a constraint on populist erosion of democratic institutions. Observing the U.S. or Brazil or India, the specter of corruption never seems far from populist strongmen, even if by no means limited only to such rulers. Anticorruption vigilance has two features that suggest potential points of limitation on some of the freewheeling, anti-institutional features of populism.

First, unlike broad human rights claims or claims based on the integrity of democracy, anticorruption efforts tend to engage a broader swath of the ordinary state-enforcement apparatus. In the wake of 1989, virtually all new democracies created specialized apex courts to address fundamental questions of state conduct. These courts were invariably modeled on the German Constitutional Court and seemed to respond to multiple concerns in the transition period. These courts stood apart from the ordinary judiciary, and their judges were typically recruited through distinct mechanisms that bypassed the career track. In countries that had been compromised under autocratic rule, this allowed a necessary retention of the career judges (who had been Nazi judges, apartheid judges, communist judges, etc.) while creating a new oversight body devoted to new constitutional values. The brute reality is that no country has a reserve body of judges capable of taking up the ordinary fare of contracts and torts in case of a complete lustration of those associated with the past.

These newly created constitutional courts could also claim fraternity with other apex courts in developing a broad-scale liberal agenda of rights, even social rights.[2] These courts faced down the first Ukrainian power grab in 1994, the lack of entrenchment of individual rights in the first South African Constitution in 1996, efforts by presidents to extend their terms of office, the failure of corrupt or incompetent governments to deliver on social promises—the list goes on at some length.

Unfortunately, students of comparative constitutional law were not the only ones to take note of this phenomenon. From Yeltsin and Putin in Russia, to more recent developments in Poland and Hungary, illiberal democracies discovered that constitutional courts could be made and unmade, and the same elements of administrative independence could well serve regimes if these courts could be captured. A heroic decision, such as denying President Uribe a third term in Colombia, could quickly be distorted into a servile decision to strike down as antidemocratic a constitutional limitation on multiple terms for President Morales in Bolivia.[3]

As wonderfully captured by Madhav Khosla, these independent courts "were once seen as shields against the tyranny of majority and autocratic drifts within the state, and as the defenders of liberty and enforcers of accountability. Sadly, courts today have become silent bystanders and complicit actors."[4] Writing before the current populist wave, I speculated about how long courts could hold out against challenges from within democracy, as opposed to those from the autocratic past:

> Courts are in a more precarious situation because their claim to authority is not the importance of constitutional democracy against vestiges of an autocratic past, but of a superior set of constitutional values against democratic claims to power. Courts are not simply a central part of the transition to democracy, but are the enforcers of limits on majoritarian prerogatives, of what in contemporary European debates is referred to as "constrained democracy." The difficulty inheres in that these cases pit the branch with the least democratic authority against the popularly elected political branches, generally over matters within the confines of formal legality.[5]

A recent trip to Poland presented this issue in a revealing light. Postcommunist Poland has two apex courts, a constitutional court modeled after the German court, and a supreme court that operates as the equivalent of the French Cour de Cassation as the final arbiter of ordinary appeals. The former is a stand-alone institution and wielded its power broadly in the period of transition to democracy. But that court has been largely neutered after relentless assault. Government reforms that changed the retirement age, withheld funds for the publication of court rulings, and swamped the docket effectively humbled the constitutional court. The attacks on the constitutional court prompted grassroots resistance loosely organized around the Committee in Defense of Democracy (KOD), which invoked the defense of the Constitution against PiS. At one point, the best-selling book in Poland was the Constitution itself, seen as a point of resistance against the government's efforts to trample state institutions. In the end, however, the claimed power of election overwhelmed the opposition. As urged by Polish de facto head of state Jarosław Kaczyński: "In a democracy, the sovereign is the people, their representative in Parliament and, in the Polish case, the elected president. . . . If we are to have a democratic state of law, no state authority, including the Constitutional Tribunal, can disregard legislation."[6]

Meanwhile, the other high tribunal, the Supreme Court, has more limited powers over the national government. It does not sit as a constitutional tribunal able to condemn government action; instead, it sits as the final arbiter in cases that come up through the ordinary pathways of the law. While its jurisdictional reach is narrower, the Supreme Court is an integrated part of the national judiciary, with deeply embedded institutional pathways. Whereas the constitutional court is composed of justices selected by the legislature, the Supreme Court has a bureaucratic system of nomination, leading to a final selection by the president. Its judges are career jurists who train and are qualified as such, and who progress along a civil servant track. The current PiS government viewed both the constitutional court and the Supreme Court as impediments to its political agenda, although its initial fury was directed at the constitutional court because of its broader mandate over the outputs of government decision-making.

Paradoxically, the extraordinary nature of the constitutional court and the more customary quality of the Supreme Court left their capacity to resist standing in inverse relation to their power. The willow may bend and the oak tree may break in a squall, as it were. The government easily dominated the constitutional court by manipulating its composition, while finding the bureaucratic mechanisms of the Supreme Court more of an obstacle. Embedded civil service bureaucracies are less sweeping in their mandate but more difficult to overwhelm by sheer executive fiat. While the PiS government harassed individual members of the Supreme Court,[7] it was only after the re-election of President Duda in 2020 that the PiS attempted to neuter the Supreme Court wholesale. The new regime reduced the number of judges from ninety-seven to somewhere in the twenty to thirty range, thereby overwhelming the Court's capacity to act effectively.[8] This was well after the de facto disabling of the constitutional court.

PiS legislation under President Duda also attempted to circumvent the Supreme Court's decision-making process altogether by furthering what Wojciech Sadurski describes as "Jarosław Kaczyński's dominant idea that all the wrongness of the old system related to the people who served in it: replace the people with better ones and you will change the system of PiS."[9] To neuter the career judges that could not be ousted, PiS created a new Supreme Court chamber on "extraordinary review and public affairs,"[10] consisting of twenty judges appointed by the PiS-controlled National Council of the Judiciary (KRS). As the Venice Commission noted, "the result of this design will be that 'judges appointed by a [KRS] dominated by the current political majority would decide on issues of particular importance, including the regularity of elections.'"[11] Indeed, one of the visible targets of the new process was Professor Sadurski, who having been found not guilty of criminal defamation in charges brought by the state-controlled TV station, then had to face review by this new Star Chamber.[12]

This then leads to the second observation. Prohibitions on corruption engage a broader domain of law than either human rights or the entrenchment of democracy. Centralized capture may prove more difficult where authority is diffuse and integrates more easily with the ordinary administration of law. While the current design trend in constitutionalism is to have independent agencies with specific power over questions of corruption, the argument here is that ordinary law in the hands of ordinary justice may prove most effective.[13]

The U.S. provides a ready example. Checks on presidential misbehavior are difficult in the face of the presidential pardon power and the centralized command structure of the Department of Justice. Impeachment requires Congress to challenge the president by abandoning political alignment in favor of institutional loyalty, a difficult process in an era of heightened polarization. By contrast, the confrontations with President Trump show that the ordinary mechanisms of criminal and administrative review allow dozens of investigations to go forward outside the direct control of the president or the attorney general. Some of these were handled by local federal prosecutors whose independence could be attacked. But many were in the hands of state investigators and promulgated through ordinary civil lawsuits seeking discovery of bank records and similar potential evidence of misconduct. It may well be that fiscal inducements on the eve of an election are difficult to prohibit. Yet the political processes that yield to the ready use of the state coffers to reward or to selectively punish may also provide a basis for legal accountability for populist excesses. The inquiry becomes the effectiveness of ordinary legal constraints against the more direct forms of corruption that are likely to emerge from this form of populist rule.

As discussed, the concept of corruption is broad and may be pushed to include the deformation of judgment,[14] or even the loss of citizen equal treatment, either through "drowned voices" or a "dispirited public."[15] In the present context, however, corruption stands for the more mundane concern regarding the violation of well-established prohibitions on the personal enrichment of public officials as a result of trading power for money. This is not a broad theory of equality in either political inputs or outputs. It is purely an instrumental account that seeks to enlist well-established prohibitions to limit certain political liabilities. This definition attempts neither to give a full account of proper functioning of democratic institutions nor a comprehensive view of improper motives that might compromise democracy. In this sense, the limited definition of corruption is once again "derivative" from other concerns about the political process.[16] But the objective is to focus on corruption standing on its own as a "policing concept,"[17] allowing the normal operation of the law to check the degradation of democracy in circumstances where other avenues of judicial concern for rights and democratic structures might not reach.

I. South Africa

South Africa is the most salient example of corruption becoming a central axis of legal challenge to populist unilateralism. Although South Africa served and continues to serve as the greatest hope for a negotiated transition to democracy under strong constitutional oversight, the legacy is more complicated. The post-apartheid South African Constitution vests too much power in the president, who serves as head of government, head of state, and head of the military. The president is selected by the National Assembly, which means the chief executive is also the head of the largest political party and is able to command a legislative majority. The initial hope was that this would be tempered by political competition at the legislative level and by the protections of federalism. This approach fared poorly as the African National Congress (ANC) leveraged its inherited authority from the anti-apartheid struggle to become a hegemonic political force, both at the national and at almost all provincial levels. In the absence of meaningful political challenge, South Africa followed the path of Mexico under the Partido Revolucionario Institucional (PRI), a state with elections for office but under the control of only one party. As the revolutionary ethos ebbed across the succeeding presidencies of Mandela to Mbeki to Zuma, an era of repeated corruption scandals came to define state authority, again following the trajectory of PRI-dominated Mexico after Lázaro Cárdenas.

Extractive economies, like South Africa's, are rife with the potential for corruption. The state tends to play an oversized role in owning and regulating economic activity. South Africa had a further mandate to redistribute ownership away from the whites-only apartheid economy, made all the more urgent by the burgeoning black political power of post-apartheid rule. Privileged members of the civil service and other politically connected entrepreneurs became the new owners of important shares of central businesses and the beneficiaries of high government employment and lucrative contracts. These "tenderpreneurs"[18] became a new governing class, but one whose existence and protection depended on relations to governmental power.

The programs designed to stimulate the creation of a black entrepreneurial class were fraught with the risk of misuse in the hands of a government eager to expand its authority into an unaccountable economic role, as was well evident under President Jacob Zuma. The redistributive programs were rhetorically forceful as a repudiation of apartheid, unobjectionable in principle as necessary to black economic empowerment, yet selective and nontransparent in their application. The driving consideration was invariably proximity to political power, thereby cementing the relationship between politics and economic returns. Not surprisingly, the culture of dispensing patronage wealth in this fashion translates readily to outright corruption, all the way to the highest levels of government.

While corruption emerged as a problem from the founding of the post-apartheid state, it was tempered by the presence and moral probity of Nelson Mandela. Only under President Zuma did corruption appear to lose all sense of boundaries. The embedded power of the executive as the head of the dominant political party and the largest parliamentary bloc made Parliament passive, if not complicit, in the relation between the ANC and governmental largesse. This left the Constitutional Court as the primary situs for confronting the dominant power of the executive, evidenced in a series of rulings whose cumulative effect was to prod parliamentary action. As the South African Constitutional Court said in its decision in *Glenister v. President of South Africa and others*, "corruption threatens to fell at the knees virtually everything we hold dear and precious in our hard-won constitutional order. It blatantly undermines the democratic ethos, the institutions of democracy, the rule of law and the foundational values of our nascent constitutional project."[19]

Corruption proved to be the pivotal legal confrontation with the Zuma regime. Throughout his tenure in office, President Zuma attempted to strip any vestige of independence of the National Prosecuting Authority (NPA). Repeatedly, heads of the NPA were removed from office in favor of more pliable officials. Courts sought to restrict the ability to fire prosecutors and strengthen independence as an eligibility criterion for appointment. These decisions were noteworthy not for predetermining the outcome of claims against Zuma but for imposing process obligations for the anticorruption efforts, something that in turn could potentially prod the legislative branch to exercise its countervailing authority.[20] As evidence of the extent of corruption mounted, and as the Parliament remained unable to resist the entrenched executive and the commands of the ANC, the Constitutional Court found itself repeatedly confronting Zuma's efforts to compromise prosecutorial independence and official resistance to repaying the staggering sums that Zuma had spent on his personal estate.[21] When Zuma finally forced the resignation of yet another public prosecutor amid increasing controversy over his corruption, it was the courts that led the response.

In due course, the matter ended up before the High Court, Gauteng Division.[22] Notably, the pathway did not begin with direct claims to a constitutional court but to the ordinary judiciary. The High Court wasted no time rejecting Zuma's claim of unilateral presidential authority: "In a rights-based order it is fundamental that a conflicted person cannot act; to act despite a conflict is self-evidently to pervert the rights being exercised as well as the rights of those affected."[23] The High Court ruling built on a decade of increasing court intervention that established a "politics of accountability," empowering other state institutions to investigate elected officials for corruption and make recommendations for addressing such corruption.[24]

Of more immediate interest is the decree that followed. The court reversed all the efforts of President Zuma to control anticorruption efforts and ordered that "as long as the incumbent President is in office, the Deputy President is responsible for decisions relating to the appointment, suspension or removal of the National Director of Public Prosecutions."[25] Further, the court declared the unconstitutionality of the National Prosecuting Authority Act and offered a rewritten Act that would cure the constitutional defect of allowing presidential authority over an investigation of the president. But the court suspended the statutory revision for eighteen months and referred the entire matter to Parliament to cure the constitutional defect on its own. The effect was to weaken Zuma, force Parliament to act, and ultimately set the stage for Zuma's compelled and long-overdue resignation.

As with the Brexit decision of the British Supreme Court, the effect of referring the matter to Parliament to act forced the democratic institutions to perform their constitutional functions. Stu Woolman well captures the spillover effects of confronting the ANC even if limited to the question of corruption:

> By the beginning of 2016, the media, the Public Protector and our appellate courts had rattled the cage. Rattling had discernible knock-on effects. Public support for a two-term President and the ANC waned. That disenchantment took the form of victories by (coalitions of) minority parties in the 2016 municipal elections. Two international rating institutions lost faith in the current regime's ability to govern effectively and downgraded the country's sovereign credit status from investment grade to junk. Against the background of the President's and the ANC's diminished status, the Constitutional Court continued to hold state actors accountable.[26]

Corruption continued to define the efforts to restore democratic functioning in South Africa under President Cyril Ramaphosa.[27] A commission of public inquiry headed by Deputy Chief Justice Raymond Zondosoon ran into Zuma's refusal to appear before the inquiry.[28] The commission filed an application to the Constitutional Court, requesting Zuma be found in contempt of court and sentenced to two years in prison for defying summonses to testify.[29] The application states that "the seriousness of the threat that Mr. Zuma's conduct poses to public trust in, and respect for, the authority of the courts and the rule of law requires this court to intervene and assert its authority without delay."[30] Justice Zondo has separately stated that "if [Zuma's behavior] is allowed to prevail, there will be lawlessness and chaos in the courts. There may be other people who will decide to follow his example when they are served with summons in other court processes.... If the message that is sent out is that people can ignore or disregard summons and orders of courts with impunity, there will be very little that will be left of our democracy."[31]

The showdown with Zuma presents the long-overdue accounting for the unchecked political power of the ANC. Under pressure, the ANC becomes less an integrated political force and more "an alliance of many different identities, political factions and financial interests held together by its compulsion to hold on to power, make money and the legacy of being seen as a liberation movement."[32] The ANC under President Ramaphosa was unable to command Zuma to submit to questioning, "a sign of the party's inability to hold its senior leadership accountable."[33] In fact, in fashion similar to the fractures in the Republican Party after the U.S. 2020 election, Zuma launched a full-fledged attack on the ANC, accusing it of "not having his back and instead looking the other way while he is the subject of state capture allegations."[34] In yet another parallel to the U.S., in late May of 2021, Zuma had to appear in court to answer to bribery charges related to a 1990s arms deal prior to his time as president.[35] These charges were first brought against Zuma in the mid-2000s and resurrected in 2018 as a separate corruption investigation into the former president—again showing the dispersion of prosecuting authority for charges of straightforward corruption. Finally, at the end of June 2021, the Constitutional Court ordered Zuma jailed for fifteen months for his refusal to appear before the commission on corruption.[36]

As of this writing, the saga continues. In some parts of the country, Zuma loyalists initially took to the streets in acts ranging from protest to civil disobedience to outright gang criminality. Perhaps most ominously, the appeal to support Zuma seems to resonate most strongly across the lines of long-held tribal grievances, with Zuma loyalists unabashedly invoking Zulu clan allegiances as grounds to resist the ANC government. If anything, the violence and tribal base of the current upheaval shows how far South African democracy had been degraded during the Zuma period. Perhaps obvious, but it bears emphasizing that such politics of criminality would have been inconceivable under the presidency of Nelson Mandela.

At the same time, also deserving emphasis is the fact that it was the issue of corruption that finally brought about the confrontation with the degraded state of South African democracy. Despite all the efforts to diminish the institutional capabilities of the judiciary and the independent anticorruption authorities, the seeming boundlessness of Zuma's corrupt empire is what caused the ultimate confrontation. And here, as Mark Tushnet tellingly notes, South Africa "shows that investigations of high-level corruption can exist even in a system with a dominant party."[37]

II. Systematic Misbehavior

The relation of corruption to lack of political accountability is ever present: "In countries with populist or autocratic leaders, we often see democracies in decline and a disturbing pattern of attempts to crack down on civil society, limit press freedom, and weaken the independence of the judiciary. Instead of tackling crony capitalism, those leaders usually install even worse forms of corrupt systems," as expressed by José Ugaz, the chair of Transparency International.[38] Some of this takes the form of corrupt dealings with foreign autocracies, primarily Russia, but mostly it appears endemic to the regimes led by a domestically grown populist.[39]

In short, the ability to dispense patronage, to let government contracts, to command media attention through the powers of the office, and to allocate social benefits during the electoral period yield a controlling authority that often dovetails with populist political claims. In turn, the ability to turn on and off the spigot of government largesse invites corruption of public institutions. The question is whether the ensuing propensity toward corruption highlights the importance of challenging *intralegal* abuse through the mechanisms of ordinary law rather than extraordinary constitutional claims. As the South African example suggests, this form of "apex criminality" may be of a sort that "cannot be mitigated by formal constitutional rules,"[40] yet may be addressed through other legal means.

Even here, an important distinction must be made in the aims of corruption. Many electoral systems are plagued by imprecise sources of funding for political parties and electoral campaigns. Argentina, for example, has an elaborate mechanism of controls on party funding, yet the vast majority of electoral activity is conducted through cash contributions and cash expenditures, a destructive invitation to nefarious practices of circumvention. Further, a significant amount of electoral campaigning is underwritten by use of public funds from a provincial or municipal government controlled by one political faction or another. This is corrupt in the sense of being occult and not formally permitted by law. But it is not necessarily the form of personal enrichment that lends itself readily to criminal prosecution—although use of private funds for underwriting the activity of the Workers' Party did lead to the impeachment and removal of President Dilma Rousseff in Brazil in 2016,[41] or at least that was the formal charge in a fraught political drama.

There is social science evidence that citizen moral intuitions follow this distinction between lubricating the political skids and personal engorgement, particularly as polarization hardens into an us-versus-them existential battle. One social science study in Poland found that voters were tolerant of PiS commandeering public resources so long as it was directed to the party itself rather than individual enrichment of party functionaries. Most simply, "a politician will not lose the confidence of voters for breaking the law in a way that benefits the party."[42]

Poland may be the exception to the pervasiveness of simple, ordinary corruption in populist regimes. Perhaps the single most bizarre incident occurred in Argentina when, at the end of the Cristina Kirchner presidency in 2016, José

López, a secondary minister in the government, was arrested while throwing sacks of cash totaling $8.9 million over the wall of a convent in the middle of the night, an almost cartoonish version of theft by public officials.[43] More common is the direction of public contracts to cronies of the regime whose resulting fortunes seem suspiciously close to the personal assets of the supreme leader, whether it be Zuma or Putin or Orbán. In a particularly Hungarian euphemism, Prime Minister Orbán referred to the doling out of government contracts as "the reinforcement of the national capitalist class," a class defined primarily by political proximity to Orbán himself.[44] Thus, in the seemingly independent economic realm, "these industries' success is heavily reliant on government contracts, subsidies and favourable regulations. As a result, none of the 'national capitalists' are able to go against the executive power's will without risking everything they own."[45]

The swirl of corruption rarely stops at the awarding of benefits to others. Examples of family members implicated in corruption scandals spread around the populist movements. The key is not the particulars but the general, overall pattern of breaking down institutional constraints on how governmental functions are organized and regulated. In the U.S., the repeated transgressions of official conduct at some point or other lead back to corruption itself. At least a half dozen close associates of President Trump were jailed or indicted for improprieties related to the campaign or governance of the administration— although several benefited from last-minute pardons by the outgoing president.[46] Even the re-election war chest in 2020 burned cash at extraordinary levels under a series of interlocking contracts among campaign officials, family members, and the inevitable hangers-on.[47]

Much as some individual acts were just greed and nothing more, the picture is more troubling. A campaign and administration that prided itself on transgressing customary norms invites miscreant behavior. When President Trump hawked the canned products of a political backer in a photo opportunity from the Resolute desk in the Oval Office, there was not a direct payment in sight. But the same impulse infuses using official channels to fast-track trademark approval for Ivanka Trump products in China or Japan. And it allows requests to the ambassador to the United Kingdom to lobby for holding the British Open at a Trump golf resort. It redirects official travel to Trump properties overseas or allows another Trump property to be hawked as the site for a G7 summit.[48] Can the FBI move out of its outdated Washington headquarters? Not if its iconic building can be redeveloped into a competitor to an adjacent Trump hotel. The list goes on and on, beginning from the refusal to divulge tax returns and continuing through the constant interaction between family business and the presidency.

Once the boundaries are breached, then public policy follows individual preferences in attempting legal sanctions against disfavored entities such as

Google or Amazon, in manipulating venerated institutions such as the Post Office or the U.S. Census, and in mobilizing against the electoral system itself. Legal institutions flail against such an overwhelming assault. Law requires an internalization of customs among the population as the state cannot possibly impose police vigilance on a self-governing polity. When transgression becomes the rallying point among the governing class, the threat becomes existential.

Here again, there is a distinction between politically motivated misbehavior and illicit behavior, including graft, even if the boundaries might not be precise in practice. In some instances, the executive is the one charged with illicit behavior directed only at self-enrichment. For example, in the battles over accountability of President Trump, the Supreme Court drew a distinction between congressional demands for accountability and the ordinary workings of the law against the person occupying the Oval Office. In *Trump v. Vance*,[49] which involved a local state prosecutor in New York City seeking financial records as part of a fraud investigation, the Supreme Court invoked two centuries of practice to find that presidents had always been subject to the subpoena powers of federal criminal proceedings.[50] That left only the question whether some special immunity attached when the grand jury inquiry came under the auspices of a state court rather than a federal court. Finding no historical basis for such an immunity, the Court could conclude that "a President does not possess absolute immunity from a state criminal subpoena," as framed by Justice Kavanaugh, himself appointed to the Supreme Court by President Trump.[51] Indeed, in the wake of *Vance*, a New York State judge ordered President Trump and his immediate family to sit for depositions in the state's inquiry into their financial practices, although there has been spotty upshot so far.[52]

In other cases, the lines are blurred in ways that damage democratic integrity altogether. Here, the lead example is Brazil. The sprawling "car wash" (*Lava Jato*) payment scheme by construction giant Odebrecht involved extraordinary payments to politicians and other government officials for favorable contract engagements, frequently run through the state-dominated petroleum firm, Petrobras. Some payments went to state officials themselves, with culprits reaching all the way to the top. But more interesting than simple corruption was the use of these illicit funds to maintain government coalitions under the shaky party-alliance system necessary for a Brazilian president to construct a government coalition. In fact, the impeachment of President Dilma Rouseff, almost a congressional coup in its execution, seized on allegations that she used misbegotten funds to lubricate congressional support, that of the same Congress that then impeached her when her coalition faltered.[53]

III. A Billiard Shot

As understood since Archimedes, the shortest distance between two points will be a straight line. The more direct the aim, the more likely the objective is to be reached and reached effectively. If the concern about populism is that it systematically undermines the institutional buffers of democratic governance, then the road to protecting democracy should run through the institutions at risk. The aim of this chapter is to suggest that the propensity for corruption might be a source of legal vulnerability that may serve to constrain destructive behavior in a less linear, more complicated way. Al Capone and tax evasion, if you will.

Clearly this is not the most direct fashion of addressing the problem of executive misbehavior, and it certainly would not count as the Archimedean direct path. Ideally, the constraints should be institutional and should correspond to guardrails that prevent popular sovereignty from being hijacked. There are many institutional buffers that offer oversight by one branch of government over others. In the classic separation of powers envisioned by Montesquieu, the division of authority among distinct branches of government served as a bulwark against tyranny. Madison similarly hoped that the pull of institutional prerogatives would make each organ of government a jealous overseer against overreach by any other governmental authority. Yet, as Professors Levinson and Pildes observe, this institutional gambit quickly succumbed to the power politics of partisanship:

> The success of American democracy overwhelmed the Madisonian conception of separation of powers almost from the outset, preempting the political dynamics that were supposed to provide each branch with a "will of its own" that would propel departmental "ambition . . . to counteract ambition." The Framers had not anticipated the nature of the democratic competition that would emerge in government and in the electorate. Political competition and cooperation along relatively stable lines of policy and ideological disagreement quickly came to be channeled not through the branches of government, but rather through an institution the Framers could imagine only dimly but nevertheless despised: political parties.[54]

At the institutional level, generalized barriers to claims of authority constantly cede before the momentary demands for action now. But the risks come not just from the ordinary urges toward executive power but also from the hardening of political lines. Political parties should serve as the brokers for a broader aim of national advancement as opposed to the myopic re-election concerns of incumbents. But in times of hardening of politics around issues of immediate partisan gain, party increasingly means us opposed to them. Justice Jackson noted long ago, with regard to presidential power, "party loyalties and interests, sometimes more binding than law, extend his effective control into branches of government other than his own and he often may win, as a political leader, what he cannot command under the Constitution."[55] Bob Bauer and Jack Goldsmith soberly caution that

> in the polarized politics of our time, the extent to which Congress is motivated to inquire likely depends on which of the parties commands the majority at any one time. A president's party is not a reliable inquisitor. The reluctance of parties to police their own is a feature of hardcore contemporary partisanship: Neither party wants to open up lines of attack for the opposition.[56]

Parties play an indispensable role in democratic governance in organizing governance around a shared set of policy commitments. If that is the noble or high road of partisanship, there is unfortunately a low road as well:

> The low partisanship that motivates blind opposition to everything associated with the opposition party is incompatible with a separation-of-powers constitution. The separation of powers and bicameralism prevent narrow and evanescent majorities from passing legislation. They necessitate compromise: building a large, diverse, and enduring majority. Parties, which once made the constitution work by doing exactly this, now impede it by creating narrow and ephemeral majorities fueled by low partisan passions.[57]

In the U.S., the parties have aligned themselves into non-overlapping worlds of conflict. By standard measures, the most conservative Democrat is more liberal than the most liberal Republican and vice versa. This yields an extraordinary level of roll-call discipline on matters put up for congressional votes. But partisan homogeneity expressed in voting does not translate into strong parties capable of forging policy-driven governance. Parties are overwhelmingly defined in terms of opposition to the other but lack the internal strength actually to engage on matters of governance.

If partisan exchange cannot yield governance, other institutions must step into the fray. In the first wave of democratization following the fall of the Soviet bloc, much hope was placed on independent constitutional courts to hold the balance as the institutions of democracy matured—particularly political parties, an independent media, and a vibrant legislative arena. The courts held admirably to this role, leading enthusiasts to hope that a constitutional temporizing strategy could yield democratic stability. I cheerfully include myself among these enthusiasts, and my book *Fragile Democracies* was an effort to give coherence to the challenges being faced in so much of the newly democratizing world.

Courts proved resilient in the face of political uncertainty and the lack of any clear democratic mandate for the first officeholders. Countries recently emerging from some form of authoritarian past had imperfectly formed democratic institutions. But they also had weak state apparatuses and immature claim to power based on a short-term electoral mandate. Once political power consolidated, however, oppositional courts risked being overwhelmed, particularly when confronting a single-party state. What followed were not the bruising confirmation battles that have galvanized Supreme Court appointments into a wedge political issue in the U.S. Instead, what followed was a combination of changed rules of judicial authority and, in many cases, the simple act of appointing supplicants to judicial office. At the end came the incapacity of courts to stand up to political power, the abdication of the counter-majoritarian role of constitutional oversight. The Supreme Court of India may have inspired the constitutional world with its protection of the "basic structures" of democracy against the Indira Gandhi state of emergency. But the same Supreme Court today has not deigned to attend to even a single petition for habeas corpus when the Hindu nationalist government of Prime Minister Modi places Kashmir, the only majority Muslim section of the country, under martial law.[58]

Unfortunately, polarization does not only compromise the ability of institutional buffers to hold. That same polarization defeats normal boundaries set by the broad center of politics. In a period of "weak parties, strong polarization," institutional constraints succumb to a political environment in which even the integration of information is subject to what has been termed "tribal epistemology."[59] As Ezra Klein observes, rather ominously, "toxic systems compromise good individuals with ease . . . not by demanding we betray our values but by enlisting our values such that we betray each other."[60]

The problem of institutional capture is exacerbated by what is, in effect, the capturing of the electorate through appeals to emotion rather than reason, to fear rather than hope, to specific group antagonism rather than the more abstract sense of common purpose. "Political parties and interest groups strive to make their concerns become current triggers of your moral modules. To get your vote, your money, or your time, they must activate at least one of your moral foundations."[61] Contemporary research points to a neurological foundation for what Emile Durkheim's work described as a collective "passion and ecstasy that [is created by] group rituals."[62] Thus, this line of thinking ultimately concludes that even sudden moral judgments are the direct result of "a social process, [rather than] . . . a private act of cognition."[63] In turn, the search for clear markers rewards partisan excess: "When candidates take extreme positions, they emit very strong partisan cues, which makes it harder for voters to recognize when a candidate in the opposing party might actually be closer to their own preference."[64]

Increasingly, politics is not the domain of policy divergences but of core identity issues of voters who use politics to "express who they are, who they support, and who they loathe."[65] Politicians respond to the clear voter invitation to play on those identities, to place themselves increasingly on the edges of the political spectrum, and to drive a wedge into the partisan divide that exists. This polarizing choice, moreover, cannot be stopped by a party that has already given itself over to the partisan choices of the most active wing of its voting base.[66] When the parties cannot prevent the divide driven by a base, the electoral arena opens up further avenues for extremists to wind their way into positions of power and consequently speed up this downward spiral.[67] Every election becomes a "do or die" moment that serves to cast aside the historic moderating controls that had been in place to regulate political behavior, what colorfully is expressed as the Flight 93 rush-the-cockpit moment.[68]

Corruption as an issue may serve to restore some respect for legal norms while not exacerbating the polarized divides. Take for example the illegality that swirled around the prosecution of the war on terror under the Bush administration. Accusations of unlawful conduct steadily emerged from black-site renditions, from the introduction of torture, and from related departures from the laws of war and legal constraints on American officials. The period was awash in what came to be known as "lawfare," the persistent question of illegality surrounding official conduct and the constant legal challenges from individuals subject to detention in the U.S. to those at Guantanamo. The unpopularity of the Iraq War and the aimlessness of the engagement in Afghanistan sapped political support from the administration, led to a Democratic sweep in the midterm elections of 2006, and brought the election of Barack Obama as president in 2008.

With the new administration came the question of how to assess the conduct of the prior presidency. Amid repeated claims for criminal accountability of leading Bush era officials, presumably extending up to Vice President Dick Cheney, the Obama administration quickly decided that it would not seek prosecutions.[69] Instead, the new administration allowed the election to serve as the judgment of history on a series of failed policy undertakings that had fueled the descent into illegality. Politics and a new administration then addressed the disputed conduct rather than the criminal justice system.

Were it otherwise, the foundations of democracy would be imperiled. If democracy rests on accepting the notion of repeat play, criminal liability for the acts of state risks placing incumbents at existential rather than political peril with each election cycle. Simply put, democracies cannot permit jailing former heads of state for anything reflecting the official acts of office, even those conducted in the fog of wartime engagements. Autocrats tend to leave office in a body bag or trembling in exile. Democracies offer a place of honor, a presidential library, and an ability to continue public engagements, even following electoral repudiation. As a result, autocracies end amid demands for human rights accountability and freighted negotiations over amnesty. By contrast, democracies transfer power as a matter of routine, something made all the more pressing by the storming of Congress on January 6, 2021, and the repeated efforts of defeated President Trump to thwart the election outcome.

At the same time, not everything a head of state does is official conduct. Daphna Renan disaggregates the "president's two bodies," the distinction between the officeholder and the office. The two aspects are necessarily intertwined during the tenure in office of any individual president, but the accumulated powers and prerogatives of office must endure.[70] The closer any retrospective accountability comes to the discharge of public functions, even where the conduct borders on the unimaginable, the more difficult it is to retain the loyalty of the opposition. Civilized nations have long repudiated any categorical defense of "following orders" for individual soldiers or state functionaries, and the act of state doctrine cannot be a guarantee of legal immunity, regardless of the conduct. But when state actions are aligned to public objectives that are tied to election and democratic accountability, the introduction of criminal prosecutions raises the potential stakes beyond what a consensual political order can ordinarily tolerate.

The first impeachment of Donald Trump unfortunately moved too close to the conduct of the presidency and not to the failing of the individual. The specific charges of using the foreign policy of the U.S. to further electoral prospects and resisting congressional inquiry pushed untested boundaries of executive privilege. Such claims stood little chance of breaking the bounds of partisan loyalty and failed accordingly. Impeachment was unfortunately viewed as a partisan attack on an unpopular presidency—an unsuccessful replay of the Brazilian impeachment of President Rousseff—rather than a challenge to a simpler and more vulgar form of personal enrichment at the expense of the public.

While Republican allies of the president wasted no time rallying in opposition to impeachment, they remained quiet in the face of the personal corruption stories, running from hush payments to a former porn star paramour to the revelations of tax manipulation. Were Donald Trump to be tried after his time in office for anything resembling a policy directive of his presidency, the likely reaction would be a rekindling of intense polarization in a do-or-die moment. By contrast, a prosecution for tax evasion, even for tax returns filed when president of the U.S., isolates the individual as president from the political institution which must remain contested terrain.

Al Capone once again.

IV. Holding Corruption at Bay

Writing in the democratizing England of the late 19th century, William Gladstone noted that wise government ultimately depends heavily on "the good faith of those who work it."[71] The current period of democratic disrepair tests the institutional fortitude of elected governments in an era conspicuously lacking in such good faith. The question presented here is whether law may serve as a credible backstop in cases of democratic erosion along two principal dimensions that characterize the era. The first is the propensity of certain regimes to pull up the drawbridge behind them. They limit their electoral accountability or the ability of their political rivals to exercise power. The second is the temptation in executive-dominated governments toward the dispensation of discretionary favors, ultimately leading to outright enrichment of the head of state. I term both of these corruption. The first is the corruption of the process of electoral accountability. The second is the more classic corruption of the illicit quid pro quo in which payment of tribute becomes a necessary feature of life under a regime that commandeers state power.

As to the first "corrupt" efforts to unwind the democratic bargain, the tools of constitutional law have thus far been substantially effective in enough settings to confirm their importance. Emerging constitutional principles cordoning off the "basic structures" of democratic governance have prevented significant democratic erosion in a surprising number of countries. Unfortunately, the lesson of enabled constitutional courts has not been lost on populists bent on consolidating power. The example of Evo Morales in Bolivia shows how a captured constitutional court can use the same argument about enabling democracy to remove constitutional barriers to multiple elections of the same head of state, thereby eliminating the accompanying constriction of competitive accountability.

Corruption redirects the inquiry to actual conduct in office. Fiscal discipline requires long-term vision. By contrast, populism feeds on immediate gain and lives by the dictates of the next election cycle. While every president wants the head of the Federal Reserve to embrace short-term stimulus measures as an election approaches, populists break the bank. Trump—as a self-professed "king of debt" during his earlier life as a businessman—was already comfortable borrowing and unabashed about defaulting. This became his government's credo.

When a stimulus was clearly needed to confront the pandemic's impacts, Trump rushed to take credit, even hijacking the stimulus payout as a propaganda coup, forcing the IRS to print his name on checks mailed around the country.[72] But the raid on the fisc began well before COVID-19. Trump and other elected Republicans eagerly capitalized on opportunities for deficit spending to advantage wealthy allies. Congressional Republicans and administration negotiators wove in provisions for specific industries and interest groups. Instead of policy, there were one-off payments (the "deals") dispensed by the president as a new dole to the politically connected or to politically salient constituencies, such as farmers.

This is selective deficit spending for political credit and private profit, with little regard for the well-being of citizens beyond a select circle. Some of this is not new to the American political landscape nor limited to which party is in power. What's different here is how these spoils are used in combination with the aggregation and exercise of autocratic powers.

The most intriguing argument then, and the most untested, is whether the ordinary instrumentalities of law can thwart some of the illicit bargains that typically accompany populist rule. Can the ordinary judicial system and vigilance against common forms of corruption rein in the anti-institutionalist form of governance associated with populism? Perhaps. Anticorruption tends to engage a broader cross-section of the judiciary than just the structurally isolated constitutional courts that have dominated the post-1989 legal environment. While these regular judicial institutions can in turn be captured, the process may prove more laborious than replacing the five or six justices needed to neuter a constitutional court.

Ultimately, however, the corruption of politics under populism is the corruption of popular sovereignty. Populism tends to pitch itself to base impulses, to desires for immediate reward, to disregard for the future. The demands of immediacy may yield the destruction of the rain forest, the prorogation of Parliament, or the momentary inflation of the currency. For the past several centuries, democracies have balanced the need for majority rule with the institutionalization of democratic politics in a way that tempers demands for immediate rewards. Law can only go so far in restraining these tendencies toward the here and now, toward the us or them, in the absence of institutional frameworks that moderate the popular will into sustainable forms of governance.

At the same time that populism tempts the populace with immediate rewards, it also tempts the leaders with the prospect of plunder free of institutional constraints. There is something in the genetics of populist governance that invites corruption. The transactional relations with constituents provides the first step: "Clientelism often evolves into pure corruption because politicians have the power to distribute public resources as they wish; money that could go

to clients often ends up in their own pockets."[73] The anti-institutionalism of populist rule breaks down the governmental structures that should brake corruption
as democratic societies mature.

If the mechanisms of political accountability or impeachment or even constitutional scrutiny become compromised in an era of angry political polarization,
the hope is that the instrumentalities of ordinary law can fill the void. Individual
accountability, including to the criminal law, may indeed provide a mechanism
to strip government officials of the cloak of popular approbation. Doing so
means isolating specific individual acts of illegality from what may appear to be
governmental policy, attacking misbehavior as a matter of individual transgression, not as a matter of political misdirection.

Two years ago, on the eve of a tightly contested presidential election in
Poland, I created a bit of a stir in a public speech to opposition leaders. The election seemed to offer the prospect of defeating the PiS government of Jarosław
Kaczyński, ultimately a failed hope, and the question of the day in liberal circles
in Poland was what would come next. For many, the degradations of governance
under PiS needed a strong-hand reply and, by extension, the use of prosecutorial
powers against the displaced leaders. I strongly urged restraint, observing simply
that the history of democracies that jail their former heads of state is generally
the history of ex-democracies.

Now those questions return full circle in the U.S. There has never been a regime as notoriously self-dealing as the Trump administration. And there was a
constitutional crisis created by extending that same form of institutional corruption to the conduct of the 2020 presidential election, to the attempt to sabotage
the vote count in various states, and ultimately to the dramatic assault upon the
Capitol. The question is whether the criminal law should attempt to frame the
response to these outrageous acts.

Here I return to the position I took in Poland. There is no problem with a political repudiation of President Trump, either electorally or through the constitutional processes of impeachment, as difficult as those are to mobilize. Hopefully
the defeat by the largest margin in the history of the popular vote and the record
of two impeachments, with the second receiving a substantial majority of Senate
votes for conviction, serve to start redirecting American politics. But it remains
doubtful that using the criminal law for the acts of governance, no matter how
outrageous, will do anything but compromise the Biden administration as
simply another self-interested actor.

By contrast, if now-former President Trump were prosecuted civilly or crim-
inally by Georgia officials for vote tampering, or by New York officials for tax
evasion and financial fraud, this strips the person of President Trump from the
office he held, at least for purposes of accountability. Similarly, an investigation
by Congress into the assault on that institution itself has a different feel than

relying primarily on the criminal law to render accounts with the former president. Finally, it is far different for individuals injured on January 6th to sue for damages as a result of instigation than for the Department of Justice to dedicate itself to the prosecution of its former executive head. The former looks like the law working itself through difficult cases; the latter would be seen as an attempt to use prosecutorial authority to cement in place the outcome of the last election. There is a symmetry in the style of rule of President Trump and President Zuma. There may be symmetry in their eventual downfall.

Institutional Wreckage

The modern democratic era dates from the American presidential election of 1800. The transformative success of the Broadway musical *Hamilton* focuses attention on the dramatic question of *who* should have been declared the president in that famous election. Because of a defect in the selection mechanism, both the presidential candidate Thomas Jefferson and his vice-presidential running mate Aaron Burr received the same number of electoral votes. The election was thrown into the House of Representatives until enough of the Federalists, inspired in part by Alexander Hamilton, swung the tally to Jefferson, who then assumed the presidency. This much of the story is familiar to theatergoers the world over thanks to the genius of Lin-Manuel Miranda's inspiring production.

Left unsaid in the theatrical production, as well as assumed for much of subsequent American history, is that the winner of the election under existing rules should indeed have assumed office. Much as this is the presumed logic of electoral democracy, there was no history prior to 1800 of a head of state yielding office to a challenger as a result of an election—and a much disputed election to boot. Missing from Miranda's play is John Adams, the incumbent president of the United States and the defeated candidate for re-election. In retrospect, we might take for granted that Adams would have relinquished office at the end of his elected term, just as George Washington had done four years prior. But Washington had not been defeated. Instead, in the manner of the American Cincinnatus, he retreated to his domestic pursuits having righted the ship of state.

Yet the assumption that elections should determine the presidency is so ingrained in the American political psyche that the U.S. held contested elections even during the Civil War and World War II. This is decidedly not the norm in other democracies—Churchill, for example, faced no new parliamentary elections during the war. But in the U.S., elections historically have gone forward, with the ordinary forms of election administration determining the winner, and, most critically, the ordinary forms of rotation in office playing out, even in fraught election periods.

Until January 6th.

I. A Tragedy Averted

It is hard to overstate the unprecedented nature of the violent assault on the Capitol as the Congress met to solemnize the results of the 2020 presidential election. The congressional count of the Electoral College votes has long been part and parcel of the orderly transfer of power that has defined democratic accountability in the United States. On occasion, as with Richard Nixon in 1960 and Al Gore in 2000, the ceremonial vice-presidential task of ordaining the result has fallen to the defeated presidential candidate—with far more legitimate concern about electoral shenanigans in those years than in 2020. And yet, across wars, changes in political fortunes, and deep political dissensus, the process has been orderly and dignified.

At the same time, it is important not to exaggerate what happened on January 6th. This was not an attempted coup d'état in the fashion of Latin American dictators of the late 20th century. There was no effort to take over the nerve centers of power, no attempt to control broadcasting, no round-up of enemy politicians, no meaningful effort to mobilize the military. Even the *autogolpes* of presidents overthrowing their own civilian rule had a military component to solidify state authority. Instead, as violent and damaging as the assault on the Capitol may have been, it had the unmistakable air of a Trump production: malevolent, exploitative, and lazy.

President Trump drew heavily on the *caudillo* style that is associated with Latin American strongman presidents. The key to this style of governance, whether in the hands of President Trump or any of this fraternity across the globe, is the penchant for unilateral action. There is no patience for the niceties of process, and, as discussed previously on juridical responses, even a conservative Supreme Court recognized the style's conflict with constitutional norms in cases pertaining to the census and immigration.[1] The simple populist expectation is that governance is the exercise of power at the whim of the elected boss.[2] As political scientist Nadia Urbinati writes, populists in power "treat procedures and political cultures as a matter of property and possession."[3]

The pandemic put many of these tendencies on display across the world. It offered an opening for Modi to mobilize India against Muslims,[4] Orbán to rail against the threat from outsiders and consolidate formal control,[5] Bolsonaro to petition for military intervention,[6] and so on. Trump seemed to follow suit.

He repeatedly proclaimed his authority and made fleeting and often ineffectual gestures to restrict travel and immigration. He dismissed CDC guidelines,[7] withdrew unilaterally from the World Health Organization,[8] commanded states to allow churches to reopen, and threatened (hollowly) to "override the governors" if they balked.[9]

Most notable in the American context is that, rhetoric aside, most of these pronouncements had limited practical impact. Fortunately, President Trump was drawn to the pomp of high office but not so much to the circumstances of having to work the levers of power. Unlike the serious agglomeration of unilateral power in the hands of foreign strongmen, the most striking legacy of Trump is not the consolidation of power in an enhanced executive branch but the systematic erosion of state capacity. Although Trump made much of his power under the Defense Production Act, for example, he hesitated to bring its force to bear.[10] His invocation of absolute authority regarding reopenings met swift and predictable legal backlash.[11]

Claims of unilateral command under the Trump administration served more as a stage for performance than as a leadership strategy. Trump made bombastic claims that the president "calls the shots. . . . When somebody's the president of the United States, the authority is total."[12] But after the news cycle would pass, there was usually no follow-up. Cabinet members and senior officials learned they could slow-walk any demand so as to avoid implementing the president's most outrageous dictates, knowing his attention would flag.[13] Trump may have asserted the power to override governors at will, but the federal government abandoned national leadership in the pandemic. Unlike many foreign despots on the rise, Trump's recurring pattern was to claim ultimate authority while eschewing responsibility.[14] This was command without substance. On this president's Resolute desk one could find an apparent infomercial for the cans of Goya beans manufactured by a supporter (Figures 8.1a & b),[15] but certainly the buck did not stop there.

(a)

Figure 8.1a   A post shared by President Donald J. Trump (@realdonaldtrump) on Jul. 15, 2020

Source: https://www.instagram.com/p/CCrAzKiBFUQ/

Figure 8.1b   Former US President Truman sits at a recreation of his Oval office at the Truman
Library in 1959 with the famous "The Buck Stops Here" sign located on his desk.

Not surprisingly then, on January 6th, Trump could incite the crowd to violence but then retreat to the White House to watch on television. One shudders
to think what a shrewder would-be despot might have wrought.

II. Weaponizing the Electoral Process

That January 6th was more spectacle than coordinated threat should not dis-
count the seriousness of the breach of democratic norms. Even after the shock
of a violent assault, 139 House Republicans and eight Republican senators
voted against certifying the 2020 election results,[16] effectively transforming
an administrative symbol of orderly democratic governance into cynical
partisan theater. In turn, as the rhetorical assault on the supposedly stolen
election persisted, 70 percent of surveyed Republicans rejected the Biden
election as fraudulent.[17] As well captured by long-time Republican strate-
gist Stuart Stevens, even before the assault on the Capitol, "much of a major
party has turned against democracy. It's foolish to believe that does not have
consequences."[18]

In practical terms this means that the Republican Party has set its sights on
voting and election administration as the prime culprit for losing the presidency.
There are ominous turns, as with the targeting of poll workers in Anchorage,
that threaten to unleash on a lower scale the same violent impulses seen in the
attack on the Capitol. In the aftermath of a hotly contested and particularly
nasty mayoral race that displayed "name-calling and allegations of campaign finance violations" between the Republican Dave Bronson and Democrat Forrest
Dunbar, the Anchorage municipal clerk reported "unprecedented harassment of
election officials."[19] This meant repeated frivolous challenges to ballot counting
coupled with assaults on poll workers in a manner "geared towards intimidating"
them.[20]

Of greatest concern is the effort to solidify party control of election mechanisms, turning the ordinary task of tabulating election results into an opportunity for partisan mischief. Such appeals to immediate partisan gain are a chronic problem for election administration across the world. Thus, the European Commission for Democracy through Law (known as the "Venice Commission"), the EU's preeminent institution on democratic best practices,[21] sets as one of its categorical building blocks that "an impartial body must be in charge of applying electoral law."[22] Drawing on the experience of sixty-one countries, the Venice Commission decrees that "where there is no longstanding tradition of administrative authorities' independence from those holding political power, independent, impartial electoral commissions must be set up at all levels, from the national level to polling station level."[23]

The United States is notably derelict in this regard. Elections are generally under the supervision of partisan officials, usually the secretary of state, but that is only where ultimate authority resides. In reality, the election process is highly decentralized and usually left to the hands of bipartisan local bodies. Whereas democratic best practices would insulate election mechanics from partisanship, the U.S. substitutes a nonprofessional administration that is bipartisan, not nonpartisan. Perhaps this is not the platonic ideal, but it has generally been good enough to muddle through. So long as each of the major parties could vigilate the other, a commitment to electoral competition, repeat play, and basic values of popular sovereignty kept temptations to cheat reasonably at bay. American democracy is marred by a long history of franchise restrictions. But apart from scattered episodes of one-party local control, like that of Jim Wells County in Lyndon Johnson's 1948 Senate election,[24] American election results have basically corresponded to the votes actually cast.

Over the course of the 2020 election and its various challenges, the institutions responsible for election administration proved remarkably resistant to the demands of the Trump campaign to set aside voting totals or to declare the results illegitimate. It is easy to be distracted by the cartoonish legal figures holding press conferences in the parking lot of a lawn care company or advancing legal claims so outlandish that they succeeded only in launching efforts to disqualify the lawyers involved for professional misdeeds. But what should not be overlooked is the institutional resilience in the face of extraordinary pressures from President Trump and his acolytes.

A comprehensive examination by researchers at Stanford and MIT concluded, "in the end, poll workers, election administrators, and the courts rose to the occasion and professionally resolved each of these [election lawsuit] challenges in accordance with law and established procedures. None of the recounts, election challenges, audits, or lawsuits turned up any significant fraud or had any impact on the outcome of the election in any state."[25] The state-by-state review revealed that "the electoral system confronted and passed its most severe test in recent memory. Any fair appraisal would focus on the heroism of election officials, civil society actors, and voters, who turned out in record numbers despite the threat of the pandemic."[26]

Notwithstanding the political pressures placed on election officials, the system held up remarkably well. From secretaries of state to local election boards to courts tasked with overseeing election disputes, the Trump claims of fraud and malfeasance failed and failed again. These institutions held a reservoir of what Swedish political scientist Bo Rothstein terms "knowledge realism," or an "assured knowledge of what is true and what is not."[27]

Having run elections year in and year out, these local officials were able to maintain their bearings even under the extraordinary strains of the pandemic. If the electorate divides along partisan lines on the use of early voting, for example, there is nothing suspicious about early vote trends not matching final results. Years of experience and plain common sense discounted claims that ballots might contain bamboo that would indicate Chinese infiltration in Arizona, or charges that the historically less than formidable Italian military had designed space-based technology to flip ballots from Trump to Biden. Seen from afar, these claims will seem the stark madness of the moment. For those on the front line of elections, however, these were assertions contrary to detailed experiential knowledge of how elections operate and appeared so in real time.

Much of this knowledge is remarkably localized. Take Michigan, for example, one of the true battleground states with a Democratic governor, a gerrymandered Republican legislature, and a small popular vote margin for Biden over Trump. Michigan is one of twenty states that maintains township governments, an American pattern dating from 17th-century New England, and decentralized local control of most governmental functions, including administration of elections: "Involving 83 county clerks, 280 city clerks and 1,240 township clerks, Michigan's elections system is administered by 1,603 county and local election officials making it the most decentralized elections system in the nation."[28] Each county has a local canvassing board, and it is "virtually unheard-of for canvassers to do anything but do the job of certifying their county's results, then sending them on to the Board of State Canvassers to do the same."[29] Indeed, "it is the settled law of this State that canvassing boards are bound by the return, and cannot go behind it, especially for the purpose of determining frauds in the election. Their duties are purely ministerial and clerical."[30] The multiple levels of Michigan state election administration produced reliable results because of a high level of bureaucratic routinization and a bipartisan commitment to adhere to centuries of custom: "Bureaucracy is viewed favorably as capable of advancing the common good, and everyone is expected to participate in the community's political affairs."[31]

But the stability of these structures depends on a long-haul bipartisan commitment to repeat engagements, a commitment anathema to the demands of populist immediacy. And, historically, these essential functions of democracy were carried out by governmental entities who labored in the bureaucratic shadows. These deservedly obscure local agencies and officials were targeted by President Trump as a vulnerability in the process of certifying election results. All of a sudden there was an unprecedented test in whether bipartisanship, rather than serve as a guarantee of common enterprise, could be manipulated through partisan appeals. The predicate of course was the claim of fraud. Trump filled the air with inflammatory claims of a captured election process: "In Detroit, there are FAR MORE VOTES THAN PEOPLE. Nothing can be done to cure that giant scam. I win Michigan!"[32] The means chosen to unearth this putative fraud was to destroy a century of public decency for momentary political gain.

Bowing to pressure from the White House, two Republican members of the Detroit-centered Wayne County Board of Canvassers initially refused to certify the election results[33] in the heavily Democratic county,[34] citing small discrepancies between the precinct officials' recorded number of voters and the actual number of votes cast.[35] The mild discrepancies were nothing surprising to experienced election officials; some voters show up, get discouraged by lines, and leave, while others simply do not cast ballots.

But the actions taken by the Republican canvassers was completely unheard of. The county-level board of canvassers was assigned only the ministerial task of checking that all precinct level returns are received. After, they forward the tabulations up the chain to the state board. The canvassers do not serve as judges of electoral outcomes. The Wayne County actions provoked great public outcry, and ultimately the Republican board members reversed course and voted with their Democratic counterparts to certify the election results,[36] although, they later attempted to recant their votes after a phone call from President Trump.[37] President Trump also attempted to influence the state election board, which is also equally divided along party lines; but that body voted to certify, albeit 3-0 with one Republican abstention.[38] All of a sudden, the country was in suspense as to whether Michigan could complete its election process, which generally has all the excitement and uncertainty of watching paint dry. In blunt form, "when Boards of Canvassers meeting[s] become exciting, things have stopped being normal."[39]

Ultimately, this time around, normalcy prevailed. The Michigan State Senate, which is majority Republican, convened an Oversight Committee chaired by Senator Ed McBroom, a public and highly vocal Trump supporter.[40] The Committee concluded there was no widespread vote fraud in the 2020 election in Michigan, and McBroom attributes this to "the extent to which our elections officials go to facilitate our elections."[41] The report ends by stating:

We commend the innumerable clerks, canvassers, staff, workers, and volunteers across Michigan that make the enormous complexity of elections operate so smoothly, so often. The complexity of the work and the dedication we discovered are astounding and worthy of our sincerest appreciation. . . . If all citizens remain vigilant and involved, we will emerge stronger after any challenging time.[42]

III. Institutional Destruction of Electoral Administration

The ability of election administrators to hold the line in 2020 should not breed complacency. The intensity generated by the Trump campaign claim of fraud sparked extralegal attacks on election officials, of a sort that threatens the ability of the election system to function at all. A false accusation that the Erie County postmaster in Pennsylvania had backdated mail-in ballots resulted in vigilante harassment. That official had to abandon his home to take his family into hiding.[43] Similar threats were reported across the country, most notably in Georgia, where Trump supporters, in addition to staking out the house of Georgia Secretary of State Brad Raffensberger, "also harassed ground-level election workers, none of whom enjoyed police protection [like Raffensberger did]. Ruby Freeman was in hiding, for instance. Ralph Jones, who helped oversee voter registration, had endured vile online messages, slurs, and threats."[44]

Once election officials come under personal threat, and once these routine, bureaucratic processes are weaponized, however—as undertaken by the Trump camp in 2020—can the normalcy chronicled by the Michigan Senate Report be maintained? At this point, the particulars of the 2020 election merge into the broader theme of populism as a corrosively anti-institutional form of governance.

In the wake of the 2020 election, many Trump-infused, Republican-controlled state legislatures have either proposed or enacted legislation—invariably under the guise of election security—that would dismantle the decentralized and bipartisan machinery of election administration in favor of immediate control by the state legislature, which in these cases are at present majority Republican.[45] *Nemo judex in causa sua* is the maxim inherited from Roman law, the simple proposition that no man should be a judge in his own case. The effort to wrest control of the election process from the realm of administration and deliver it to the political threatens to destroy any claim of democratic legitimacy in popular election of government.

Most of the hue and cry over Republicans' election-related lawmaking has focused on the efforts to limit voter registration and restrict the casting of ballots. By and large, these efforts have had at best modest impact on actual voter turnout. As evident in the massive turnouts in the 2020 presidential election cycle, voters are highly adaptive in how they vote. It may be that drop boxes were used successfully to facilitate voting under COVID-19 protocols. It does not mean that if drop boxes are restricted or eliminated, the voters who took advantage of this highly rational mechanism in 2020 will not vote. In all likelihood, determined voters will find another electoral outlet, as they did under the extraordinary conditions of the COVID pandemic. As the Stanford-MIT study summarized:

> The most basic measure of the success of an election is turnout. By this metric, the 2020 election was an unalloyed success by U.S. standards. Nearly 160 million votes were cast in 2020, up by more than 20 million from 2016.... Turnout as a percentage of the voting-eligible population increased in every state.[46]

The Trump obsession of the Republican Party has channeled much of the reform effort into restructuring voting so that pro-Biden votes could not have been cast in the same fashion. While the result is a more restrictive voting environment than in 2020, the likely impact of these alterations remains unclear; by and large voting will still be easier than it was a decade ago, and voters remain motivated by the partisan divide. More ominous, however, is the proliferation of strategically aimed voting legislation—more than 400 bills introduced at the state level in the first six months of 2021 alone—that do not affect the casting of ballots. Rather, these are bills that increase partisan control of the counting and certification of ballots. These proposals typically allow state legislatures to control election certification, to override mechanisms of local control, or strip state executives—like the Georgia secretary of state who did his job in the 2021 Senate elections—of power over election administration. Perhaps most dangerous are bills that politicize election security by empowering partisan "poll watchers" to be more active in their roles and intervene in ballot counting,[47] inviting the threats already seen in Anchorage. Given the apocalyptic rhetoric of current elections, these bills threaten to expose every voting site to a mini-January 6th insurrection.

These rapid-fire changes, all invoking the putative fraud of the Trump electoral defeat, involve no systematic scheme of administrative reform. They are simple-minded reactions to what happened in 2020. If the Georgia secretary of state refused Trump's demand to "find" a few thousand extra votes, then move administrative power to a different set of

officials. A perfect example is found in the most recent overhaul of election administration in Arizona, in which a surprise Democratic victory in
2020 was followed by a bizarre private "audit" of the ballots. It turned up
nothing. As of this writing, Arizona has a Republican attorney general and a
Democratic secretary of state; the latter historically supervises the election
process, including any litigation or challenges to election outcomes. In late
June 2021, the Republican legislature passed and the governor signed a bill
relocating authority over election challenges from the secretary of state to
the attorney general.[48]

In principle, there is no normative reason that authority over election
challenges should rest in one elected state office or another; either one might
be tempted to engage in partisan manipulation or high-profile grandstanding
to enhance future prospects for higher office. Curiously, however, the new law
provides that the power would rest with the attorney general only until January
2, 2023.[49] Why that date? That is when the next elected attorney general will be
sworn in, and that could conceivably be a Democrat. This is one and done with
a vengeance, to return to basketball terminology. There is not even a pretense
of preserving institutional authority, simply a short-term calculus of immediate
political return.

The attacks on American election administration echo a recurring pattern internationally, for a repeated populist goal is to subordinate any independent electoral authority. In Hungary, upon taking power in 2010, Prime Minister Orbán
suspended the tenure of the Electoral Commission and forced each Commission
member to be reelected by Parliament following each national election.[50]
Because Orbán's Fidesz was the majority party in Parliament, the new Election
Commission included no opposition members.[51] In 2013, Fidesz reorganized
the Commission again to place the power of nomination directly in parliamentary hands.[52] Further, while the administrative Election Office is staffed by civil
service employees, it too is led by Fidesz party officials.[53] Not surprisingly, in
subsequent elections, the Commission has signed off on misinformation and
false advertising campaigns, including incorrect election instructions directed at
voters likely to vote for the opposition.[54]

A similar pattern followed in Poland's 2015 election of Jarosław Kaczyński's
Law and Justice Party (PiS). The party claimed (but never established) a need
to address "monstrous irregularities in voting."[55] Key to controlling election administration was the capture of the National Electoral Commission. While the
entire Commission had been appointed by the judiciary, a new law provided
for seven of the nine members on the Commission to be directly appointed by
Parliament—the remaining two by the constitutional court, another institution
that had already been captured by PiS.[56] As Wojciech Sadurski summarized,
"The electoral process will be thus fully controllable by the ruling party, either

by the parliamentary majority or by the minister of the Interior who is a member of the narrow party leadership."[57]

The pattern recurred in Turkey with the packing of the Turkish Higher Electoral Commission (YSK).[58] In the inimitable words of Turkish President Recep Erdoğan, the game plan is simple: "You ride [democracy] until you get to your destination . . . and then you step off."[59]

Similarly in India, the independent Election Commission has been a critical target of Prime Minister Narendra Modi and the Bharatiya Janata Party (BJP),[60] and part of Modi's wave of deinstitutionalization.[61] While elections do go forward in India, they are now deeply compromised by the manipulation of election rules over when voting could occur, as in the recent 2021 state elections in Tamil Nadu and West Bengal.[62] Ominously, when the BJP nonetheless lost in West Bengal, Modi initiated prosecution of political opponents, including four ministers from the winning party.[63] The BJP has also sought to reshape the electorate in ways that seem beyond even the imagination of the U.S. Republican Party. In particular, the Citizenship Act of 2019 would have granted citizenship to undocumented religious minorities in India except Muslims (on the ground that they were not "indigenous" Indians).[64] The law systematically disfavored a bloc of voters who would almost certainly vote for the opposition.[65]

As chronicled in 2021 by the Citizen's Commission on Elections, a group of former Indian government officials led by retired Supreme Court Justice Madan Lokur, the government's control over the Election Commission has facilitated BJP efforts to exclude minority groups likely opposed to the BJP from voter rolls, to politicize the scheduling of elections, and to issue locally expedient but inconsistent rulings on election administration.[66] The Citizen's Commission report concludes that the Election Commission (and perhaps India more generally) has "morphed into an 'unelected autocracy.'"[67]

Nor is the populist assault on electoral integrity limited to the right side of the political ledger. In 2018, Andrés Manuel López Obrador was elected president of Mexico as a left-wing populist, understood to be the antiestablishment candidate.[68] Upon taking office, López Obrador set his sights on the independent National Electoral Institute (INE) and Electoral Tribunal of the Federal Judiciary (TEPJF), particularly after these institutions prevented two López Obrador–backed candidates from running in elections. López Obrador declared that these bodies were formed to "prevent democracy"[69] and were corrupt.[70] López Obrador has sought to put those critiques into policy, proposing reforms to disband the INE and TEPJF and replace them with a body of directly elected members selected on political criteria to manage state and local elections.[71] A majority of Mexicans support López Obrador's reform package.[72] As it happens, these independent electoral institutions, which are constitutionally recognized autonomous organizations,[73] had allowed Mexico in the 1990s to emerge from one-party rule by the Partido Revolucionario Institucional (PRI).[74] Having buttressed Mexico's tenuous hold on democracy since the fall of the PRI, those institutions now loom as impediments, and are in turn vulnerable to, López Obrador's effort to consolidate power, an effort strengthened by Morena's resounding victory in state elections in Mexico over four of six states they had not yet controlled.[75]

IV. The Broader Attack on State Competence

The efforts to compromise impartial election administration, while perhaps especially toxic to democracy, are in turn but a subset of the populist challenge to the modern state. Because the modern would-be autocrats claim legitimacy from the fact of having been elected, the mechanics of voting have a particular salience in bending state institutions to the populist will. The destructive claims of electoral fraud—from Trump throughout his time in politics and from others like Bolsonaro anticipatorily in case of electoral defeat—serve both to buttress shaky claims to popular approbation and to remove a source of institutional resistance. Election administration offers populists a particularly propitious opportunity to "aggressively leverage institutional power and do so for partisan ends."[76]

At the same time, election administrators share with other elements of the modern administrative state a core of bureaucratic authority. This authority is based on specialized expertise, certainty in command structures, continuity of institutional presence, and established forms of decision-making. Together these form the essence of bureaucratic governance in the modern state, identified by Max Weber and by generations of specialists in administration who have followed. While bureaucracies may fall vulnerable to becoming stale and encrusted over time, they provide indispensable order to the complex functions of state organization that have emerged over the past two centuries.

For the great sociologist of the modern state, Max Weber, the effective modern bureaucracy required professional independence and selection based upon objective standards of merit.[77] By design, the bureaucracy had to be not only politically independent but also able to resist political pressure. This is primarily guaranteed by the use of objective criteria for hiring, such as civil service exams, and by protection of career civil servants against removal without proof of good cause.

In the election context, this structured independence translated to the ability of election officials in Georgia and Arizona to resist President Trump's demands that vote counting either be halted or that a few thousand extra votes be redirected to his statewide totals. These American election officials did not have formal civil service protection, but they nonetheless discharged established institutional responsibilities. They relied on a shared bipartisan environment to protect them from unilateral partisan retaliation.

Whether in the form of nonpartisan independent election administration in other countries, and even in the American bipartisan election structures, election commissions are centerpieces of what Mark Tushnet dubs institutions for protecting democracy.[78] Modern constitutions, such as South Africa's, recognize the independent status of the institutions that do not guide democratic governance, but instead guarantee the continued vitality of democratic norms. Even when independent election administration bodies do not have direct constitutional protections, they are legally insulated from pressure and are expected to operate free from partisan interference, as in Canada.[79]

More broadly, bureaucratic authority rests on a normative commitment to resist the politics of the moment in favor of the dictates of expertise, experience, and reasoned study. The modern administrative bureaucracy derives its authority from "modern tenets such as *specified rules, spheres of competence*, and the systematic division of powers."[80] In turn, this yields expertise that is "loaded with authority and power,"[81] which then relies on the production of "neutral information that is necessary to the operation of modern democracies."[82]

In other words, the Weberian ideal form of bureaucratic rationality relies ultimately on professionalism and a commitment to scientific knowledge, the heart of Enlightenment values. Weber identified three kinds of claims to political legitimacy: those rooted in traditional authority, those emanating from charismatic authority in the political sphere, and those grounded in rational-legal principles. The basic machinery of the modern state hews most closely to rational-legal authority, with its internal operations following prescribed practices, such as with the American Administrative Procedure Act.[83] The state bureaucracy has no direct claim to the traditional authority of a monarch, has no independent democratic status, and operates best when it proceeds anonymously as the executor of pre-existing mandates. By contrast, the individual authority claimed by populist heads of state emerges from an electoral mandate and is typically carried forth by individuals with charismatic authority.

Modern organizational theory posits that institutions of governance are not simply tools constructed for accomplishing a specific task—say, measuring contaminants in a stream—but become "infused with value beyond the technical requirements of the task at hand."[84] Martin Krygier adds that such "institutionalization occurs as a spontaneous social *process* over time, as people develop particular habits, relationships, networks, ties, loyalties, and attachments in the course of living and working together, participating in activities and sharing and learning values, symbols, myths, and so on."[85] These embedded pathways no doubt can lead to bureaucratic sluggishness as habits may become encrusted. But it is this history of "consistent conduct and supportive belief" reinforcing a sense of "regularity and legitimacy"[86] that allowed the election boards of Michigan to perform their duty. A commitment to that sort of process regularity—and to distinguishing fact from fantasy—is what allows an investigation by the Republican-led Michigan state legislature, under the authorship of an open Trump supporter, to conclude that Trump had indeed lost the election in Michigan and that the claims of fraud were unfounded.

To cut to the chase, the angry populism of the day has no use for any of the values associated with rational-legal authority, from nonpolitical competence to the testing of falsifiable propositions. Again and again, the populist challenge to inherited state institutions is bound up with claims of "alternative facts" that fit poorly into the test-and-validate approach taken from science. The modern administrative state is built around technical competence and procedural transparency that cannot tolerate an alternative fact universe. As a result, the current strain of populists defy bureaucracy not simply to push through specific policy initiatives, but instead as part of a wholesale war against modern notions of science and proof. "Knowledge realism," to return to Bo Rothstein's account of the gains from experience-based inquiry, is one of the enemies of anti-institutional populism.

Unfortunately, these pathologies of incompetence, antipathy to technical expertise, and magical thinking converged in the deadly context of the COVID-19 pandemic. For Bolsonaro, Brazilians' natural vigor would repel any rapacious virus—and even as Brazil became one of the countries most devastated by the virus, he countenanced no public health measures.[87] Both Bolsonaro and Trump trumpeted hydroxychloroquine,[88] which became an elixir of faith, until in turn supplanted by ivermectin, a horse worm medication of all things.[89] Trump went so far to speculate at a news conference (to the evident dismay of public health officials) that internal application of household disinfectants or strong lights could wipe out the virus;[90] he also blocked a COVID-ridden ship from docking to keep its infection numbers off the books.[91]

Even after Trump's defeat, the attack on science and public health remains a mainstay of Trump-inspired Republican politics. Over Republican Governor Mike DeWine's veto, the more Trumpian Ohio legislature enacted Senate Bill 22, which allows the legislature to terminate a state of emergency declared by the governor after thirty days and to rescind any stay-at-home or mask mandates issued pursuant to the state of emergency declaration, and it also blocks local health departments from restricting large gatherings or closing schools.[92] Similar legislation is now commonplace across the denial-belt. For example, in Kansas, a state with only about 40 percent of its population vaccinated as of July of 2021,[93] the state legislature responded to resurgent infection levels not with public health measures but with restrictions on state health capability. The new legislation not only limited the powers of local health officials and the governor to issue emergency orders,[94] but it also created an extraordinary private right to sue for individuals "burdened" by a state or local health order; already challenged public health officials were required to provide a hearing on all such challenges within seventy-two hours.[95] Not to be outdone, state Republicans in Tennessee prohibited all vaccine outreach to teenagers by the state—all, not just for COVID-19—and forced the firing of the state's top vaccine official.[96]

But none of this—the denigration of expertise and facts—began with COVID-19. During his campaign, President Trump promised to "drain the swamp,"[97] expunging the malign "deep state." But the "deep state" turned out to include essentially all long-time civil servants and scientists. Trump's presidency witnessed an unprecedented exodus of experts—some fired, others resigning in dismay. The pattern of hostility to government capabilities was not an aberration but a central feature of Trump's charismatic claims to unbridled authority.

Michael Lewis beautifully chronicles the manifest disinterest in governance from even before the Trump administration formally took office. One evolved routine is that a presidential "transition team" from the winning campaign is assisted in learning about the detailed operations of the government agencies that it would soon be overseeing. And so:

> On the morning after the election, November 9, 2016, the people who ran the U.S. Department of Energy turned up in their offices and waited. . . . The Department of Energy staff planned to deliver to Trump's people the same talks, from the same five-inch-thick three ring binders with the Department of Energy seal on them, that they would have given to the Clinton people. . . . By afternoon the silence was deafening. "Day 1, we're ready to go," says a former senior White House official. "Day 2 it was, 'Maybe they'll call us?' " . . .
>
> On the Monday after the presidential election, the same thing that happened across the rest of the U.S. government happened inside the Department of Commerce: nothing. Dozens of civil servants sat all day waiting to deliver briefings that would, in the end, never be heard.[98]

That pattern would persist throughout the Trump years. The Trump administration significantly cut staffing related to "regulation, enforcement, civil rights, worker safety, and other areas" with considerable cuts to, for example, the number of inspectors, IRS officers tasked with collecting overdue taxes, soil scientists, and public health educators.[99] A particular target was the State Department, where ambassadorial vacancies lasted for years, and nearly half the top positions remained unfilled two years into Trump's term.[100] In order to bypass the Federal Vacancies Reform Act, the administration left open positions requiring Senate confirmation and staffed the government with a series of interim appointees with colorful titles, such as the "deputy director exercising the authority for the National Park Service" and the "senior official performing the duties of the director at U.S. Immigration and Customs Enforcement."[101] Where the appointment power ran out, career civil servants found themselves shunted to basement offices, banned from decision-making meetings, and faced with executive orders removing job protections for long-term employees. "Bending the apparatus of the state to his own will—there's an authoritarian tint to that that is impossible to escape."[102]

Once again, when viewed internationally, the Trump approach finds ready echoes in other populist regimes that without fail seek to tame "autonomous bureaucratic capacity, insulated from political control at the day-to-day level."[103] Hungary provides a perfect example of how the capture of the administrative powers of the state can insulate a populist regime, even were it to lose its electoral command. One of Fidesz's first acts in power was to change civil service labor laws to remove job security protections. Orbán quickly fired thousands of civil service employees who opposed Fidesz, and, even though this move was ultimately declared unconstitutional, by the time the protections were back in place, they were protecting Fidesz loyalists who had been installed instead of the previous employees.[104] Party loyalists were quickly appointed into previously independent positions in the Audit Office or the anticorruption ombudsman, and the Fidesz-controlled Parliament quickly gave those officials extended tenure.[105] The aim was twofold. First, even were Fidesz to lose an election, they would have control of critical portions of the state. Second, Orbán used this control over government agencies such as the Audit Office or the Prosecutors Office to launch investigations to weaken political opponents and limit electoral accountability altogether.[106]

Similarly in Poland, actions by the PiS under Andrzej Duda and Jarosław Kaczyński since their election in 2015 mimic Orbán's efforts to hollow out democratic institutions.[107] Unlike Fidesz, PiS never had a sufficient parliamentary majority to amend the Constitution freely, making the institutional moves all the more important. The first target was the Constitutional Court, effectively rendered powerless through a combination of court packing and surgical legislation, such as the prohibition on publishing the opinions of the Court.[108] Legislation had turned the civil service into a political body with all high-level officials now appointed by PiS and even most low-level positions flowing through party control.[109] New government agencies, such as the Internal Security Agency, gave the government broad investigatory powers under the guise of protecting against terrorism.[110]

Although the details vary from country to country, the same pattern of undermining institutional resistance stretches across the populist spectrum. In Mexico, López Obrador enacted budget cuts that gutted the civil service, reduced salaries, and fired many nonpartisan officials who might push back against the regime.[111] He also slashed the budgets of various independent agencies by as much as 20 percent.[112] In order to prevent judicial pushback, López Obrador packed the court with loyalists, cut judicial salaries, and extended the terms of sympathetic judges.[113] For those agencies and individuals that he has not been able to reach through executive powers, he has turned to media criticism and criminal investigation.[114]

Meanwhile in the most autocratic of these countries, Turkey, the failed 2016 coup gave Erdoğan cover to declare a state of emergency, bypass the legislative process, and dissolve government institutions. In addition to depriving individuals of civil liberties, Erdoğan proceeded to purge government institutions, to install loyalists throughout the military and police, and to detain or fire over 3,000 judges and 100,000 civil service employees.[115] As a parting shot, just before the end of the state of emergency in 2018, Erdoğan fired an additional 18,000 civil service employees.[116]

Populist assaults on pockets of resistance are not limited to governmental institutions. NGOs and media outlets have been subject to increased restrictions—though not usually through formal state repression, as in dictatorships of old. In India, for example, the BJP has used intimidation and harassment, including direct attacks on dissenting journalists, to inspire fear and caution in the media.[117] Correspondingly in Poland, Fidesz and PiS have used all manner of regulatory authority to tie up media authorities and other civil society groups.[118] In Hungary, the mobilization of a series of onerous tax and regulatory mechanisms forced parts of the Central European University (a private institution established by George Soros) to leave the country altogether.[119] The attack on university independence is echoed in India where the BJP government has used taxing and regulatory power to squeeze private universities, such as Ashoka. The government forced the resignation of leading public critic Pratap Banhu Mehta first from his rectorship and then ultimately from his professorship as well.[120] BJP-aligned student groups have also targeted dissident professors and students as "anti-national," triggering violent protests reminiscent of the Cultural Revolution.

V. Bureaucracy and Resistance

No doubt, countries like India and Mexico are plagued by a sclerotic civil service that is bloated, inefficient, and frequently corrupt. Even in less-corrupt countries there is often a gap between the promise of bureaucratic expertise and the public performance that grows over time. "Bureaucrats came to be more interested in protecting their budgets and jobs than in the efficient performance of their mandates. And they clung to old mandates even when both science and the society around them were changing."[121] The dynamic is well captured by Francis Fukuyama: "The very stability of institutions is also the source of political decay."[122] Unfortunately, the same insulation from electoral politics that might reinforce democracy by resisting power grabs might also lead to the capture of institutions by interest groups or a minority of powerful elites.[123]

What animates populism, however, is not an effort to improve responsiveness or realize efficiencies through reorganization, but simply to curtail institutional resistance to autocratic rule.[124] The "sabotage" of legislatively enacted administrative authority represents an undemocratic privileging of "the president's views about the desirability of maintaining statutory programs over congressional judgments expressed in law."[125]

Efforts to eliminate entrenched bureaucratic authority follow a standard pattern across illiberal populist regimes, all designed to break the will of government officials who might claim an independent source of authority.[126] The gameplan runs through centralization of governmental power, firing civil servants and hollowing out the bureaucracy through not appointing replacements, the constant threats to retaliate against administrators not under the direct appointment control of the executive, and, finally, the expansion of executive authority outside customary checks and balances.[127] But at heart, the mechanism is intimidation: "The power to remove government officials and replace them with the chief executive's preferred people provides a powerful weapon to convert the government from an instrument of law into the instrument of an autocratic chief executive."[128]

The effort to tame the bureaucracy invariably introduces a decreased level of competence in state activities and puts pressure on populists in power. Neutering the bureaucracy deprives populist governments of the specialized technical knowledge necessary to "respond with flexibility and precision to specific problems."[129] This too then accelerates the push toward greater autocratic independence from electoral accountability, regardless of the particular political organizations in different countries. While Erdoğan and Orbán had sufficient parliamentary sway to amend their national constitutions, most of the populist assaults on state institutions have occurred within existing constitutional parameters. Orbán achieved constitutional reform; Kaczyński did not. Orbán is prime minister; Kaczyński is formally a backbencher in Parliament. Putin consolidated his rule as both president and prime minister, as did Erdoğan. The forms of government appear to matter less than the relentless assault on the institutions that undergird democracy.[130]

So while the American state and political culture had sources of resilience and resistance that many newer democracies lacked, Trump's assaults on institutions followed similar patterns with similarly corrosive effects. As the administration progressed, it came to be filled by cronies. To the frustration of others in the administration, subordinates tied to Trump by blood or marriage played an outsized role and enjoyed unparalleled access to the Oval Office. As detractors were pushed out, the family remained, most notably the minister-without-portfolio (or with multiple portfolios), son-in-law Jared Kushner. There is of course nothing unprecedented in presidents' depending on a pre-existing inner circle, even on family. First ladies have often been influential. John Kennedy appointed his brother attorney general. But the narrowing circle of trust under Trump took place outside any of the formal structures of governance, as best exemplified by Ivanka Trump and Jared Kushner being charged with everything from pandemic responses to pacifying the Middle East.

Populists govern in a swirl of cronyism and clientelism, using public funds for private power. Whether Putin's oligarchs, Zuma's "tenderpreneurs," Orbán's beneficiaries of public contracts, or any number of other arrangements, the unifying theme is the use of government expenditures to enrich those with personal connections to the regime. But such transactional relations are necessarily unstable, unlike family that cannot escape the association. Populism tends toward a hollowing out not only of the competent parts of the state apparatus but also the circles of cronyist confidence.

The departed Trump administration left behind a staggering number of deaths from COVID-19, social upheaval triggered by police brutality, unemployment levels not seen since the Depression, and an increasingly burned-over political landscape. It is too easy to focus on high-profile policy disasters and the political and cultural flashpoints that roiled Twitter on any given day. And it may be tempting to hope that a calm and rational presence in the White House will itself restore national political culture. But it will not be so easy to reverse the steady erosion of the norms and institutional arrangements that have defined our democracy.

Knowledge of how democracy has been dismantled or defended across other countries might help provide a roadmap for the reforms that will be required to get the United States back on a democratic track. Even in Britain, the fount of an idealized parliamentary regime, Aileen Kavanagh notes the confluence of the incendiary exploitation of "growing popular distrust of elected politicians; the erosion of shared political norms amongst the governing elites; the contracting out of key public services; and the tyranny of the tabloids, to name but a few."[131] By the time the UK Supreme Court asserted itself in its Brexit rulings, parliamentarism was increasingly subsumed by the "expanding power of the Executive, the changing nature of political parties, and the weakening of the civil service"—all contributing to what Erin Delaney terms "the UK's constitutional distress."[132]

A confluence of anti-institutionalist moves over Trump's four years has shown the vulnerability of a stable constitutional democracy. The Trump presidency witnessed a concentration of discretionary authority in the hands of the president, the dismantling of the federal government's institutional resources, and a degeneration of policy and budgeting into a short-term horizon focusing exclusively on immediate political gain—and often on cronyist profit. One need not have been inside the room with John Bolton to see how deinstitutionalized governance and discretionary power yield a *caudillo* or despotic style, which leaves only a semblance of democracy in the claim that elections are periodically held. As expressed by Bob Bauer and Jack Goldsmith, both former senior officials, one serving under Obama and the other under George W. Bush, the question just starting with the executive branch is "how to reconstruct the battered and much-changed presidency that Trump will have left behind."[133]

Partisans tend to exaggerate the significance of any one election. For generations in the United States, political control has flipped back and forth between the two major parties. We have lived through scandals and wars, social upheavals, and dramatic transformations. But considered in retrospect and with the benefit of hindsight, the forms of governance have all been recognizable. The way that government functions has been largely maintained. While progress has been agonizingly slow at times, the bent of the political universe has not fundamentally been called into question.

The four years of the Trump presidency marked a profound shift in the United States. This change in the very nature of political practice far exceeds any easily identified policy demarcations. We have begun to see the unwinding of modern America. The effects did not simply evaporate when Trump left office. Lasting damage has been done to public trust in democratic institutions, government capability, the status of news media, the ability to invoke science and proof, and more. Putting our political culture and democratic system back together will require more than mere policy repair. That will be the issue in the final part of this book.

PART III

A DEMOCRATIC RESTORATION?

The Exposed Underpinnings
of American Democracy

Political engagement is not the ordinary state of affairs for most people. Rather, "it is conflict that involves people in politics and the nature of the conflict determines the nature of the public involvement."[1] The long-run viability of democratic governance turns on the ability to manage deep divergences among the citizenry and offer the prospect of future gains to deal with the necessary disappointment of a system in which some win but others lose. Healthy democratic elections turn on counterpoised visions of potential policy directions in which contestants are accountable for past leadership results and future prospects. By contrast, elections fueled by rage, with the potential for violence lurking in the background, portend poorly for the stability of a democracy.

There are as many problems to be solved as there are roots of populist anger. The last period of democratic politics has assumed the feel of tribal divisions, and there has been a corresponding coarsening of the terms of political engagement. Public expression of group hatred—from the anti-Muslim indignities in India to outright racism in the United States to public incitement of antisemitism in Hungary—defies formal antidiscrimination norms and the core values of liberal tolerance. The fragmentation of political authority allows public indignation to be stoked by political provocateurs competing for extremist attention in the byways of social media. As political scientists Amy Fried and Douglas Harris wrote in assessing the transformed political environment in 2016, "Trump used language that was more directly and explicitly anti-immigrant and overtly race based than any major party presidential candidate after World War II."[2] And central to it all—particularly still in the midst of the COVID-19 body blows—is the sense that democratic authorities lack the capacity, care, and even compassion for addressing the travails of their laboring classes, historically the heart and soul of the struggle for the franchise and the belief in popular sovereignty.

The confluence of the assaults on democracy give rise to a myriad set of concerns and proposals for redress. The need for a diagnostic response is overwhelming in writing on the topic. Particularly if the reaction to the populist moment is driven by fear for what has been lost, it seems almost irresponsible to not offer a program of remediation. By and large, the responses proposed follow from the main channel of inquiry. If the central problem addressed is racism or communal violence, then the response takes form around constraints on speech and demands for communal reparations. If populism emerges from the maldistribution of wealth, the entry point shifts accordingly. Similarly, if the question is one of political authority or state competence, that too yields a different set of diagnostic responses. All too often, the proposals for repair dovetail with the political priors of the writer in a way that democratic repair is ill-distinguished from a distinct political platform.

While each of the central concerns weighs on the prospects for democratic revival, the focus of this book has been on the forms of populist governance and its dismantling of the institutions that make popular sovereignty possible—or at least have played that role historically. It is institutions that have channeled passions into practice, that have blunted the edges of group animus, that have provided increased welfare protections for the bulk of the citizenry, and that have compelled accountability to a broader range of the society. Tocqueville commented two centuries ago on the propensity of Americans to join associations and to come together in pursuit of shared aims.[3] What he saw in the new Republic were the embryonic forms of institutional life that would guide the expanding democratic world even through the cataclysms of the 20th century.

So the concluding discussion is directed along the same institutional lines, and it is more American centered than the overall themes of this book would suggest. While some of what follows has generalized import, attention to institutional detail requires some more focused national setting. Nonetheless, the inquiry yields four major themes:

1. Restoring government capability and the ability to deliver public goods.
2. Revitalizing the legislative branch and restricting the push toward unilateral executive authority.
3. Reengaging the citizenry.
4. Recentering the institutional forms of democratic politics.

Simply presenting a list underscores the difficulty of the undertaking. If the problem were simply one of executive overreach, the remedy would likely take the form of increased institutional checks on executive authority. Similarly, if the issue were simply that of state capability, the answer would largely take the form of simplifying the exercise of governmental authority. Just these two would likely point in different directions and would be challenging enough. Current difficulties unfortunately run deeper and run to the core of public values and the capacity of democratic politics to engage the citizenry.

A reader should be justly skeptical of any three-point program that promises restoration by formula. Such skepticism should increase as the number of points to the program grows exponentially. Many of the needed responses can only emerge from the bottom up as new forms of political and social organization, just as they have throughout the history of efforts at democratic self-governance. A new set of mandatory rules, no matter how well intentioned, are unlikely to reset democracy on its institutional moorings.

We are now two decades into what can only be understood as a sustained period of democratic decline. New democracies are not emerging, and fragile new post-1989 entrants into the democratic orbit are being pulled centripetally into increasingly autocratic orbits. Most ominously, the disengagement from democratic governance has spread to the heartlands of democracy. According to the most recent OECD survey data, in only sixteen countries did more than half of respondents report having confidence in their governments.[4]

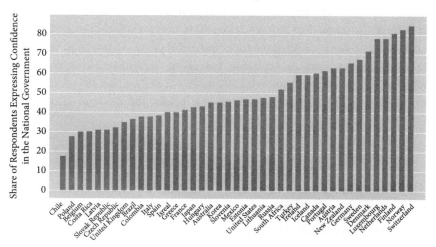

Figure 9.1   Share of respondents expressing confidence in the national government

OECD, *Trust in Government*, https://data.oecd.org/gga/trust-in-government.htm.

As reflected in Figure 9.1, the figure in the United States was below 47 percent, which is higher than it was through most of the preceding decade, when confidence in government measured in the 30's.[5] Indeed, the 47 percent confidence level during the pandemic represents a respite from "the near complete collapse" in recent confidence in the U.S. government.[6] But, by way of comparison, the recent rise to 47 percent still leaves the United States lower than the comparable data in Russia prior to the invasion of Ukraine. France is lower yet at 41 percent, which is a figure lower than that registered in Hungary. And the United Kingdom lags at an astonishing 35 percent, lower in turn than Brazil. In other words, many of the mainstays of democracy generate lower levels of citizen faith than their autocratic counterparts. Were it not for Germany, Switzerland, and the Nordic belt, the democratic world would lag the bastions of illiberalism.

Surveys are no doubt imperfect, and they may measure momentary partisan disengagement more than long-term hostility to democracy as such. Yet to the extent that democracy requires optimism for gain from repeated electoral engagements, the disenchantment with democratic governments portends poorly. Confidence in government draws from all the central concerns about poor state capacity, weakness of political institutions, and citizen sense that little is being done to address the travails of their lives. Moreover, the data measure the period before the full dislocations of the COVID-19 pandemic created new grounds for uncertainty and anger over government intrusion on private lives, regardless of whether such anger is well founded.

Using poor citizen confidence as a ready proxy for state and political dysfunction leads to avenues of reform across all these dimensions, as daunting as that might be. Again, a caution: what follows is a partial list of critical considerations in each of the subjects of inquiry. It is neither comprehensive nor even necessarily responsive to the most pressing challenges of the moment. At any given moment, issues turning on economic inequality, racial justice, climate change, inflation, or crime might command the public's eye. The discussion that follows is attentive to the central concern of this book—the decayed institutional foundations of democratic governance.

I. Government Capability

In 2004, Thomas Frank published his lament over the politics of his native state under the evocative title *What's the Matter with Kansas?* The central theme was that the economic populism that drove the politics of the American prairie heartland a century ago had turned decidedly angry and right-wing:

> Out here the gravity of discontent pulls in only one direction: to the right, to the right, further to the right. Strip today's Kansans of their job security, and they head out to become registered Republicans. Push them off their land, and next thing you know they're protesting in front of abortion clinics. Squander their life savings on manicures for the CEO, and there's a good chance they'll join the John Birch Society. But ask them about the remedies their ancestors proposed (unions,

antitrust, public ownership), and you might as well be referring to the days when knighthood was in flower.[7]

The crux of the "matter" with Kansas was the failure to follow economic dictates rather than other political markers. This argument both overstates the centrality of economic concerns—one might as well ask what is wrong with Cambridge, Massachusetts, and its notorious failure to follow simple economic interest— and understates the perceived failure of government to respect and reward the life ambitions of the laboring classes.

Part of the evident despair fueling populism comes from the view of the state as a privileged elite domain, incapable of addressing the concerns of ordinary citizens and disrespecting the central cultural markers of their lives. This is compounded by the perceived failure of democratic government to deliver social benefits to disenchanted citizens. Here the challenge is substantially to the core of basic state capability, defined as "the ability of a state to collect taxes, enforce law and order, and provide public goods."[8] To return to the opening discussion of this book, it is not clear that the democratic world any longer holds an advantage over more autocratic regimes (think China or Singapore) in the ability to create public goods or even to manage public crises, as with COVID-19. Note that the Chinese response to President Biden's late 2021 democracy summit was entitled, "China: Democracy That Works." As President Xi Jinping defiantly told a party leadership group: "Democracy is not an ornament to be used for decoration; it is to be used to solve the problems that the people want to solve."[9]

A reinvigoration of state capability lies at the heart of the liberal response to the challenges of both autocracy and illiberal populism. A commitment to governmental delivery of social goods was the immediate key to the platforms of President Joe Biden in the United States and Chancellor Olaf Scholz in Germany, to pick the two leading examples. Each has pledged to modernize the country's economic foundations, with both placing a heavy emphasis on large state-directed initiatives on infrastructure.[10] These ambitious programs range from 21st-century digital pathways and environmentally sustainable energy programs, to the most basic of 19th- and 20th-century public works, and attention to roads, bridges, and rails. And each has turned to debt financing to both fund the capital outlays and, hopefully, to stimulate the economy to pay for the undertaking.

Having lived in Argentina during the hyperinflationary period of the mid-1980s, my confidence in the certainty of economic expansion resulting from aggressive assumptions of governmental debt is shaky at best. Yet it seems inescapable that a central part of the ability to wrest popular support for democracy back from authoritarian demagogues must be a restored sense that democratic governments can indeed constructively address the issues of the day. Taking up this challenge strains modern state capabilities and is not without risk on grounds of both feasibility and political will. But I focus on two issues that exemplify needed state initiatives, infrastructure support and the question of immigration. Both not only tax the capabilities of current democratic governments to deliver but also challenge the political foundations of liberal coalitions. While there are many other issues that could be chosen—race relations, climate change, and wealth redistribution come readily to mind—I have suggested these two because of their salience in the battle with populism.

A. Shovels in the Ground

The problem of state capacity is no doubt context specific, but attention to the United States provides a stand-in for the challenges facing democratic states in the current period. No doubt the most expansive state undertaking of the recent past was the Affordable Care Act, the signature initiative of the Obama administration. The Act combined a governmental commitment to increased healthcare, particularly for the most vulnerable Americans, with an elaborate workaround to avoid direct confrontation with vested health insurance concerns. The Act passed Congress only through a legislative maneuver (the so-called reconciliation process) but has not been revisited with much needed fixes in the decade since its initial adoption. More ominously, the rollout of the internet portal, healthcare.gov, was an embarrassing disaster.

State incapacity is increasingly seen as a decisive challenge by critics across the political spectrum:

> Inflexible procedural rules are a hallmark of the American state. The ubiquity of court challenges, the artificial rigors of notice-and-comment rulemaking, zealous environmental review, pre-enforcement review of agency rules, picayune legal rules governing hiring and procurement, nationwide court injunctions—the list goes on and on. Collectively, these procedures frustrate the very government action that progressives demand to address the urgent problems that now confront us.[11]

The procedural blockages, enforced through boundless litigation, have been forcefully ventilated by Philip Howard as what he terms a "common sense" challenge to America's stagnation.[12]

Some of the efforts to handicap the state are no doubt ideological and draw from antiregulatory demands of well-heeled enterprises. But the issue runs deeper and taps a reservoir of suspicion of the state across the political divide. Lindsey Brink well addresses the American manifestation of this pathology:

On the right, the abiding worry has been that big government will throttle the dynamism of American business and foster sloth and dependency. For the left, meanwhile, the anxiety runs in the other direction—namely, that big business and the rich and powerful will subvert the state to do their bidding at others' expense. The fears of both sides are well grounded enough, but, ironically, each side has taken actions that have undermined effective governance—and, in the process, ended up helping to make its own darkest fears come true.[13]

Though the actual sources are no doubt complex, the result is limited government capability as simply a technical matter. For example, during the pandemic, many states found their ability to process expanded unemployment relief frustrated by the inability of their computer systems to handle the altered requirements, many of which were still coded in antediluvian languages such as Fortran.[14]

Outdated computer code is symptomatic of the fact that government has ceased to drive the technological advance of the society. Federal investment in research and development has notably lagged, even in areas such as technology and pharmaceuticals where government undertakings are paired with a dynamic private sector. Between 1964 and 2020, for example, federal spending on R&D dropped from 1.8 percent of GDP to 0.7 percent. That is substantially less than China and several countries that enjoy much higher popular perceptions of state capability, such as Germany, Norway, and Sweden.[15] It also means a smaller cadre of government officials are accustomed to the demands of technological innovation or have the skills to secure successful implementation. Government capability eroded significantly during the period when the populist objective was, in the words of Steve Bannon, "to deconstruct the administrative state."[16]

Beyond the question of government capacity to execute is the mismatch between the political objectives of stemming the populist tide and the means chosen through investment in infrastructure redevelopment. As President Obama learned when structuring the stimulus program in response to the 2008 financial meltdown, there are few "shovel-ready" programs on stand-by to be excavated at a moment's notice. Stable democracies are able to commit to the space program or the highway investments that realize gains over the long haul. But under pressure from populist destabilization, the impulse toward a short-term rapid response is great. Reduced to the immediate, democratic governments are forced to compete on the compressed timeframe of populism and to sacrifice the capacity for long-term investment that is the hallmark of stable political regimes. It is also likely that the payoff for either the economic benefits of the public undertaking or even the realization of its immediate utility will be years in the making. The Empire State Building may have been built in a year, but that is no longer within the capabilities of our society. The result is that those who expend the

political will on such undertakings will likely not be the ones to benefit electorally from gains that only come into focus well down the road.

Moreover, the weakness of state institutions over time compromises their capacity to "respond with flexibility and precision to specific problems."[17] There
is an unfortunate spiral, well captured by Ezra Klein, under which "a key failure
of liberalism in this era is the inability to build in a way that inspires confidence
in more building. Infrastructure comes in overbudget and late, if it comes in at
all. The political problem is if people keep watching the government fail to build
things well, they won't believe the government can build things well. So they
won't trust it to build. And they won't even be wrong."[18]

Finally, social investment is not an unbounded good. Even wealthy societies
have limited resources and have to trade off among competing demands for attention. Historically, this is the operational core of politics, usually negotiated
in back rooms, and with accountability in the final instance before the voters in
the electoral arena. In turn, the ability to structure deals based on compromised
claims to governmental attention requires political leadership. The fracas over
President Biden's efforts at broad-scale investment shows how weak political
parties spill over into governmental incapacity. The Biden administration spent
valuable time in the early stages of the Administration because the Democratic
Senate leadership was able to broker a deal that would balance the social welfarist impulses of the party's left-wing against the fiscal concerns of the more centrist wing. In the age of perpetual Twitter storms, a topic addressed more fully
shortly, there was no longer the political cushion of time and repeat interactions
to find a governing path.[19]

B. Politics Beyond the Short Term

Recapturing the faith of working-class voters is not simply a matter of improving
economic conditions. Rather, there is the growing estrangement from the core
of liberal democracy, fueled substantially by what Republican Senator Ben Sasse
framed as the protracted Trump effort to "weaponize distrust."[20] The distrust
is fueled by the sense that heartland values and beliefs are derided by powerful
elites who attend to a different set of norms and even speak a different language.
For example, whereas 60 percent of Americans who trace their heritage to Latin
America or Spain use the term "Hispanic" to describe themselves, the discourse
among university elites is to employ the term "Latinx," used by a scant 2 percent
of the relevant population, which a majority of Hispanics find offensive,[21] and
that does not even lend itself to easy pronunciation in Spanish.

Perhaps no area of distrust is as pronounced as the immigration issue. There
is simply no escaping the immigration question in the inflamed politics of

populism. West Germany undertook the integration of East Germany, despite the economic and cultural dislocations that would be required. But German reunification could be presented as an act of national solidarity. The rise of menacing right-wing politics in the former East is a reminder how much this remains an act in process. By contrast, the German decision to admit 1 million refugees, mostly from Syria, in 2015 provoked an immediate decline in support for Chancellor Angela Merkel's coalition and triggered the rise of the right-wing populist Alternative for Germany (AfD) Party.[22] By 2017, AfD had grown to be the third-largest vote getter in the German federal elections.[23]

The sense of inclusive commitment to a joint undertaking has been key to successful democratic state building. Mancur Olsen set the foundations in his classic work on collective enterprise: "Stable societies with unchanged boundaries tend to accumulate more collusions and organizations for collective action over time. The longer the country is stable, the more distributional coalitions they're going to have."[24] Immigration, no matter how necessary to the revitalization of a country or to expand its workforce or to address humanitarian crises, represents an inevitable disruption of established networks of trust. Immigration also carries the flashpoints of race, religion, and ethnicity that threaten more homogeneous communities. The claim of the nation overrun by foreigners allows a more polite introduction of a toxic mix of xenophobia and out-and-out racism into national political discourse.

Most critically, immigration seems to paralyze liberal democrats who are too often infused with a sense of cosmopolitan skepticism to national barriers. Any real immigration law reform has to reject the claim for open borders, either as a formal matter or practically as the result of efforts to procedurally tie up the ability to enforce whatever immigration controls are in place. For liberal democrats, this is a difficult issue that clashes with a political outlook heavily focused on the victims of life's many lotteries. It is no coincidence that liberal parties around the world have failed to articulate any position on immigration except to demand more process rights for asylum seekers and easier paths to citizenship for those who are in the country. The question of borders and of national control over immigration flows is largely left untouched, most notably by the Democratic Party in the U.S., which in turn provides a ripe medium for right-wing agitation.

Some of the difficulty is that immigration is only partly about immigrants. It serves as a stand-in for the effects of globalization that robs communities of earlier forms of economic activity that provided sources of both wealth and inclusiveness. As summarized by Cynthia Estlund: "The major trends in the organization of work since the 1970s—the shift from manufacturing to services, shorter job tenures, more precarious and contingent work, the 'fissuring' of supply chains, and the rise of the gig economy and independent contracting versus employment—seem likely to undercut the potency of work as a source of connectedness and social solidarity."[25] Rather than an attachment to a job and community, "what matters now are innovation, flexibility, entrepreneurialism, and a constant willingness to learn new skills."[26] Not surprisingly, many workers "bridle at the demand to reinvent themselves as the jobs they once held are outsourced to low-wage countries or assigned to robots."[27]

Take as an example the coal-mining regions that prospered in earlier stages of industrialization but now provide ready bases of support for populist insurgents. In these regions, concern for immigration is readily expressed, though the consequence of foreign interaction is not that there are large numbers of immigrants moving into depressed areas such as Appalachia. Immigration here is not a matter of people moving in, but instead one of the jobs once in these regions having either been lost or moved abroad. Oxford Professor Paul Collier describes the demise of his steelmaking hometown of Sheffield during his lifetime amid the economic growth of London. The changed trajectory begins just with a simple examination of the demographics of the two regions. London's population in 2011 was 37 percent first-generation immigrants, a figure that would have been negligible right after World War II.[28] Those immigrants were part of the economic transformation of London into one of the true world centers of the 21st century. By contrast, Sheffield stagnated and declined from the stable village life of the 1950s to a world of industrial decay.[29] Sheffield has not been a magnet for migrants or economic transformation. Paradoxically, Adam Smith described 18th-century Sheffield as being a center of new industry that drew enterprising workmen with the promise of higher wages.[30]

The voting on Brexit captured how the world outlooks of cosmopolitan London and the hollowed out industrial cities of the Midlands diverge considerably. The immigrants and the successful elite of London—Collier disparagingly calls the latter the "smug skilled"—have no strong solidaristic attachment to Sheffield or the struggling belt of yesterday's England. For those left behind in the areas that delivered the Industrial Revolution centuries ago, foreign attachments are a process of disruption of expectation of community, language, and even food. By contrast, the elites of London would be readily at home walking the streets of Paris or Brussels, but certainly not of Sheffield. Michael Sandel well captures the core insight that

> many working-class supporters of Trump, Brexit, and populist parties
> in other countries seemed less interested in promises of upward mo-
> bility than in reassertions of national sovereignty, identity and pride.
> They resented meritocratic elites, expert, and professional classes
> who had celebrated market-driven globalization, reaped the benefits,

consigned working people to the discipline of foreign competition, and who seemed to identify more with global elites than with their fellow citizens.[31]

Immigration arouses the worst of nativist impulses, typically freely adorned with xenophobic and even racist imagery. The readiness of the populist descent into such rage makes it all too easy for the underlying concerns to be dismissed out of hand in politically righteous discourse. But if immigration is in part a place-holder for those increasingly at risk of social and economic marginalization, then failing to address it is paving the path to populist ascendency. Immigration is one of a number of issues on which progressive elites seem out of touch with the concerns of those who fear being forgotten and left behind. In the language of populism, immigration symbolizes the inability of government to address core concerns of dignity and respect that are inflamed by reference to "deplorables" or dismissive gestures to the beleaguered working classes. In significant part, that working class will still draw heavily from whites and males. Failure to take up immigration indicates state incapacity to craft a serious program of immigration goals that includes not only rights for lawful immigrants but also border controls and meaningful limits. Failure to do so is not only bad public policy but guarantees readily combustible fuel for the flames of populism.

II. The Executive Bounded: Reining in the *Caudillo* State

Political scientists have long debated the competing strengths and weaknesses of presidential versus parliamentary regimes.[32] The general line of division was that presidential selection forces coalitions to form ahead of the elections and to be accountable for the conduct of the party in office at the time of the election. By contrast, proportional representation systems require governing coalitions to be assembled after the vote and frees each narrower party to run on its aspirations rather than on what the previous government had actually brought about. Presidentialism offers broad-tent parties that leave many or most voters distant from the electoral platform. Parliamentary systems offer incentives for narrower tracked parties that align more directly with voter preferences and are more nimble in responding to shifting sentiments. Heads of government in a parliamentary system are never far from legislative accountability, and political shifts or unforeseen events may prompt easier transitions to new elections and new governors.[33] Presidential regimes offer the benefit of having the head of the government run for election before all the voters and therefore retain authority even if legislative politics break down.

Critics of presidentialism go further to charge that the nature of the unitary executive promotes a breakdown of legislative power and a push toward autocratic governance. For example, Dean Bertil Oder describes the residual role of the Parliament in Turkey even as the Erdoğan government became increasingly authoritarian:

> The centrality of the parliament in the political system did not lead to consensual and less polarized politics, but it did secure inclusionary political practices with regard to the opposition. The presidential system attacks this longstanding embodiment of postulates and conventions in Turkish politics that have shaped it. As opposed to the unipersonal and "winner takes all" structure of presidentialism, the parliamentary system operated more inclusively by enabling the opposition and political parties as powerful actors.[34]

While this is an apt description of Turkish developments, it is hard to disentangle causation from correlation. The processes described by Oder have a familiar ring across the democratic world as the executive increasingly dominates the legislative branches, regardless of whether the executive is elected singularly as president or as prime minister heading the legislative majority. A look across the illiberal states shows that the process may arguably be simpler in a presidential regime, but that this is hardly a make-or-break distinction. In Turkey, for example, the marginalization of the opposition was underway before Erdoğan's formal rebranding as president rather than prime minister. Similarly, Putin also found it possible to consolidate power as both prime minister and president, and the illiberal states are led by Orbán and Kaczyński, one serving as prime minister, the other in a presidential system.

Perhaps more telling is that power has concentrated in the hands of the chief executive in classically parliamentary countries such as Britain and Canada. The strength of the legislative branch seems to be more a function of the capacity of political parties to organize the terms of governance through the legislative factions. The fragmentation of political authority, as well as the rise of the legislator as lone venturer along the lines of a Ted Cruz or an Alexandria Ocasio-Cortez, emerges as the driving force weakening the legislative branch's capacity for collective action. That pattern is visible around the world in both presidential and parliamentary systems, limiting the explanatory power of political arguments that focus on how the chief executive is chosen. Put another way, it is unlikely that parliamentarism will emerge as the check on populist aggrandizement of the executive. Notably, in the European context, domination by the executive is a constant across the countries and even at the EU-level, which in turn, "is exacerbated by the opaqueness of the EU political system, and by the technocratic and complex workings of the EU supranational institutions which are highly inaccessible to citizens and make it hard for them to feel adequately represented."[35]

A. Federalism

One common way to prevent over-concentration of power is to divide authority between centralized and local units of government in a federal structure. The classic formulation is from William Riker, describing federalism as "a political organization in which the activities of government are divided between regional governments and a central government in such a way that each kind of government has some activities on which it makes final decision."[36] While federalism takes many forms—ranging from economic coordination to governance by councils selected from regional constituencies—the modern forms increasingly gravitate to a model of a representative central government with separately selected local governments having varying levels of autonomous control over the welfare of their citizens.[37] A recent study by Robert Inman and Daniel Rubinfeld provides a thorough account of how federalism yields both political and economic gains that reinforce democratic governance. Under conditions of full participation and cross-cutting areas of local and federal control, federalism harnesses greater levels of citizen engagement in governance and corresponding attentiveness to local preferences. If successfully implemented—and Inman and Rubinfeld were consultants to the attempts to divide power along federalism lines in South Africa—federalism necessarily limits the scope of a single executive's unilateral authority.

Yet the defining feature in Inman and Rubinfeld's account is the need for coordination and specialization in a common project. Their meticulous examination of the conditions under which federalism succeeds concludes with the importance of a shared enterprise: on their account, arguments for federalist structures "will then be most persuasive for new and evolving democratic states where citizen preferences for public goods and services vary but where there is sufficient goodwill and respect for differences that compromise is possible."[38]

Federalism is not designed as a check on executive power as such, even if its institutional design looks heavily toward shared representation of various local constituencies in the national legislature to cement the local/national bond. As with the use of the ordinary criminal law to check the populist impulse toward freewheeling rewards to regime loyalists, sometimes a less direct path may be politically advantageous. Because federalism operates to fractionate political power, it might also serve to check the centrifugal pull toward executive unilateralism visible across the democratic world. A secondary benefit might thus be realized. Further, the empowerment of local officials in a federalized polity creates stakeholders in checking executive authority. "Ambition must be made to counteract ambition," as Madison famously set out in *Federalist*, no. 51.[39]

But where political compromise is not possible, federalism raises the prospect of yet another means to frustrate government capability by opening up myriad institutional obstacles to the achievement of national objectives. "Partisan federalism" emerges as a strategy to "involve political actors' use of state and federal governments in ways that articulate, stage, and amplify competition between the political parties."[40] As developed by Jessica Bulman-Posen, federalist obstruction may involve (1) litigation claiming infringement of state sovereignty by federal actors,[41] (2) state legislative action running counter to the agenda the federal government is pursuing,[42] and (3) "uncooperative federalism" whereby state governments push back on federal policy through their oversight on implementation.[43]

The stage was set in the United States with the war on the Affordable Care Act (ACA). A Republican commitment to undermining the Act was announced the day it was enacted,[44] and federalism provided a significant part of the arsenal. Eighteen states enacted statutory or constitutional provisions banning enforcement of the ACA's individual mandate of obligatory insurance coverage, and nineteen states enacted laws that limited and regulated the function of "navigators" who help consumers select and purchase health insurance.[45] Republican-led states across the country refused to cooperate in implementing the ACA, even though the federal government covered the full cost of Medicaid expansion.[46] Many oppositional states then turned to litigation, which achieved a small victory when the Supreme Court struck down the individual mandate in *NFIB v. Sebelius*.[47] The result was that "during both the Trump and Obama presidencies, AGs found a new way to use litigation to advance their political ambitions—to litigate *as partisans* around a polarized issue."[48] Margaret Lemos terms this "horizontal" state activity in which litigation is used by the attorney general of one state to attack the partisan agenda of other states.[49]

While the pattern developed most forcefully in the Obama years, it did not stop there. Correspondingly, Democratic state and local officials used federalism to thwart many aspects of the immigration programs under President Trump. Without regard to the desirability of the underlying federal policies, the similarity of the tactics across the divide highlights the role of partisan federalism in a politics of obstruction.[50] Federalism allowed California to threaten to divest its public pension fund from companies that helped build the border wall, a well-known campaign promise of the former president.[51] Further, because federal immigration enforcement relies heavily on state and local cooperation, Democratic states and cities quickly declared themselves "sanctuaries," passing legislation that barred cooperation with federal immigration officials aiming to implement President Trump's immigration policy.[52]

COVID-19 provides the key example of federalism not only being a point of political obstruction but also undermining the effectiveness of a needed coordinated response. Early on in the pandemic, public health experts warned of the "dark side of federalism":

> [Federalism] encourages a patchwork response to epidemics. States and localities may decide to implement aggressive disease-mitigation measures, but need not do so. The defining feature of the U.S. response to Covid-19 therefore continues to be localized action against a threat that lost its local character weeks ago.[53]

In the first throes of the pandemic, this federal structure resulted in states competing for crucial PPE and medical equipment.[54] With the change of administration, efforts to impose mask or vaccine mandates were repeatedly challenged or undermined. After the CDC recommended mask mandates in schools and other public locations, state officials in Florida,[55] Texas,[56] and Arizona[57] responded with legislation banning or restricting the implementation of mask mandates. President Biden announced workforce vaccine mandates, stating that " 'if those governors won't help us beat the pandemic, I will use my power as president to get them out of the way.' "[58] In response, Florida passed legislation countering such measures, and Republican state officials called a special session to plan for ways to push back on the president's pandemic response.[59] Ten states, all but one with Republican attorneys general, filed suit seeking to block federal vaccine mandates for workplaces.[60]

The collapse of federalism into a secondary battlefield under conditions of sharp partisan polarization mirrors the subordination of institutional prerogatives in Congress to the demands of partisanship. The framers assumed—or at least, hoped—that limits could be induced by the institutional rivalries among the coordinate institutions of the federal government. Madison's solution for political excesses was to fractionate power among the different branches of government. That prescription relies on the institutional interests of each branch being distinct to that branch and further that each branch will jealously protect its prerogatives against incursion. For Montesquieu, in the formulation that inspired the American founding generation, "ballast to one, in order to enable it to counterpoise the other."[61]

That means that Congress as an institution, and through its members, will see its aims realized as being the legislative branch. But if the Congress is simply an organ of partisan divides, then it has no ambition as such and serves simply as a situs for partisan aims. As Vernon Bogdanor summarized from the British perspective, "the dominance of party politics in modern democracies" results in "the practice of bicameralism [that] bears very little relation to the theory."[62]

Consider as just one example the Republican response to President Obama's assumption of office amid the worst financial crisis in several generations. A meeting of key Republican leaders on Inauguration Day featured the pledge "to stick together" around a simple strategy: "Show united and unyielding opposition of the president's economic policies."[63]

While the extreme version of burn-it-down politics during the Obama period prepared the electoral turf for President Trump, it was by no means new. The emergence of a strong Republican caucus in the House of Representatives in the 1990s transformed the role of the congressional opposition from gaining incrementally through constituent services and shaping legislation to outright obstruction. Even before Republicans captured Congress in 1994 under the "Contract with America" program, they learned that partisans could be mobilized in opposition to any initiative of President Bill Clinton. What ensued was later characterized by the Clinton administration as "a decision not to give the President any victories, for if they did not, they could potentially gain significantly at the midterm elections."[64] However novel that may have seemed thirty years ago, it has become standard fare in the interim.

B. Empowering the Opposition

There are mechanisms that offer opposition parties the capacity to present an alternative system of showing strength by political example rather than mere objection. If the opposition had the right to offer programs that had to be voted on or was able to call some number of legislative hearings, the parliamentary arena could be the focus of policy engagement over the directions of governance. The aim is to create a desire on the part of all parties to invest in the institutions that they might soon take over, and "to make the legislature work as a forum for genuine critical debate."[65] This hearkens back to the view of party politics in a mature democracy as a regulated rivalry, per Nancy Rosenblum.[66]

In fact, many countries around the world have procedures and structures in place that empower the opposition to serve as a balance on the party (or individual) in power.[67] Not only do such structures allow the opposition to check majority power, these structures often give such opposition parties a share in governance: "Government in opposition rules prevent excesses of power, because even if a political movement wins all different kinds of elections for all different kinds of positions, they still do not control all of the winners' powers."[68] In effect, an official role for the opposition is what Adrian Vermeule terms a "submajority rule" that lowers the threshold necessary for registering concern through official channels that the majority powers are overreaching.[69] Such submajority rules for airing concern may combine with supermajority voting rules to "curb the abuses of unfettered majoritianism."[70]

Formalizing the role of the opposition may perform five key functions: "1) resisting integration into the regime; 2) guarding zones of autonomy against it; 3) disputing its legitimacy; 4) raising the costs of authoritarian role; and 5) creating a credible democratic alternative."[71] The best known of such opposition roles is the shadow cabinet in the United Kingdom, designated as "Her Majesty's Loyal Opposition." Under such a regime, the "dispositions of Opposition and government members to regard each other as constitutional actors—not enemies in a civil war—are facilitated and encouraged by the swing of the pendulum. The alternation of office between two main political parties promotes the understanding that the Opposition is the government-in-waiting and, correspondingly, that the government is the Opposition-in-waiting."[72] As Sujit Choudhry summarizes:

> Regimes of opposition rights have three components. First, they create an opposition team through provisions that encourage the aggregation of, or coordination among, opposition legislators to act collectively. Second, they confer rights exercisable by the opposition team or its recognized leaders that further one or both of the key functions of opposition parties: (a) to scrutinize the conduct of the executive and hold it accountable through powers of oversight; and (b) to provide a government-in-waiting through agenda-setting powers. Third, they contain an enforcement mechanism, consisting of constitutional court referrals and/or speakers of the legislature.[73]

The aim is not formalized power sharing or the diminution of the ability of the prevailing party to form a government independent of the losing opposition. Rather, the goal is to empower the minority with procedural rules that hold the majority to account in its legislative agenda. By forcing such high-stakes decisions to be made more publicly, minority parties are able to better ensure that the majority is aware of public accountability, reducing the likelihood for it to circumvent democracy and empower itself.[74]

Notably, illiberal regimes around the world have eliminated such formal opposition roles in their quest to consolidate strongman power. In Russia, opposition parties have been harassed out of existence, with members arrested and jailed on "minor offenses."[75] In Hungary, Viktor Orbán changed procedures in Parliament, stripping the opposition of the ability to speak on the floor and challenge legislation.[76] The Law and Justice Party (PiS) in Poland eliminated the role of the opposition completely by limiting floor speech time, voting on legislation "*en bloc*" to prevent debate, and sanctioning opposition MPs for minor offenses to exclude them from attending Parliament at all.[77] In India, the Indian National Congress (INC) was without a Leader of the Opposition for several years as the ruling BJP has refused to recognize an opposition leader on the grounds that the INC does not have sufficient numbers.[78]

Any success for empowering the opposition turns on the shared dedication to governance. While that is a noble aim, it cannot be assumed. On this score, recent American political history inspires no confidence. The mechanisms that may help fractionate political power may also serve to frustrate the effective capacity to govern. During the last period of President Obama's second term, the Republicans controlled both houses of Congress. Because the United States is a presidential rather than parliamentary system, this gave the Republicans unlimited ability to set the congressional agenda, in effect a boundless minority platform to show off a different agenda for governing.

The results were not encouraging. In the run-up to the 2016 election, with Hillary Clinton the presumptive nominee, one of the main Republican legislative agenda items was the limitless revisiting of the 2012 attack on the U.S. diplomatic outpost in Benghazi, Libya, while Clinton had been secretary of state in Obama's first administration. Eight different subcommittees held many dozens of hearings on the attacks, continuing the political theater past the election of President Trump.[79] By contrast, even with command of both chambers after 2016, and the presidency, the Republicans advanced no legislation on critical issues such as healthcare or immigration reform.[80]

C. *Independent Oversight*

Both federalism and the formalization of the role of the opposition are premised on divided authority within a shared enterprise. Neither is sustainable if it serves only as a locus of disruption of the ability of the prevailing governing party to govern effectively. Both geographic division of authority and independent oppositional authority within the central government serve to contest unilateral assertions of authority by the dominant executive—the *caudillo* threat to democracy—but do so by increasing the potential veto points that may undermine state competence—another of the deficits of modern democracies. In the popular recounting in the 2021 dystopian political satire movie *Don't Look Up*, the combination of populist agitation and hyper-partisan dysfunction leaves government unable to respond to catastrophic threats to global survival. Fill in climate change, viral pandemics, financial meltdowns, and the picture is all too familiar.

Under conditions of high polarization and relative balance of core constituencies, the contending political parties have a reasonable short-term prospect of capturing both the presidency and Congress. When out of office, the risk is that each party will see immediate gain in frustrating the capability of the governing party and thereby enhance its electoral prospects down the road. At each stage, the risk is that the needs of state are subordinated to future partisan aims. Frances Lee concluded that in positions of rough parity, where each party has a realistic chance to take office, "an out party does not win a competitive edge by participating in, voting for, and thereby legitimating the in party's initiatives. Instead, an out party angling for partisan advantage will look for reasons to withhold support and oppose."[81]

If rival democratic actors cannot contest presidential unilateralism without threatening core state competencies, what is left are strategies for what Cristina Rodriguez refers to as "decentering the presidency," a view that tolerates expanded executive authority not because of its ultimate subservience to the president's electoral mandate, but because of its competence-based ability to respond to political urgency.[82] As Rodriguez frames it, an approach that is more risk seeking, one that seeks to harness the potential of the modern state, must rest on "a conception of politics and politically driven decisionmaking that justifies executive policymaking," a justification that ultimately rests on the need for action and is "much less tied to the Madisonian separation of powers and flawed assumptions about presidential accountability."[83]

No doubt, modern statecraft routinely confronts the moments where, as expressed by Justice Elena Kagan, "the law runs out and policy-laden choice is what is left over."[84] But such moments are ones of risk if there are no institutional partners who, while sharing the aims of the enterprise, push back at how far the executive branch may lead on its own accord. If the institutional response does not come from other governmental actors, at either the state or national levels, then eyes necessarily turn to mechanisms that either reform the internal workings of the executive or create independent oversight entities. These may not be the first best strategies of formal separation of powers across the organs of government, but they may be the best available in a time of partisan dysfunction and the need to rein in unilateral executive authority.

On this score, the careful analysis by Bob Bauer and Jack Goldsmith in *After Trump* bears particular attention.[85] Having respectively served as White House counsel under President Obama and head of the Department of Justice Office of Legal Counsel under President George W. Bush, the authors examine the exploitation of structural weaknesses in formal lines of legal authority during the Trump years and recommend a series of direct reforms to address these. With the exception of a few assessments of foreign relations and war powers, the recommendations are almost all internal to the executive and seek to thwart the ability of a norm-busting president to break through the weak institutional barriers to abuse. Specific protections include shoring up the independence of the Office of Legal Counsel and moving the bulk of the White House Counsel office out of the White House and into the Department of Justice. These are efforts to wall off agency functioning from personalistic power grabs by a rogue president. Other recommendations attempt to ratchet up legal vulnerability for the misuse of the pardon power, while some reinforce shaky ethics and disclosure requirements dealing with conflicts of interest.

Such reforms do not open the process of governing to the opposition; hence, neither offer the prospect of invigorating democratic politics nor the risk of gumming up the process of governance for partisan gain. Internal constraints on the president exercising excess power through the executive branch are not reforms aimed at restoring democratic integrity. These reforms are targeted at an immediate concern over executive excess. They may be joined with other poles of independence in the executive, such as the role of the inspector generals in overseeing both legal compliance and fiscal integrity inside executive agencies. Sadly, this may be the most critical short-term response to further populist assault on norms of governance.

At the same time, these reform efforts are less far-reaching than efforts to create a body outside the formal organs of governance to monitor areas of anticipated governmental misconduct, such as human rights violations. Virtually all European democracies have such an ombudsman or parliamentary minister who is empowered to investigate and challenge official misconduct.[86] Even in an illiberal democracy such as Poland, the ombudsman has proved to be a thorn in the side of efforts by PiS to retaliate against political opponents, particularly the press.[87]

Perhaps most immediately pressing is the reform of election administration. As discussed in Chapter 8, the American experiment with bipartisan oversight of election officials drawn from within the political process came under serious challenge in 2020, and it may not survive another assault in 2024. The efforts to weaponize election administration, drive experienced poll workers out of the enterprise, and hold the entire process hostage to the dictates of legislative majorities spell the end of even the most rudimentary conceptions of elections as moments of popular sovereignty.[88] A system built on reasonable boundaries of trust and forbearance cannot be reconstructed without institutional reform. Trust, once broken, is a lost institutional achievement. The toothpaste does not readily reenter the tube.

III. Democratic Citizens

For as long as there has been popular sovereignty, there have been debates about the level of virtue that such governance demands from its citizens. Going back to

Aristotle, there was an examination of an enhanced capacity in citizens coming together, what today we term the wisdom of the masses: "For even where there are many people, *each has some share of virtue* and practical wisdom; and when they are brought together, just as in the mass they become as it were one man with many pairs of feet and hands and many senses, so also do they become one in regard to character and intelligence."[89]

The governance of a free people required, for Aristotle, that "the good citizen must have the knowledge and ability both to rule and be ruled. That is what we mean by the virtue of a citizen—understanding the governing of free men."[90] Without this foundation of "justice and virtue," the state "cannot be managed at all."[91] The demands for virtue among the citizens continued into the founding era of the American Republic, most forcefully expressed by John Adams in 1776:

> There must be a possitive [*sic*] Passion for the public good, the public Interest, Honour, Power, and Glory, established in the Minds of the People, or there can be no Republican Government, nor any real Liberty. And this public Passion must be Superiour to all private Passions. Men must be ready, they must pride themselves, and be happy to sacrifice their private Pleasures, Passions, and Interests, nay their private Friendships and dearest Connections, when they Stand in Competition with the Rights of society.[92]

Ultimately, the Constitution rested on institutional design rather than faith in citizen virtue. "The idea that people would consistently sacrifice their own good for that of the public struck Madison as a credulous fantasy."[93] And yet, even for Madison, who posited in *Federalist* no. 51 that the structures of government must reflect the fact that men are not angels,[94] there was the nagging sense that a democratic republic must lay claim to some sense of enlightened nobility among the citizenry: "To suppose that any form of government will secure liberty or happiness without any virtue in the people, is a chimerical idea."[95]

Madison's distinction between the inescapability of citizen regard for self-interest and the need for some level of civic virtue defines the precarious balance in democratic sustainability. Inescapably, there must be some level of citizen engagement with democracy as a shared enterprise. The heart of modern commitments to pluralism is a convergence on the process of democratic deliberation even if rival interests constantly exert centripetal pressures. Hence Michael Ignatieff's formulation of democracy turning on a challenge between rivals but not enemies.[96]

It is not just populist rhetoric that challenges the sense of shared enterprise; it is citizens' values themselves. To take but one snapshot, consider polling in the United States that over half of Biden voters and Trump voters strongly agree with the proposition that elected officials of the other party are "presenting a clear and present danger to American democracy"; meanwhile 80 percent or more of respondents somewhat agree with this proposition.[97] When party affiliation is not just a matter of interest or persuasion but becomes a form of blood oath, the capacity of democratic processes to intermediate and channel discord is strained. We enter a world long ago described by David Hume as "when in a faction, [people] are apt, without shame or remorse, to neglect all the ties of honour and morality, in order to serve their party."[98] At the same time, and perhaps paradoxically, under different circumstances it is these same parties that provide the longer view and the need for accommodation. Thus, for political scientists, such as Steven Levitsky and Daniel Ziblatt, democracy turns on the internalization of the norms of forbearance and tolerance, the acceptance of institutional constraints on the exercise of power and acceptance of political opposition as part of a shared and legitimate collective enterprise in self-governance.[99]

To the extent that the institutionalization of a longer view that promotes forbearance and tolerance has been political parties, that transmission mechanism stands in disrepair. Political parties are simply no longer the participatory vehicle of democracy. Well before the emergence of social media, technology had already moved the citizenry to a different engagement with politics:

> The dominance of the television party goes a long way to explain the detachment between citizenship and institutions, voters and elites, which we have experienced in recent years. With its mediatisation of politics, the television party type has eroded the role of the "party on the ground" and strongly contributed to generating a passive attitude in the electorate, reminiscent of the "couch potato" lifestyle attributed to TV viewers. In so doing, it has engendered political apathy, registered in nosediving citizens' trust in political parties and in the severe decline of membership in mainstream parties registration in recent decades.[100]

The ills of political parties in the world of mass media pales before the loss of cohesion introduced by social media. As Nathaniel Persily observes, "traditional media, which had long played a 'gatekeeper' role in setting the agenda for campaign discourse, had been losing ground for some time even before the rise of the Internet. The 2016 contest saw legacy media slip even further."[101] The ensuing triumph of "cheap speech"[102] in turn "undermined mediating and stabilizing institutions of American democracy including newspapers and political parties, with negative social and political consequences."[103] Richard Hasen argues this point forcefully: "Rather than democratizing our politics, cheap speech appears to be hastening the irrelevancy of political parties by facilitating the ability of demagogues to secure support from voters by appealing directly to them, sometimes with incendiary appeals."[104]

In recent elections in the U.S. and abroad, new algorithmic warriors, such as Cambridge Analytica, offered a destructive vision of narrow-cast, retail politics that could appropriate social media algorithms for polarizing campaign efforts. No meaningful content filters were evident in social media platforms that lent themselves to this new political medium. Nor was it clear that there was any longer a scaled return to cost for those who mastered the new political environment. Trump boasted, apparently correctly for once, that he underspent his outmaneuvered political rivals in 2016, especially the established candidates like Jeb Bush and then Hillary Clinton, who both relied primarily on expensive television ads to communicate their campaign messages.[105]

Political parties that had provided the legions of election workers needed for labor-intensive campaigns adapted to mass media by becoming access to capital for mass communication, with parties serving as the "key fundraisers for national candidates, providing expertise and scale, thereby allowing candidates to spend sums necessary for effective advertising."[106] Social media represents the next step in the evolution, allowing candidates to reach out and secure support from voters directly.[107]

Nor is this phenomenon limited to the United States. According to the Italian Five Star Movement's leader, the internet is a powerful tool for directly removing political parties as an intermediary, since "the use of [*sic*] Internet is supposed to allow voters to directly participate in the political process, according to the model of e-democracy, and thus increase transparency and political accountability."[108] When placed on top of an already polarized political system, there is bound to be "a precipitous decline in public confidence in election integrity" and the broader political system.[109] Not only is there a corresponding drop in the readership and success of traditional news media,[110] but also the ensuing distrust in elections is likely to become justified in light of "hyperpolarization mak[ing] partisans far more willing to engage in anti-democratic measures."[111]

It is a short step from politics through social media to what one RAND study captivatingly labeled "truth decay."[112] Social media algorithms create feedback mechanisms that reward radicalization of content[113] and risk fractionating the body politic into a "billion private realities."[114] When listeners hear only what furthers their prior assumptions, they fall prey to a "Credulous Bayesianism" by which the normal filters of checking background reliability of information are suspended.[115] While tech companies may try to moderate the content on their platforms, the scale is overwhelming, and the efforts to use artificial intelligence mechanisms either with or especially without human controllers have thus far been disappointing.[116] Because of the democratic implications of the power to remove speech from the realm of political discourse, efforts have been made to create a species of "digital constitutionalism."[117] The most prominent example is Facebook's Oversight Board, a court-like body comprised of an exemplary group of academics and civic leaders from around the world.[118]

A. *Meeting Demand*

Three forms of response immediately present themselves: market, internal, and regulatory. Ideally, of course, there would be a market for a centrist return to filtered content. The experience with social media thus far is that simple market mechanisms are unlikely to restore democratic norms to social media-generated content. Jack Balkin well captures the incentives toward polarization:

> Market competition won't produce the kind of culture and knowledge necessary for democratic self-government, democratic culture, or the growth and spread of knowledge. Markets will underproduce the kinds of speech and knowledge goods that support political and cultural democracy; they will underproduce the kinds of institutions that will reliably discover and spread knowledge. Conversely, market incentives will overproduce conspiracy theories and speech that undermines democratic institutions. When social media are dominated by a small number of powerful economic actors, their incentives are not much better.[119]

In an ideal environment, one could also rely upon internal guidance within the operation of the tech firms that would, in turn, produce the professional norms necessary to promote the "democratic competence" of today's sources of information production.[120] Canada, with limited results, has tried an information-forcing regime of disclosure of the sources of partisan messaging through the Election Modernization Act.[121] The main problem is that the ultimate consumer of this information, the social media user prone to hyperpolarized rhetoric, may simply not care. Many of the reform proposals assume that distorted depictions of the world are foisted upon citizens who would prefer to know something that in the spirit of the Enlightenment would be known as truth. All evidence seems to point in the opposite direction.[122] The sorting algorithms used by the various social media platforms may exacerbate the insularity of incoming information, but it is hard to believe that the problem is entirely supply driven by the profit motives of social media. Unfortunately, a large part of this polarizing phenomenon rests on the demand side of the equation.

Proposals that try to dampen polarization by allowing social media users to score the reliability of sources,[123] run into the same problem that social media might well be delivering what users desire. Perhaps those preferences might be altered by educating citizens "to critically assess online information, to recognize malicious interference, to avoid online manipulation, and to engage effectively in public debate."[124] But, at bottom, social media evidently fills a demand, and social media companies "were not created principally to serve democratic values and do not have as their lodestar the fostering of a well-informed and critically minded electorate."[125]

In turn, this leads to proposals that forgo citizen self-help and instead mandate filters through the social media platforms. The significance of this shift should not be lost. It represents an abandonment of the marketplace-of-ideas concept that has, for at least a century, dominated American thinking on efforts to limit speech. Not surprisingly, efforts to address social media polarization through legislative restrictions on content have been tentative and have largely stalled around the world, confronting the inevitable risk of suppressing disfavored political speech.[126] This is particularly true in the United States, where any "laws restricting the Internet must meet strict scrutiny . . . plac[ing] the Internet in the same, protected media category as newspapers."[127]

This leaves the paradoxical demand that private capital assumes a power to regulate speech that would be questionable under European or American law if claimed by the state. Take, for example, the most high-profile case of a social media blackout, the banning of *President* Trump in the aftermath of January 6th. The highlighting of president underscores the fact that he was still the democratically elected president of the U.S., yet banned from a major source of public information by the unilateral action of dominant private actors. Facebook suspended his account on January 7, and Twitter banned him on January 8. The precipitating event was a video Trump posted on social media at 4:21 PM on January 6, urging the mob to "go home" while praising their actions and perpetuating the claims that the election was fraudulent.[128] About an hour and a half later, Facebook removed the post for violating its Community Standards.[129] At 6:07 PM, President Trump posted a written statement on Facebook claiming that he had truly won the election in a landslide and claimed that "great patriots" were stripped of their victory.[130] Eight minutes later, Facebook removed the post.[131] The next day, Facebook, after reviewing President Trump's posts, his off-platform communications, and additional information about violence at the Capitol, blocked President Trump's account "indefinitely and for at least the next two weeks until the peaceful transition of power is complete."[132]

Facebook's Oversight Board upheld the immediate suspension as having "struck an appropriate balance in light of the continuing risk of violence and disruption,"[133] but it rescinded Trump's indefinite suspension. Now comes the paradox. The decision of Facebook and Twitter to remove Trump from social media probably did more than anything else to dampen the level of social unrest in the period between January 6th and the inauguration of President Biden. In the period between the election and January 6th, Trump turned to Twitter more than 400 times to attack the legitimacy of the election.[134] After January 6th, there was silence.

At the same time, the stated rationale for the social media ban was that Trump applauded those who had engaged in violence and mayhem, not that his post on January 6th speech met the First Amendment definition of incitement, framed narrowly as "advocacy [that] is directed to inciting or producing imminent lawless action and is likely to incite or produce such action."[135] Even under European proportionality rules, there would have to be a heightened showing of the ineffectuality "of setting specific limits to the authorisation or to the prohibition."[136] In other words, had the silencing of Trump come as a result of government action, it is likely that American and European law would have condemned that as a violation of fundamental speech liberties.

Unfortunately, there is no escaping the dilemma that any effort at "content moderation" necessitates the suppression of non-conforming speech regardless of whether the source is state authority or private capital. Whether in the ad hoc fashion employed in Turkey or in the dystopian interventions under China's "Golden Shield," the result is a powerful system of censorship that can easily be harnessed by the world's repressive regimes. Meanwhile other autocrats, as in Brazil, use state authority not to modulate content but to disable the disablers by forbidding internet platforms from removing content.[137] There are innumerable legal issues raised by the efforts to regulate speech, as in the United States under the First Amendment[138] and Section 230 of the Communications Decency Act,[139] which limits the liability of social media companies. But the most pressing issue is not the question of the application of particular legal regimes but the difficulty of framing the objectives of any response to the fragmenting power of social media.

One person's moderation easily becomes another person's power to silence. In 2016, the European Commission and large social media companies voluntarily agreed to work in tandem to remove hate speech promptly from their platforms once those posts were identified.[140] Germany went even further and established stringent timelines for mandating removal of speech it deemed unlawful while also imposing heavy penalties for any company that failed to comply within the appropriate period.[141] The types of unlawful speech covered by those requirements "includ[e] . . . hate speech, public incitement to crime, dissemination of depictions of violence, forming criminal or terrorist organizations, and defamation," among others.[142] Considering such broad measures, there are concerns about the removal of these posts as being tantamount to censorship.[143] But the larger concern is that the policies have seemed to backfire, as those who have had posts taken down are using "censorship" as a sign of legitimacy for their radical viewpoints.[144]

Adam Littlestone-Luria well captures the further paradox of how models devised in democratic regimes quickly become their opposite:

> Germany's Network Enforcement Act (NetzDG)[145]—a stringent intermediate liability regime requiring immediate removal of material deemed "obviously illegal" according to standards defined by government—has become a paradigm that other nations in Europe and around the world now use as a model, sometimes allowing regimes with authoritarian tendencies to invoke the Germany model as a fig-leaf for suppression.[146]

Notably, when Vladimir Putin sought to ensure monochromatic presentation of the war against Ukraine as the final battle of the anti-Nazi crusade of World Warr II, one of his first moves was to shut down Facebook and Instagram.[147] The danger of government control of speech is not behind us.

Finally, there is the question of the efficacy of using prohibition against mass movements with ample bases of support. Once banned, Trump's favorability ratings rebounded, and the ban itself has been a source of political mobilization among his supporters.[148] The banning of Trump, whether directly or implicitly, also galvanized the legal challenge to tech immunity, including from leading jurists such as Supreme Court Justice Clarence Thomas and D.C. Circuit Judge Laurence Silberman.[149]

C. Small Bore Reform

Much of the controversy over the power of the social media giants turns on issues tangential to the problem addressed here of the distancing of the citizenry from collective engagement with democratic society. Social media facilitates a descent into non-overlapping existences. The ability to have a curated engagement with facts or falsehoods about the world voids the collective sense of what Emile Durkheim in the realm of religion called "group rituals."[150] The loss of the coordinating references of another era—the soothing voice of Walter Cronkite on the evening news comes readily to mind—translates into a lack of shared references among the society. Neither breaking up the social media giants under the force of antitrust law nor changing liability rules is likely to have much impact on the risk of tribalism. It may be that democracy requires first and foremost an identification of the citizenry as part of the "demos" that frames the society. In the absence of a sense of belonging to a demos, societies risk a "tribal epistemology"[151] in which "toxic systems compromise good individuals with ease . . . not by demanding we betray our values but by enlisting our values such that we betray each other."[152]

Perhaps there are moderating institutional arrangements, even if quite limited. There are mechanisms drawn from other domains that serve to coordinate conduct around best practices, without intrusive government regulation. Standards-setting organizations, such as the International Organization for Standardization (ISO), provide a way of coordinating practices from railroad gauges to film speeds to the size of nuts and bolts (literally). Such coordination "reduc[es] information and bargaining costs for producers and consumers, and by obviating duplicative systems,"[153] allowing firms to realize network benefits without either costly negotiation or trial and error.[154] Standardization organizations, without the power to censor, serve across a number of domains. For example, the Entertainment Software Ratings Board (ESRB) sets the standard for what *voluntary* labels are placed on video games based on the content of the game.[155] Similarly, the Motion Picture Association of America (MPAA) was generated by both the need to set "guidelines for acceptable film content" and to avoid the uncertainty of being unable to match government censorship standards.[156]

In some circumstances, standards plus certification has a way of warning consumers, as with the Good Housekeeping Seal of Approval, the Wirecutter recommendations from the *New York Times,* or the Michelin restaurant ratings. None of these has the force of government behind it, yet all steer conduct. These standards empower the consumer to act on the basis of greater information and force information to be disclosed in a coherent way that facilitates informed consumer decision-making. The critical issue, however, is trust in the expertise and the disinterestedness of the reviewers. Unfortunately, the prevailing climate is one of distrust in expertise and the ensuing disputation of claims of authority.

Hostility to claims of objective authority by experts is especially rampant in an era of "fake news" and "alternative truths." The ability to mobilize user awareness through the *Washington Post*'s Fact Checker and its Pinocchio ratings is likely to be seen as determined by the fairly transparent editorial preferences of that paper and its owner, Jeff Bezos. One example is a Facebook effort to return control to the user, who can alter the information received through a "scoring system" of the trustworthiness of news sources.[157] Similarly, Facebook has attempted to prioritize sources based on the response it has on other users, measured by comments or shares.[158] Although this latter structure is a relatively cheap method to check information and shields the company from criticism that they selectively target certain viewpoints, the crowd-sourced method of ranking content is unlikely to convert the faithful. It remains easy to dismiss a menu of reliable sources as being just one more example of fake news.[159] Moreover, leaving it to the large tech companies to foster democratic spirit runs up against the reality that they are profit-seeking enterprises not organized around democratic principles.[160]

So far, the most promising, if limited, efforts aim at having "Internet corporations . . . develop some tools for de-indexing fake new [*sic*] websites after their nature is checked by independent authorities."[161] The desire for disclosure and transparency is seen in other arguments that social media companies should be viewed as "information fiduciaries," which would impose on them a "duty of loyalty, good faith, and candid disclosure regarding how user data is employed" and how information is disseminated on their platforms.[162]

One feature of social media does seem redressable, even if a limited issue. The scoring algorithms themselves suggest content that reinforces the push toward extremes. The compounding effect of inflammatory sites leading to similar sources and creating a closed loop is one issue that does seem addressable, even if the specifics of how to do so are beyond this inquiry. As discussed above in the European context, there are some effective efforts to remove hate speech, a more limited problem than dissemination of falsehoods. The types of unlawful speech covered by those requirements "includ[e] . . . hate speech, public incitement to crime, dissemination of depictions of violence, forming criminal or terrorist organizations, and defamation," among others.[163] Unfortunately, this content is a manifestation of the core problem of social media breaking down collective identities. It is not the central issue in democratic disengagement.

Sadly, little in our collective experience thus far suggests a ready path to repair fostering collective understandings. Perhaps one technological fix can slow the rate of acceleration of polarization, even if not addressing the fundamental underlying political dynamics. Recent attention has focused not on social media as such but on the rewards to polarization as a function of how communication goes viral. The origins of the current conception of viral content can be traced to 2009, when both Facebook and Twitter launched the "like" and "retweet" features, respectively.[164] In 2012, Facebook introduced the "share" button to its mobile app, allowing users to quickly share content from their mobile phones, as opposed to the desktop landing page, and other platforms followed suit.[165] Social media increasingly provided a platform where confirmation and negativity bias flourished with algorithmic guidance.[166] In 2019, the Senate Select Committee on Intelligence highlighted how foreign entities had used fake journalists at shell publications to exploit viral networks in a campaign of disinformation.[167]

In turn, increased virality on Facebook and Twitter is tied to political media content, with negative, political out-group language being shared more likely.[168] Content containing criticism of the opposing political party creates the most engagement among both liberal and conservative leaders, the rewards to "going negative."[169] The resulting "attention economy" incentivizes the creation of viral content despite the negative externalities this creates.[170] In the realm of politics, social media has become one of the dominant ways constituents interact with their representatives and political organizations, or express their own opinions and views.[171] Overall, the factors contributing to increasing virality include out-group subjects, negativity, and having an in-group source.[172]

The early optimism created by the role of social media during the Arab Spring[173] soon gave way to what Martin Gurri has termed a "universal solvent," highlighting its ability to disintegrate modes of governances without providing alternative visions of organization or governance.[174] Both Jonathan Haidt and Jonathan Rauch tie the views together by seeking to disable the like, retweet, and other functions that both facilitate dissemination and promote a certain type of virality.[175]

Slowing down human response time might seem an odd step to control the destructive potential of new technology, but it is not without analogues. For example, the modern QWERTY keyboard was apparently created to manage jamming typewriters and slow down typists before they made a mistake.[176] Early typists were simply too fast for the machine's primitive stroke and reset function. While path dependence has left us with an inefficient key template in the age of computer keyboards, the progress of technology nonetheless required an early intervention when human capabilities outstripped social utility. Removing the easy mechanisms for inflammatory content to go viral may serve a similar training function for how humans use machines.

IV. The Future of Democratic Politics

Two hundred years ago, Benjamin Constant presented his famous lecture in Paris titled *The Liberty of the Ancients Compared with That of the Moderns*. Writing in the aftermath of the French Revolution, Constant framed the concept of liberty around the form of governance that differentiated the relation of the governed to the direction of society. For Constant, the "liberty of the ancients consisted in carrying out collectively but directly many parts of the over-all functions of government, coming together in the public square" for common deliberation and decision.[177] By contrast, the modern conception of liberty was premised centrally on the autonomy of the individual, the freedom from arbitrary use of state authority, and the ability to participate in the selection of those to whom governance is entrusted. Modern citizens "no longer experience political participation as an intrinsically rewarding form of action."[178]

This contrast in the relation of the citizen to governing institutions continues to define the struggles of democracies. To the extent that democracy can permit direct participation, the problem of political elites imposing their will is reduced.

But citizens confront the limitations of experience and time. Decisions ranging from long-term fiscal integrity to military preparedness will likely prove beyond the ability of lay generalists. Representative government filters decision-making through institutional actors who can draw on broader knowledge, but in so doing invariably introduce the costs that arise between principals and their agents. For Madison, writing in *Federalist*, no. 10, the intermediation of representation was an added virtue that allowed the expanded geographic scale of the Republic to overcome the passion and parochialism associated with the small domain of direct decision-making.[179] But the distance between the governors and the governed risks estrangement. If citizens are not going to take up the responsibility of governing directly, some other form of engagement in democracy must be found. Elections alone do not suffice.

The past several centuries of Western democracy have largely been organized around institutional forms of channeling citizen input, primarily political parties and other instruments of civil society that act as an intermediate between the individual and the state. These intermediaries represent the citizens before the representatives, as it were. This role is rarely formalized, and the American founding generation unwisely thought that separation of authority would exist only at the level of formal government institutions.

These intermediaries are now in a state of serious disrepair. The erosion of participatory endeavors, what Robert Putnam captured as *Bowling Alone*,[180] is reflected in decreasing membership in unions, churches, civic associations, and the other places were citizens reach beyond themselves. Without input from civil society, there is an increasingly plebiscitary air to even formally representative democracies. Time has also not been kind to the Madisonian insight that the scale of the Republic would defeat factional interests. Technology shrunk the geographic divide and allowed the modern political parties to exist across broad territories. And the rise of digital communication has allowed a plebiscitary world to engage the citizens directly and frequently.

Not surprisingly, the ease of communication has revitalized claims favoring deliberative forms of democracy. Consider two of the more prominent. For the past thirty years, American political scientist James Fishkin has not just advocated but also put into practice in a number of countries a program of what he terms deliberative polling.[181] The practice involves gathering random citizens to spend days in study of contemporary governance issues with the aim "not just to ask them their impression of sound bites and headlines as in conventional polling, but rather to engage them in many moderated small group discussions with trained moderators who help them engage with balanced and evidence based materials."[182] In turn, the hope is that these individuals would emerge as opinion leaders for those citizens not selected or unable to devote the intensive time required.[183] Rather than trusting institutional actors, such as political parties, to educate the rationally uninformed voters, the proposals by Fishkin and his collaborators would trust that process to be conducted by expert facilitators, a difficult proposition in a polarized political environment.

By contrast, political theorist Hélène Landemore bypasses any concept of expert education in favor of the inherent "wisdom of the masses," an application of the mathematical principles of large numbers yielding more reliable results, as first formulated in the 18th century by the Marquis de Condorcet. For Landemore, inherent in democracy and majority rule is the power of this statistical principle, allowing a well-constructed system of government to maximize the chances that a country picks the "best" political answer.[184] The Condorcet rule requires a single dimension (go to war or remain at peace) and that individuals have a more likely than not chance of knowing the right answer, and that they do so in isolation from each other.[185] Condorcet formulated his theory as a maxim for jury determinations of guilt or innocence. There the jury is convened for only one task, and its decisional framework is preset.

None of these conditions can be assumed in the real world of political governance. Few political choices other than selecting one of two candidates comes prepackaged as a binary choice, and the assumption of greater than 50 percent chance of having accurate knowledge is fanciful, particularly when the issues are ones of contested policy, rather than true/false fact. And in a world of echo chambers driven by social media,[186] there is no prospect of what Condorcet would have termed juror independence.[187] Nonetheless, the Condorcet models continue to have support in the fact that there is wisdom in more rather than less.[188]

Perhaps more interesting is that Landemore goes further by taking up the concept of direct citizen governance, in the style of the Greeks of old. If the wisdom truly resides in the citizens in the aggregate, why not let them govern directly, also without intermediation? Hence the resurrection of the lottery as a randomized draw upon the time of individual citizens to assume the role of state officials.[189] As Landemore explains, the proposal is not unlike jury duty:

> Lottocratic representatives are selected by lot and frequently rotated. The combination of sortition and rotation ensures that lottocratic assemblies are accessible and "open" to all, not spatially speaking, since those not selected are excluded, but over time. . . . One might think of the open mini-public as a supersized version of the criminal jury in the American system. . . . The open mini-public is meant to be to the criminal jury what a full-grown tree is to a bonsai: a much larger, less constrained, and more empowered entity, fully expressing the

democratic potential of trusting a larger, descriptively representative group of ordinary citizens.[190]

Whatever the practicalities of these claims to direct citizen involvement, it is notable that both Fishkin and Landemore begin with individuals untethered to any form of institutional participation. Both begin with random lotteries that bring together diverse cuts of the American public, Fishkin in order to improve each voter as an example, and Landemore to tap their already existing collective wisdom. Each represents a vision of politics shorn of institutional engagements. Each has found small measures of support as political parties are seen as diminished entities. Yet, if such politics without parties sounds fanciful, as it no doubt will after centuries of democracy centered on nonstate political institutions, the question is what is the alternative?

The postwar period of optimism, cresting in the post-1989 aftermath of the fall of the Soviet empire, had its great exposition in the rise of social democracy. It was not only that parties defined the politics of the time but also that the divide between them framed the broad contours of democracy struggling against its authoritarian rivals. Regardless of whether the center-left or center-right was in power in Europe, the core tenets of both market freedoms and welfarist protections defined the postwar consensus of politics. The period preceding the rise of populism also marked the demise of social democratic ascendency. It is hard to carry forward that optimism about the future prospects of political parties as they have existed through most of the 19th and 20th centuries. A quick glimpse at the state of the major parties in France and Germany confirms the earlier discussion about the conditions for party erosion (Figures 9.2 a &b).[191]

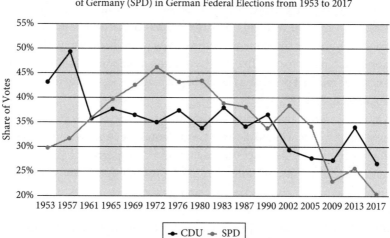

Share of votes for the Christian Democratic Union (CDU) and Social Democratic Party of Germany (SPD) in German Federal Elections from 1953 to 2017

Figure 9.2a   *Source:* https://www.statista.com/statistics/1037985/cdu-and-spd-vote-share-by-election/

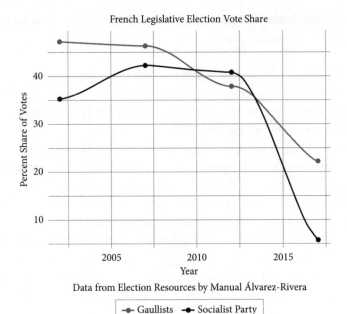

French Legislative Election Vote Share

Data from Election Resources by Manual Álvarez-Rivera

—•— Gaullists —•— Socialist Party

Figure 9.2b   *Source:* electionresources.org/fr/

These rates of decline are dramatic for the parties that essentially defined the postwar consensus. The loss of political parties compromises the ability to integrate disparate interests in common enterprise. Social scientists use the concept of "pernicious polarization" to describe a level of political divide that crosses over from contestation to enmity. As described by the authors of the leading Carnegie Endowment study note: "The rise of an 'us versus them' mindset and political identity in American sociopolitical life is evident in everything from the rise of highly partisan media to the decline in Americans' willingness to marry someone from the opposing political party."[192] The conclusion is far from rosy: "The most common outcome of episodes where democracies reached pernicious levels of polarization was some form of major democratic decline."[193]

Time may prove that parties can reconstitute themselves more easily in Europe than in the United States. Continental election systems allow for greater party creative destruction because of the proportional representation system. Basically, a disenchanted rump of a former party can reorganize itself and seek participation in a coalition government. Or, as in the case of Emanuel Macron in France, the technocratic remnants of the Socialist Party could be hastily reorganized to compete in the multiple-round presidential election.

In the U.S., as well as in countries that have a single winner for elected office, the pressure of the electoral system pushes to reliance on two and only two parties. Dubbed Duverger's law,[194] any effort to form a third party in a single-peaked election means pulling votes from the nearest political ally in favor of the most distant party. In simple terms, the Tea Party never left the Republicans, for fear of dividing the conservative vote and delivering elections to the Democrats. Similarly, the various more left-wing forces among the Democrats hesitate to spin off and compromise the prospects of their traditional allies.

Yet, in the array of populist forces that have claimed electoral mandates in recent years, the U.S. is the only case of the subversion of democracy having been launched from within one of the established parties. It is inconceivable that a democracy would last long without electoral contestation between political rivals that accept the basic tenets of democratic competition. The question seems to be less of prognosticating the exact form that the reconstruction of political competition will take and more preserving as much as possible of the foundations for the future. To return to Tocqueville's early observation about the prospects of the American Republic, the question is to have the breathing space to make retrievable mistakes.

If indeed the future holds a form of democratic politics with different central institutions than the ones we have known thus far, time will no doubt tell. But in the interim, it is possible to address specific barriers to the effectiveness of political parties that may slow down their decline or perhaps even restore a measure of institutional responsibility to democratic politics. The fact that the phenomenon of party decline is so consistent in the democratic world invariably leads the inquiry to broader trends. Nonetheless, the general should not crowd out the particular. There are national-level rules and procedures governing the electoral process that may accelerate or retard the collapse of political parties. Two examples from the U.S. address the distinct problems created by the private funding of political campaigns and by the nomination process of candidates for office.

A. *Funding the Parties*

Beginning with the post-Watergate reforms, particularly after the concerns over soft money in the 1990s, campaign finance reform laws have increasingly squeezed money out of the political parties. The trend for money to flow to alternative avenues of influence, what Pamela Karlan and I termed the "hyrdraulics of campaign finance," began more than twenty years ago,[195] only increased after the ill-fated McCain-Feingold amendments to federal campaign law. The result has been to incentivize lone-wolf fundraising and to push the financing of elections away from the party and toward the candidates.[196] Lost in the trade was the capacity of parties to "create[] mutually beneficial arrangements to satisfy those willing to join the party coalition against rivals who might take benefits away."[197] Because these benefits are up for grabs in every election, electoral competition creates for the parties a necessary "incentive[] to avoid extremism that might jeopardize seats in the legislature . . . [and as a result, moderation becomes the] . . . byproduct of their pursuit of power."[198] The historic trend away from this moderating role for parties is compounded by "social-media-driven fundraising, often fueled by hyperpartisan or inflammatory statements. Some new members come into office with large followings and the ability to raise huge sums of money independently. Those members have been willing to publicly break with their party's leadership or harshly criticize other members."[199] As one representative noted, "You're often awarded for the most extreme things you say and the biggest attacks you launch."[200]

In effect, there are currently no limits on contributions into politics, save through official channels. Super PACs and other organizations can funnel unlimited amounts of money into support of individual candidates, and candidate-affiliated super PACs dominate fundraising at the individual level. Some money comes in from small donors, but that exacerbates polarization by fueling extreme candidates.[201] The result is an institutional shift toward the extremes because "as donors become more ideologically extreme, they tend to prefer giving directly to candidates . . . that reflect their ideological preferences."[202] As political scientists La Raja and Schaffner conclude, "when the pragmatic party organization has a restricted role in elections, the opportunities expand for more ideological elements to support party candidates. As candidates rely increasingly on the purists for their campaigns, the collective party becomes more ideological and distinctive."[203]

In turn, the party organization loses not only power but also relevance, with political "leadership lack[ing] the disciplinary power over their members that they once held" because the "financial support for candidates has now shifted . . . to outside organizations, such as super PACs and their formidable war chests."[204] Because money is the capital of elections, when super PACs are the financing operations, politicians who depend more heavily on these outside donors are more likely to curry their favor.[205] These outside influences on voting behavior also open the door for "free agent successors" to challenge and ultimately replace party crusaders, which in turn "fragment[s] the party's voting cohesion."[206] By contrast, La Raja and Schaffner find that when states place "few[er] restrictions" on party campaign financing, there is "less polarization of parties."[207]

A proposal suggests itself from the following pieces: (a) money outside the parties polarizes; (b) money in the parties does not polarize to the same extent; (c) the limitations on money in politics have not worked; and (d) that the hydraulic pressures of money lead finance to the paths of least resistance. The conclusion is as evident as it is a shocking departure from current practice. The time has come to abandon the current system of campaign finance. We should permit money to flow freely to political parties with only disclosure as a condition. Right now, that system exists—but only to outside organizations and only with partial levels of disclosure. Better to have the money flow to the parties and through them to provide some protection to less extreme candidates who now fear donor retaliation. Money in the parties also gives more power to efforts to legislate for the longer term—not just for Twitter.

There remain many technical details to resolve, including the form of disclosure, what the right levels for disclosure should be, and how to police against the introduction of foreign money, if that continues to be prohibited. These are important questions of application, but beyond what is necessary to address here. The main point is that if parties play a useful filtering role on passion and polarization, and if a central objective is to thwart the tendency toward tribalized politics, it is time to put our money where our mouths are, almost literally.

B. *Breaking the Tyranny of the Minority of the Majority*

Invariably, we return to the time horizon of populism as opposed to the forms of democratic governance associated with stable political parties. Most colorfully expressed, "strong party government is like a marriage, which enables its members to invest and plan for the whole family and for the long term. By contrast, in the colorful language of Argentinian commentator Eduardo Fidanza, weak parties are prone to patronage deals that are more like sex for pay."[208]

If political institutions matter, so does the manner in which those institutions operate. As party control has waned in the U.S., the primaries have emerged as the fulcrum of electoral politics, especially as court doctrine has allowed partisan gerrymandering a relatively free hand.[209] The single most salient characteristic of primaries is that they have low turnout and that those voters who do turn out represent the extremes of the party, far from the median voter.[210] Not for nothing, the emergence of the menacing political verb phrase "to primary" demonstrates the threatened vengeance of the activist wings of the parties on any candidate who dares depart from the polarizing direction of American politics. And with the fragmentation of political authority and the veto power of the polarized wings of the parties comes the general inability to govern, to compromise, to act for ends beyond the immediate. This is the spiral that yields what William Galston beautifully quipped as "the tyranny of the minority of the majority."

It may be impossible to restore the parties to the role they played when they stood as the expositors for mass institutions, but that does not mean that ill-considered legal regulations should not be reevaluated, particularly when they exacerbate institutional frailty. Consider the proposals of Frances Rosenbluth and Ian Shapiro with regard to the problem of extreme activists using low turnout in primaries to hijack the will of the parties.[211] While our democratic ethos may make it impossible to get rid of primaries altogether, even where voter turnout is shockingly low, this does not exhaust the range of potential reforms:

> Getting rid of primaries is likely impossible, but a rule that declared Convention delegates unbound by primary results in which turnout fell below, say, 75 percent of the party's vote share in the previous general election would blunt the power of activists at party extremes. Still better would be reforms that allowed the party's sitting representatives and senators to select the candidate if the 75 percent threshold was not met. Rule changes of this kind might not be such a difficult sell politically, because proposing them would highlight the exceedingly low turnout in most primary races.[212]

The use of voting rules to blunt the effects of polarization does resonate in recent experience. These mechanisms may restore to some extent the attentiveness of the parties to the median voter. The most interesting recent example comes in Virginia, a state that Joe Biden carried with 10 percent of the vote in 2020,[213] but the governor's office was won a year later by a Republican, Glenn Youngkin, with an almost 2 percent advantage in the popular vote.[214] While the electorate may be somewhat different in presidential and off-year elections, and while Biden's popularity was in precipitous fall by November 2021, the real explanation lies elsewhere. The Republican Party chose to hold a nominating convention rather than a primary and then selected the candidate through ranked-choice voting rather than the plurality winner who would typically emerge from a primary. As explained by one of the leaders of the state Republican Party, this two-prong approach both reinforced the collective enterprise of the state party and then filtered candidates toward moderation:

> First, the convention efficiently reconciled the pro-Trump and Trump-skeptical wings of the Republican Party in a nomination contest featuring seven gubernatorial candidates from across the Republican

spectrum. In a state like Virginia, where Democrats have won state-wide elections for a decade, both wings of the party are essential to victory. A primary that turned into a "who is the most Trump-like candidate" would have lost the Trump-skeptical voters, and a primary that produced a Trump-skeptical general election candidate would have struggled with Trump-supporting Republicans. We couldn't afford to lose either group. By using ranked-choice voting, we ensured our nominees represented the broad consensus of Republicans.[215]

Other states experiment with mechanisms that force a second round in elections before a winner is declared. There are competing mechanisms to facilitate a pathway for more centrist candidates to bypass the polarizing pull of the primary system. These may include a second round that demands a clear majority winner or forcing a second round of the "top two" system in California, where the top vote getters advance to the general election regardless of party, or as in Alaska, the "Nonpartisan Top Four Primary Election."[216] These mechanisms do not allow a thin plurality in a low-turnout election to control. They require a second stage to secure that effect, something that ranked choice allows in a one-step primary.

Consider the 2021 Buffalo mayoral election as a cautionary note. Buffalo is a one-party Democratic town, with a multiple term incumbent mayor, Byron Brown. In the party primary, Brown was narrowly defeated by a declared socialist, India Walton, who drew support from national party progressives, such as Alexandria Ocasio-Cortez. Walton received 11,000 of the 21,000 votes cast.[217] Brown was forced to run for re-election as a write-in candidate, appearing nowhere on the ballot—in fact, there were no other candidates on the ballot other than Walton. Brown managed to win almost 60 percent of the votes, despite not being on the ballot, in an election where over 64,000 voters turned out.[218] Though Brown may have been out of touch and lackluster as a mayor—the socialist label did not command support in Buffalo overall, just among a large enough slice to prevail in the low-turnout primary.

Buffalo shows the paradox captured by Galston's concern about the minority of the majority having too much power. With the weakness of the parties in terms of money and messaging, they too readily become subject to takeover by an activist minority, fueled by small donors or a few large benefactors and committed to the margins of electoral politics, not to governing.

Ranked-choice voting and run-offs will not check the fractionating pressures on American politics in an era of weak parties and strong polarization. Nor will pulling money into the parties of itself arrest the decline of democratic politics in an era when the political class is increasingly distanced from the intermediary institutions that ground successful democratic politics. Somehow the institutional forms of a new democratic politics will need to develop in the shadow of democratic decline. These small steps may arrest the complete collapse of our politics or slow down the process so that time will allow new institutional mechanisms to emerge. To return to Tocqueville once again, the populist period underscores the importance of allowing all systems to make retrievable mistakes.

EPILOGUE

Glimmers of Hope?

Back in the post-1989 period, the rise of liberal democracy may have seemed inevitable, perhaps even the final stage of historical development. There is the risk that the illusion of the inevitable good will cede to the passive acceptance of the predestined bad. This book chronicles enough frailties of democratic governance to reinforce a sense of gloom. In the spirit of never leaving a dinner party, even a dreary one, without complimenting the host on the food, so too it would be improper to end simply on a tone of despair.

It is important to recall that the first recent populist upsurge took place in Latin America and collapsed in relatively short order from the chaos and corruption that plague anti-institutional governance. So too the weakness of democratic governments in the recent past should not equate to an overestimation of the current wave of populists in office. History may show that, as exemplified by Donald Trump, their reign was more characterized by the weaknesses they could exploit than what they could create as an alternative. The same problems of chaos and corruption that plagued the first round of late 20th-century populists are never far from the 21st-century variants.

The polarization of politics, the dissolution of a common understanding of facts and history, and the distrust of science and expertise are looming dangers. But a large number of institutions held up relatively well during the period of populist assault, most forcefully orchestrated by President Trump after losing the 2020 election. Some of the institutions were no doubt so far removed culturally and politically that there was little chance of succumbing to direct White House pressure—the most obvious example would be the universities. Another example would be the mass media, again skewing decidedly against Trump as a matter of politics, but constantly challenging falsehoods on matters ranging from COVID-19 to the election. These media may be in decline in importance and general acceptance, but they provided important counternarratives to the barrage of outrage on Twitter. Other institutions stayed the course and refused to lend their authority to a repudiation of democratic norms—with the courts providing the clearest example in the post-election period.

Less visible, but perhaps equally important, was resistance from quarters not inclined to public intervention. Chaos and corruption may serve the populist moment, but it threatens institutions beyond the narrow realm of politics: "When domestic and foreign businesses invest in the United States—helping to create jobs—or when investors buy U.S. Treasuries—helping to fund the government programs on which Americans depend—they are relying on [the rule of law as a] bedrock."[1] Ceaseless attacks on core American institutions spill over into critical domains of economic security. As I addressed with Robert Rubin, the former secretary of the treasury: "Business decisions are enormously affected by confidence, and the rule of law is integral to confidence. Businesses must be confident that contracts will be enforced and property rights will be honored. If that confidence is shaken by such a fundamental matter as setting aside the voters' choices in favor of legislatures' dictation of an election's outcomes, the consequences could be devastating."[2]

As discussed in Chapter 8, the political institutions and electoral apparatus held in Michigan in 2020 in the face of unprecedented pressure from a president seeking to overturn election results. Alongside the laudable institutional resilience was the less visible backing of the mainstay economic bastions of Michigan. Fearing an economic environment in which President Trump's continued onslaught on the truth divides consumer bases, business leaders in Michigan wrote to the state Republican Party urging them not to push restrictive election laws through the state legislature.[3] In the letter, business leaders noted that "government has a responsibility to continuously improve and strengthen election administration, because public faith in the security and integrity of our elections is fundamental."[4] The polarized atmosphere that stems from weakened democratic institutions and populist attacks on government forces business to "pick sides" between divided consumer bases,[5] an environment not welcoming to would-be investors. Even after President Trump's defeat, these trends have persisted. On the one-year anniversary of the January 6th insurrection, businesses across the country released statements condemning the events, highlighting again the choices businesses are forced to make as political polarization spreads even to consumer markets.[6]

In their book *How to Save a Constitutional Democracy*, Tom Ginsburg and Aziz Huq address the themes mentioned here, highlighting the ways the weakening of institutions of democratic governance can have implications outside the political arena. Ginsburg and Huq discuss countries that "stav[ed] off a slide from democracy," noting that often this involved unexpected alliances between parties on the right and the left rooted in a shared conviction of "the importance of political support for democracy as a going concern."[7] Perhaps this is the path by which the business community, typically shy in taking political stances, provides ballast for efforts to push back against the antidemocratic actions of the Republican Party.

At the same time, the handful of case studies of nations that pulled back from the brink is missing one key ingredient. Typically, the way back was led by the parties who rallied to thwart the advance of antidemocratic elements. The era of weak political parties is an ongoing concern, as has been documented throughout this book. Still, and again returning to Tocqueville, democratic societies are replete with nonstate civil institutions that in ways large and small help guide through troubled historical times. The basic institutions of American society have held through a civil war, the dismantling of the slave economy, presidential assassinations, world wars, domestic intrigue, and all manner of civil unrest as the society's democratic promises were grudgingly extended to the victims of history. There should be enough resilience to survive the populist assault, even when led by a sitting president.

Finally, some glimmer of hope may have been provided from the unlikeliest of sources, Vladimir Putin. It is much too early to draw any definitive historic balance sheet of the horrific invasion of Ukraine. But even as of this writing, the leader of the illiberals of the modern stage proved to be less capable, less militarily savvy, and less imposing than expected. The resilience of the Ukrainian will to resist, ceding to calls from an unexpectedly forceful democratically elected president, has been an inspiration of democratic solidarity. Even the seemingly dependable Putin coterie of Erdoğan and Orbán wavered in their attachment to Russia, and Poland threw its lot in quickly with European and American resistance to the invasion. Instead of showing the weakness of the West, "Ukraine's tenacity and creativity have ignited civil-society energy, corporate strength, and humanitarian assistance."[8]

If Ukraine, with a weak history of governance and surrounded on all sides by the furies of anti-liberalism, can somehow hold on to its tentative efforts at democracy, perhaps there is hope for others as well.

ACKNOWLEDGMENTS

This book has been a long undertaking. There are many colleagues who have provided comments, encouragement, critical exchanges, and all the other indispensable pieces of an intellectual project. Among the many colleagues I have engaged over the period of working on these issues are Justice Luís Roberto Barroso, Robert Bauer, Violeta Besirevic, Bruce Cain, Sujit Choudhry, Pablo De Greiff, Rosalind Dixon, John Ferejohn, Willy Forbath, Heather Gerken, Benjamin Ginsberg, Mark Graber, Moshe Halbertal, Stephen Holmes, Ira Katznelson, Tarunabh Khaitan, Madhav Khosla, Lord Mervyn King, Mattias Kumm, Sandy Levinson, Marcin Matczak, Troy McKenzie, Pratap Bantu Mehta, Conrado Huber Mendes, Trevor Morrison, Pasquale Pasquino, Nancy Rosenblum, Wojciech Sadurski, András Sajó, Adam Samaha, Mark Tushnet, Renáta Uitz, Jeremy Waldron, Joseph Weiler, and Po Jen Yap.

It is a source of particular pride that I have many former students and supervisees who have gone on to leading academic careers of their own or are in the process of doing so. Among this group, several provided comments or assistance during the formative stages of this volume: Vicente Benítez-Rojas, Colin Bradley, Alvin Cheung, Erin Delaney, Aziz Huq, Teddy Rave, Yvonne Tew, and Sergio Verdugo.

Special acknowledgment to my long-time collaborators on the Law of Democracy project, Pamela Karlan and Richard Pildes, as well as to my newest coauthors in this venture, Nathaniel Persily and Franita Tolson. Also, in this special group I have to add Tom Ginsburg, who agreed to review the entire manuscript, as well as to two anonymous reviewers who provided careful comments and suggestions. And, of course, the most merited thanks to she who is most burdened by my undertakings, Cynthia Estlund.

Along the years, I have had an amazing group of research assistants without whom this would never have come to fruition. In this group I thank Eloise

Ackman, Elaine Andersen, Alexander Arnold, Rupsha Basu, Alexandra Bursak, Gregory Crane, David Drew, Jonas Elfman, Christopher Graham, Jacob Hansen, Will Hughes, Isaac Inkeles, Joseph Krakoff, Stephen Levandoski, Adam Littlestone-Luria (including as a coauthor), William North, Alexandra Origines, Mitchell Pallaki, Libby Rozbruch, Jonathan Steinberg, Caroline Tan, and Joshua Zakharov. Here too there are several people meriting special acknowledgment for their work on checking, editing, and revising the final manuscript: Jonathan Goldberg, Deven Kirschenbaum, and Benjamin Shand.

Some of the material presented here draws from earlier work, which should also be acknowledged: *Constitution by Convention,* 108 CAL. L. REV. 1913 (2020) (with Trevor Morrison); *The Corruption of Popular Sovereignty,* 18 INT'L J. CONSTIT. L. 1 (2020); *Democracy's Deficits,* 85 U. CHI. L. REV. 485 (2018); *Outsourcing Politics: The Hostile Takeover of Our Hollowed Out Political Parties,* 54 HOUSTON L. REV. 845 (2017); *The Plebiscite in Modern Democracy,* in HANDBOOK OF ILLIBERALISM (2021) (with J. Colin Bradley) (András Sajó, Renáta Uitz, & Stephen Holmes, eds); *Populism Versus Democratic Governance,* in CONSTITUTIONAL DEMOCRACY IN CRISIS? (Mark Graber, Sanford Levinson, & Mark Tushnet, eds., 2018); *The Demise of Government: The Grim Task of Undoing Trump's Damage,* https://www.justsecurity.org/71092/the-demise-of-government-the-grim-task-of-undoing-trumps-damage/, July 1, 2020 (with Adam Littlestone-Luria). An excerpt from Chapter 8 previously appeared in Stanford Law Review Online at 74 *Stan L. Rev. Online* (2021), and that excerpt may be found at the Law Review website.

NOTES

Introduction

1. Daryl Levinson & Richard Pildes, *Separation of Parties, Not Powers*, 119 HARV. L. REV. 2311 (2006).
2. Venezuela's GINI coefficient score by the end of the 1990s was 48.3 and rising, whereas other high regional scores in Colombia, Brazil, Argentina, and Costa Rica were all declining. Moisés Naím, *High Anxiety in the Andes: The Real Story Behind Venezuela's Woes*, 12 J. DEMO. 17, 21 (2001).
3. *See, e.g.*, Anatoly Kurmanaev, *Venezuela's Collapse Is the Worst Outside of War in Decades, Economists Say*, N.Y. TIMES (May 17, 2019), https://www.nytimes.com/2019/05/17/world/americas/venezuela-economy.html (noting that Venezuela was "Latin America's wealthiest country" in the 1990s).
4. Jason Margolis, *Venezuela Was Once the Richest, Most Stable, Democracy in Latin America. What Happened?*, WORLD (Feb. 7, 2019), pri.org/stories/2019-02-07/venezuela-was-once-richest-most-stable-democracy-latin-america-what-happened (by the end of the 20th century, Venezuela's GINI coefficient was at 48.30, one of the world's highest).
5. *See* Naím, *High Anxiety in the Andes* at 17–18.
6. *Id.* at 19.
7. *It Takes Two to Disentangle*, THE ECONOMIST (April 3, 2021), at 29 (quoting the Argentinian president's political advisors).
8. I borrow this formulation from Dieter Grimm. Correspondence to author, Dec. 4, 2019.
9. *See* Samuel P. Huntington, *The Third Wave: Democratization in the Late Twentieth Century*, 2 J. OF DEMOCRACY 12 (1991). Huntington was the first to use the idea of "waves of democratization."
10. ALEXIS DE TOCQUEVILLE, DEMOCRACY IN AMERICA 232 (J. P. Mayer ed., George Lawrence trans., 1988) (1835).
11. Michael Ignatieff, *Enemies vs. Adversaries*, N.Y. TIMES (Oct. 16, 2013), https://www.nytimes.com/2013/10/17/opinion/enemies-vs-adversaries.html.
12. Isaiah Berlin et al., *To Define Populism*, 3 GOV'T & OPPOSITION 137, 174 (1968).
13. *See* YASCHA MOUNK, THE PEOPLE VS. DEMOCRACY: WHY OUR FREEDOM IS IN DANGER AND HOW TO SAVE IT (2018).
14. *See* PIPPA NORRIS & RONALD INGLEHART, CULTURAL BACKLASH: TRUMP, BREXIT, AND AUTHORITARIAN POPULISM (2019).
15. *See* LARRY DIAMOND, ILL WINDS: SAVING DEMOCRACY FROM RUSSIAN RAGE, CHINESE AMBITION, AND AMERICAN COMPLACENCY (2019).
16. *See* BENJAMIN MOFFITT, THE GLOBAL RISE OF POPULISM: PERFORMANCE, POLITICAL STYLE, AND REPRESENTATION (2016).
17. STEVEN LEVITSKY & DANIEL ZIBLATT, HOW DEMOCRACIES DIE (2018).
18. *See* JAN-WERNER MÜLLER, WHAT IS POPULISM? (2016).

19. SAMUEL ISSACHAROFF, FRAGILE DEMOCRACIES: CONTESTED POWER IN THE ERA OF CONSTITUTIONAL COURTS (2015).

20. Cas Mudde & Cristóbal Rovira Kaltwasser, *Exclusionary vs. Inclusionary Populism: Comparing Contemporary Europe and Latin America*, 48 GOV'T & OPPOSITION 147, 160 (2013).

21. Cas Mudde, *The Populist Zeitgeist*, 39 GOV'T & OPPOSITION 541, 547–48 (2004).

22. STEVEN LEVITSKY & LUCAN A. WAY, COMPETITIVE AUTHORITARIANISM: HYBRID REGIMES AFTER THE COLD WAR 27 (2010).

23. *Id.* at 5.

24. *See* MÜLLER, WHAT IS POPULISM?

25. LEVITSKY & ZIBLATT, HOW DEMOCRACIES DIE.

Chapter 1

1. Sarah Repucci & Amy Slipowitz, *Freedom in the World 2021: Democracy Under Siege*, FREEDOM HOUSE (Mar. 3, 2021), https://freedomhouse.org/report/freedom-world/2021/democracy-under-siege (noting the "long democratic recession" continues to deepen fifteen years after the decline of democracy began in 2006).

2. Lucan A. Way, *Authoritarian State Building and the Sources of Regime Competitiveness in the Fourth Wave: The Cases of Belarus, Moldova, Russia, and Ukraine*, 57 WORLD POL. 231, 232 (2005) (describing early elections as reflecting not the ascendance of democracy, but rather the momentary "inability of incumbents to maintain power or concentrate political control by preserving elite unity").

3. PHILIP BOBBITT, THE SHIELD OF ACHILLES: WAR, PEACE, AND THE COURSE OF HISTORY xxi–xxii (2002) ("This war . . . began in 1914 and only ended in 1990. The Long War, like previous epochal wars, brought into being a new form of the State—the market-state.").

4. Franklin D. Roosevelt, Annual Message to Congress (Jan. 6, 1941), *in* 87 Cong. Rec. 44 (1941).

5. ZACHARY D. CARTER, THE PRICE OF PEACE: MONEY, DEMOCRACY, AND THE LIFE OF JOHN MAYNARD KEYNES 314–15 (2020).

6. F. A. HAYEK, THE ROAD TO SERFDOM: TEXT AND DOCUMENTS, THE DEFINITIVE EDITION 78 (Bruce Caldwell, ed., 2014) (1944).

7. FRIEDRICH HAYEK, THE MIRAGE OF SOCIAL JUSTICE 104 (1976).

8. *The Two Worlds: A Day-Long Debate*, N.Y. TIMES (July 25, 1959), at 3, https://timesmachine.nytimes.com/timesmachine/1959/07/25/issue.html.

9. *See* GERD HORTEN, DON'T NEED NO THOUGHT CONTROL: WESTERN CULTURE IN EAST GERMANY AND THE FALL OF THE BERLIN WALL 41–43 (2020) (noting East German viewers' satisfaction with the TV coverage of the 1972 Olympic Games).

10. The single best treatment of the decline in innovation and productivity enhancements is ROBERT J. GORDON, THE RISE AND FALL OF AMERICAN GROWTH (2016).

11. A powerful illustration is found in ANNE CASE & ANGUS DEATON, DEATHS OF DESPAIR AND THE FUTURE OF CAPITALISM (2020). A sharper focus on the rise of opioids and addiction may be found in SAM QUINONES, DREAMLAND: THE TRUE TALE OF AMERICA'S OPIATE EPIDEMIC (2015).

12. *See* NIHEER DASANDI, IS DEMOCRACY FAILING?: A PRIMER FOR THE 21ST CENTURY (2018) (focusing on the financial crisis); JOHN B. JUDIS, THE POPULIST EXPLOSION: HOW THE GREAT RECESSION TRANSFORMED AMERICAN AND EUROPEAN POLITICS (2016) (same).

13. Robin Greenwood & David Scharfstein, *The Growth of Finance*, 27 J. ECON. PERSPS. 3, 3 (2013).

14. *See* Stephen G. Cecchetti & Enisse Kharroubi, *Why Does Financial Sector Growth Crowd Out Real Economic Growth?* 25 (Bank for Int'l Settlements, Working Paper No. 490, 2015).

15. *See* Branko Milanovic, *Global Income Inequality by the Numbers: In History and Now—An Overview* 7–8 (World Bank Dev. Research Grp., Working Paper No. 6259, 2012), http://documents1.worldbank.org/curated/en/959251468176687085/pdf/wps6259.pdf [http://perma.cc/Q3U3-5EL8] (comparing different measures of global inequality and concluding that the period of globalization running from 1988 to 2008 witnessed "a decline in global inequality" for "perhaps . . . the first time since the Industrial Revolution").

16. Subsequent research has challenged some of the foundations for the "trough" in the elephant curve—that is, whether the working class in the rich world experienced an actual decline in wages, stagnation in wages, or merely slower comparative growth. Regardless, what is clear (and relevant for the purposes of this chapter) is that working-class wages in the rich world have not kept pace with the shift in world income. *Compare* Adam Corlett, *Examining an Elephant: Globalisation and the Lower Middle Class of the Rich World*, RESOLUTION FOUNDATION (September 2016) *with* Christoph Lakner & Branko Milanovic, *Response to Adam Corlett's* "Examining an Elephant: Globalisation and the Lower Middle Class of the Rich World" (September 2016).

17. PAUL COLLIER, THE FUTURE OF CAPITALISM: FACING THE NEW ANXIETIES 52 (2018) (footnote omitted).

18. This tradition is clearest in the breach. *See* Thomas R. Rochon & Ravi Roy, *Adaptation of the American Democratic Party in an Era of Globalization*, 31 INT'L J. POL. ECON. 12, 18–24 (2001) (documenting Democrats' shift from a primarily working-class to middle-class party and the ensuing changes in trade policy in the 1990s). Thus, the North American Free Trade Agreement (NAFTA) was pitched by not only the Reagan and Bush administrations but also by the Clinton administration as protecting jobs and ensuring popular demand for accessible consumer goods. *See* Michael Wilson, *The North American Free Trade Agreement: Ronald Reagan's Vision Realized*, HERITAGE FOUND. (Nov. 23, 1993), https://www.heritage.org/trade/report/the-north-american-free-trade-agreement-ronald-reagans-vision-realized [http://perma.cc/6Q46-LFN5].

19. *See* Mark Muro & Sifan Liu, *Another Clinton-Trump Divide: High-Output America vs Low-Output America*, BROOKINGS INST.: THE AVENUE (Nov. 29, 2016), https://www.brookings.edu/blog/the-avenue/2016/11/29/another-clinton-trump-divide-high-output-america-vs-low-output-america/ [http://perma.cc/63QB-BS4J]; Jim Tankersley, *Donald Trump Lost Most of the American Economy in This Election*, WASH. POST (Nov. 22, 2016), https://www.washingtonpost.com/news/wonk/wp/2016/11/22/donald-trump-lost-most-of-the-american-economy-in-this-election/ [http://perma.cc/3U86-WRUD].

20. *EU Referendum: The Result in Maps and Charts*, BBC (June 24, 2016), https://www.bbc.com/news/uk-politics-36616028 [http://perma.cc/4JN2-5SSM].

21. While President Emmanuel Macron bested Marine Le Pen in all but two departments during the final round of voting, Le Pen's support was strongest in the rural, deindustrialized northeast and the southern coast. *See* Seán Clarke & Josh Holder, *French Presidential Election May 2017—Full Second Round Results and Analysis*, THE GUARDIAN (May 26, 2017), https://www.theguardian.com/world/ng-interactive/2017/may/07/french-presidential-election-results-latest [http://perma.cc/6VKE-8BPS].

22. *See* Steven Mufson, *Why Obama Says Bank Reform Is a Success but Bernie Sanders Says It's a Failure*, WASH. POST: WONKBLOG (Mar. 7, 2016), https://www.washingtonpost.com/news/wonk/wp/2016/03/07/doddfrank0308/ [http://perma.cc/6N6T-9BSN] (discussing internecine debates surrounding failure to prosecute bankers and break up banks postcrisis); *see also* Justin Fox, *What We've Learned from the Financial Crisis*, HARV. BUS. REV., (Nov. 2013), https://hbr.org/2013/11/what-weve-learned-from-the-financial-crisis [http://perma.cc/9L4E-TP4L] (noting how "unanimity [of opinion on macroeconomic policy] quickly unraveled" among economists after the 2008 financial bailout).

23. For an exploration of the postcrisis class rift on the American right, see Vanessa Williamson, Theda Skocpol, & John Coggin, *The Tea Party and the Remaking of Republican Conservatism*, 9 PERSP. ON POL. 25, 32–34 (2011) (noting that Tea Party conservatives' embrace of social-safety-net spending is at odds with Republican orthodoxy); *see also* David Frum, *The Great Republican Revolt*, THE ATLANTIC (Jan./Feb. 2016), https://www.theatlantic.com/magazine/archive/2016/01/the-great-republican-revolt/419118/ [http://perma.cc/Y2CD-TBDZ] (tracking the class divide in the Republican Party through Trump support in the 2016 primary).

24. YASCHA MOUNK, THE PEOPLE VS. DEMOCRACY: WHY OUR FREEDOM IS IN DANGER AND HOW TO SAVE IT 159 (2018).

25. MICHAEL J. SANDEL, THE TYRANNY OF MERIT: WHAT'S BECOME OF THE COMMON GOOD? 71–72 (2020).

26. Among those that emphasize the link between downward mobility, globalization of markets, and the rise of populism are MOUNK, THE PEOPLE VS. DEMOCRACY (focusing on globalization); PETER MAIR, RULING THE VOID: THE HOLLOWING OF WESTERN DEMOCRACY (2013) (same); DASANDI, IS DEMOCRACY FAILING? (focusing on the financial crisis); and JUDIS, THE POPULIST EXPLOSION (same).

27. *See generally* ALEN TOPLIŠEK, LIBERAL DEMOCRACY IN CRISIS: RETHINKING RESISTANCE UNDER NEOLIBERAL GOVERNMENTALITY (2019).

28. PIPPA NORRIS & RONALD INGLEHART, CULTURAL BACKLASH: TRUMP, BREXIT, AND AUTHORITARIAN POPULISM 15 (2019).

29. *See* LARRY DIAMOND, ILL WINDS: SAVING DEMOCRACY FROM RUSSIAN RAGE, CHINESE AMBITION, AND AMERICAN COMPLACENCY 72–76 (2019) (discussing the rise in immigration and the resulting "growing anxiety" and "fear that foreigners are taking over their countries and endangering their way of life," which has enabled a surge in illiberal populism in some of the most established democracies on earth, as "right-wing populist parties generate, stoke, and mobilize the fear that immigration will erase cultural heritages and national identities") (footnote omitted).

30. *See id.* at 72–73.

31. CARL SCHMITT, THE CRISIS OF PARLIAMENTARY DEMOCRACY 9 (Ellen Kennedy trans., 1985) (1923).

32. *Id.*

33. THE FEDERALIST NO. 2, at 9 (John Jay) (Jacob E. Cooke, ed., 1961) (1787).

34. JOHN STUART MILL, CONSIDERATIONS ON REPRESENTATIVE GOVERNMENT 344–45 (2009) (1861).

35. JOHN RAWLS, THE LAW OF PEOPLES: WITH, THE IDEA OF PUBLIC REASON REVISITED 106 (1999).

36. NANCY L. ROSENBLUM, ON THE SIDE OF THE ANGELS: AN APPRECIATION OF PARTIES AND PARTISANSHIP 266–67 (2010).

37. Larry Bartels, *The "Wave" of Right-Wing Populist Sentiment Is a Myth*, WASH. POST (June 21, 2017), https://www.washingtonpost.com/news/monkey-cage/wp/2017/06/21/the-wave-of-right-wing-populist-sentiment-is-a-myth/.

38. *Portugal's Flourishing Far Right Target Roma Ahead of Vote*, FRANCE 24 (Jan. 25, 2022), https://www.france24.com/en/live-news/20220125-portugal-s-flourishing-far-right-target-roma-ahead-of-vote; *Portugal's Ruling Socialists Win Re-election with Outright Majority*, FRANCE 24 (Jan. 30, 2022), https://www.france24.com/en/europe/20220130-portugal-s-ruling-socialists-and-far-right-party-chega-eye-gains-in-snap-legislative-elections.

39. *See* Robert D. Putnam, E Pluribus Unum: *Diversity and Community in the Twenty-First Century*, 30 SCANDINAVIAN POL. STUD. 137, 141–54 (2007) (discussing the relationship between diversity—and, by extension, immigration—and social isolation in American communities); *see also* Dora L. Costa & Matthew E. Kahn, *Civic Engagement and Community Heterogeneity: An Economist's Perspective*, 1 PERSP. ON POL. 103, 105–7 (2003) (charting heterogeneity and voluntary civic participation in 20th-century America).

40. *See* Oliver Balch, *Africa Droughts Prompt Calls to Start Pumping Untapped Groundwater*, THE GUARDIAN (Aug. 18, 2016), https://www.theguardian.com/sustainable-business/2016/aug/18/africa-drought-untapped-groundwater-aquifers-water-stress-ngo-partnership-ethiopia.

41. STEPHEN SMITH, THE SCRAMBLE FOR EUROPE: YOUNG AFRICA ON ITS WAY TO THE OLD CONTINENT 4–5 (2019).

42. *See* Maggie Michael, Lori Hinnant, & Renata Brito, *Making Misery Pay: Libya Militias Take EU Funds for Migrants*, AP NEWS (Dec. 31, 2019), https://apnews.com/article/9d9e8d668ae4b73a336a636a86bdf27f.

43. Bartels, *The "Wave" of Right-Wing Populist Sentiment Is a Myth*.

44. M. Murat Ardag et al., *Populist Attitudes and Political Engagement: Ugly, Bad, and Sometimes Good?*, 56 J. REPRESENTATIVE DEMOCRACY 1, 3 (2019), http://archive.ceu.hu/sites/default/files/publications/populist-attitudes-and-political-engagement-ugly-bad-and-sometimes-good.pdf.

45. David Brady, John A. Ferejohn, & Aldo Paparo, *Populism in the Electorate: Explaining the "Populist Vote"*, (Aug. 8, 2020) (working manuscript) (on file with author).

46. *Id.*

47. *Id.*

Chapter 2

1. In Singapore, initial firm state oversight of financial and labor markets coupled with aggressive solicitation of foreign investment achieved rapid growth in the decades following independence. See generally W. G. Huff, *What Is the Singapore Model of Economic Development?*, 19 CAMBRIDGE J. ECON. 735 (1995). While China's general rise is well known, less focus has been placed on its advances in infrastructure. It has spent 8.5 percent of its GDP since the 1990s on infrastructure, and now outpaces both the U.S. and the EU in absolute spending. While gains are lopsided by sector, it has rapidly built its infrastructure stock to compete with developed nations. *See* Yougang Chen, Stefan Matzinger, & Jonathan Woetzel, *Chinese Infrastructure: The Big Picture*, MCKINSEY Q. (June 2013), http://perma.cc/3U7V-2SF7.

2. *See* Francis Fukuyama, *America: The Failed State*, PROSPECT 30, 31 (Jan. 2017).

3. *Id.* at 31.

4. Patient Protection and Affordable Care Act, Pub L No 111-148, 124 Stat. 119 (2010).

5. *See* Alexander Bolton, *GOP Facing Likely Failure on ObamaCare Repeal*, THE HILL (Sept. 25, 2017), http://perma.cc/M3W9-5SP3 (discussing congressional Republicans' likely prospect of failing in a "nine-month odyssey" to repeal Obamacare).

6. DAVID M. ESTLUND, DEMOCRATIC AUTHORITY: A PHILOSOPHICAL FRAMEWORK 8 (2008).

7. SAMUEL ISSACHAROFF, FRAGILE DEMOCRACIES 158 (2015).

8. Balkans in Europe Policy Advisory Group, *The Crisis of Democracy in the Western Balkans. Authoritarianism and EU Stabilitocracy* 7 (Mar. 2017), http://perma.cc/3W9S-3SM8.

9. Interview by Razia Iqbal with Norman Foster, Senior Exec. Partner, Foster + Partners, BBC, in London, UK, June 16, 2013 (transcript at http://perma.cc/G5V6-W3R7).

10. *Id.*

11. *Id.* at *10–11.

12. Matthew Yglesias, *NYC's Brand New Subway Is the Most Expensive in the World—That's a Problem*, VOX (Jan. 1, 2017), http://perma.cc/XT5A-BJJZ.

13. *See* Alon Levy, *US Rail Construction Costs*, PEDESTRIAN OBSERVATIONS (May 16, 2011), http://perma.cc/MNW2-RWKB.

14. *See* George Packer, *The Empty Chamber*, NEW YORKER (Aug. 9, 2010), http://perma.cc/SR7D-72JJ.

15. Hitler's regime consolidated power through a number of direct referenda in the 1930s, including those withdrawing Germany from the League of Nations and combining the offices of chancellor and president into that of the *führer*. These referenda were initiated and controlled by the German executive branch. *See generally* Arnold J. Zurcher, *The Hitler Referenda*, 29 AM. POL. SCI. REV, 91 (1935). In Italy, Mussolini maneuvered to give the Fascist Grand Council the power to approve election lists throughout the 1920s, shifting the Italian Parliament from a deliberative (though gridlocked) electoral body to a single-party "Corporative Chamber" approved by popular plebiscite: "Our aim is to create a Corporative Chamber without an opposition. We have no desire nor need for any political opposition." *The Fascist Grand Council and the Italian Election*, 5 BULL INT'L NEWS 3, 4 (1929) (quoting Mussolini).

16. CONRADO HÜBNER MENDES, CONSTITUTIONAL COURTS AND DELIBERATIVE DEMOCRACY 14 (2013).

17. *Id.* at 15.

18. *Statistics and Historical Comparison*, GOVTRACK, http://perma.cc/3BVH-AT7D (last visited Oct. 4, 2021) (showing that the 95th Congress passed 804 bills while the 114th Congress passed 329).

19. Jane Mayer, *Enabler-in-Chief: Mitch McConnell's Refusal to Rein in Trump Is Looking Riskier than Ever*, NEW YORKER (April 20, 2020), at 64.

20. Julia Azari, *A President's First 100 Days Really Do Matter*, FIVETHIRTYEIGHT (Jan. 17, 2017), http://perma.cc/852T-G5DF.

21. Jordan Fabian, *Trump "Disappointed" in Congressional GOP*, THE HILL (Apr. 28, 2017), https://thehill.com/homenews/administration/331140-trump-disappointed-in-congre ssional-gop (explaining that while twenty-eight pieces of legislation were passed and signed during President Trump's first hundred days, "thirteen . . . measures roll back Obama-era regulations . . . [and] most others are small-scale measures that appoint personnel, name federal facilities or modify existing programs").

22. James Crump, *Biden's First 100 Days in Numbers, from Executive Orders to Vaccines*, THE GUARDIAN (Apr. 27, 2021), https://www.independent.co.uk/news/world/americas/us-politics/biden-100-days-bills-executive-orders-b1838313.html.

23. The major congressional actions took the form of an expedited procedure to withdraw regulatory decrees within a fast-track window. There were no new legislative initiatives of any substance. *See* David Leonhardt, *Donald Trump's First 100 Days: The Worst on Record*, N.Y. TIMES (Apr. 26, 2017), http://nyti.ms/2pleYVE.

24. Maegan Vazquez, Kate Sullivan, Tami Luhby & Katie Lobosco, *Biden's First 100 Days: What He's Gotten Done*, CNN (Apr. 28, 2021), https://www.cnn.com/2021/04/28/politics/presid ent-biden-first-100-days/index.html.

25. Emily Cochrane, *Congress Clears $1.9 Trillion Aid Bill, Sending It to Biden*, N.Y. TIMES (Mar. 30, 2021), https://www.nytimes.com/2021/03/10/us/politics/covid-stimulus-bill.html.

26. Joshua Cohen, *Deliberation and Democratic Legitimacy*, *in* THE GOOD POLITY: NORMATIVE ANALYSIS OF THE STATE 17 (Alan Hamlin & Philip Pettit, eds., 1989).

27. JOSEPH A. SCHUMPETER, CAPITALISM, SOCIALISM AND DEMOCRACY 250 (1976) (1942).

28. Cohen, *Deliberation and Democratic Legitimacy* at 21–26.

29. *See* SCHUMPETER, CAPITALISM, SOCIALISM AND DEMOCRACY at 247–49.

30. *See* Cohen, *Deliberation and Democratic Legitimacy* at 18–20.

31. SCHUMPETER, CAPITALISM, SOCIALISM AND DEMOCRACY at 248–49.

32. EZRA KLEIN, WHY WE'RE POLARIZED 3 (2020).

33. RAYMOND J. LA RAJA & BRIAN F. SCHAFFNER, CAMPAIGN FINANCE AND POLITICAL POLARIZATION: WHEN PURISTS PREVAIL 3 (2015).

34. Nadia Urbinati, *Liquid Parties, Dense Populism*, 45 PHIL. & SOC. CRITICISM 1069, 1076 (2019)(citations and footnotes omitted).

35. Fernando Bizzarro et al., *Party Strength and Economic Growth*, 70 WORLD POL. 275 (2018).

36. *Id.* at 290.

37. *Id.* at 293.

38. *See* Kenneth J. Arrow, *A Difficulty in the Concept of Social Welfare*, 58 J. POL. ECON. 328, 328–31 (1950) (discussing the confusion attendant to any attempt to amalgamate the social and voting preferences of a diverse whole).

39. *See generally id.* (laying out Arrow's impossibility theorem and the inevitability of preference cycling). *See also* Richard H. Pildes & Elizabeth S. Anderson, *Slinging Arrows at Democracy: Social Choice Theory, Value Pluralism, and Democratic Politics*, 90 COLUM. L. REV. 2121, 2183–86 (1990) (arguing that institutional arrangements may mediate Arrow's predicted cycling).

40. *Ray v. Blair*, 343 U.S. 214, 221 (1952).

41. *See generally* Samuel Issacharoff & Richard H. Pildes, *Between Civil Libertarianism and Executive Unilateralism: An Institutional Approach to Rights During Wartime*, 5 THEORETICAL INQUIRIES L. 1 (2004)(surveying the response of American courts in periods of crisis when the executive asserts a need for unilateral action).

42. *Youngstown Sheet & Tube Co. v. Sawyer*, 343 U.S. 579, 636–38 (1952) (Jackson, J., concurring).

43. *Id.* at 637.

44. *Id.*

45. How this conflict plays out is the subject of Rosalind Dixon & Samuel Issacharoff, *Living to Fight Another Day: Judicial Deferral in Defense of Democracy*, WIS. L. REV. 683, 706 (2016).

46. *See generally* SELECT COMMITTEE ON THE CONSTITUTION, WAGING WAR: PARLIAMENT'S ROLE AND RESPONSIBILITY, 2006, HL 236-I (UK), http://perma.cc/MF99-F78K.

47. Pub. L. No. 93-148, 87 Stat. 555 (1973), codified as amended at 50 U.S.C. § 1541 et seq.

48. SELECT COMMITTEE ON THE CONSTITUTION, WAGING WAR, at 5. ("The purpose of our inquiry has been to consider what alternatives there are to the use of the Royal prerogative

power in the deployment of armed force . . . and in particular whether Parliamentary approval should be required for any deployment of British forces outside the United Kingdom."). In the following years, the interplay between the prime minister and Parliament developed informally, until the point in 2014 when "the prime minister acknowledged that a convention of Commons approval now existed." Philippe Lagassé, *Parliament and the War Prerogative in the United Kingdom and Canada: Explaining Variations in Institutional Change and Legislative Control*, 70 PARLIAMENTARY AFFS. 280, 289 (2017).

49. *Brown Calls for MPs to Decide War*, BBC NEWS (Apr. 30, 2005), http://perma.cc/ 86MH-QDHX.

50. *See* THE REPORT OF THE IRAQ INQUIRY: EXECUTIVE SUMMARY, 2016, HC 264, at 58, 83 (UK), http://perma.cc/H5T3-EWNR (critiquing Blair's actions, the report noted that "there should have been a collective discussion by a Cabinet Committee or small group of Ministers on the basis of inter-departmental advice agreed at a senior level between officials at a number of decision points which had a major impact on the development of UK policy before the invasion of Iraq").

51. *See, e.g.*, MICHAEL FOLEY, THE BRITISH PRESIDENCY: TONY BLAIR AND THE POLITICS OF PUBLIC LEADERSHIP 108 (2000) (noting "that Blair and his followers operated on the assumption that parliament was no longer a central force of political significance"); Zachary Karabell, *How the GOP Made Obama One of America's Most Powerful Presidents*, POLITICO (Apr. 14, 2016), http://perma.cc/AN8D-BBHE (positing that Republicans in Congress as "the so-called Party of No only provoked the Obama administration into finding innovative ways to exercise [greater unilateral] power. . . . Rather than containing the White House, congressional Republicans liberated it").

52. *See generally, e.g.*, Anu Bradford, *The Brussels Effect*, 107 NW. U. L. REV. 1 (2012) (describing how regulations passed in Brussels can result in the globalization of standards); Cynthia R. Farina, *Congressional Polarization: Terminal Constitutional Dysfunction?*, 115 COLUM. L. REV. 1689 (2015) (synthesizing political science literature about congressional polarization); Mattias Kumm, *The Legitimacy of International Law: A Constitutional Framework of Analysis*, 15 EUROPEAN J. INTL. L. 907 (2004)(discussing conflicts between international law and national domestic self-government); Juan J. Linz, *The Perils of Presidentialism*, 1 J. OF DEMOCRACY 51 (Winter 1990) (arguing that presidentialism is less conducive to democracy than parliamentarism); Melanie Amann, Thomas Darnstädt, & Dietmar Hipp, *Is Germany's Parliamentary Hurdle Obsolete?*, SPIEGEL ONLINE (Oct. 4, 2013), http://perma.cc/9GG5-RT8Z (surveying political scientists' critiques of the Bundestag's 5 percent hurdle to seat parties). *See also, e.g.*, Richard H. Pildes, *Romanticizing Democracy, Political Fragmentation, and the Decline of American Government*, 124 YALE L. J. 804, 809 (2014) (positing that political fragmentation is a cause of recent government dysfunction, such as "the inability of party leaders to bring along recalcitrant minority factions of their parties").

53. An astonishing number of Brazil's members of Congress have faced indictment in recent years. *See, e.g.*, Anthony Boadle & Alonso Soto, *Brazil's Indicted Senate Head Removed by Supreme Court*, REUTERS (Dec. 5, 2016), http://perma.cc/34HH-ER3N (reporting the removal of the Senate president following an indictment); Paul Kiernan, *Brazil Former Official Is Sentenced*, WALL ST. J. (Mar. 31, 2017), at A7 (reporting the sentencing of the former House Speaker Eduardo Cunha to prison for corruption "in a case that has landed scores of politicians and businessmen behind bars"); Dom Phillips, *Prominent Leader Is Sentenced in Brazil*, N.Y. TIMES (Mar. 31, 2017), at A9 (reporting the sentencing of the former House Speaker to "one of [the] stiffest penalties meted out to a top political figure in Brazil in recent years," as part of an investigation that "has shaken Brazil's political and business establishments to their core"). The problem is not limited to Congress, as shown by the conviction and sentencing of former President Luiz Inácio Lula da Silva, *see* Ernesto Londoño, *Ex-President of Brazil Sentenced to Nearly 10 Years in Prison for Corruption*, N.Y. TIMES (July 12, 2017), http://www. nytimes.com/2017/07/12/world/americas/brazil-lula-da-silva-corruption.html, and by the explosive public removal trial of current President Michel Temer, resulting in a divided vote of the Electoral Court on his removal, *see* Simon Romero & Dom Phillips, *Court in Brazil Clears President Michel Temer in Campaign Finance Case*, N.Y. TIMES (June 9, 2017), http:// www.nytimes.com/2017/06/09/world/americas/brazil-michel-temer.html. *See also* Dom

Phillips, *President Michel Temer of Brazil Is Charged with Corruption*, N.Y. TIMES (June 26, 2017), http://www.nytimes.com/2017/06/26/world/americas/brazil-temer-corruption-charge-joesley-batista.html (detailing new bribery allegations against Temer).

54. Daniel Cohn-Bendit, *Presidentialism: The French Disease*, ESPRIT (Feb. 22, 2012), http://perma.cc/BCS7-HHDT.

55. The *caudillo* is the military man on a horse leading a highly personalized political movement based on swashbuckling individual authority, rather than lasting political institutions. The 19th-century form of *caudillo* command, called the "caudillaje," is the precursor of both pop-ulism and military rule. *See* Eric R. Wolf & Edward C. Hansen, *Caudillo Politics: A Structural Analysis*, 9 COMPAR. STUD. SOC'Y & HIST. 168, 168–69 (1967); *see also* Diego von Vacano, *Trump Embraces Caudillo Politics as Latin America Shuns It*, NBC NEWS (Nov. 22, 2016), https://www.nbcnews.com/news/latino/opinion-trump-embraces-caudillo-politics-latin-america-shuns-it-n686861.

56. *See* Cohn-Bendit, *Presidentialism*.

57. *See* J. Benson Durham, *Economic Growth and Political Regimes*, 4 J. ECON. GROWTH 81, 93 (1999) (explaining that democratic governance "assumes a modicum of wealth" and discussing empirical studies around country wealth and form of government).

58. *See* Michael L. Ross, *What Have We Learned About the Resource Curse?*, 18 ANN. REV. POL. SCI. 239, 248–50 (2015)(discussing theoretical research and empirical studies finding a link between new resource wealth as a result of oil and weakened institutional capacity, impeding democratic development).

59. *See* Elena Kagan, *Presidential Administration*, 114 HARV. L. REV. 2245, 2266–67 (2001).

60. *Id.* at 2272.

61. *Id.* at 2313 n.271 (quoting James Bennet, *True to Form, Clinton Shifts Energies Back to U.S. Focus*, N.Y. TIMES (July 5, 1998), § I, at 10 (quoting Paul Begala, former counselor to President Clinton).

62. Noah Rosenblum, *The Antifascist Roots of Presidential Administration*, 122 COLUM. L. REV. 1, 3 (2022).

63. Issacharoff & Pildes, *Between Civil Libertarianism and Executive Unilateralism* at 4.

64. THE FEDERALIST NO. 51, at 382 (James Madison) (Amazon Classics ed., 2017).

65. Gillian Metzger, *Foreword: 1930s Redux*, 131 HARV. L. REV. 1, 75 (2017)

66. Rosenblum, *The Antifascist Roots of Presidential Administration*.

67. *See* Trevor M. Morrison, *Constitutional Alarmism*, 124 HARV. L. REV. 1688 (2011).

68. *See* Samuel J. Rascoff, *Presidential Intelligence*, 129 HARV. L. REV. 633 (2016).

69. *See* SAI PRAKASH, THE LIVING PRESIDENCY: AN ORIGINALIST ARGUMENT AGAINST ITS EVER-EXPANDING POWERS (2009).

70. *See* Jon D. Michaels, *An Enduring, Evolving Separation of Powers*, 115 COLUM. L. REV. 515 (2015).

71. Kagan, *Presidential Administration* at 2332.

72. Seila Law LLC v. Consumer Fin. Prot. Bureau, 140 S. Ct. 2183, 2203 (2020).

73. BERNARD MANIN, THE PRINCIPLES OF REPRESENTATIVE GOVERNMENT 8 (2020).

74. ARISTOTLE, POLITICS bk. VI, at 176 (C. D. C Reeve trans., 1998) (c. 384 B.C.E.).

75. Philip Stephens, *Thatcher Was Right About Referendums*, FIN. TIMES (Sept. 10, 2007), https://www.ft.com/content/d620b8c6-5fc9-11dc-b0fe-0000779fd2ac.

76. Rosenblum, *The Antifascist Roots of Presidential Administration*.

77. ROBERT DAHL, A PREFACE TO DEMOCRATIC THEORY 4 (2006).

78. WILLIAM G. HOWELL & TERRY M. MOE, PRESIDENTS, POPULISM, AND THE CRISIS OF DEMOCRACY 63 (2020).

79. *Id.* at 219.

80. *See, e.g.,* TOM GINSBURG & AZIZ Z. HUQ, HOW TO SAVE A CONSTITUTIONAL DEMOCRACY 211–12 (2018).

Chapter 3

1. E. E. SCHATTSCHNEIDER, PARTY GOVERNMENT 1 (1942).

2. *See* Richard H. Pildes, *Romanticizing Democracy, Political Fragmentation, and the Decline of American Government,* 124 YALE L. J. 804, 809 (2014).
3. *See* Grundgesetz [GG] [Basic Law], art. 21 (Ger.), translation at http://www.gesetze-im-internet.de/englisch_gg/index.html.
4. Zachary Elkins, *Militant Democracy and the Pre-emptive Constitution: From Party Bans to Hardened Term Limits,* 29 DEMOCRATIZATION 174, 184 (2022).
5. *See* Tom Ginsburg, *Constitutions as Political Institutions, in* ROUTLEDGE HANDBOOK OF COMPARATIVE POLITICAL INSTITUTIONS 101, 106 (Jennifer Gandhi & Rubén Ruiz-Rufino, eds., 2015) ("In the nineteenth century . . . few constitutions mentioned political parties, while most written in the twentieth century do so.").
6. ALEXIS DE TOCQUEVILLE, DEMOCRACY IN AMERICA 979 (Henry Reeve trans., 2009) (1840).
7. *See* V. O. KEY JR., POLITICS, PARTIES, AND PRESSURE GROUPS 210–11, 244 (1942).
8. *See id.* At 243–44; Samuel Issacharoff, *Outsourcing Politics: The Hostile Takeover of Our Hollowed-Out Political Parties,* 54 HOUSTON L. REV. 845, 858 (2017).
9. *See id.* at 866–70.
10. Adam Winkler, *Voters' Rights and Parties' Wrongs: Early Political Party Regulation in the State Courts, 1886–1915,* 100 COLUM. L. REV. 873, 876 (2000).
11. BRUCE E. CAIN, DEMOCRACY MORE OR LESS: AMERICA'S POLITICAL REFORM QUANDARY 6 (2015).
12. *See* Gerald F. Davis, Kristina A. Diekmann, & Catherine H. Tinsley, *The Decline and Fall of the Conglomerate Firm in the 1980s: The Deinstitutionalization of an Organizational Form,* 59 AM. SOCIO. REV. 547, 563 (1994) (discussing the rapid shift away from the conglomerate form in the 1980s, including Gulf & Western's reorganization as Paramount Communications); John G. Matsusaka, *Corporate Diversification, Value Maximization, and Organizational Capabilities,* 74 J. BUS. 409, 412–14 (2001) (charting acquisitions and divestments by Gulf & Western and ITT from 1958 to 1988); *see also* Edward B. Rock, *Adapting to the New Shareholder-Centric Reality,* 161 UNIV. PA. L. REV. 1907, 1921–22 (2013) (describing incentives for conglomerates to spinoff "unrelated businesses" and noting such spinoffs by Sears, CBS, DuPont, and AT&T).
13. *See generally* DAVID WEIL, THE FISSURED WORKPLACE: WHY WORK BECAME SO BAD FOR SO MANY AND WHAT CAN BE DONE TO IMPROVE IT (2014).
14. For a more detailed discussion of how direct-democratic procedures, such as direct appeals to voters by populist candidates, weaken political parties, see Emanuel V. Towfigh et al., *Do Direct-Democratic Procedures Lead to Higher Acceptance Than Political Representation? Experimental Survey Evidence from Germany,* 167 PUB. CHOICE 47, 49 (2016).
15. *Id.* At 48–49.
16. PETER MAIR, RULING THE VOID: THE HOLLOWING OF WESTERN DEMOCRACY 43 (2013).
17. *See generally* Chris J. Bickerton & Carlo Invernizzi Accetti, *Democracy Without Parties? Italy After Berlusconi,* 85 POL. Q. 23 (2014) (describing fragmentation across the spectrum of Italian politics); *see also* Marc Bühlmann, David Zumbach, & Marlène Gerber, *Campaign Strategies in the 2015 Swiss National Elections: Nationalization, Coordination, and Personalization,* 22 SWISS POL. SCI. REV. 15, 25 (2016) ("The personalization with nationwide 'party stars' is a new phenomenon in Switzerland.").
18. *See, e.g.,* Hermann Schmitt, Sara Hobolt, & Sebastian Adrian Popa, *Does Personalization Increase Turnout?* Spitzenkandidaten *in the 2014 European Parliament Elections,* 16 EUROPEAN UNION POL. 347, 347–48 (2015):
    "The 2014 European Parliament elections were the first elections where the major political groups each nominated a lead candidate (*Spitzenkandidat*) for the Commission presidency in the hope that this would increase the visibility of the elections and mobilize more citizens to turn out. . . . The potential to increase political participation was . . . at the heart of the European Commission's support for the *Spitzenkandidaten* innovation, as they hoped this could "contribute to raising the turnout for European elections."
19. *See* Pedro O. S. Vaz de Melo, *How Many Political Parties Should Brazil Have? A Data-Driven Method to Assess and Reduce Fragmentation in Multi-Party Political Systems,* 10 PLOS ONE 1, 2 (Oct. 14, 2015), http://perma.cc/27ZA-2EY2.
20. MAIR, RULING THE VOID at 16.

21. Jeremy Shapiro, *Brexit Was a Rejection of Britain's Governing Elite. Too Bad the Elites Were Right*, VOX (June 25, 2016), http://perma.cc/9586-AQA7.

22. *See* Jason Horowitz, *Italy's Premier, Matteo Renzi, Says He'll Resign after Reform Is Rejected*, N.Y. TIMES (Dec. 4, 2016), http://www.nytimes.com/2016/12/04/world/europe/italy-matteo-renzi-referendum.html?smid=pl-share&_r=0 ("Prime Minister Matteo Renzi said he would resign after voters decisively rejected constitutional changes.").

23. Russell J. Dalton, Wilhelm Bürklin, & Andrew Drummond, *Public Opinion and Direct Democracy*, 12 J. OF DEMOCRACY 141, 141 (2001).

24. *What's Gone Wrong with Democracy*, THE ECONOMIST (Mar 1, 2014), http://perma.cc/2KWC-8XCH.

25. *Trends in Party Identification, 1939–2014*, PEW RESCH. CENTER (Apr. 7, 2015), http://perma.cc/N9C8-SZBM.

26. *See generally* J. DAVID GREENSTONE, LABOR IN AMERICAN POLITICS (1969) (documenting American labor's symbiotic relationship with the Democratic Party through the first half of the twentieth century); Peter L. Francia, *Assessing the Labor–Democratic Party Alliance: A One-Sided Relationship?*, 42 POLITY 293 (2010) (contrasting modern organized labor's continued support for Democratic candidates with Democratic failures to deliver pro-labor policy).

27. *See generally* DANIEL ZIBLATT, CONSERVATIVE PARTIES AND THE BIRTH OF DEMOCRACY (2017) (chronicling the organizational rise of the British and German conservative parties).

28. Tom O'Grady, *Careerists Versus Coal Miners: Welfare Reforms and the Substantive Representation of Social Groups in the British Labour Party*, 52 COMPAR. POL. STUD. 544, 547 (2018).

29. MEGAN DUNN & JAMES WALKER, U.S. BUREAU OF LAB. STAT., UNION MEMBERSHIP IN THE UNITED STATES 2–4 (2016), http://perma.cc/5VPC-YDKB.

30. The concern over the legal implications of the distinct role of public-sector unionism in the United States goes back at least to Harry Wellington and Ralph Winter. Harry H. Wellington & Ralph K. Winter Jr, *The Limits of Collective Bargaining in Public Employment*, 78 YALE L. J. 1107, 1116, 1124–25 (1969).

31. Matthew Yglesias, *Scott Walker's Plan to Crush American Labor Unions, Explained*, VOX (Sept. 18, 2015), https://www.vox.com/2015/9/18/9345805/scott-walkers-union-plan ("Walker repeatedly refers to unions as 'special interests' and public sector unions (which, these days, account for most union members) as 'big-government special interests'").

32. David Brodwin, *The Chamber's Secrets*, U.S. NEWS & WORLD REPS. (Oct. 22, 2015), http://perma.cc/8SJU-E53D. *See also generally* ALYSSA KATZ, THE INFLUENCE MACHINE: THE U.S. CHAMBER OF COMMERCE AND THE CORPORATE CAPTURE OF AMERICAN LIFE (2015).

33. Brodwin, *The Chamber's Secrets*. The article goes on to state:

> Founded in 1912, the U.S. Chamber of Commerce has been shaped by its CEO Tom Donohue into a powerful lobbying and campaigning machine that pursues a fairly narrow special-interest agenda. It's now the largest lobbying organization in the U.S. (ranked by budget). It mostly represents the interests of a handful of so-called "legacy industries"—industries like tobacco, banking and fossil fuels which have been around for generations and learned how to parley their earnings into political influence. The Chamber seeks favorable treatment for them, for example, through trade negotiations, tax treatment, regulations and judicial rulings.

34. *Id.*; *see also* KATZ, THE INFLUENCE MACHINE at xiii (discussing the "undisclosed financial contributions to the U.S. Chamber of Commerce" made by "industries that provide vital goods and services but at mounting costs to society").

35. Ronald Coase, *The Nature of the Firm*, 4 ECONOMICA 386 (1937).

36. *Id.* at 390–91.

37. *Id.* at 388.

38. *Id.* at 390.

39. *Id.* at 393.

40. Oliver E. Williamson, *The Modern Corporation: Origins, Evolution, Attributes*, 19 J. ECON. LITERATURE 1537, 1540–42 (1981).

41. KEY, POLITICS, PARTIES, & PRESSURE GROUPS.

42. Nathaniel Persily & Bruce E. Cain, *The Legal Status of Political Parties: A Reassessment of Competing Paradigms*, 100 COLUM. L. REV. 775, 778 (2000) (citations omitted) (citing v. o. KEY, JR., POLITICS, PARTIES AND PRESSURE GROUPS 163–65 (5th ed., 1964) [hereafter KEY (5th ed.)]).

43. KEY (5th ed.), at 164.

44. *Id.*

45. *Id.* (providing as examples national committeemen, state central committees, county chairmen, and organizational staffers).

46. *Id.*

47. Of course, corporations also confront complexity in the form of principal-agent problems, competing short- and long-term objectives, and uncertain payoffs for investment opportunities.

48. *See generally* JOSEPH SCHUMPETER, CAPITALISM, SOCIALISM AND DEMOCRACY (1942) (discussing creative destruction).

49. *See* ALBERT O. HIRSCHMAN, EXIT, VOICE AND LOYALTY: RESPONSES TO DECLINE IN FIRMS, ORGANIZATIONS, AND STATES (1990).

50. *See* Roger D. Congleton, *The Median Voter Model*, *in* 1 THE ENCYCLOPEDIA OF PUBLIC CHOICE 382, 384 (Charles K. Rowley & Fredrich Schneider, eds., 2004).

51. KEY (5th ed.), at 212.

52. *See, e.g.*, MORRIS P. FIORINA, HOOVER INSTITUTION, HAS THE AMERICAN PUBLIC POLARIZED? 10–12 (Sept. 14, 2016), http://www.hoover.org/sites/default/files/research/docs/fior ina_finalfile_0.pdf.

53. *See, e.g.*, Jay K. Dow, *A Comparative Spatial Analysis of Majoritarian and Proportional Systems*, 20 ELECTORAL STUDIES 109, 111 (2001); FERDINAND A. HERMENS, DEMOCRACY OR ANARCHY? A STUDY OF PROPORTIONAL REPRESENTATION 19 (1941); KEY (5th ed.), at 220 (footnote omitted) ("The diversity of pressures from within the party upon the leadership drives it to-ward moderation. . . . The situation generates a radically different sort of imperative for the leadership than does the context in which party leaders of a multiparty system operate: they may be driven to accentuate the separatism of their electoral following.").

54. FIORINA, HAS THE AMERICAN PUBLIC POLARIZED? at 2–5.

55. KEY (5th ed.), at 316 ("Collaboration comes about, to the extent that it does come about, through a sense of common cause rather than by the exercise of command.").

56. *Id.* at 323.

57. *Id.* at 331.

58. *Id.* at 341 ("Tightly managed statewide organization has become exceptional and has been replaced by a fractionalized system of personal and fractional cliques of professionals within each party."). Key links this decentralizing upheaval to both a decline in patronage, disruptive new mass media technologies, and the adoption of direct primaries. *Id.* at 342. Those factors have only intensified in the intervening period.

59. CAIN, DEMOCRACY MORE OR LESS, at 134–35 (identifying the majoritarian consolidation of power in the House and anti-majoritarian "holds, unanimous consent, and cloture rules" in the Senate).

60. *See* Dennis C. Mueller, *Public Choice: An Introduction*, *in* 1 THE ENCYCLOPEDIA OF PUBLIC CHOICE 32 (Charles K. Rowley & Fredrich Schneider, eds., 2004).

61. Ray v. Blair, 343 U.S. 214, 221 (1952).

62. *See* Bernard Grofman, *Public Choice, Civic Republicanism, and American Politics: Perspectives of a "Reasonable Choice" Modeler*, 71 TEX. L. REV. 1541, 1558–59 (1993). For some examples of cycling in legislative settings, see William H. Riker & Steven J. Brams, *The Paradox of Vote Trading*, 67 AM. POL. SCI. REV. 1235, 1246–47 (1973).

63. *E.g.*, consider a situation where there are 19 voters on an issue with three choices. 8 voters prefer option B the most, followed by option C, and then option A (B>C>A). 6 voters prefer option C, followed by option A, then option B (C>A>B). Finally, 5 voters prefer option A, followed by option B, followed by option C (A>B>C). Here, it is difficult to model what choice would win in a vote. A is preferred over B by 11 out of 19 voters, C is preferred over A by 14 out of 19 voters, and B is preferred over C by 13 out of 19 voters. For a further il-lustration of this example, *see* Jan Kok, Clay Shentrup, & Warren Smith, *Condorcet Cycles*,

RANGEVOTING.ORG, http://rangevoting.org/CondorcetCycles.html (last visited Sept. 15, 2021).

64. *See Texas Senate Changes Majority Rules to Benefit Republicans*, CBS AUSTIN (Jan. 13, 2021), https://cbsaustin.com/news/local/texas-senate-changes-majority-rules-to-benefit-republicans (explaining how the two-thirds rule became the three-fifths rule and then became the five-ninths rule).

65. *Why Is the Lieutenant Governor the Most Powerful Office in Texas? And Who Wants That Power?*, KUT 90.5 (Oct. 16, 2014), http://kut.org/post/why-lieutenant-governor-most-powerful-office-texas-and-who-wants-power ("The lieutenant governor appoints all the committee chairs of the committees in the Senate, determines where the bills are going to be sent and to what committees and the timing.").

66. KEY (5th ed.), at 219 ("The makeup of each party also restrains the zeal of the leadership in the advocacy of the cause of any single element within the party. Leaders in congressional districts may be extremists . . . nevertheless, that segment of the party leadership with a national outlook—fundamentally those concerned with victory in presidential elections—must keep in view all elements within the party.").

67. JOHN H. ALDRICH, WHY PARTIES? THE ORIGIN AND TRANSFORMATION OF POLITICAL PARTIES IN AMERICA 4 (1995) (describing governance in the U.S. as being the ultimate litmus test for party success).

68. Michael S. Kang, *The Hydraulics and Politics of Party Regulation*, 91 IOWA L. REV. 131, 166 (2005).

69. SETH E. MASKET, THE INEVITABLE PARTY: WHY ATTEMPTS TO KILL THE PARTY SYSTEM FAIL AND HOW THEY WEAKEN DEMOCRACY 18 (2016).

70. Justin A. Nelson, *The Supply and Demand of Campaign Finance Reform*, 100 COLUM. L. REV. 524, 539 (2000).

71. Samuel Issacharoff & Pamela S. Karlan, *The Hydraulics of Campaign Finance Reform*, 77 TEX. L. REV. 1705, 1708 (1999).

72. Carroll Doherty, *Seven Things to Know About Polarization in America*, PEW RESCH. CTR. (June 12, 2014), http://www.pewresearch.org/fact-tank/2014/06/12/7-things-to-know-about-polarization-in-america/ (finding higher rates of political donations amount "ideologically consistent" partisans).

73. RAYMOND J. LA RAJA & BRIAN F. SCHAFFNER, CAMPAIGN FINANCE AND POLITICAL POLARIZATION: WHEN PURISTS PREVAIL 59 (4th ed., 2015).

74. Issacharoff & Karlan, *The Hydraulics of Campaign Finance Reform* at 1717–18.

75. Colorado Republican Fed. Campaign Comm. v. FEC (*Colorado Republican I*), 518 U.S. 604, 614 (1996) (recognizing protection of party independent expenditures so long as not coordinated with any candidate).

76. FEC v. Colorado Republican Fed. Campaign Comm. (*Colorado. Republican II*), 533 U.S. 431, 453 (2001).

77. *See* Stephen Ansolabehere & James M. Snyder, Jr., *Soft Money, Hard Money, Strong Parties*, 100 COLUM. L. REV. 598, 614–15 (2000).

78. *See id.* at 606–7 (roughly 15 percent held back by state parties); PETER REUTER & EDWIN M. TRUMAN, CHASING DIRTY MONEY: THE FIGHT AGAINST MONEY LAUNDERING 36 (2004) ("Experienced investigators refer to a general price range of 7 to 15% for laundering for drug dealers, but some reports are inconsistent with such estimates.").

79. *See* Andy Kroll, *Follow the Dark Money*, MOTHER JONES (July/Aug. 2012), http://www.motherjones.com/politics/2012/06/history-money-american-elections.

80. *See, e.g.*, Stephen Labaton, *House Aide Links a Top Lawmaker to Embezzlement*, N.Y. TIMES (July 20, 1993), https://nyti.ms/1FHybBd; Press Release, *Former Delegate Fauntroy Is Charged, Agrees to Plead Guilty* (Mar. 22, 1995), https://www.justice.gov/archive/opa/pr/Pre_96/March95/153.txt.html.

81. Kevin R. Kosar, *Shutdown of the Federal Government: Causes, Effects, and Process*, CRS REP. FOR CONGRESS 2 (Sept. 20, 2004), http://archives.democrats.rules.house.gov/archives/98-844.pdf.

82. *How the Senators Voted on Impeachment*, CNN (Feb. 12, 1999), http://www.cnn.com/ALLPOLITICS/stories/1999/02/12/senate.vote/.

83. For example, much of the "Republic Revolution" of 1994 was driven by a united attack by the Republican Party on Bill Clinton's healthcare reform and perceived liberalism. *See* Stuart Rothenberg, *How High the Wave? Don't Just Think 1994; Think 1974, 1958, 1982*, INSIDE ELECTIONS (Oct. 26, 2006), http://insideelections.com/news/article/how-high-the-wave-dont-just-think-1994-think-1974-1958-1982.

84. Jeffrey B. Gayner, *The Heritage Lectures: The Contract with America: Implementing New Ideas in the U.S.*, HERITAGE FOUND. 1–2 (1995), http://s3.amazonaws.com/thf_media/1995/pdf/hl549.pdf.

85. The best account of the transformation of the Republican Party around the coordinating force of Newt Gingrich is found in JULIAN E. ZELIZER, BURNING DOWN THE HOUSE: NEWT GINGRICH, THE FALL OF A SPEAKER, AND THE RISE OF THE NEW REPUBLICAN PARTY (2020).

86. Bipartisan Campaign Reform Act of 2002, Pub. L. No. 107-155, 116 Stat. 81 (2002); Robert Kelner & Raymond La Raja, Opinion, *McCain-Feingold's Devastating Legacy*, WASH. POST (Apr. 11, 2014), https://www.washingtonpost.com/opinions/mccain-feingolds-devastating-legacy/2014/04/11/14a528e2-c18f-11e3-bcec-b71ee10e9bc3_story.html.

87. In the 2000 election cycle, the Center for Responsive Politics reports that independent expenditures totaled $5,095,476, across all federal elections. The 2008 total was $64,122,607, representing a 1,258 percent increase. Ctr. For Responsive Pol., *Total Outside Spending by Election Cycle, Excluding Party Committees*, OPENSECRETS.ORG, http://www.opensecrets.org/outsidespending/cycle_tots.php?cycle=2014&view=Y&chart=N (last visited Feb. 4, 2017).

88. Michael J. Malbin, *McCutcheon Could Lead to No Limits for Political Parties—With What Implications for Parties and Interest Groups?*, 89 N.Y.U. L. REV. ONLINE 92, 99–100 (2014).

89. Joseph Fishkin & Heather K. Gerken, *The Two Trends That Matter for Party Politics*, 89 N.Y.U. L. REV. ONLINE 32, 35 (2014).

90. *See, e.g., id.* (providing an overview of the law of super PACs and their role in recent campaigns); Terence Dougherty, *Section 501(c)(4) Advocacy Organizations: Political Candidate-Related and Other Partisan Activities in Furtherance of the Social Welfare*, 36 SEATTLE U. L. REV. 1337 (2013) (summarizing the treatment of 501(c)(4) organizations and their political activities); Michael S. Kang, *The Year of the Super PAC*, 81 GEO. WASH. L. REV. 1902 (2013) (discussing the influence of super PACs in the 2012 presidential election cycle); Garrick B. Pursley, *The Campaign Finance Safeguards of Federalism*, 63 EMORY L.J. 781 (2014) (tracing the rise of super PACs and their weakening of federalism); Bradley A. Smith, *Super PACs and the Role of "Coordination" in Campaign Finance Law*, 49 WILLAMETTE L. REV. 603 (2013) (describing the rise of super PACs and the anti-coordinating requirements); Molly J. Walker Wilson, *Financing Elections and "Appearance of Corruption": Citizen Attitudes and Behavior in 2012*, 63 CATH. U. L. REV. 953 (2014) (reviewing the rise of super PACs and their effect on voters' perceptions of political corruption).

91. In the 2008 cycle, Barack Obama raised approximately $750 million from donors, while John McCain raised roughly $238 million from donors. Tahman Bradley, *Final Fundraising Figure: Obama's $750M*, ABC NEWS (Dec. 5, 2008), http://abcnews.go.com/Politics/Vote2008/story?id=6397572&page=1.

92. Twenty-four percent of Barack Obama's $746.1 million in contributions in the 2008 cycle (pre-nomination and general election contributions combined) came from donors who gave less than $200. *All CFI Funding Statistics Revised and Updated for the 2008 Presidential Primary and General Election Candidates*, CAMPAIGN FIN. INST. (Jan. 8, 2010), http://www.cfinst.org/press/releases_tags/10-01-08/Revised_and_Updated_2008_Presidential_Statistics.aspx.

93. *See* Nicholas Confessore & Nick Corasaniti, *Small Donations Help Trump Cut Fund-Raising Gap*, N.Y. TIMES (Aug. 3, 2016), at A1, A12 ("Mr. Trump has the potential to be the first Republican nominee whose campaign could be financed chiefly by grass-roots supports pitching in $10 or $25 apiece, echoing the success of Senator Bernie Sanders of Vermont during the Democratic primary.").

94. *See, e.g.* Ollie Gratzinger, *Small Donors Give Big Money in 2020 Election Cycle*, OPENSECRETS (Oct. 30, 2020), https://www.opensecrets.org/news/2020/10/small-donors-give-big-2020-thanks-to-technology (noting the importance of small dollar donations for Biden, Trump, and several congressional candidates); Susan Davis, *"Fundraging" Fuels Democratic Money Advantage Over GOP in Most Races*, NPR (Oct. 22, 2020), https://www.npr.org/

2020/10/22/925892007/fundraging-fuels-democratic-money-advantage-over-gop-in-most-races (explaining that much of the money donates to high-profile congressional races comes from small dollar donations); Elena Schneider, *ActBlue's Stunning Third Quarter: $1.5 Billion in Donations*, POLITICO (Oct. 15, 2020) (referencing the power of small-dollar donors in the 2020 Democratic primary).

95. CAIN, DEMOCRACY MORE OR LESS at 202.

96. *See* Fredreka Schouten, *2016 Hopefuls Gear Up For "Koch" Primary*, USA TODAY (July 29, 2015), http://www.usatoday.com/story/news/politics/elections/2016/2015/07/29/charles-koch-donors-meeting-california/30803357/ ("GOP candidates are headed to California to tout their conservative credentials in person before [the Kochs] and . . . hundreds of wealthy donors. . . . [The candidates] will participate in question-and-answer sessions during the gathering of about 450 contributors who have pledged to spend nearly $900 million ahead of the 2016 election.").

97. Karen Yourish, Larry Buchanan, & Alicia Parlapiano, *More Than 160 Republican Leaders Don't Support Donald Trump. Here's When They Reached Their Breaking Point*, N.Y. TIMES (Oct. 9, 2016), https://nyti.ms/2kBZfQ6.

98. KEY (5th ed.), at 348.

99. *Compare* MICHAEL KAZIN, THE POPULIST PERSUASION: AN AMERICAN HISTORY 288 (1998) (discussing how American political parties ideologically adapted in order to avert challenges by third parties), *with* MARTIN & SUSAN TOLCHIN, TO THE VICTOR . . . : POLITICAL PATRONAGE FROM THE CLUBHOUSE TO THE WHITE HOUSE 300–02 (1971) (portraying New Deal programs as patronage disguised as ideological concessions in order to "neutralize and incorporate the disaffected groups").

100. *See* BRUCE F. BERG, NEW YORK CITY POLITICS: GOVERNING GOTHAM 165, 253 (2007).

101. Wolfgang C. Müller, *Party Patronage and Party Colonization of the State, in* HANDBOOK OF PARTY POLITICS 189, 191 (Richard S. Katz & William Crotty, eds., 2006).

102. CAIN, DEMOCRACY MORE OR LESS at 159.

103. LEON D. EPSTEIN, POLITICAL PARTIES IN WESTERN DEMOCRACIES 105, 110, & n.25 (1979).

104. CARL RUSSELL FISH, THE CIVIL SERVICE AND THE PATRONAGE 156 (1905).

105. By introducing the "spoils system" for federal employment Andrew Jackson aimed to "democratize public service by expanding the class of persons eligible for public positions, ensuring bureaucratic responsiveness to the popular will, and limiting the extent to which corruption developed during lengthy tenure in office might taint the public service." Note, *Developments in the Law: Public Employment*, 97 HARV. L. REV. 1611, 1624 (1984).

106. EPSTEIN, *supra* note 103, at 106 (citing HAROLD F. GOSNELL, MACHINE POLITICS: CHICAGO MODEL (1937)).

107. WILLIAM L. RIORDON, PLUNKITT OF TAMMANY HALL 3–4 (Terrence J. McDonald, ed., 1994) (1905).

108. KEY (5th ed.), at 337 ("Patronage is an important factor in building up lines of command and in establishing internal cohesion and discipline in the machine.").

109. James Q. Wilson, *The Economy of Patronage*, 69 J. POL. ECON. 369, 373 (1961). Wilson describes the conflict inherent in different uses of patronage: maintaining boss's power, controlling elected officials, maximizing the vote, and attracting party workers, at 371.

110. KEY (5th ed.), at 338 (quoting CARROLL HILL WOODDY, THE CHICAGO PRIMARY OF 1926: A STUDY IN ELECTION METHODS 7–8 (1926)).

111. Wilson, *The Economy of Patronage* at 372 (noting that there were only 115–120 jobs available in New York at the same time).

112. Pendleton Civil Service Reform Act, ch. 27, 22 Stat. 403 (1883).

113. V. O. KEY, JR. POLITICS, PARTIES & PRESSURE GROUPS 390 (4th ed., 1958).

114. *Id.*

115. *Id.* at 391.

116. *Id.* at 391–92.

117. 427 U.S. 347 (1976).

118. *Id.* at 369 (footnote omitted).

119. Rutan v. Republican Party of Illinois, 497 U.S. 62, 103–04 (1990) (Scalia, J., dissenting).

120. *Id.* at 106.

121. *Id.* at 109.
122. SCHATTSCHNEIDER, PARTY GOVERNMENT at 64.
123. *Boris Johnson Wins Race to Be Tory Leader and PM*, BBC (July 23, 2019), https://www.bbc.com/news/uk-politics-49084605.
124. *See* Heather Stewart, *Boris Johnson Elected New Tory Leader*, THE GUARDIAN (July 23, 2019), https://www.theguardian.com/politics/2019/jul/23/boris-johnson-elected-new-tory-lea der-prime-minister.
125. WILLIAM P. CROSS, OFER KENIG, SCOTT PRUYSERS, & GIDEON RAHAT, THE PROMISE AND CHALLENGE OF PARTY PRIMARY ELECTIONS 6 (2016).
126. Ray v. Blair, 343 U.S. 214, 221 (1952).
127. DANIEL H. LOWENSTEIN ET AL., ELECTION LAW 415 (5th ed., 2012) (discussing *Ray v. Blair*, 343 U.S. 214 (1952)).
128. Winkler, *Voters' Rights and Parties' Wrongs* at 877.
129. *Id.* at 876.
130. Robin Miller, Annotation, *Constitutionality of Voter Participation Provisions for Primary Elections*, 120 A. L. R. 5th § 2 (2004).
131. *See, e.g.*, Whitney v. California, 274 U.S. 357, 373 (1927) (Brandeis, J., concurring); Olmstead v. United States, 277 U.S. 438, 471 (1928) (Holmes, J., dissenting).
132. Winkler, *Voters' Rights and Parties' Wrongs* at 879.
133. *Id.*
134. ALAN WARE, THE AMERICAN DIRECT PRIMARY: PARTY INSTITUTIONALIZATION AND TRANSFORMATION IN THE NORTH 227 (2002).
135. JAMIE L. CARSON & JASON M. ROBERTS, AMBITION, COMPETITION, AND ELECTORAL REFORM: THE POLITICS OF CONGRESSIONAL ELECTIONS ACROSS TIME 35–36 (2013).
136. *Id.* at 43–44.
137. *Id.* at 92–93.
138. WARE, THE AMERICAN DIRECT PRIMARY at 251–52.
139. *Id.* at 252.
140. *Id.* at 253.
141. Drew Desilver, *So Far, Turnout in This Year's Primaries Rivals 2008 Record*, PEW RESCH. CTR. (Mar. 8, 2016), http://www.pewresearch.org/fact-tank/2016/03/08/so-far-turnout-in-this-years-primaries-rivals-2008-record. In Nevada, for example, Clinton won the 2008 state Democratic caucuses with fewer than 20,000 people participating, in a state with a population of 2.7 million. *See Election 2008 Nevada Caucus Results*, N.Y. TIMES (Jan. 19, 2008), http://politics.nytimes.com/election-guide/2008/results/states/NV.html; Tim Richardson, *Nevada Falls to No. 8 in Population Growth*, L.V. SUN (Dec. 22, 2008), https://lasvegassun.com/news/2008/dec/22/nevada-falls-no-8-population-growth.
142. Jonathan Rauch, *How American Politics Went Insane*, THE ATLANTIC (July/Aug. 2016), https://www.theatlantic.com/magazine/archive/2016/07/how-american-politics-went-insane/485570.
143. *See* CAIN, DEMOCRACY MORE OR LESS at 89 ("Voters compensate for [their] knowledge deficiency by relying heavily on electoral appeals and voting cues communicated by more 'expert' individuals and groups th[r]ough paid and unpaid media. Ballot box measures, consequently, give well-organized and well-resourced interest groups an additional avenue of influence beyond lobbying and donating to candidates.").
144. Rauch, *How American Politics Went Insane* (describing Eric Cantor, "the Republican House majority leader who, in a shocking upset, lost to an unknown Tea Partier in his 2014 primary"). For other examples of successful incumbent challenges in primary contests brought about by ideological activists and low voter turnout, see CAIN, DEMOCRACY MORE OR LESS at 9.
145. CARSON & ROBERTS, AMBITION, COMPETITION, AND ELECTORAL REFORM at 143.
146. MASKET, THE INEVITABLE PARTY at 133 (quoting La Follette in an 1897 address).
147. *Id.* at 147.
148. Andrew Prokop, *The Democratic Platform, Explained*, VOX (Aug. 18, 2020), https://www.vox.com/2020/8/18/21322685/democratic-convention-platform-controversy.

149. *See generally* Landon Schnabel, *When Fringe Goes Mainstream Again: A Comparative Textual Analysis of the Tea Party Movement's Contract from America and the Republican Party Platform,* 15 POL., RELIGION & IDEOLOGY 604 (2014).

150. Interview by Jeff Stein with David A. Hopkins (July 12, 2016), https://www.vox.com/2016/7/12/12060358/political-science-of-platforms ("The platform can serve as an easy giveaway for presidential nominees looking to placate fired-up ideological activists—precisely because it lacks any real enforcement mechanism.").

151. *Id.* ("The activists can get something of a free hand with the platform because they can be the only ones who care,' Hopkins says. 'And then the candidates will think, "Well, if this makes the activists happy, and nobody else is paying attention, then there's no harm done."'").

152. *See* Julia Beth Fierman, *"We Are Peronists, We Are Organic": Discipline, Authority, and Loyalty in Argentine Populism,* 10 SOC. SCIS. 326, 326 (2021) (evaluating Peronism to "elucidate how populist movements valorize discipline and loyalty in order to unify their ranks around sentiment and ritual in the absence of more stable programmatic positions").

153. Reid J. Epstein, *The G.O.P. Delivers Its 2020 Platform. It's From 2016,* N.Y. TIMES (Aug. 25, 2020), https://www.nytimes.com/2020/08/25/us/politics/republicans-platform.html.

154. *See* Republican Nat'l Comm., 2016 Republican Party Platform (2016), https://prod-cdn-static.gop.com/static/home/data/platform.pdf.

155. Republican Nat'l Comm., Resolution Regarding the Republican Party Platform (2020), https://prod-cdn-static.gop.com/media/documents/RESOLUTION_REGARDING_THE_REPUBLICAN_PARTY_PLATFORM.pdf?_ga=2.109560193.504857691.159 8219603-2087748323.1598219603.

156. Pildes, *Romanticizing Democracy* at 809–10.

157. *See* Katherine Krimmel, The Efficiencies and Pathologies of Special Interest Partisanship 5 (June 22, 2015) (unpublished manuscript on file with author) (quoting E. E. Schattschneider, *Pressure Groups Versus Political Parties,* ANNALS AM. ACAD. POL. & SOC. SCI. (Sept. 1948), at 18). Professor Krimmel's doctoral dissertation appears to be the first effort to take seriously the Coasean insights into the nature of a firm for the role of political parties. Professor Krimmel focuses on the ability and incentives for political parties to outsource communication functions to interest groups as a contributing factor to the polarization of political parties at present.

Chapter 4

1. STEVEN LEVITSKY & LUCAN A. WAY, COMPETITIVE AUTHORITARIANISM: HYBRID REGIMES AFTER THE COLD WAR 5 (2010).

2. Orbán pre-COVID had popularity ratings of about 66 percent, which rose to 74 percent during the pandemic. Dénes Albert, *Hungary: PM Orbán Is 5th Most Popular EU Leader During Coronavirus Crisis,* REMIX NEWS (Apr. 14, 2020), https://rmx.news/article/article/hungary-pm-orban-is-5th-most-popular-eu-leader-during-coronavirus-crisis. Modi was about 74 percent pre-COVID; then up to 82 percent. Katharina Buchholz, *World Leaders' Approval Suffers as COVID Crisis Drags On,* STATISTA (May 3, 2021), https://www.statista.com/chart/21812/world-leader-approval-ratings/. Erdoğan pre-COVID was at 41.9 percent in February; up to 55.9 percent in March with the pandemic. *Pandemic Boosts Support for Europe's Autocrats,* REPORTING DEMOCRACY (May 6, 2020), https://balkaninsight.com/2020/05/06/pandemic-boosts-support-for-europes-autocrats/.

3. *Freedom in the World 2017,* FREEDOM HOUSE (2017), https://freedomhouse.org/sites/defa ult/files/FH_FIW_2017_Report_Final.pdf. As populism consolidates, the figure drops with eighty-three countries labeled "free;" sixty-three "partly free;" and forty-nine "not free." *Freedom in the World 2020,* FREEDOM HOUSE (2017), https://freedomhouse.org/sites/defa ult/files/2020-02/FIW_2020_REPORT_BOOKLET_Final.pdf.

4. JOSEPH A. SCHUMPETER, CAPITALISM, SOCIALISM, AND DEMOCRACY 269–73 (3d ed., 2008) (1950).

5. JAN-WERNER MÜLLER, WHAT IS POPULISM? 41–49 (2016).

6. Isaiah Berlin et al., *To Define Populism,* 3 GOV'T & OPPOSITION 137, 174 (1968).

7. ERIC A. POSNER, THE DEMAGOGUE'S PLAYBOOK: THE BATTLE FOR AMERICAN DEMOCRACY FROM THE FOUNDERS TO TRUMP 8 (2020).

8. Ming-Sung Kuo, *Against Instantaneous Democracy*, 17 INT'L J. CON. L. 554, 562 (2019).

9. SCHUMPETER, CAPITALISM, SOCIALISM, AND DEMOCRACY at 258–59.

10. *See, e.g.,* ARLIE R. HOCHSCHILD, STRANGERS IN THEIR OWN LAND: ANGER AND MOURNING ON THE AMERICAN RIGHT (2016); KATHERINE J. CRAMER, THE POLITICS OF RESENTMENT: RURAL CONSCIOUSNESS IN WISCONSIN AND THE RISE OF SCOTT WALKER (2016).

11. Rogers Brubaker, *Why Populism?*, 46 THEORY & SOC'Y 357, 363 (2017).

12. RICHARD HOFSTADTER, THE PARANOID STYLE IN AMERICAN POLITICS AND OTHER ESSAYS 3 (1965).

13. DAVID RUNCIMAN, HOW DEMOCRACY ENDS 171 (2018).

14. IVAN KRASTEV & STEPHEN HOLMES, THE LIGHT THAT FAILED: WHY THE WEST IS LOSING THE FIGHT FOR DEMOCRACY 140 (2020).

15. *See* NANCY ROSENBLUM, ON THE SIDE OF ANGELS: AN APPRECIATION OF PARTIES AND PARTISANSHIP 121 (2008) (invoking Edmund Burke's idea of regulated rivalry).

16. Kuo, *Against Instantaneous Democracy* at 554.

17. LARRY DIAMOND, ILL WINDS: SAVING DEMOCRACY FROM RUSSIAN RAGE, CHINESE AMBITION, AND AMERICAN COMPLACENCY 62 (2019).

18. ETHAN B. KAPSTEIN & NATHAN CONVERSE, *Why Democracies Fail, in* POVERTY, INEQUALITY, AND DEMOCRACY 29, 29 (Francis Fukuyama et al. eds., 2012).

19. Dylan Lino, *Albert Venn Dicey and the Constitutional Theory of Empire*, 36 OXFORD J. LEGAL STUD. 751, 777 (2016).

20. SIR IVOR JENNINGS, THE LAW AND THE CONSTITUTION 135 (1959).

21. P. S. ATIYAH, PROMISES, MORALS AND LAW 116 (1982); *see also* DAVID HUME, *A Treatise of Human Nature, in* MORAL PHILOSOPHY 12, 87–99 (2006) (identifying institutional arrangements that arise not from formal consent but from shared benefits from the utility of the practice).

22. Ernest Young, *Rediscovering Conservatism: Burkean Political Theory and Constitutional Interpretation*, 72 N. CAROLINA L. REV. 619, 649 (1994).

23. GEOFFREY MARSHALL, CONSTITUTIONAL CONVENTIONS: THE RULES AND FORMS OF POLITICAL ACCOUNTABILITY 4 (1987).

24. A. V. DICEY, INTRODUCTION TO THE STUDY OF THE LAW OF THE CONSTITUTION 431 (10th ed., 1985).

25. EDMUND BURKE, REFLECTIONS ON THE REVOLUTION IN FRANCE 18 (Frank Turner, ed., 2003) (1790).

26. Ivan Krastev, *Age of Populism: Reflections on the Self-Enmity of Democracy*, 10 EUR. VIEW 11, 12–14 (2011).

27. *Id.* at 12–13.

28. Martin Krygier, *The Challenge of Institutionalisation: Post-Communist "Transitions," Populism, and the Rule of Law*, 15 EUR. CONST. L. REV. 544 (2019)

29. *See* ALEN TOPLIŠEK, LIBERAL DEMOCRACY IN CRISIS: RETHINKING RESISTANCE UNDER NEOLIBERAL GOVERNMENTALITY (2019).

30. For a systematic catalog of the president's major outlandish claims, see Christian Paz, *All the President's Lies About the Coronavirus*, THE ATLANTIC (Nov. 2, 2020), https://www.theatlantic.com/politics/archive/2020/11/trumps-lies-about-coronavirus/608647/.

31. MÜLLER, WHAT IS POPULISM? at 20.

32. ADAM PRZEWORSKI ET AL., DEMOCRACY AND DEVELOPMENT: POLITICAL INSTITUTIONS AND WELL-BEING IN THE WORLD, 1950–1990 18–27 (2000).

33. BERNARD MANIN, THE PRINCIPLES OF REPRESENTATIVE GOVERNMENT 29 (1997).

34. Kuo, *Against Instantaneous Democracy* at 561.

35. ALEXIS DE TOCQUEVILLE, DEMOCRACY IN AMERICA 232 (J. P. Mayer, ed., George Lawrence, trans.) (1835).

36. Everything old is, of course, new again. Steve Inskeep, *Donald Trump and the Legacy of Andrew Jackson*, THE ATLANTIC (Nov. 30, 2016), https://www.theatlantic.com/politics/archive/2016/11/trump-and-andrew-jackson/508973/.

37. TOCQUEVILLE, DEMOCRACY IN AMERICA at 35.

38. SAMUEL ISSACHAROFF, FRAGILE DEMOCRACIES 223–25 (2015).

39. TOM GINSBURG, JUDICIAL REVIEW IN NEW DEMOCRACIES: CONSTITUTIONAL COURTS IN ASIAN CASES 22–30 (2003).

40. As with all reforms examined one by one, the risks of the filibuster run heavily toward a minority hold-out veto and an ability of a partisan minority to attempt to defeat governance altogether. *See, e.g.,* MIMI MARZIANI, FILIBUSTER ABUSE (2010); Catherine Fisk & Erwin Chemerinsky, *The Filibuster,* 49 STAN. L. REV. 181 (1997); Gerard N. Magliocca, *Reforming the Filibuster,* 105 NW. U. L. REV. 303 (2011); Benjamin Eidelson, *The Majoritarian Filibuster,* 122 YALE L. J. 980 (2013).

41. *See* MASHA GESSEN, THE FUTURE IS HISTORY: HOW TOTALITARIANISM RECLAIMED RUSSIA (2017).

42. Rachelle Krygier & Anthony Faiola, *Venezuela's Pro-Government Assembly Moves to Take Power from Elected Congress,* WASH. POST (Aug. 18, 2017), https://www.washingtonpost.com/world/venezuelas-pro-government-assembly-moves-to-take-power-from-elected-congress/2017/08/18/9c6cd0a2-8416-11e7-9e7a-20fa8d7a0db6_story.html.

43. Richard Fausset, *North Carolina Governor Signs Law Limiting Successor's Power,* N.Y. TIMES (Dec. 16, 2016), https://www.nytimes.com/2016/12/16/us/pat-mccrory-roy-cooper-north-carolina.html. After courts blocked portions of the law, efforts redoubled. Mark Joseph Stern, *North Carolina GOP Votes to Dilute Governor's Power and Curtail Voting Rights—Again,* SLATE: THE SLATEST (Apr. 12, 2017), http://www.slate.com/blogs/the_slatest/2017/04/12/north_carolina_republicans_dilute_governor_s_power_and_curtail_voting_rights.html.

44. NOAH FELDMAN, THE THREE LIVES OF JAMES MADISON: GENIUS, PARTISAN, PRESIDENT 112–15 (2017).

45. Müller, WHAT IS POPULISM? at 20.

46. NANCY ROSENBLUM, ON THE SIDE OF THE ANGELS: AN APPRECIATION OF PARTIES AND PARTISANSHIP 11 (2008).

47. My thanks to Donald Verrilli for this helpful formulation.

48. Mfuneko Toyana, *South African Court Rules Zuma Appointment of State Prosecutor Invalid,* REUTERS (Dec. 8, 2017), https://www.reuters.com/article/us-safrica-zuma/south-african-court-rules-zuma-appointment-of-state-prosecutor-invalid-idUSKBN1E2151; Daniel Boffey & Christian Davies, *Poland Cries Foul as EU Triggers "Nuclear Option" over Judicial Independence,* THE GUARDIAN (Dec. 20, 2017), https://www.theguardian.com/world/2017/dec/20/eu-process-poland-voting-rights; Andrew Byrne, *Orban Goads Soros with Hungarian University Laws,* FIN. TIMES (Mar. 29, 2017), https://www.ft.com/content/3a125962-148c-11e7-80f4-13e067d5072c.

49. NIELS PETERSEN, PROPORTIONALITY AND JUDICIAL ACTIVISM: FUNDAMENTAL RIGHTS ADJUDICATION IN CANADA, GERMANY AND SOUTH AFRICA 19–21 (2017).

50. *Id.*

51. *See* Maoz Rosenthal, Gad Barzilai, & Assaf Meydani, *Judicial Review in a Defective Democracy: Judicial Nominations and Judicial Review in Constitutional Courts,* 9 J. L. & CTS. 137, 143–45 (2021) (giving an overview of Israeli high court reform).

52. Daniel Politi, *Cristina and the Supremes,* N.Y. TIMES: LATITUDE (July 5, 2013), https://latitude.blogs.nytimes.com/2013/07/05/cristina-and-the-supremes/.

53. Poland's attacks have come in waves. In 2015, it imposed a supermajority vote requirement on its constitutional court. *Poland: Law Altering Top Court Goes into Effect Despite Criticism,* N.Y. TIMES (Dec. 28, 2015), https://www.nytimes.com/2015/12/29/world/europe/poland-law-altering-top-court-goes-into-effect-despite-criticism.html. In December 2017, it targeted judges on the Supreme Court with age limits. Marc Santora & Joanna Berendt, *Poland Overhauls Courts, and Critics See Retreat From Democracy,* N.Y. TIMES (Dec. 20, 2017), https://www.nytimes.com/2017/12/20/world/europe/eu-poland-law.html. Orbán pledged "solidarity" after the move, having led his own judicial purge in 2013. Andrew Byrne, *Hungary's Orban Vows to Defend Poland from EU Sanctions,* FIN. TIMES (July 22, 2017), https://www.ft.com/content/b1bd2424-6ed7-11e7-93ff-99f383b09ff9.

54. *Donald Trump's Judicial Appointments May Prove His Most Enduring Legacy*, THE ECONOMIST (Jan. 11, 2018), https://www.economist.com/news/united-states/21734409-everything-else-could-theory-be-reversed-his-effect-law-will-be-profound-donald.

55. DAVID COLE, ENGINES OF LIBERTY: THE POWER OF CITIZEN ACTIVISTS TO MAKE CONSTITUTIONAL LAW (2016); JACK GOLDSMITH, POWER AND CONSTRAINT: THE ACCOUNTABLE PRESIDENCY AFTER 9/11 (2012).

56. As of December 2017, Turkey was responsible for seventy-three of the 262 journalists jailed worldwide. Sewell Chan, *Number of Jailed Journalists Hits Record High, Advocacy Group Says*, N.Y TIMES (Dec. 13, 2017), https://www.nytimes.com/2017/12/13/world/europe/journali sts-jailed-committee-to-protect-journalists.html.

57. MÜLLER, WHAT IS POPULISM? at 35.

58. E. E. SCHATTSCHNEIDER, PARTY GOVERNMENT 1 (1942).

59. Robert A. Dahl, *Reflections on Opposition in Western Democracies*, 1 GOV'T & OPPOSITION 7, 21 (1965).

60. PETER MAIR, RULING THE VOID: THE HOLLOWING OF WESTERN DEMOCRACY 138 (2013).

61. Ed Turner, *The Countries That Get By Without a Government*, BBC (Jan. 8, 2018), https://www.bbc.com/news/uk-politics-42570823.

62. KRASTEV & HOLMES, THE LIGHT THAT FAILED at 9.

63. *Id.*

64. ADAM PRZEWORSKI, CRISES OF DEMOCRACY 163 (2019).

65. *Id.* at 163–64.

66. MICHAEL E. SHIN & JOHN A. AGNEW, BERLUSCONI'S ITALY: MAPPING CONTEMPORARY ITALIAN POLITICS 73–85 (2008).

67. The phrase is often attributed to former assistant secretary of state and U.S. ambassador to Syria and Egypt Edward Djerejian. For further discussion, see Ali Khan, *A Theory of Universal Democracy*, 16 WIS. INT'L L. J. 61, 106 (1997).

68. ISSACHAROFF, FRAGILE DEMOCRACIES at 248–64.

69. Andrew England, *South Africa Corruption Fears Grow*, FIN. TIMES (Mar. 25, 2015), https://www.ft.com/content/b7564954-c896-11e4-b43b-00144feab7de.

70. Kuo, *Against Instantaneous Democracy* at 558.

71. Sujit Choudhry, *"He Had a Mandate": The South African Constitutional Court and the African National Congress in a Dominant Party Democracy*, 2 CONST. CT. REV. 1, 26 (2009).

72. Niv Elis, *CBO Says It Can't Do Full Score of Tax Bill Before House Vote*, THE HILL (Nov. 13, 2017), https://thehill.com/policy/finance/360188-cbo-says-it-cant-do-full-score-of-tax-bill-before-house-vote.

73. Dylan Matthews, *The Republican War on the CBO, Explained*, VOX (July 19, 2017), https://www.vox.com/policy-and-politics/2017/7/19/15967224/congressional-budget-office-cbo-war-explained.

74. Glenister v. President of the Republic of South Africa and Others 2011 ZACC 6 (S. Afr.).

75. Steven Levitsky & Daniel Ziblatt, *How a Democracy Dies*, THE NEW REPUBLIC (Dec. 7, 2017), https://newrepublic.com/article/145916/democracy-dies-donald-trump-contempt-for-american-political-institutions.

76. DICEY, INTRODUCTION TO THE STUDY OF THE LAW OF THE CONSTITUTION at 24.

77. *Quoted in The Referendums and the Damage Done*, THE ECONOMIST (June 1, 2019), at 17.

78. SCHUMPETER, CAPITALISM, SOCIALISM, AND DEMOCRACY at 261.

79. NLRB v. Noel Canning, 573 U.S. 513, 525 (2014) (first quoting Marbury v. Madison, 1 Cranch 137, 177 (1803); and then McCulloch v. Maryland, 4 Wheat 316, 401 (1819)).

80. *Id.*

81. Letter from James Madison to Spencer Roane (Sept. 2, 1819), *in* THE WRITINGS OF JAMES MADISON 447, 450 (G. Hunt, ed., 1908).

82. Curtis A. Bradley & Trevor W. Morrison, *Historical Gloss and the Separation of Powers*, 126 HARV. L. REV. 411, 427 (2012).

83. For a clear exposition of the view of constitutionalism as a form of coordination, see RUSSELL HARDIN, LIBERALISM, CONSTITUTIONALISM, AND DEMOCRACY 5 (1999) ("Where there is broad consensus on order, we do not need Hobbes's autocrat to rule us," nor a contract to keep us from dominating each other).

84. Gerald J. Postema, *Implicit Law*, 13 LAW & PHIL. 361, 361 (1994).
85. ANDREW SABL, HUME'S POLITICS: COORDINATION AND CRISIS IN THE "HISTORY OF ENGLAND" 6 (2012).
86. Cass Sunstein, *Impeaching the President*, 147 U. PA. L. REV. 279, 295 (1998).
87. *See* EZRA KLEIN, WHY WE'RE POLARIZED (2020).
88. Ricardo Moraes, *Brazil's Bolsonaro Says Democracy, Liberty Depend on Military*, REUTERS (Mar. 7, 2019), https://www.reuters.com/article/us-brazil-politics/brazils-bolsonaro-says-democracy-liberty-depend-on-military-idUSKCN1QO2AT.
89. Vindu Goel & Jeffrey Gettleman, *Under Modi, India's Press Is Not So Free Anymore*, N.Y. TIMES (Apr. 2, 2020), https://www.nytimes.com/2020/04/02/world/asia/modi-india-press-media.html.
90. *Orbán's Obsession with Order*, THE ECONOMIST (Jan. 7, 2011), https://www.economist.com/charlemagne/2011/01/07/orbans-obsession-with-order.
91. Benjamin Novak, *Hungary Moves to End Rule by Decree, but Orban's Powers May Stay*, N.Y. TIMES (Sept. 24, 2020), https://www.nytimes.com/2020/06/16/world/europe/hungary-coronavirus-orban.html; *Hungary's Orban Extends Emergency Powers, Points to Ukraine*, DEUTSCHE WELLE (May 25, 2022), https://www.dw.com/en/hungarys-orban-extends-emergency-powers-points-to-ukraine/a-61918348.
92. David G. Timberman, *Philippine Politics Under Duterte: A Midterm Assessment*, CARNEGIE ENDOWMENT FOR INST. PEACE (Jan. 10, 2019), https://carnegieendowment.org/2019/01/10/philippine-politics-under-duterte-midterm-assessment-pub-78091.
93. SCHUMPETER, CAPITALISM, SOCIALISM, AND DEMOCRACY at 260.

Chapter 5

1. CARL SCHMITT, CONSTITUTIONAL THEORY 370 (Jeffrey Seizer trans., 1928).
2. NADIA URBINATI, ME THE PEOPLE: HOW POPULISM TRANSFORMS DEMOCRACY 4 (2019).
3. MASHA GESSEN, SURVIVING AUTOCRACY 6 (2020).
4. JAMES COMEY, A HIGHER LOYALTY: TRUTH, LIES, AND LEADERSHIP 221–22 (2018).
5. Nadia Urbinati, *Liquid Parties, Dense Populism*, 45 PHIL. & SOC. CRITICISM 1069, 1075 (2019) (footnote omitted). This immediacy helps explain populism's "'impatience' with constitutional rules and divisions of powers." *Id.* at 1070.
6. IVAN KRASTEV & STEPHEN HOLMES, THE LIGHT THAT FAILED: WHY THE WEST IS LOSING THE FIGHT FOR DEMOCRACY 98 (2019).
7. Urbinati, *Liquid Parties, Dense Populism* at 1076 (footnote omitted).
8. Nicholas Chesterley & Paolo Roberti, *Populism and Institutional Capture*, 53 EUR. J. POL. ECON. 1, 3 (2018).
9. Sujit Choudhry, *"He Had a Mandate": The South African Constitutional Court and the African National Congress in a Dominant Party Democracy*, 2 CONST. CT. REV. 1, 34 (2009).
10. Rosalind Dixon & David Landau, *Transnational Constitutionalism and a Limited Doctrine of Unconstitutional Constitutional Amendment*, 13 INT'L J. CONST. L. 606, 613 (2015).
11. *See id.*; YANIV ROZNAI, UNCONSTITUTIONAL CONSTITUTIONAL AMENDMENTS: THE LIMITS OF AMENDMENT POWERS (2017).
12. Alvin Y. H. Cheung, An Introduction to Abusive Legalism (Mar. 19, 2019) (unpublished manuscript), https://osf.io/preprints/lawarxiv/w9a6r/.
13. Daryl Levinson & Benjamin I. Sachs, *Political Entrenchment and Public Law*, 125 YALE L. J. 400, 402 (2015).
14. *See, e.g.*, Aziz Huq & Tom Ginsburg, *How to Lose a Constitutional Democracy*, 65 UCLA L. REV. 78 (2018); Richard Albert, *Constitutional Amendment and Dismemberment*, 43 YALE J. INT'L L. 1 (2018); MARK A. GRABER, SANFORD LEVINSON & MARK TUSHNET, CONSTITUTIONAL DEMOCRACY IN CRISIS? (2018); David Landau, *Abusive Constitutionalism*, 47 U.C. DAVIS L. REV. 189 (2013).
15. Madhav Khosla & Milan Vaishnav, *The Three Faces of the Indian State*, 32 J. DEMOC. 111, 123 (2021).
16. WOJCIECH SADURSKI, POLAND'S CONSTITUTIONAL BREAKDOWN (2019).

17. Tarunabh Khaitan, *Killing a Constitution with a Thousand Cuts: Executive Aggrandizement and Party-State Fusion in India*, 14 L. & ETHICS HUM. RTS. 49 (2020).
18. TOM GINSBURG & AZIZ Z. HUQ, HOW TO SAVE A CONSTITUTIONAL DEMOCRACY 91 (2018).
19. *Id.* at 17.
20. URBINATI, *Liquid Parties, Dense Populism* at 6 (internal quotation marks and footnote omitted).
21. ERIC POSNER, THE DEMAGOGUE'S PLAYBOOK: THE BATTLE FOR AMERICAN DEMOCRACY FROM THE FOUNDERS TO TRUMP (2020).
22. Ozan O. Varol, *Stealth Authoritarianism*, 100 IOWA L. REV. 1673, 1721 (2015).
23. *The 40-Year Itch: Populism and Polarisation Threaten Latin America*, THE ECONOMIST (May 11, 2019), https://www.economist.com/briefing/2019/05/09/populism-and-polarisation-threaten-latin-america.
24. MANUEL JOSÉ CEPEDA ESPINOSA & DAVID LANDAU, COLOMBIAN CONSTITUTIONAL LAW: LEADING CASES 357 (2017).
25. SADURSKI, POLAND'S CONSTITUTIONAL BREAKDOWN at 20; Daniel Kalan, *A Tale of Two Polands*, FOREIGN POLICY (Oct. 11, 2019), https://foreignpolicy.com/2019/10/11/pis-centuries-old-divides-polands-east-west-elections/.
26. FRANCIS FUKUYAMA, POLITICAL ORDER AND POLITICAL DECAY: FROM THE INDUSTRIAL REVOLUTION TO THE GLOBALIZATION OF DEMOCRACY 482 (2014).
27. Loveday Morris, *How Do Poland's Ruling Populists Remain So Popular? Follow the Money*, WASH. POST (Oct. 11, 2019), https://www.washingtonpost.com/world/europe/how-do-polands-ruling-populists-remain-so-popular-follow-the-money/2019/10/11/6ae9f886-eb73-11e9-a329-7378fbfa1b63_story.html.
28. Chesterly & Roberti, *Populism and Institutional Capture* at 3.
29. Jeffrey D. Sachs, *Social Conflict and Populist Policies in Latin America* 10 (Nat'l Bureau of Econ. Research Working Paper Series, Working Paper No. 2897, 1989).
30. The major work on the tension involved in efforts in more powerful states to regulate bribery in weaker states is KEVIN E. DAVIS, BETWEEN IMPUNITY AND IMPERIALISM: THE REGULATION OF TRANSNATIONAL BRIBERY (2019).
31. CEPEDA ESPINOSA & LANDAU, COLOMBIAN CONSTITUTIONAL LAW at 356.
32. *See* Samuel Issacharoff, Santiago Garcia-Jaramillo, & Vicente F. Benítez, *Judicial Review of Presidential Re-election Amendments in Colombia*, in MAX PLANK ENCYCLOPEDIA OF COMPARATIVE CONSTITUTIONAL LAW (2020).
33. *The End of Kirchnerismo: And the Beginning of Saner Economic Policies, Perhaps*, THE ECONOMIST (Oct. 22, 2015), https://www.economist.com/the-americas/2015/10/22/the-end-of-kirchnerismo.
34. CAS MUDDE & CRISTÓBAL ROVIRA KALTWASSER, POPULISM: A VERY SHORT INTRODUCTION 110–11 (2017).
35. Presidency Conclusions, European Council in Copenhagen (Jun. 21–22, 1993), https://www.europarl.europa.eu/enlargement/ec/pdf/cop_en.pdf.
36. Urbinati, *Liquid Parties, Dense Populism* at 1077 (first emphasis added) (citing GIANROBERTO CASALEGGIO & BEPPE GRILLO, SIAMO IN GUERRA: PER UNA NUOVA POLITICA 86 (2011)).
37. FUKUYAMA, POLITICAL ORDER AND POLITICAL DECAY at 148.
38. THOMAS HOBBES, Chapter 19, *in* THE LEVIATHAN (1651).
39. THUCYDIDES, THE HISTORY OF THE PELOPONNESIAN WAR (Donald Lateiner & Richard Crawley trans., 2006).
40. Lawrence Lessig, *What an Originalist Would Understand "Corruption" to Mean*, 102 CALIF. L. REV. 1, 11 (2014).
41. Nathaniel Persily & Kelli Lammie, *Perception of Corruption and Campaign Finance: When Public Opinion Determines Constitutional Law*, 153 U. PA. L. REV. 119, 156–59 (2004).
42. THOMAS BYRNE EDSALL, THE NEW POLITICS OF INEQUALITY X (1984).
43. Brown v. Hartlage 456 U.S. 45, 49 (1982) (quoting KY. REV. STAT. § 121.055 (1982)).
44. *Id.* at 56.
45. *See* Brett Arends, *Trump's Tax Cuts Are Punishing States That Voted for Clinton, Data Suggest*, MARKETWATCH (Mar. 8, 2019), https://www.marketwatch.com/story/trumps-tax-cuts-are-punishing-states-that-voted-for-clinton-data-suggests-2019-03-07.

46. DENNIS THOMPSON, ETHICS IN CONGRESS: FROM INDIVIDUAL TO INSTITUTIONAL CORRUPTION 28 (1995).

47. Deborah Hellman, *Defining Corruption and Constitutionalizing Democracy*, 111 MICH. L. REV. 1385, 1396 (2013).

48. LAURA S. UNDERKUFFLER, CAPTURED BY EVIL: THE IDEA OF CORRUPTION IN LAW 69 (2013).

49. SARAH CHAYES, THIEVES OF STATE: WHY CORRUPTION THREATENS GLOBAL SECURITY 54–57 (2015).

50. *Id.* at 112.

51. *Id.* at 111.

52. Frank Michelman, *Law's Republic*, 97 YALE L. J. 1493, 1502 (1988)(discussing the "jurisgenerative" effects of deliberative politics).

53. Melani Barlai & Zsófia Banuta, *Irregularities in the 2019 European Parliamentary and Local Elections in Hungary Discovered*, UNHACK DEMOCRACY (2020), 25.

54. Samuel Issacharoff, *On Political Corruption*, 124 HARV. L. REV. 118, 127–30 (2010).

55. Daniel Lederman, Norman V. Loayza, & Rodrigo R Soares, *Accountability and Corruption: Political Institutions Matter*, 17 J. ECON. & POL. 1, 4 (2005)(reviewing empirical literature).

56. SUSAN ROSE-ACKERMAN, CORRUPTION & GOVERNMENT: CAUSES, CONSEQUENCES, AND REFORM (1999).

57. JOEL SIMMONS, THE POLITICS OF TECHNOLOGICAL PROGRESS: PARTIES, TIME HORIZONS AND LONG-TERM ECONOMIC DEVELOPMENT 36 (2016).

58. *Id.* at 5.

59. Scott Gehlbach & Philip Keefer, *Private Investment and Institutionalization of Collective Action in Autocracies: Ruling Parties and Legislatures*, 74 J. POL. 621 (2012).

60. *See* Andrew Prokop, *Why Republicans Didn't Write a Platform for Their Convention This Year*, VOX (Aug. 24, 2020), https://www.vox.com/2020/8/24/21399396/republican-convent ion-platform-2020-2016 ("The party's true priority is supporting Donald Trump.").

61. Jeff Stein, *New Tax Plan from Leading GOP Senator Would Require All Americans to Pay Federal Income Taxes*, WASH. POST (Feb. 24, 2022), https://www.washingtonpost.com/us-policy/ 2022/02/23/rick-scott-campaign-plan/.

62. THOMAS HOBBES, LEVIATHAN 89 (1996)(1651).

63. TOM GINSBURG, DEMOCRACY AND INTERNATIONAL LAW: THE TRIALS OF LIBERALISM (2022).

64. DAVID HUME, THAT POLITICS MAY BE REDUCED TO A SCIENCE (1741).

65. Fernando Bizzarro et al., *Party Strength and Economic Growth*, 70 WORLD POL. 275, 281 (2018).

66. *Id.* at 290.

67. *Id.* at 310.

68. V.O. KEY JR., SOUTHERN POLITICS IN STATE AND NATION 303 (1949).

69. PRATAP BHANU MEHTA, THE BURDEN OF DEMOCRACY 6 (2003).

70. Luigi Guiso et al., *Populism: Demand and Supply* 38 (CEPR Discussion Paper No. DP11871, 2017).

71. Jane Mayer, *How Mitch McConnell Became Trump's Enabler-in-Chief*, NEW YORKER (Apr. 12, 2020), https://www.newyorker.com/magazine/2020/04/20/how-mitch-mcconnell-bec ame-trumps-enabler-in-chief (quoting Norman Ornstein).

Chapter 6

1. STEPHEN HOLMES, PASSIONS AND CONSTRAINT: ON THE THEORY OF LIBERAL DEMOCRACY 134–77 (1995).

2. David Landau & Rosalind Dixon, *Abusive Judicial Review: Courts Against Democracy*, 53 U.C. DAVIS L. REV. 1313 (2020).

3. BRENNAN CTR. FOR JUSTICE, VOTE SUPPRESSION, https://www.brennancenter.org/issues/ens ure-every-american-can-vote/vote-suppression (last visited May 21, 2021).

4. Guillermo Fontana, *Argentina Drops Its Voter Age to 16*, CNN (Nov. 1, 2012), https://www. cnn.com/2012/10/31/world/americas/argentina-youth-vote/index.html.

5. *See Corrupt*, MERRIAM-WEBSTER, https://www.merriam-webster.com/dictionary/corrupt ("to cause disintegration or ruin").

6. Tom Ginsburg, *Authoritarian International Law?*, 114 AM. J. INT'L L. 221, 229 (2020).

7. Mila Versteeg et al., *The Law and Politics of Presidential Term Limit Evasion*, 120 COLUM. L. REV. 173, 200 (2020).

8. *See* PAUL STARR, ENTRENCHMENT: WEALTH, POWER, AND THE CONSTITUTION OF DEMOCRATIC SOCIETIES 187 (2019).

9. Daryl Levinson & Benjamin I. Sachs, *Political Entrenchment and Public Law*, 125 YALE L. J. 400, 409 (2015).

10. ADAM PRZEWORSKI ET AL., DEMOCRACY AND DEVELOPMENT: POLITICAL INSTITUTIONS AND WELL-BEING IN THE WORLD, 1950–1990 15 (2000).

11. Richard Albert, *Constitutional Amendment and Dismemberment*, 43 YALE J. INT'L L. 1, 5 (2018).

12. *Id.*

13. These changes are summarized in Michael J. Klarman, *Foreword: The Degradation of American Democracy—and the Court*, 134 HARV. L. REV. 1, 60–61 (2020).

14. Aziz Huq & Tom Ginsburg, *How to Lose a Constitutional Democracy*, 65 UCLA L. REV. 78, 138 (2018).

15. David Landau, *Constitution-Making and Authoritarianism in Venezuela, in* CONSTITUTIONAL DEMOCRACY IN CRISIS? (Mark A. Graber, Sanford Levinson, & Mark Tushnet, eds., 2018).

16. STEPHEN WOJCIECH SADURSKI, POLAND'S CONSTITUTIONAL BREAKDOWN 163 (2019).

17. David Landau, *Abusive Constitutionalism*, 47 U.C. DAVIS L. REV. 189, 237 (2013).

18. Rosalind Dixon & David Landau, *Transnational Constitutionalism and a Limited Doctrine of Unconstitutional Constitutional Amendment*, 13 INT'L J. CONST. L. 606, 613 (2015).

19. GRUNDGESETZ [GG] [BASIC LAW], arts. 1, 20, translation at https://www.gesetze-im-internet. de/englisch_gg/.

20. *See generally* Aharon Barak, *Unconstitutional Constitutional Amendments*, 44 ISR. L. REV. 321, 333 (2011) (discussing judicial interpretation of unamendable provisions); Yaniv Roznai, *Unconstitutional Constitutional Amendments—The Migration and Success of a Constitutional Idea*, 61 AM. J. COMP. L. 657, 676 (2013).

21. Kesavananda Bharati v. Kerala, (1973) 4 SCC 225 (India). For exposition of the doctrine, see SUDHIR KRISHNASWAMY, DEMOCRACY AND CONSTITUTIONALISM IN INDIA 24–26 (2009).

22. IR Coelho v. Tamil Nadu, AIR 2007 SC 861, para. 151(ii) (India).

23. *Id.* at para. 70.

24. Indira Gandhi v. Raj Narain, AIR 1975 SC 2299 (India).

25. *Id.*; IR Coelho v. Tamil Nadu, AIR 2007 SC 861 (India). *See* Virendra Kumar, *Basic Structure of the Indian Constitution: Doctrine of Constitutionally Controlled Governance*, 49 J. INDIAN L. INST. 365, 390–91 (2007).

26. SANJAY RUPARELIA, DIVIDED WE GOVERN: COALITION POLITICS IN MODERN INDIA (2015).

27. Corte Cost., 15 dicembre 1988, n. 1146, Gazz. uff. 1989, 2, 627 (It.), *translated in* Lois F. del Duca & Patrick del Duca, *An Italian Federalism? The State, Its Institutions and National Culture as Rule of Law Guarantor*, 54 AM. J. COMP. L. 799, 800–1 (2006).

28. *See* YANIV ROZNAI, UNCONSTITUTIONAL CONSTITUTIONAL AMENDMENTS: THE LIMITS OF AMENDMENT POWERS (2017).

29. Nález Ústavního soudu ze dne 10.09.2009 (ÚS) [Decision of the Constitutional Court of September 9, 2009], ÚS 27/09 (Czech), *available in English at* https://perma.cc/P8XL-VFYB.

30. Corte Constitucional [C.C.] [Constitutional Court], febrero 26, 2010, Sentencia C-141/10 (Colom.), *translated in* MANUEL JOSÉ CEPEDA ESPINOSA & DAVID LANDAU, COLOMBIAN CONSTITUTIONAL LAW: LEADING CASES 354–55 (2017).

31. SAMUEL ISSACHAROFF, FRAGILE DEMOCRACIES 146–47 (2015).

32. *Id.*

33. Corte Constitucional [C.C.] [Constitutional Court], febrero 26, 2010, Sentencia C-141/10 (Colom.), *translated in* Cepeda Espinosa & Landau, COLOMBIAN CONSTITUTIONAL LAW at 354–55.

34. *See* Carlos Bernal-Pulido, *Unconstitutional Constitutional Amendments in the Case Study of Colombia: An Analysis of the Justification and Meaning of the Constitutional Replacement Doctrine,* 11 INT'L J. CONST. L. 339 (2013).

35. Vicente F. Benítez-R, *We the People, They the Media: Judicial Review of Constitutional Amendments and Public Opinion in Colombia, in* CONSTITUTIONAL CHANGE AND TRANSFORMATION IN LATIN AMERICA 143 (Richard Albert, Carlos Bernal Pulido, & Juliano Zaiden Benvindo, eds., 2019).

36. Samuel Issacharoff, Santiago García-Jaramillo, & Vicente F. Benítez-Rojas, *Judicial Review of Presidential Re-Election Amendments in Colombia, in* MAX PLANK ENCYCLOPEDIA OF COMPARATIVE CONSTITUTIONAL LAW 13, 13 (2020).

37. ZHONGHUA MINGUO XIANFA ZENGXIU TIAOWEN [Additional Articles of the Constitution of Taiwan] 5th Revision (1999), *available in English at* https://english.president.gov.tw/page/93.

38. *Id.*

39. *See* Yen-Tu Su, Political Antitrust: Rethinking the Constitutional Law of Competitive Democracy 189–90 (2000) (unpublished Ph.D. dissertation) (on file with author).

40. J.Y. Interpretation No. 499 (Taiwan Const. Ct. Mar. 24, 2000), https://web.archive.org/web/20171025024050/http://www.judicial.gov.tw/constitutionalcourt/en/p03_01.asp?expno=499.

41. *Id.; see also* Ming-Sung Kuo, *Moving Towards a Nominal Constitutional Court? Critical Reflections on the Shift from Judicial Activism to Constitutional Irrelevance in Taiwan's Constitutional Politics,* 25 WASH. INT'L L. J. 597, 600 (2016) (arguing that Interpretation No. 499 is "the foremost example . . . to constitutional politics" of Taiwan Court).

42. For arguments that courts buttress their domestic authority by invoking international norms, see Vicki Jackson, *Unconstitutional Constitutional Amendments: A Window into Constitutional Theory and Transnational Constitutionalism, in* DEMOKRATIE-PERSPEKTIVEN: FESTSCHRIFT FÜR BRUN-OTTO BRYDE ZUM 47, 70 (Brun-Otto Bryde et al. eds., 2013).

43. Chilima and Another v. Mutharika and Others (Ruling on App for Suspension) (Constitutional Reference No. 1 of 2019) [2020] MWHC 1 (12 February 2020), 31.

44. Jason Burke & Charles Pensulo, *Malawi Court Annuls 2019 Election Results and Calls for New Ballot,* THE GUARDIAN (Feb. 3, 2020), https://www.theguardian.com/world/2020/feb/03/malawi-court-annuls-2019-election-results-calls-new-ballot.

45. TOM GERALD DALY, THE ALCHEMISTS: QUESTIONING OUR FAITH IN COURTS AS DEMOCRACY-BUILDERS 269–70 (2017).

46. *Compare* Kuo, *Moving Towards a Nominal Constitutional Court?* at 603 (arguing that the Court has been "sidelined in the arena of constitutional politics" in the 21st century), *with* Tzu-Yi Lin, Ming-Sung Kuo, & Hui-Wen Chen, *Seventy Years On: The Taiwan Constitutional Court and Judicial Activism in a Changing Constitutional Landscape,* 48 H.K. L. J. 995, 1014 (2018) (arguing that the Court has taken on a "role as the defender of constitutional principles in the face of social dissensus" in the 21st century).

47. STEPHEN GARDBAUM, THE NEW COMMONWEALTH MODEL OF CONSTITUTIONALISM: THEORY AND PRACTICE 37 (2013).

48. *See, e.g.,* Rasiah v. Badan Peguam Malaysia & Anor [2010] 3 CLJ 507, 517 (HC) ("Unless sanctioned by the Constitution itself, any statute (including one amending the Constitution) that offends the basic structure may be struck down as unconstitutional.").

49. YVONNE TEW, CONSTITUTIONAL STATECRAFT IN ASIAN COURTS 63 (2020) (quoting Indira Gandhi a/p Mutho v. Pengarah Jabatan Agama Islam Perak & Ors. [2018] 1 MLJ 545, 587 (FC)).

50. *See* Indira Gandhi a/p Mutho v. Pengarah Jabatan Agama Islam Perak & Ors. [2018] 1 MLJ 545, 586–87 (FC).

51. Versteeg et al., *The Law and Politics of Presidential Term Limit Evasion* at 179.

52. Landau & Dixon, *Abusive Judicial Review* at 1353–63.

53. *See* Tom Ginsburg, *International Courts and Democratic Backsliding,* 37 BERK. J. INT'L L. 263, 279–80 (2019)

54. *See* Decision N. 84 of 2017, Nov. 28, 2017 (C.C. Bolivia).

55. *See* TOM GINSBURG, JUDICIAL REVIEW IN NEW DEMOCRACIES: CONSTITUTIONAL COURTS IN ASIAN CASES 25 (2003).

56. Samuel Issacharoff, *Constitutional Courts and Democratic Hedging*, 99 GEO L. J. 961 (2011).

57. Sergio Verdugo, *The Fall of the Constitution's Political Insurance: How the Morales Regime Eliminated the Insurance of the 2009 Bolivian Constitution*, 17 INT'L J. CONST. L. 1, 24 (2019).

58. NOAH FELDMAN, THE THREE LIVES OF JAMES MADISON: GENIUS, PARTISAN, PRESIDENT 112–15 (2017).

59. CHARLES WARREN, THE MAKING OF THE CONSTITUTION 194 (1928).

60. *See, e.g.,* Donald Trump (@realDonaldTrump), TWITTER (Dec. 22, 2016, 11:41 AM) ("Someone incorrectly stated that the phrase 'DRAIN THE SWAMP' was no longer being used by me. Actually, we will always be trying to DTS."); [archived at https://web.archive.org/web/20170301202022/https:/twitter.com/realDonaldTrump/status/811975049431416832]; Donald Trump (@realDonaldTrump), TWITTER (May 17, 2019, 7:00 AM), https://twitter.com/realDonaldTrump/status/1129340814080040961 ("DRAIN THE SWAMP!") [archived at https://web.archive.org/web/20190518143612/https:/twitter.com/realDonaldTrump/status/1129340814080040961].

61. *See generally* Peter W. Stevenson, *A Brief History of the "Lock Her Up!" Chant by Trump Supporters Against Clinton*, WASH. POST (Nov. 22, 2016), https://www.washingtonpost.com/news/the-fix/wp/2016/11/22/a-brief-history-of-the-lock-her-up-chant-as-it-looks-like-trump-might-not-even-try/?noredirect=on.

62. *See* Robert A. Dahl, *Myth of the Presidential Mandate*, 105 POL. SCI. Q. 355, 360 (1990).

63. Kim Lane Scheppele, *Autocratic Legalism*, 85 U. CHI. L. REV. 545, 549 (2018).

64. *Id.*

65. ANDRÁS SAJÓ & RENÁTA UITZ, THE CONSTITUTION OF FREEDOM: AN INTRODUCTION TO LEGAL CONSTITUTIONALISM 284–85 (2017); *see also* Renáta Uitz, *Courts and the Expansion of Executive Power: Making the Constitution Matter, in* THE EVOLUTION OF THE SEPARATION OF POWERS: BETWEEN THE GLOBAL NORTH AND THE GLOBAL SOUTH 85 (David Bilchitz & David Landau, eds., 2018).

66. Samuel Issacharoff & Richard H. Pildes, *Politics as Markets: Partisan Lockups of the Political Process*, 50 STAN. L. REV. 643, 648–49 (1998).

67. *See, e.g.,* Reynolds v. Sims, 377 U.S. 533, 562 (1964) ("Since the right to exercise the franchise in a free and unimpaired manner is preservative of other basic civil and political rights, any alleged infringement of the right of citizens to vote must be carefully and meticulously scrutinized.").

68. Pamela S. Karlan, *Reapportionment, Nonapportionment, and Recovering Some Lost History of One Person, One Vote*, 59 WM. & MARY L. REV. 1921, 1940 (2018).

69. *See* Samuel Issacharoff, *Regulating the Electoral Process, Judging Politics: The Elusive Quest for Judicial Review of Political Fairness*, 71 TEX. L. REV. 1643, 1665 (1993).

70. PAUL T. DAVID & RALPH EISENBERG, DEVALUATION OF THE URBAN AND SUBURBAN VOTE 3 (1961) (noting a disparity of 987 to 1 in Vermont's lower house).

71. Baker v. Carr, 369 U.S. 186, 258–59 (1962) (Clark, J., concurring).

72. Dylan Lino, *Albert Venn Dicey and the Constitutional Theory of Empire*, 36 OXFORD J. LEGAL STUD. 751, 777.

73. W. IVOR JENNINGS, THE LAW AND THE CONSTITUTION 135 (1948).

74. P. S. ATIYAH, PROMISES, MORALS, AND LAW 116 (1982); *see also* DAVID HUME, *A Treatise of Human Nature, in* MORAL PHILOSOPHY, 12, 87–99 (2006).

75. Ernest Young, *Rediscovering Conservatism: Burkean Political Theory and Constitutional Interpretation*, 72 N.C. L. REV. 619, 649 (1994).

76. GEOFFREY MARSHALL, CONSTITUTIONAL CONVENTIONS: THE RULES AND FORMS OF POLITICAL ACCOUNTABILITY 4 (1987).

77. A. V. DICEY, INTRODUCTION TO THE STUDY OF THE LAW OF THE CONSTITUTION 426 (10th ed., 1985).

78. EDMUND BURKE, REFLECTIONS ON THE REVOLUTION IN FRANCE 18 (Frank M. Turner ed., 2003) (1790).

79. Erin Delaney, *Brexit Optimism and British Constitutional Renewal, in* CONSTITUTIONAL DEMOCRACY IN CRISIS? 11 (Mark A. Graber, Sanford Levinson, & Mark Tushnet, eds., 2018).

80. DICEY, INTRODUCTION TO THE STUDY OF THE LAW OF THE CONSTITUTION at 96–97.

81. Lord Mervyn King, *How Brexit Broke British Politics*, BLOOMBERG (May 30, 2019), https://www.bloomberg.com/opinion/articles/2019-05-30/mervyn-king-on-how-brexit-broke-british-politics.

82. *Id.*

83. *See* Sara B. Hobolt, *The Brexit Vote: A Divided Nation, a Divided Continent,* 23 J. EUR. PUB. POL'Y 1259, 1260 (2016) ("British Leave voters were motivated by anti-immigration and anti-establishment feelings. They also reveal stark demographic divides, as the less well-educated and the less well-off voted in large majorities to leave the EU, while the young graduates in the urban centres voted to stay. This divide between those who feel left behind by the forces of globalization and mass immigration and those who welcome such developments is also a driving force behind the increasing support for Eurosceptic parties on the radical right and left across Europe.").

84. R v. Sec'y of State [2017] UKSC 5, [28], https://www.supremecourt.uk/cases/docs/uksc-2016-0196-judgment.pdf.

85. *Id.*

86. *Quoted in* Claire Mills, *Parliamentary Approval for Military Action* 8 (HC Library, Briefing Paper No. 7166, 2018).

87. *Id.* at 10–13 (discussing government deployment of British troops from WWII through Kosovo).

88. This is discussed in Samuel Issacharoff, *Political Safeguards in Democracies at War,* 29 OXFORD J. LEGAL STUD. 189 (2009).

89. Charlie Cooper, *Historic Defeat for Theresa May on Brexit Vote,* POLITICO (Jan. 15, 2019), https://www.politico.eu/article/brexit-deal-rejected-by-432-votes-to-202-2/.

90. Trollope's Palliser novels chronicled the dislocation in British politics following the franchise reforms in the 19th century. *See, e.g.,* ANTHONY TROLLOPE, THE PRIME MINISTER (1876).

91. R v. Prime Minister [2019] UKSC 41 (appeal taken from [2019] EWHC 2381 and [2019] CSIH 49), ¶ 37.

92. *Id.* at ¶ 1.

93. *Id.* at ¶ 50.

94. *Id.* at ¶ 56.

95. *Id.* at ¶ 1.

96. *Id.* at ¶ 50.

97. John Finnis, *The Unconstitutionality of the Supreme Court's Prorogation Judgment, with Supplementary Notes* 3 (Oxford Legal Stud. Research Paper No. 6/2020, Notre Dame Legal Stud. Paper. No 200304, 2020), https://ssrn.com/abstract=3548657.

98. *Id.* at 15.

99. *Id.* at 36 (quoting Lord Sumption's evidence at a Select Committee).

100. *The Executive Unchained; Constitutional Reform,* THE ECONOMIST (Nov. 21, 2020), at 49–51.

101. Tarunabh Khaitan, *On Coups, Constitutional Shamelessness, and Lingchi,* U.K. CONST. LAW BLOG (Sept. 6, 2019), https://ukconstitutionallaw.org/2019/09/06/tarunabh-khaitan-on-coups-constitutional-shamelessness-and-lingchi/.

Chapter 7

1. Samuel Issacharoff, *On Political Corruption,* 124 HARV. L. REV. 118, 126 (2010).

2. *See* ANNE-MARIE SLAUGHTER ET AL., THE EUROPEAN COURT AND NATIONAL COURTS DOCTRINE AND JURISPRUDENCE: LEGAL CHANGE IN ITS SOCIAL CONTEXT (1998).

3. *See* David Landau & Rosalind Dixon, *Abusive Judicial Review: Courts Against Democracy,* 53 U.C. DAVIS L. REV. 1313, 1356 (2020).

4. Madhav Khosla, *With Freedom at Stake, Courts Are Collapsing,* N.Y. TIMES (Sept. 9, 2020), https://www.nytimes.com/2020/09/09/opinion/hungary-turkey-india-courts.html?action=click&module=Opinion&pgtype=Homepage.

5. SAMUEL ISSACHAROFF, FRAGILE DEMOCRACIES: CONTESTED POWER IN THE ERA OF CONSTITUTIONAL COURTS 276–77 (2015). For discussion of the concept of constrained democracy, see Jan Werner-Müller, *Beyond Militant Democracy?,* 73 NEW LEFT REV. 39, 44 (2012) (speaking of the "post-war European understanding of constrained democracies"); *see also* Jürgen Habermas, *Constitutional Democracy: A Paradoxical Union of Contradictory Principles?,* 29 POL. THEORY 766 (2001). For a broader application of the importance of

constraints on democratic prerogatives, see DARON ACEMOGLU & JAMES A. ROBINSON, ECONOMIC ORIGINS OF DICTATORSHIP AND DEMOCRACY 33–34 (2006).

6. Marc Santora, *Amid Growing Uproar, Poland to Remove 27 Supreme Court Justices*, N.Y. TIMES (July 3, 2018), https://www.nytimes.com/2018/07/03/world/europe/poland-supreme-court-judiciary.html (quoting Jarosław Kaczyński in a 2016 speech and detailing how Poland's governing party harassed, threatened, and removed opposing members of the Supreme Court).

7. *Id.*

8. *See Poland Plans Further Reforms at Its Supreme Court, Says Newspaper*, REUTERS (Sept. 8, 2020), https://www.reuters.com/article/uk-poland-judiciary/poland-plans-further-refo rms-at-its-supreme-court-says-newspaper-idUKKBN25Z10W.

9. WOJCIECH SADURSKI, POLAND'S CONSTITUTIONAL BREAKDOWN 98 (2019).

10. *Id.* at 113.

11. *Id.* (quoting *Opinion of the European Commission for Democracy Through Law on the Draft Act Amending the Act on the National Judiciary Council*, at 10, CDL-AD(2017)031 (Dec. 11, 2017)).

12. Max Shanahan, *USyd Law Professor Not Guilty; Legal Battles Continue*, HONI SOIT. (Mar. 8, 2021), http://honisoit.com/2021/03/usyd-law-professor-not-guilty-legal-battles-continue/.

13. *See* Aziz Z. Huq, *Legal or Political Checks on Apex Criminality: An Essay on Constitutional Design*, 65 UCLA L. REV. 1506, 1518–19 (2018).

14. Deborah Hellman, *Defining Corruption and Constitutionalizing Democracy*, 111 MICH. L. REV. 1385, 1395 (2013).

15. Zephyr Teachout, *The Anti-Corruption Principle*, 94 CORNELL L. REV. 341, 387 (2009).

16. David A. Strauss, *Corruption, Equality, and Campaign Finance Reform*, 94 COLUM. L. REV. 1369, 1370 (1994).

17. Hellman, *Defining Corruption* at 1421.

18. Minister Albert Fritz, Western Cape Provincial Parliament, Speech During a House Debate on "Tenderpreneurship" (Sept. 4, 2014), https://www.gov.za/tenderpreneurship-stuff-croo ked-cadres-fighters.

19. Glenister v. President of the Republic of South Africa and Others 2011 ZACC 6 at para. 166 (S. Afr.).

20. *See, e.g.*, United Democratic Movement v. Speaker of the National Assembly and Others 2017 ZACC 21 at para. 97 (S. Afr.) (requiring secret ballots on no confidence motions); Oriani-Ambrosini, MP v. Sisulu, MP Speaker of the National Assembly 2012 ZACC 27 at para. 51 (S. Afr.) (protection of rights of legislative participation and speech by minority parties); Mazibuko v. Sisulu and Another 2013 ZACC 28 at para. 45 (S. Afr.); Democratic Alliance v. Speaker of the National Assembly and Others 2016 ZACC 8 at para. 45 (S. Afr.) (same).

21. Economic Freedom Fighters v. Speaker of the National Assembly and Another 2017 ZACC 47 (S. Afr.); Democratic Alliance v Speaker of the National Assembly and Others 2016 ZACC 11 at para. 105 (S. Afr.).

22. Corruption Watch (RF) NPC and Another v. President of the Republic of South Africa and Others; Council for the Advancement of the South African Constitution v. President of the Republic of South Africa and Others 2017 ZAGPPHC 743 (S. Afr.).

23. *Id.* at para 112.

24. Stu Woolman, *A Politics of Accountability: How South Africa's Judicial Recognition of the Binding Legal Effect of the Public Protector's Recommendations Had a Catalysing Effect That Brought Down a President*, 8 Const. Ct. Rev. 155, 156 (2018).

25. *Corruption Watch (RF) NPC* at para 128.

26. Woomlan, *A Politics of Accountability* at 185.

27. Adam Forrest, *Cyril Ramaphosa Promises a South Africa "Free From Corruption" as He Is Sworn in as President*, INDEPENDENT (May 25, 2019), https://www.independent.co.uk/news/world/africa/cyril-ramaphosa-south-africa-president-corruption-zuma-anc-gupta-scandal-a8930321.html; George Matlala, *Cyril Ramaphosa Vows to Bring the Corrupt to Book*, SUNDAY WORLD (Jan. 25, 2020), https://sundayworld.co.za/politics/cyril-ramaphosa-vows-to-bring-the-corrupt-to-book/.

28. *Zuma Corruption Claims: South Africa State Capture Inquiry Opens*, BBC (Aug. 20, 2018), https://www.bbc.com/news/world-africa-45245121.

29. *See* Emsie Ferreira, *Zondo Asks Constitutional Court to Jail Zuma for Two Years for Continued Defiance*, MAIL & GUARDIAN (Feb. 22, 2021), https://mg.co.za/politics/2021-02-22-zondo-asks-constitutional-court-to-jail-zuma-for-two-years-for-continued-defiance/.

30. *Id.*

31. Jason Burke, *Jacob Zuma Faces Jail After Failing to Appear at Anti-Corruption Inquiry*, GUARDIAN (Feb. 15, 2021), https://www.theguardian.com/world/2021/feb/15/jacob-zuma-faces-jail-failing-appear-anti-corruption-inquiry.

32. Lynsey Chutel, *Zuma Risks Arrest After Defying South Africa Corruption Inquiry*, N.Y. TIMES (Feb. 15, 2021), https://www.nytimes.com/2021/02/15/world/africa/zuma-corruption-imprisonment-threat.html (quoting Professor Susan Booysen at the University of the Witwatersrand); *see also* Mogomotsi Magome, *South Africa's President Fights Own Party Over Corruption*, AP NEWS (Feb. 19, 2021), https://apnews.com/article/coronavirus-pandemic-cyril-ramaphosa-africa-south-africa-courts-9536bc1063cc5cb748a7b16b0081dff3.

33. *Id.* (quoting Professor Booysen).

34. Thabo Baloyi, *Jacob Zuma Reveals All About ANC Top Six Meeting*, S. AFRICAN (Apr. 5, 2021), https://www.thesouthafrican.com/news/jacob-zuma-reveals-all-about-anc-top-six-meeting/; Nonkululeko Njilo, *Jacob Zuma Slams ANC for Not Protecting Him in Recent Years*, TIMES LIVE (Apr. 5, 2021), https://www.businesslive.co.za/bd/.

35. Andrew Harding, *Jacob Zuma: South Africa's Ex-President Pleads Not Guilty for Multi-Billion Dollar Arms Deal*, BBC (May 26, 2021), https://www.bbc.com/news/world-africa-57246802.

36. Alexander Winning, *Former S. African Leader Zuma Sentenced to 15 Months in Jail*, REUTERS (June 29, 2021, 9:44AM), https://www.reuters.com/world/africa/south-africas-top-court-says-ex-leader-zuma-contempt-absences-2021-06-29/.

37. MARK TUSHNET, THE NEW FOURTH BRANCH: INSTITUTIONS FOR PROTECTING CONSTITUTIONAL DEMOCRACY 119 (2021).

38. *Corruption Perceptions Index 2016: Vicious Circle of Corruption and Inequality Must Be Tackled*, TRANSPARENCY INT'L (Jan. 25, 2017), https://www.transparency.org/en/press/corruption-perceptions-index-2016-vicious-circle-of-corruption-and-inequali#.

39. Caleb Groen, *Corruption: The Gravedigger of Populism*, BERKELEY POL. REV. (Sept. 15, 2020), https://bpr.berkeley.edu/2019/11/08/corruption-the-gravedigger-of-populism/.

40. Huq, *Legal or Political Checks on Apex Criminality* at 1510.

41. *See* Simon Romer, *Dilma Rousseff Is Ousted as Brazil's President in Impeachment Vote*, N.Y. TIMES (Aug. 31, 2016), https://www.nytimes.com/2016/09/01/world/americas/brazil-dilma-rousseff-impeached-removed-president.html.

42. PRZEMYSŁAW SADURA & SŁAWOMIR SIERAKOWSKI, POLITICAL CYNICISM: THE CASE OF POLAND 12 (2019), https://globalconpop.files.wordpress.com/2019/09/sadura-and-sierakowski-2019-in-english.pdf.

43. *See* Uki Goñi, *Argentina Gripped by Mystery: The Ex-minister, a Convent and Bundles of Cash*, GUARDIAN (June 17, 2016), https://www.theguardian.com/world/2016/jun/17/argentina-ex-minister-convent-cash-jose-lopez.

44. *See* Szabolcs Panyi, *A Brief History of Graft in Orbán's Hungary*, EURACTIV (Feb. 19, 2020), https://www.euractiv.com/section/justice-home-affairs/opinion/a-brief-history-of-graft-in-orbans-hungary/.

45. *Id.*

46. *See* Ursula Perano & Shawna Chen, *Trump Grants Flurry of Last-Minute Pardons*, AXIOS (Jan. 20, 2021), axios.com/trump-pardons-list-657cc832-f3ee-4940-92b6-dbe40aa2e9cb.html.

47. *See* David A. Graham, *Trump Is Running His Campaign Like He Ran His Businesses*, THE ATLANTIC (Sept. 9, 2020), https://www.theatlantic.com/ideas/archive/2020/09/how-donald-trump-blew-1-billion-fundraising-lead/616156/.

48. *See* Dan Alexander, *Trump Shifted Campaign-Donor Money Into His Private Business After Losing the Election*, FORBES (Feb. 5, 2021), https://www.forbes.com/sites/danalexander/2021/02/05/trump-shifted-campaign-donor-money-into-his-private-business-after-losing-the-election/?sh=37a0923b4418.

49. 140 S. Ct. 2412 (2020).

50. *Id.* at 2423.
51. *Id.* at 2431 (Kavanaugh, J., concurring).
52. Josh Gerstein, *Judge Orders Trump to Sit for Deposition in New York Investigation*, POLITICO (Feb. 17, 2022, 1:57 PM), https://www.politico.com/news/2022/02/17/trump-deposit ion-new-york-probe-00009847.
53. The ins and outs of the Brazilian corruption scandals and their taint reaching all the way to the eligibility for re-election of former President Lula da Silva is not only ongoing as of this writing, but far too complex for a simple telling. For a cogent and informed account in English, see TUSHNET, THE NEW FOURTH BRANCH at 99–110.
54. Daryl J. Levinson & Richard H. Pildes, *Separation of Parties, Not Powers*, 119 HARV. L. REV. 2311, 2313 (2006) (quoting 1 FEDERALIST NO. 51, at 321–22 (Alexander Hamilton) (Clinton Rossiter, ed., 1961)).
55. Youngstown Sheet & Tube Co. v. Sawyer, 343 U.S. 579, 654 (1952) (Jackson, J., concurring).
56. BOB BAUER & JACK GOLDSMITH, AFTER TRUMP: RECONSTRUCTING THE PRESIDENCY 62 (2020).
57. Russell Muirhead & Jeffrey K. Tulis, *Will the Election of 2020 Prove to Be the End or a New Beginning?*, 52 POLITY 339, 352 (2020).
58. *See* Shreyas Narla & Shruti Rajagopalan, *The Judicial Abrogation of Rights and Liberties in Kashmir*, ARTICLE 14 (Sept. 24, 2020), https://www.article-14.com/post/the-judicial-abr ogation-of-rights-liberties-in-kashmir.
59. EZRA KLEIN, WHY WE'RE POLARIZED 238 (2020) (quoting David Roberts, *Donald Trump and the Rise of Tribal Epistemology*, VOX (May 19, 2017, 9:58 AM), https://www.vox.com/policy- and-politics/2017/3/22/14762030/donald-trump-tribal-epistemology) (explaining tribal epistemology as only trusting information that is confirmed by or confirms the worldview of an elite or tribe).
60. *Id.* at XV.
61. JONATHAN HAIDT, THE RIGHTEOUS MIND: WHY GOOD PEOPLE ARE DIVIDED BY POLITICS AND RELIGION 134 (2012).
62. *Id.* at 226 (explaining the work of Emile Durkheim).
63. Jonathan Haidt & Fredrik Björklund, *Social Intuitionists Answer Six Questions About Moral Psychology, in* MORAL PSYCHOLOGY, VOLUME 2: THE COGNITIVE SCIENCE OF MORALITY: INTUITION AND DIVERSITY 181 (Walter Sinnott-Armstrong, ed., 2008).
64. RAYMOND J. LA RAJA & BRIAN F. SCHAFFNER, CAMPAIGN FINANCE AND POLITICAL POLARIZATION: WHEN PURISTS PREVAIL 95 (2015).
65. KLEIN, WHY WE'RE POLARIZED at 189.
66. *Id.* at 192–93 (comparing the boycott by Democrats of McGovern's candidacy with the incentives that led Republicans to vote for Trump in order to avoid a Clinton presidency).
67. *Id.* at 196 ("In an era of high polarization, weak parties, and strong partisanship, it's easy to see how extremists and, more than that, demagogues penetrate the system.").
68. *Id.* at 244.
69. *See Aide: Obama Won't Prosecute Bush Officials*, CBS NEWS (Apr. 20, 2009, 12:10 AM), https:// www.cbsnews.com/news/aide-obama-wont-prosecute-bush-officials/.
70. Daphna Renan, *The President's Two Bodies*, 120 COLUM. L. REV. 1119 (2020).
71. *The Referendums and the Damage Done*, THE ECONOMIST (June 1, 2019), at 17 (quoting William Gladstone).
72. The president is not authorized to sign for IRS disbursements, so his name had to appear on the memo line. Katelyn Burns, *Trump Wants His Name on Millions of Stimulus Checks, Even If It Delays Them*, VOX (Apr. 15, 2020, 1:40 PM), https://www.vox.com/policy-and-politics/ 2020/4/15/21222046/trump-name-stimulus-checks-delays.
73. FRANCIS FUKUYAMA, POLITICAL ORDER AND POLITICAL DECAY: FROM THE INDUSTRIAL REVOLUTION TO THE GLOBALIZATION OF DEMOCRACY 148 (2014).

Chapter 8

1. Dep't of Com. v. New York, 139 S. Ct. 2551 (2019); Dep't of Homeland Sec. v. Regents of Univ. of Cal., 140 S. Ct. 1891 (2018).

2. This is nothing new. Throughout his presidency, Trump regularly claimed an "absolute right" to undertake many actions that strain or clearly exceed the boundaries of accepted executive power. Susan B. Glasser, *Trump's Pandemic Plan: "Absolute Authority," No Responsibility*, NEW YORKER (Apr. 17, 2020), https://www.newyorker.com/news/letter-from-trumps-was hington/trumps-pandemic-plan-absolute-authority-no-responsibility. Benjamin Wittes and Susan Hennessy's UNMAKING THE PRESIDENCY: DONALD TRUMP'S WAR ON THE WORLD'S MOST POWERFUL OFFICE (2020) provides a telling account of Trump's fondness for presidential powers such as the pardon, granting and revoking security clearances, firing, and the invocation of national emergencies that allowed him to exercise completely, or even de facto, unchecked authority, and his persistent tendency to stake claims to such powers even beyond these limited arenas.

3. NADIA URBINATI, ME THE PEOPLE: HOW POPULISM TRANSFORMS DEMOCRACY 12 (2019).

4. Sameer Yasir, *India Is Scapegoating Muslims for the Spread of the Coronavirus*, FOREIGN POL'Y (Apr. 22, 2020), https://foreignpolicy.com/2020/04/22/india-muslims-coronavirus-scapeg oat-modi-hindu-nationalism/.

5. Laura Livingston, *Understanding Hungary's Authoritarian Response to the Pandemic*, LAWFARE (Apr. 14, 2020), https://www.lawfareblog.com/understanding-hungarys-authoritarian- response-pandemic.

6. Simon Romero, Letícia Casado, & Manuela Andreoni, *Threat of Military Action Rattles Brazil as Virus Deaths Surge*, N.Y. TIMES (June 18, 2020), https://www.nytimes.com/2020/06/10/ world/americas/bolsonaro-coup-coronavirus-brazil.html.

7. Jason Dearen & Mike Stobbe, *Trump Administration Buries Detailed CDC Advice of Reopening*, ASSOCIATED PRESS (May 7, 2020), https://apnews.com/article/virus-outbreak-health-us- news-ap-top-news-politics-7a00d5fba3249e573d2ead4bd323a4d4.

8. Katie Rogers & Apoorva Mandavilli, *Trump Administration Signals Formal Withdrawal from W.H.O.*, N.Y. TIMES (July 7, 2020), https://www.nytimes.com/2020/07/07/us/politics/ coronavirus-trump-who.html.

9. Anne Gearan, Lena H. Sun, Josh Dawsey, & Michelle Boorstein, *Trump Tells States to Let Houses of Worship Open, Sparking Cultural and Political Fight Over Pandemic Restrictions*, WASH. POST (May 22, 2020), https://www.washingtonpost.com/politics/trump-tells-states- to-let-houses-of-worship-open-sparking-cultural-and-political-fight-over-pandemic-restricti ons/2020/05/22/1ab1c160-9c57-11ea-ad09-8da7ec214672_story.html.

10. Alex Ward, *Exclusive: Senators Urge Trump to Use Defense Production Act to Make More COVID-19 Tests*, VOX (May 6, 2020), https://www.vox.com/2020/5/6/21249233/coronavirus-defe nse-production-act-ppe-tests-trump.

11. *See* Brian Taylor, *Fact Check: Trump Doesn't Have the Authority to Order States to "Reopen,"* NPR (Apr. 14, 2020), https://www.npr.org/2020/04/14/834040912/fact-check-trump-doe snt-have-the-authority-to-order-states-to-reopen (describing various arguments under the Constitution why President Trump did not have unilateral authority to order reopenings).

12. *Trump Insists He Has "Total" Authority to Supersede Governors*, N.Y. TIMES (Apr. 21, 2020), https://www.nytimes.com/2020/04/13/us/coronavirus-updates.html.

13. BOB WOODWARD, FEAR: TRUMP IN THE WHITE HOUSE (2018); JOHN BOLTON, THE ROOM WHERE IT HAPPENED: A WHITE HOUSE MEMOIR (2020).

14. Caitlin Oprysko, *"I Don't Take Responsibility at All": Trump Deflects Blame for Coronavirus Testing Fumble*, POLITICO (Mar. 13, 2020), https://www.politico.com/news/2020/03/13/ trump-coronavirus-testing-128971 ("I don't take responsibility at all").

15. Marc Caputo, *Struggling with Latinos, Trump Hypes Goya Food Fight*, POLITICO (July 15 2020), https://www.politico.com/news/2020/07/15/trump-latino-support-goya-2020- 364856.

16. Karen Yourish, Larry Buchanan, & Denise Lu, *The 147 Republicans Who Voted to Overturn Election Results*, N.Y. TIMES (Jan. 7, 2021), https://www.nytimes.com/interactive/2021/01/ 07/us/elections/electoral-college-biden-objectors.html.

17. Victoria Bekiempis, *Seventy Percent of Republicans Say Election Wasn't "Free and Fair" Despite No Evidence of Fraud—Study*, THE GUARDIAN (Nov. 10, 2020), https://www.theguardian. com/us-news/2020/nov/10/election-trust-polling-study-republicans.

18. Shane Goldmacher & Adam Nagourney, *Takeaways from the Electoral College's Confirmation of Biden's Win*, N.Y. TIMES (Dec. 15, 2020), at A19.

19. *See* Kavitha George, *Anchorage Clerk Reports "Unprecedented Harassment" of Election Workers During Mayoral Runoff*, ALASKA PUB. MEDIA (May 27, 2021), https://www.alaskapublic.org/2021/05/27/anchorage-municipal-clerk-describes-unprecedented-harassment-of-election-workers/.

20. Memorandum from the Mun. Clerk's Office and the Mun. of Anchorage Elections Team on the Certification of the May 11, 2021 Mayoral Runoff Election (May 25, 2021), https://www.muni.org/Departments/Assembly/Documents/AM%20341-2021%20May%2011%2c%202021%20Mayoral%20Ruoff%20Election.pdf.

21. European Commission for Democracy through Law [Venice Commission], *Code of Good Practice in Electoral Matters*, Opinion no. 190/2002, CDL-AD(2002)023rev2-cor, as revised on October 25, 2018.

22. *Id.*

23. *Id.*

24. Martin Tolchin, *How Johnson Won Election He'd Lost*, N.Y. TIMES (Feb. 11, 1990), § 1, at 30.

25. STANFORD-MIT HEALTHY ELECTIONS PROJECT, THE VIRUS AND THE VOTE: ADMINISTERING THE 2020 ELECTION IN A PANDEMIC 551 (Chelsey Davidson & Zahavah Levine, eds., 2021).

26. *Id.* at 22.

27. Bo Rothstein, *What Saved American Democracy?*, SOCIAL EUROPE (Jan. 13, 2021), https://socialeurope.eu/what-saved-american-democracy.

28. *Michigan's Elections System Structure Overview*, MICH. SECRETARY OF ST., https://www.michigan.gov/sos/0,4670,7-127-1633_8716-27476--,00.html.

29. Sarah Cwiek, *Drama at the Board of Canvassers: No, That's Not Normal. Here's What's Up*, MICH. RADIO (Nov. 20, 2020), https://www.michiganradio.org/post/drama-board-canvassers-no-thats-not-normal-heres-whats.

30. MICH. DEP'T OF ST., BUREAU OF ELECTIONS, MANUAL FOR BOARDS OF COUNTY CANVASSERS 3–8 (2020) (quoting McQuade v. Furgason, 91 Mich. 438 (1892)).

31. STEVEN F. HUEFNER, DANIEL P. TOKAJI, & EDWARD B. FOLEY, FROM REGISTRATION TO RECOUNTS: THE ELECTION ECOSYSTEMS OF FIVE MIDWESTERN STATES 87 (2007), https://moritzlaw.osu.edu/electionlaw/projects/registration-to-recounts/chapter5_85-109.pdf.

32. Donald J. Trump (@realDonaldTrump), TWITTER (Nov. 18, 2020) [archived at https://web.archive.org/web/20201118170147/https:/twitter.com/realDonaldTrump/status/1329087255168708608]; Reality Check Team, *US Election 2020: Fact-Checking Trump Team's Main Fraud Claims*, BBC NEWS (Nov. 23, 2020), https://www.bbc.com/news/election-us-2020-55016029.

33. David Landau, Hannah J. Wiseman, & Samuel Wiseman, *Federalism, Democracy, and the 2020 Election*, 99 TEX. L. REV. ONLINE 97, 111 (2021).

34. Maggie Astor, *When Michigan Republicans Refused to Certify Votes, It Wasn't Normal*, N.Y. TIMES (Nov. 18, 2010), https://www.nytimes.com/2020/11/18/us/politics/michigan-election-results.html

35. These discrepancies occur when voters sign into a polling place but leave before casting a ballot, and canvassing boards regularly certify election returns despite evidence of these small deviations in vote counts. Given that there were an estimated 357 votes out of about 250,000 affected by such inconsistencies in Wayne County, they were not significant enough to change Biden's victory in the county or in the state. Astor, *When Michigan Republicans Refused to Certify Votes.*

36. *Id.*

37. Landau, Wiseman, & Wiseman, *Federalism, Democracy, and the 2020 Election*, at 111. President Trump and other Republican Party members also initially tweeted at the board members expressing support for their initial refusal to certify the county results. *Id.* at n.68.

38. *Id.* at 111.

39. Cwiek, *Drama at the Board of Canvassers.*

40. Jonathan Oosting, *A U.P. Senator Stood up to Trump. His Career May Suffer. His Cows Don't Care*, BRIDGE MICH. (July 1, 2021), https://www.bridgemi.com/michigan-government/senator-stood-trump-his-career-may-suffer-his-cows-dont-care ("McBroom, who was a Trump delegate at the 2016 Republican National Convention, lives the kind of throwback

lifestyle the former president had put on a pedestal with his pledge to "Make America Great Again").

41. *See* MICH. SENATE OVERSIGHT COMM., REPORT ON THE NOVEMBER 2020 ELECTION IN MICHIGAN 3, 4 (2021) ("This Committee found no evidence of widespread or systematic fraud in Michigan's prosecution of the 2020 election").

42. *Id.* at 35.

43. MARK BOWDEN & MATTHEW TEAGUE, THE STEAL: THE ATTEMPT TO OVERTURN THE 2020 ELECTION AND THE PEOPLE WHO STOPPED IT 54–59 (2022).

44. *Id.* at 146.

45. *See Voting Laws Roundup: October 2021,* BRENNAN CTR. (Oct. 4, 2021), https://www.brenna ncenter.org/our-work/research-reports/voting-laws-roundup-october-2021 ("In an unprec-edented year so far for voting legislation, 19 states have enacted 33 laws that will make it harder for Americans to vote").

46. STANFORD-MIT HEALTHY ELECTIONS PROJECT, THE VIRUS AND THE VOTE at 10.

47. *See* Michael Waldman, *Who Watches the Poll Watchers,* BRENNAN CTR. (May 4, 2021), https://www.brennancenter.org/our-work/analysis-opinion/who-watches-poll-watchers (discussing state legislation empowering partisan poll watchers to observe voters and elec-tion officials and gain more access to ballot counting).

48. Michael Wines, *In Arizona, G.O.P. Lawmakers Strip Power from a Democrat,* N.Y. TIMES (July 25, 2021), https://www.nytimes.com/2021/06/25/us/Arizona-Republicans-voting.html; Ben Giles, *Arizona Republicans Strip Some Election Power from Democratic Secretary of State,* NPR (June 30, 2021), https://www.npr.org/2021/06/30/1011154122/arizona-republic ans-strip-some-election-power-from-democratic-secretary-of-state?t=1654940977080.

49. *Id.* at 48.

50. Kim Lane Sheppele, *Hungary, an Election in Question, Part 3,* N.Y. TIMES (Feb. 28, 2014), https://krugman.blogs.nytimes.com/2014/02/28/hungary-an-election-in-question-part-3/.

51. *Id.*

52. *Id.*

53. *Id.*

54. *See* Kim Lane Sheppele, *Hungary, an Election in Question, Part 4,* N.Y. TIMES (Feb. 28, 2014), https://krugman.blogs.nytimes.com/2014/02/28/hungary-an-election-in-question-part-4/ (describing the various ways the election commission appears biased towards Orbán).

55. WOJIECH SADURSKI, POLAND'S CONSTITUTIONAL BREAKDOWN 140 (2019).

56. Kamil Marcinkiewicz & Mary Stegmaier, *Democratic Elections in Poland Face a New Threat,* WASH. POST (Jan. 11, 2018).

57. SADURSKI, POLAND'S CONSTITUTIONAL BREAKDOWN at 270.

58. *See id.* at 38 (explaining that eight of eleven members of the YSK were appointed by Erdoğan's party).

59. Ozan O. Varol, *Stealth Authoritarianism in Turkey, in* CONSTITUTIONAL DEMOCRACY IN CRISIS 338 (Mark A. Graber, Sanford Levinson, & Mark Tushnet, eds., 2018) (quoting Turkish President Recep Erdoğan).

60. *See generally* RAMCHANDRA GUHA, INDIA AFTER GANDHI (2007) (discussing the independent history of the Indian Election Commission and the role it played in maintaining democracy in India).

61. *See generally* Tarunabh Khaitan, *Killing a Constitution with a Thousand Cuts: Executive Aggrandizement and Party-State Fusion in India,* 14 L. & ETHICS HUM. RTS. 49 (2020) (describing in detail the many institutions of Indian government that have fallen under Modi's influence and the subsequent frailty of Indian democracy).

62. Ramchandra Guha, *Future of Indian Democracy May Hinge on Election Commission Regaining Credibility,* SCROLL.IN (May 9, 2021), https://scroll.in/article/994395/ramachandra-guha-has-the-credibility-of-the-election-commission-ever-been-so-low.

63. Pratap Bhanu Mehta, *For the Sake of Indian Democracy, the UP Governance Model Needs to Be Challenged,* INDIAN EXPRESS (May 21, 2021), https://indianexpress.com/article/opinion/columns/for-the-sake-of-indian-democracy-the-up-governance-model-needs-to-be-challen ged-7323588/.

64. *Id.*
65. *Id.*
66. CITIZEN'S COMM'N ON ELECTIONS, REPORT OF THE CITIZEN'S COMMISSION ON ELECTIONS: VOLUME II 12–15 (2021).
67. *Id.* at 16.
68. David Luhnow & José de Córdoba, *Is Mexico's President a Threat to Its Democracy?*, WALL ST. J. (June 4, 2020), https://www.wsj.com/articles/is-mexicos-president-a-threat-to-its-democracy-11622818830.
69. *See* Alejandro García Magos, *Is AMLO Undermining Democracy in Mexico?*, OPEN DEMOCRACY (May 13, 2021), https://www.opendemocracy.net/en/democraciaabierta/democratic-backsliding-mexico-force-for-good-bad/ (explaining that the INE and TEPJF disqualified the two López Obrador–backed candidates for failing to properly file pre-campaign expenses before the INE).
70. *Id.*
71. *What Would AMLO's Election Reforms Mean for Mexico?*, INTER-AMERICAN DIALOGUE (May 13, 2022), https://www.thedialogue.org/analysis/what-would-amlos-election-reforms-mean-for-mexico/ (statement of Professor Pamela K. Starr).
72. *Id.*
73. Rodrigo Camarena González & Francisca Pou Giménez, *From Expertise to Democracy-Shaping? Constitutional Agencies in Mexico*, 56 TEX. INT'L L. J. (forthcoming 2022) (manuscript at 5–6) (on file with author).
74. SAMUEL ISSACHAROFF, FRAGILE DEMOCRACIES 206 (2015).
75. *See* Max De Haldevang, *Mexico's Ruling Party Expands Power with Local Election Wins*, BLOOMBERG (June 5, 2022), https://www.bloomberg.com/news/articles/2022-06-05/mexico-s-ruling-party-seen-expanding-control-in-local-elections#xj4y7vzkg; Lunhow & Córdoba, *Is Mexico's President a Threat to Its Democracy?* (explaining that a parliamentary majority would allow López Obrador to accomplish his goals of gaining more control over Mexican institutions, such as the Central Bank, and has been bringing other previously independent institutions under state control).
76. Miriam Seifter, *Judging Power Plays in the American States*, 97 TEX. L. REV. 1217, 1223–24 (2018).
77. MAX WEBER, ECONOMY AND SOCIETY: AN OUTLINE OF INTERPRETIVE SOCIOLOGY 998–1003 (Guenther Roth & Claus Wittich, eds., 1978).
78. MARK TUSHNET, THE NEW FOURTH BRANCH: INSTITUTIONS FOR PROTECTING CONSTITUTIONAL DEMOCRACY 119 (2021).
79. *See* Michael Pal, *Electoral Management Bodies as a Fourth Branch of Government*, 21 REV. CONSTIT. STUDIES 97 (2016).
80. Nils Gustafsson & Noomi Weinryb, *The Populist Allure of Social Media Activism: Individualized Charismatic Authority*, ORG., May 2020, at 435 (emphasis added).
81. Jarle Trondal, Zuzana Murdoch, & Benny Geys, *Representative Bureaucracy and the Role of Expertise in Politics*, 30 POLS. & GOVERNANCE, no. 1, 2015, at 28.
82. TOM GINSBURG & AZIZ Z. HUQ, HOW TO SAVE A CONSTITUTIONAL DEMOCRACY 104 (2019).
83. 5 U.S.C. §§ 551-559.
84. PHILIP SELZNICK, LEADERSHIP IN ADMINISTRATION: A SOCIOLOGICAL INTERPRETATION 17 (1984) (emphasis omitted).
85. Martin Krygier, *Polish Lessons: Backsliding, Sabotage, and the Rule of Law*, in CONSTITUTIONALISM UNDER STRESS 82 (U. Baelavusau & A. Gliszczynska-Grabias, eds., 2020).
86. PHILIP SELZNICK, THE MORAL COMMONWEALTH 232 (1992).
87. Tom Phillips, *Bolsonaro Ignores Repeated Warnings About Covid, Ex-Health Minister Says*, THE GUARDIAN (May 4, 2021), https://www.theguardian.com/world/2021/may/04/brazil-bolsonaro-coronavirus-health-minister-inquiry.
88. *See* Gabriel Stargardter & Lisandra Paraguassu, *Special Report: Bolsonaro Bets "Miraculous Cure" for COVID-19 Can Save Brazil—and His Life*, REUTERS (Jul. 8, 2020), https://www.reuters.com/article/us-health-coronavirus-brazil-hydroxychlo/special-report-bolsonaro-bets-miraculous-cure-for-covid-19-can-save-brazil-and-his-life-idUSKBN249396

(discussing Bolsonaro's public statements promoting hydroxychloroquine and noting Trump's early advocacy of the drug).

89. Emma Goldberg, *Demand Surges for Deworming Drug for Covid, Despite Scant Evidence It Works*, N.Y. TIMES (Aug. 30, 2021), https://www.nytimes.com/2021/08/30/health/covid-ivermectin-prescriptions.html.

90. *Coronavirus: Outcry After Trump Suggests Injecting Disinfectant as Treatment*, BBC NEWS (Apr. 24, 2020), https://www.bbc.com/news/world-us-canada-52407177.

91. Ben Lerner, *Trump Wants to Protect the Numbers, Not the Covid-19 Patients They Represent*, NEW YORKER (Apr. 6, 2020), https://www.newyorker.com/magazine/2020/04/13/trumps-numbers.

92. Alexa Scherzinger, *Ohio Legislature Overrides DeWine's Veto*, ADVERTISER-TRIB. (May 31, 2021), https://advertiser-tribune.com/news/312340/ohio-legislature-overrides-dewines-veto.

93. Jason Tidd, *How Bad Is the New Delta-Fueled Covid-19 Surge in Kansas? Here's What the Number Show*, TOPEKA CAP. J. (Jul. 28, 2021), https://www.cjonline.com/story/news/coronavirus/2021/07/28/kansas-covid-delta-variant-surge-cdc-new-mask-guidelines-vaccine-cases-outbreaks/5402172001.

94. Bri Smith, *Kansas Health Officials Concerned with Public Health Trends Amid Senate Bill 40 Challenges*, KAKE (Mar. 30, 2021), https://www.kake.com/story/43576386/kansas-health-officials-concerned-with-public-health-trends-amid-senate-bill-40-changes.

95. Brandan Pierson, *Lockdown Backlash Curbs Governors' Emergency Powers*, REUTERS (June 22, 2021), https://www.reuters.com/legal/government/lockdown-backlash-curbs-governors-emergency-powers-2021-06-22.

96. Brett Kelman, *Tennessee Abandons Vaccine Outreach to Minors—Not Just for COVID-19*, NASHVILLE TENNESSEAN (Jul. 13, 2021), https://www.tennessean.com/story/news/health/2021/07/13/tennessee-halts-all-vaccine-outreach-minors-not-just-covid-19/7928701002.

97. Josh Dawsey, Rosalind S. Helderman, & David A. Fahrenthold, *How Trump Abandoned His Pledge to "Drain the Swamp,"* WASH. POST (Oct. 24, 2020), https://www.washingtonpost.com/politics/trump-drain-the-swamp/2020/10/24/52c7682c-0a5a-11eb-9be6-cf25fb429f1a_story.html.

98. MICHAEL LEWIS, THE FIFTH RISK 35–36, 160 (2018).

99. Lisa Rein, *The Federal Government Puts Out a "Help Wanted" Notice as Biden Seeks to Undo Trump Cuts*, WASH. POST (May 21, 2021), https://www.washingtonpost.com/politics/2021/05/21/biden-trump-government-rebuilding.

100. Doyle McManus, *Almost Half the Top Jobs in Trump's State Department Are Still Empty*, THE ATLANTIC (Nov. 4, 2018), https://www.theatlantic.com/politics/archive/2018/11/state-department-empty-ambassador-to-australi/574831.

101. Joel Rose, *How Trump Has Filled High-Level Jobs Without Senate Confirmation Votes*, NPR (Mar. 9, 2020), https://www.npr.org/2020/03/09/813577462/how-trump-has-filled-high-level-jobs-without-senate-confirmation.

102. Lisa Rein, Tom Hamburger, Juliet Eilperin, & Andrew Freedman, *How Trump Waged War on His Own Government*, WASH. POST. (Oct. 29, 2020), https://www.washingtonpost.com/politics/trump-federal-civil-servants/2020/10/28/86f9598e-122a-11eb-ba42-ec6a580836ed_story.html (quoting Donald Kettl).

103. TOM GINSBURG & AZIZ Z. HUQ, HOW TO SAVE A CONSTITUTIONAL DEMOCRACY 102 (2019).

104. Kim Lane Scheppele, *Hungary and the End of Politics*, NATION (May 6, 2014), https://www.thenation.com/article/archive/hungary-and-end-politics/.

105. Miklós Bánkuti, Gábor Helmai, & Kim Lane Scheppele, *Hungary's Illiberal Turn: Disabling the Constitution*, 23 J. DEMOCRACY 136, 144 (2012).

106. *See How Viktor Orbán Hollowed Out Hungary's Democracy*, THE ECONOMIST (Aug. 29, 2019), https://www.economist.com/briefing/2019/08/29/how-viktor-Orbán-hollowed-out-hungarys-democracy (explaining that Orbán used the State Audit Office to launch investigations into the far-right Jobbik Party that was becoming an electoral threat).

107. *See* SADURSKI, POLAND'S CONSTITUTIONAL BREAKDOWN at 4 (explaining that PiS views Orbán as a "model" to follow).

108. *Id.* at 61–63.

109. *See id.* at 136 (explaining that civil service members must take exams administered by schools bearing the name of the former PiS president, demonstrating PiS influence over the entire civil service apparatus).

110. Wojciech Sadurski, *Constitutional Crisis in Poland, in* CONSTITUTIONAL DEMOCRACY IN CRISIS 256, 269 (Mark A. Graber, Sanford Levinson, & Mark Tushnet, eds., 2018).

111. *Id.*

112. Juan Montes & Robbie Whelan, *Mexican President Clashes with Agencies Curbing His Power*, WALL ST. J. (Feb 26, 2019), https://www.wsj.com/articles/mexican-president-clashes-with-agencies-curbing-his-power-11551186002.

113. *Id.*

114. *See* Shannon K. O'Neil, *López Obrador Is Dismantling Democracy in Mexico*, COUNCIL ON FOREIGN RELS. BLOG (Mar. 11, 2019) ("He and his political allies are using the bully pulpit, congressional inquiries and the tax authority to go after commissioners who have dared to question his methods."); Mary Beth Sheridan, *López Obrador's Bid to Alter Mexican Supreme Court Seen as Threat to Judicial Independence*, WASH. POST (Apr. 27, 2021), https://www.washingtonpost.com/world/2021/04/27/mexico-amlo-supreme-court/ (discussing López Obrador's calls to investigate a judge who had made critical comments of Morena legislation).

115. Ned Levin et al., *Inside Turkey's Irregular Referendum*, WALL ST. J. (Apr. 25, 2017), https://www.wsj.com/articles/inside-turkeys-irregular-referendum-1493150990.

116. Alina Polianskaya, *Turkey Suddenly Sacks 18,000 Officials in Emergency Decree, Days Before Erdogan Is Sworn in Again*, INDEP. (July 9, 2018), https://www.independent.co.uk/news/world/europe/turkey-sacks-18-000-officials-emergency-decree-erdogan-swears-oath-president-a8437151.html.

117. *See generally* Khaitan, *Killing a Constitution with a Thousand Cuts*, at 88–90 (2020); *Narendra Modi Threatens to Turn India into a One-Party State*, THE ECONOMIST (Nov. 28, 2020), https://www.economist.com/briefing/2020/11/28/narendra-modi-threatens-to-turn-india-into-a-one-party-state (discussing the arrest and temporary imprisonment of journalist Arnab Goswami following comments critical of the BJP).

118. *See* SADURSKI, POLAND'S CONSTITUTIONAL BREAKDOWN at 139–40, 145 (explaining PiS control over the media and how it has curtailed the influence and operations of NGOs in Poland).

119. Elizabeth Redden, *Central European U Forced Out of Hungary*, INSIDE HIGHER ED. (Dec. 4, 2018), https://www.insidehighered.com/news/2018/12/04/central-european-university-forced-out-hungary-moving-vienna.

120. *See* Amrit Dhillon, *Modi Critic's Resignation from Indian University Post Prompts Outcry*, THE GUARDIAN (Mar 19, 2021), https://www.theguardian.com/world/2021/mar/19/modi-critics-resignation-from-indian-university-post-sparks-outcry (discussing Pratap Bhanu Mehta's resignation from Ashoka University and his statements indicating he was forced out due to comments critical of the Modi government); Arunima G., *The Battle for JNU's Soul*, WIRE.IN (Dec. 25, 2018), https://thewire.in/education/the-battle-for-jnu-soul (discussing protests at Jawaharlal Nehru University that led to government crackdown and the suppression of academic freedom); Jahnavi Sen, *"Vilification" of JNU Professor Nivedita Menon as "Anti-National" Labelling Continues*, WIRE.IN (Mar. 15, 2016), https://thewire.in/politics/vilification-of-jnu-professor-nivedita-menon-as-anti-national-labelling-continues (discussing attacks on Professor Nivedita Menon by BJP student groups and state action to suppress her voice following comments critical of Modi).

121. FRANCIS FUKUYAMA, POLITICAL ORDER AND POLITICAL DECAY 460 (2014).

122. *Id.* at 463.

123. *See* Tom Ginsburg, *Democratic Erosion without Prerequisites, in* CONSTITUTIONALISM UNDER STRESS 51, 57 (Uladzislau Belavusau & Aleksandra Gliszczynska-Grabias, eds., 2020) (writing that the separation of the general public from government in large democracies reduces oversight, leading to potential democratic decline).

124. *See* David M. Driesen, *The Unitary Executive Theory in Comparative Context*, 72 HASTINGS L. J. 1, 6 (2020) ("Autocrats seeking to subvert democratic governments secure constitutional

changes restructuring the executive branch to facilitate centralized control over key bureaucracies . . . this centralization substantially impairs the rule of law by defeating the principle that the law applies equally to all").

125. *See* David L. Noll, *Administrative Sabotage*, 120 MICH. L. REV. 753 (2022) (manuscript at 11).

126. *See, e.g.,* Lisa Rein, Tom Hamburger, Juliet Eilperin, & Andrew Freedman, *How Trump Waged War on His Own Government,* WASH. POST (Oct. 29, 2020), https://www.washing tonpost.com/politics/trump-federal-civil-servants/2020/10/28/86f9598e-122a-11eb-ba42-ec6a580836ed_story.html.

127. Michael W. Bauer & Stefan Becker, *Democratic Backsliding, Populism, and Public Administration,* 3 PERSP. PUB. MGMT. GOVERNANCE 19, 23 (2020).

128. Driesen *The Unitary Executive Theory in Comparative Context,* at 42.

129. Ryan Calo & Danielle Keats Citron, *The Automated Administrative State: A Crisis of Legitimacy,* 70 EMORY L. J. 797, 816 (2021).

130. *See* JOSÉ ANTONIO CHEIBUB, PRESIDENTIALISM, PARLIAMENTARISM, AND DEMOCRACY (2006) (debunking the notion that governmental structure influences democratic decline and attributing such deterioration to countries' "authoritarian legacy").

131. Aileen Kavanagh, *Recasting the Political Constitution: From Rivals to Relationships,* 30 KING'S L. J. 43, 72 (2019).

132. Erin F. Delaney, *The UK's Basic Structure Doctrine*: Miller II *and Judicial Power in Comparative Perspective,* 12 NOTRE DAME J. INT'L & COMP. L. 22 (2022).

133. BOB BAUER & JACK GOLDSMITH, AFTER TRUMP: RECONSTRUCTING THE PRESIDENCY ii (2020).

Chapter 9

1. E. E. SCHATTSCHNEIDER, PARTY GOVERNMENT 129 (1942).

2. AMY FRIED & DOUGLAS B. HARRIS, AT WAR WITH GOVERNMENT: HOW CONSERVATIVES WEAPONIZED DISTRUST FROM GOLDWATER TO TRUMP 162 (2021).

3. 2 ALEXIS DE TOCQUEVILLE, DEMOCRACY IN AMERICA 114–118 (Henry Reeve trans., 1840) (1835).

4. *Trust in Government,* OECD, https://data.oecd.org/gga/trust-in-government.htm (choose "latest data available") (last visited Mar. 20, 2022).

5. *See id.* (highlight "United States" and toggle from 2010 to 2019).

6. FRIED & HARRIS, AT WAR WITH GOVERNMENT at 3 (2021) (quoting Marc Hetherington, *Why Polarized Trust Matters,* 3 FORUM 445, 445 (2015)).

7. THOMAS FRANK, WHAT'S THE MATTER WITH KANSAS? HOW CONSERVATIVES WON THE HEART OF AMERICA 67–68 (2004).

8. Noel D. Johnson & Mark Koyama, *States and Economic Growth: Capacity and Constraints,* 64 EXPLS. IN ECON. HIST. 1, 2 (2017).

9. Keith Bradsher & Steven Lee Myers, *Beijing Claims China Uses Its Own Variety of Democracy to Govern,* N.Y. TIMES (Dec. 8, 2021), at A6.

10. Jim Tankersley, *Biden Details $2 Trillion Plan to Rebuild Infrastructure and Reshape the Economy,* N.Y. TIMES (Mar. 31, 2021), https://www.nytimes.com/2021/03/31/business/economy/biden-infrastructure-plan.html; Bojan Pancevski, *Germany's Scholz Vows to Overhaul Economy as Next Chancellor,* WALL ST. J. (Nov. 24, 2021), https://www.wsj.com/articles/germanys-olaf-scholz-on-track-to-succeed-angela-merkel-as-chancellor-11637749450.

11. Nicholas Bagley, *The Procedure Fetish,* NISKANEN CTR. (Dec. 7, 2021), https://www.niskane ncenter.org/the-procedure-fetish/. For a fuller account of the argument, see Nicholas Bagley, *The Procedure Fetish,* 118 MICH. L. REV. 345 (2019).

12. PHILLIP K. HOWARD, THE DEATH OF COMMON SENSE: HOW LAW IS SUFFOCATING AMERICA (1995).

13. BRINK LINDSEY, NISKANEN CTR., STATE CAPACITY: WHAT IT IS, HOW WE LOST IT, AND HOW TO GET IT BACK 3 (2021), https://www.niskanencenter.org/wp-content/uploads/2021/11/brinkpaper.pdf.

14. *Id.* at 13.

15. David Leonhardt, *Effects of a Shrinking Investment in Innovation*, N.Y. TIMES (Dec. 10, 2021), at A15.

16. FRIED & HARRIS, AT WAR WITH GOVERNMENT at 164.

17. Ryan Calo & Danielle Keats Citron, *The Automated Administrative State: A Crisis of Legitimacy*, 70 EMORY L.J. 797, 816 (2021).

18. Ezra Klein (@ezraklein), TWITTER (Dec. 8, 2021, 6:00 PM), https://twitter.com/ezraklein/status/1468717212844191744.

19. *See* Eli Stokols & Jennifer Haberkorn, *With Biden's Agenda Hanging by a Thread, Democrats Question Their Leaders' Strategy*, L.A. TIMES (Feb. 12, 2022, 2:00 AM), https://www.latimes.com/politics/story/2022-02-12/with-bidens-agenda-hanging-by-a-thread-democrats-question-schumer-klain-strategy.

20. FRIED & HARRIS, AT WAR WITH GOVERNMENT at 1.

21. Natalie Colarossi, *Just Two Percent of Hispanics Use the Term "Latinx," Forty Percent Find It Offensive: Poll*, NEWSWEEK (Dec. 6, 2021), https://www.newsweek.com/just-2-percent-hispanics-use-term-latinx-40-percent-find-it-offensive-poll-1656412.

22. Jeffrey Gedmin, *Right-Wing Populism in Germany: Muslims and Minorities After the 2015 Refugee Crisis*, BROOKINGS INST. (July 24, 2019), https://www.brookings.edu/research/right-wing-populism-in-germany-muslims-and-minorities-after-the-2015-refugee-crisis.

23. Sean Clarke, *German Elections 2017: Full Results*, THE GUARDIAN (Sept. 25, 2017), https://www.theguardian.com/world/ng-interactive/2017/sep/24/german-elections-2017-latest-results-live-merkel-bundestag-afd. *But see* Emily Schultheis, *Germany's Far-Right AfD Loses Nationally, But Wins the East*, POLITICO (Sept. 28, 2021) (noting that in the 2020 elections, the AfD's voter share fell to fifth behind the Greens and Liberal Democrats).

24. MANCUR OLSON, THE RISE AND DECLINE OF NATIONS 41 (1982).

25. CYNTHIA ESTLUND, AUTOMATION ANXIETY: WHY AND HOW TO SAVE WORK 79 (2021).

26. MICHAEL J. SANDEL, THE TYRANNY OF MERIT: WHAT'S BECOME OF THE COMMON GOOD? 18 (2020).

27. *Id.* at 19.

28. PAUL COLLIER, THE FUTURE OF CAPITALISM: FACING THE NEW ANXIETIES 196 (2018).

29. *Id.* at 128–29.

30. *See* ADAM SMITH, THE WEALTH OF NATIONS 96 (2019) (1776).

31. SANDEL, THE TYRANNY OF MERIT at 71–72.

32. *See generally* Juan J. Linz, *The Perils of Presidentialism*, 1 J. DEMOCRACY 51, 52 (1990) (noting the "superior performance of parliamentary democracies," and arguing that parliamentary systems are "more conducive to stable democracy than [presidential systems]"). *But see generally* Donald L. Horowitz, *Presidents v. Parliaments: Comparing Democratic Systems*, 1 J. DEMOCRACY 73, 73–74 (1990) (responding to Linz's piece and discussing the benefits a "separate elected president can perform for a divided society"). For a discussion of differences in the approach to restraining executive power in presidential and parliamentary, contexts, see Richard Epstein, *Executive Power in Political and Corporate Contexts*, 12 J. CONST. L. 277, 281 (2010).

33. This is the argument advanced for why parliamentarism is more responsive to voter preferences. *See* Bruce Ackerman, *The New Separation of Powers*, 113 HARV. L. REV. 633, 640–41 (2000) (advancing a model of constrained parliamentarism as superior to presidentialism).

34. Bertil Emrah Oder, *Turkey's Democratic Erosion: On Backsliding and the Constitution*, 88 SOC. RESCH. 473, 482 (2021).

35. Grianne de Burca, *Reinvigorating Democracy in the European Union: Lessons from Ireland's Citizens Assembly?* 2 (N.Y.U. Sch. of L. Pub. L. & Legal Theory Paper Series, Working Paper No. 20-26, 2020), https://papers.ssrn.com/sol3/papers.cfm?abstract_id=3636244.

36. William H. Riker, *Federalism, in* HANDBOOK OF POLITICAL SCIENCE 101 (F. Greenstein & N. Polsby eds., 1975).

37. ROBERT P. INMAN & DANIEL L. RUBINFELD, DEMOCRATIC FEDERALISM: THE ECONOMICS, POLITICS, AND LAW OF FEDERAL GOVERNANCE 12 (2020).

38. *Id.* at 377.

39. THE FEDERALIST NO. 51, at 382 (James Madison) (AmazonClassics ed. 2017).

40. Jessica Bulman-Pozen, *Partisan Federalism*, 127 HARV. L. REV. 1077, 1080–81 (2014) ("Attending to partisanship reveals that our contemporary federal system generates a check on the federal government and fosters divided citizen loyalties, as courts and scholars frequently assume.... because it provides durable and robust scaffolding for partisan conflict.").

41. *Id.* at 1097–99 (pointing to Republican state litigation over the ACA and Democratic state litigation over the Defense of Marriage Act).

42. *Id.* at 1100–4 (pointing to Democratic states passing environmental protection laws under President Bush and Republican states defunding Planned Parenthood under President Obama).

43. *Id.* at 1105 (pointing to Republican states declining expanded Medicaid grants to frustrate ACA implementation and Democratic states refusing sex-ed funding that required teaching abstinence only).

44. Abbe R. Gluck, *How the G.O.P. Sabotaged Obamacare*, N.Y. TIMES (May 25, 2017), https://www.nytimes.com/2017/05/25/opinion/republicans-obamacare-aca.html ("Obamacare is not 'collapsing under its own weight,' as Republicans are so fond of saying. It was sabotaged from the day it was enacted.").

45. *Legal Cases and State Legislative Actions Related to the ACA*, NAT'L CONF. OF STATE LEGISLATURES (June 29, 2021), https://www.ncsl.org/research/health/state-laws-and-acti ons-challenging-ppaca.aspx.

46. Louise Norris, *12 Ways the GOP Sabotaged Obamacare*, HEALTHINSURANCE.ORG (July 26, 2019), https://www.healthinsurance.org/blog/12-ways-the-gop-sabotaged-obamacare/ (noting that this leaves a coverage gap of 2.3 million people).

47. 567 U.S. 519, 585 (2012) (finding that the spending clause does not permit Congress to mandate Medicaid expansion); *see also* Perry Bacon Jr., *Republicans Killed Much of Obamacare Without Repealing It*, FIVETHIRTYEIGHT (Dec. 18, 2018), https://fivethirtyeight.com/features/republicans-killed-much-of-obamacare-without-repealing-it/ (noting that elected officials joined the suit).

48. Joseph Krakoff, *Big Tech Is Not Big Tobacco: How Today's Toxic Politics Would Distort State Attorneys General Litigation Against Facebook*, JUST SECURITY (Jan. 13, 2022), https://www.justsecurity.org/79836/big-tech-is-not-big-tobacco/.

49. Margaret H. Lemos, *Aggregate Litigation Goes Public: Representative Suits by State Attorneys General*, 126 HARV. L. REV. 486 (2012).

50. *See, e.g.*, Heather Gerken, *We're About to See States' Rights Used Defensively Against Trump*, VOX (Jan. 20, 2017), https://www.vox.com/the-big-idea/2016/12/12/13915990/federalism-trump-progressive-uncooperative ("Federalism doesn't have a political valence. These days it's an extraordinarily powerful weapon in politics for the left and the right, and it doesn't have to be your father's (or grandfather's) federalism. It can be a source of progressive resistance—against President's Trump's policies, for example—and, far more importantly, a source for compromise and change between the left and the right.").

51. Katy Steinmetz, *Seven Ways California Is Fighting Back Against President Trump's Administration*, TIME (Apr. 6, 2017), https://time.com/4725971/california-resisting-trump-adminis tration/ ("This is a wall of shame and we don't want any part of it") (quoting California Assemblymember Phil Ting).

52. Kristine Cooke & Ted Hesson, *What Are "Sanctuary" Cities and Why Is Trump Targeting Them?*, REUTERS (Feb. 25, 2020), https://www.reuters.com/article/us-usa-immigration-crime/what-are-sanctuary-cities-and-why-is-trump-targeting-them-idUSKBN20J25R.

53. Rebecca L. Haffajee & Michelle M. Mello, *Thinking Globally, Acting Locally—The U.S. Response to Covid-19*, 382 NEW ENG. J. MED. e75(1), e75(2) (2020).

54. Daniel B. Rodriguez, *Professional Regulation and Federalism in the Coronavirus Crisis: Let's Remove Access Barriers*, HARV. L. REV. BLOG (Apr. 15, 2020), https://blog.harvardlawreview.org/professional-regulation-and-federalism-in-the-coronavirus-crisis-lets-remove-access-barriers/ ("COVID-19 in the United States is a national health and economic crisis, and it requires an all-hands-on-deck-approach. Our system of federalism of which we are rightly proud is poorly suited to these comprehensive national efforts. The vexing situation of states competing against one another to collect suitable PPE equipment puts this into sharp relief."); *see also* Terry Nguyen, *How the Trump Administration Has Stood in the Way of PPE*

Distribution, vox (Apr. 4, 2020), https://www.vox.com/2020/4/4/21208122/ppe-distr ibution-trump-administration-states (discussing the lack of federal response early on to the COVID-19 pandemic, resulting in state competition for crucial PPE).

55. Press Release, Taryn Fenske, Director of Communications, Governor Ron Desantis, Governor DeSantis Issues an Executive Order Ensuring Parents' Freedom to Choose (July 30, 2021), https://www.flgov.com/2021/07/30/governor-desantis-issues-an-executive-order-ensur ing-parents-freedom-to-choose/ ("Today, Governor Ron DeSantis issued Executive Order 21-175, in response to several Florida school boards considering or implementing mask mandates in their schools after the Biden Administration issued unscientific and inconsistent recommendations that school-aged children wear masks.").

56. *See* Amy B. Wang, *Texas Governor Abbott Issues Executive Order Prohibiting Cities from Requiring Masks, Vaccines,* WASH. POST (July 29, 2021), https://www.washingtonpost.com/ politics/2021/07/29/texas-gov-abbott-issues-executive-order-prohibiting-cities-requiring-masks-vaccines/ (discussing Texas's ban on mask mandates).

57. *See* Yana Kunichoff, *From Vouchers to Federal Funding, Ducey Offers Incentives to Arizona Schools, Parents, to Reject Mask Mandates,* AZCENTRAL (Aug. 17, 2021), https://www.azcent ral.com/story/news/politics/arizona-education/2021/08/17/arizona-gov-doug-ducey-offers-incentives-reject-mask-mandates/8169357002/ (noting the creation of state grant programs funding families and school districts that rejected mask mandates).

58. Jack Healy & Lauren McCarthy, *"See You in Court": G.O.P. Governors Express Outrage and Vow to Fight Biden's Vaccine Requirements,* N.Y. TIMES (Sept. 10, 2021), https://www.nytimes.com/ 2021/09/10/us/republican-governors-mandate-reaction.html.

59. John Kennedy, *DeSantis Signs Bills Blocking Biden Administration COVID Vaccine Mandates in Florida,* HERALD-TRIB. (Nov. 18, 2021), https://www.heraldtribune.com/story/news/polit ics/state/2021/11/18/desantis-signs-bills-blocking-biden-administration-covid-vaccine-mandate/8664181002/.

60. Eric Berger, *Republicans Resist Mandates to Curb Covid but Lawsuits Likely to Prove Futile,* THE GUARDIAN (Nov. 12, 2021), https://www.theguardian.com/world/2021/nov/12/us-vacc ine-mandates-workers-covid-republican-lawsuits.

61. JEREMY WALDRON, POLITICAL POLITICAL THEORY 22 (2016) (quoting BARON DE MONTESQUIEU, THE SPIRIT OF THE LAWS 68 (Thomas Nugent trans., J. V. Prichard ed., 1902) (1748)).

62. *Id.* at 82 (quoting VERNON BOGDANOR, POLITICS AND THE CONSTITUTION: ESSAYS ON BRITISH GOVERNMENT 258 (1996)).

63. FRIED & HARRIS, AT WAR WITH GOVERNMENT at 130 (quoting ROBERT DRAPER, WHEN THE TEA PARTY CAME TO TOWN xii (2012)).

64. FRIED & HARRIS, AT WAR WITH GOVERNMENT at 104 (2021) (quoting an internal White House assessment).

65. WALDRON, POLITICAL POLITICAL THEORY at 101.

66. NANCY ROSENBLUM, ON THE SIDE OF ANGELS: AN APPRECIATION OF PARTIES AND PARTISANSHIP 121 (2008) (invoking Edmund Burke's idea of regulated rivalry).

67. David Fontana, *Government in Opposition*, 119 YALE L. J. 548, 550 (2009) (explaining that countries ranging from Argentina and Chile to Germany and South Africa have structures in place to empower the opposition).

68. *See id.* (defining "government in opposition" as granting losing parties the ability to partici-pate in governing).

69. Adrian Vermeule, *Submajority Rules: Forcing Accountability upon Majorities,* 13 J. POL. PHIL. 74, 74 (2007).

70. MELISSA SCHWARTZBERG, COUNTING THE MANY: THE ORIGINS AND LIMITS OF SUPERMAJORITY RULE 7 (2014).

71. Alfred Stepan, *On the Tasks of a Democratic Opposition,* 1 J. OF DEMOCRACY 41, 44 (1990).

72. Grégoire Webber, *Loyal Opposition and the Political Constitution,* 37 OXFORD J. L. STUD. 357, 369 (2017).

73. Sujit Choudhry, Opposition Rights in Parliamentary Democracies 1 (Sept. 2020) (unpub-lished manuscript).

74. Vermeule, *Submajority Rules* at 76–84.

75. Aziz Huq & Tom Ginsburg, *How to Lose a Constitutional Democracy*, 65 UCLA L. REV. 78, 136 (2018).

76. Kim Lane Scheppele, *Autocratic Legalism*, 85 U. CHI. L. REV. 545, 550 (2018).

77. WOJCIECH SADURSKI, POLAND'S CONSTITUTIONAL BREAKDOWN 134 (2019).

78. Tarunabh Khaitan, *Killing a Constitution with a Thousand Cuts: Executive Aggrandizement and Party-State Fusion in India*, 14 L. & ETHICS OF HUM. RTS. 49, 64–65 (2020).

79. Frank Dale & Josh Israel, *Republicans Who Held Thirty-Three Hearings on Benghazi Complain That Cohen's Testimony Was a Waste of Time*, THINKPROGRESS (Feb. 28, 2019), https://archive.thinkprogress.org/after-years-of-hearings-on-benghazi-diamond-and-silk-house-gop-says-cohen-was-a-waste-of-time-c22626b510ea/.

80. *See Evaluating Trump's First 100 Days—On His Own Terms*, VOX (Apr. 28, 2017), https://www.vox.com/a/trump-first-100-hundred-days-evaluating-terms-promises-accomplishments (noting that even with an ambitious plan for his first hundred days, no major legislation was passed: "Anyone who knows anything about the legislative process could have predicted most of this, of course, though a Republican Party president being unable to write a real tax bill is odd.").

81. FRANCES E. LEE, INSECURE MAJORITIES: CONGRESS AND THE PERPETUAL CAMPAIGN 5 (2016).

82. Cristina Rodriguez, *Foreword: Regime Change*, 135 HARV. L. REV. 1, 76 (2021).

83. *Id.* at 108.

84. Kisor v. Wilkie, 139 S. Ct. 2400, 2415 (2019).

85. BOB BAUER & JACK GOLDSMITH, AFTER TRUMP: RECONSTRUCTING THE PRESIDENCY (2020).

86. *See Members of the European Network of Ombudsmen*, EUROPEAN OMBUDSMEN, https://www.ombudsman.europa.eu/en/european-network-of-ombudsmen/members/all-members (last visited Jan. 3, 2021) (noting thirty-six European countries with ombudsmen in the network).

87. *See* SADURSKI, POLAND'S CONSTITUTIONAL BREAKDOWN at 146 (noting the ombudsman's role in stopping a bill that would have given the minister of interior broad oversight of NGO fundraising); *id.* at 268 (calling the Polish ombudsman, Dr. Adam Bodnar, a "courageous, tenacious, and intelligent [ombudsman]," and arguing that he offers one pillar of hope in preventing further backsliding).

88. *SEE* RICHARD L. HASEN, ELECTION MELTDOWN: DIRTY TRICKS, DISTRUST, AND THE THREAT TO AMERICAN DEMOCRACY (2020).

89. ARISTOTLE, POLITICS bk. III, at 202 (Trevor J. Saunders trans., rev. ed., 1981) (c. 384 B.C.E) (emphasis added).

90. *Id.* at 182.

91. *Id.* at 208–9.

92. DENNIS RASMUSSEN, FEARS OF A SETTING SUN 104 (2021) (quoting letter from John Adams to Mercy Otis Warren (Apr. 16, 1776), *in* 4 PAPERS OF JOHN ADAMS 124 (Robert J. Taylor, Gregg L. Lint, & Celeste Walker, eds., 2003).

93. *Id.* at 219–20.

94. THE FEDERALIST NO. 51 (James Madison) (2012) ("If men were angels, no government would be necessary.").

95. RASMUSSEN, FEARS OF A SETTING SUN at 219–20 (quoting James Madison, Speech at the Virginia Ratifying Convention (June 10, 1788), in 11 THE PAPERS OF JAMES MADISON 163 (William T. Hutchinson & William M. E. Rachal eds., 1970).

96. *See* Michael Ignatieff, Opinion, *Enemies vs. Adversaries*, N.Y. TIMES (Oct. 16, 2013), https://www.nytimes.com/2013/10/17/opinion/enemies-vs-adversaries.html; Russell Muirhead & Nancy L. Rosenblum, *Political Liberalism vs. "The Great Game of Politics": The Politics of Political Liberalism*, PERSPS. ON POLS. (Mar. 2006), at 101.

97. UVA Center for Politics, *New Initiative Explores Deep Persistent Divides Between Biden and Trump Voters*, SABATO'S CRYSTAL BALL (Sept. 30, 2021), https://centerforpolitics.org/crystalball/articles/new-initiative-explores-deep-persistent-divides-between-biden-and-trump-voters.

98. David Hume, *On the First Principles of Government* (1741), https://davidhume.org/texts/empl1/fp.

99. STEVEN LEVITSKY & DANIEL ZIBLATT, HOW DEMOCRACIES DIE 8–9 (2018).

100. PAOLO GERBAUDO, THE DIGITAL PARTY: POLITICAL ORGANISATION AND ONLINE DEMOCRACY 35 (2019).

101. Nathaniel Persily, *Can Democracy Survive the Internet?*, 28 J. OF DEMOCRACY 63, 66 (2017).

102. The term originates with Eugene Volokh, *Cheap Speech and What It Will Do*, 104 YALE L. J. 1805 (1995).

103. Richard L. Hasen, *Cheap Speech and What It Has Done (To American Democracy)*, 16 FIRST AMEND. L. REV. 200, 201 (2018).

104. *Id.*

105. Adam Pearce, *Trump Has Spent a Fraction of What Clinton Has on Ads*, N.Y. TIMES (Oct. 21, 2016), https://www.nytimes.com/interactive/2016/10/21/us/elections/television-ads.html.

106. *Id.* at 211 (footnote omitted).

107. Richard H. Pildes, *Participation and Polarization*, 22 J. CONST. L. 341, 347 (2020) (discussing lowered transaction costs in fundraising provided by the internet).

108. *Id.* at 314.

109. Anthony J. Gaughan, *Illiberal Democracy: The Toxic Mix of Fake News, Hyperpolarization, and Partisan Election Administration*, 12 DUKE J. CONST. L. & PUB. POL'Y 57, 59 (2017).

110. *Id.* at 64; *accord id.* at 65 ("The rise of the internet has ended the monopoly exercised by the traditional news media and in the process it has made more information available to more people than ever before.").

111. *Id.* at 82.

112. JENNIFER KAVANAGH & MICHAEL D. RICH, TRUTH DECAY: AN INITIAL EXPLORATION OF THE DIMINISHING ROLE OF FACTS AND ANALYSIS IN AMERICAN PUBLIC LIFE (2018), https://www.rand.org/pubs/research_reports/RR2314.html.

113. *See, e.g.,* Joe Whittaker, Seán Looney, Alastair Reed, & Fabio Votta, *Recommender Systems and the Amplification of Extremist Content*, 10 INTERNET POL. REV. 2 (2021), https://polic yreview.info/articles/analysis/recommender-systems-and-amplification-extremist-content (documenting the effects of YouTube's algorithms in promoting extremist content while noting that the nature of the algorithms makes a difference—Reddit and Gab did not have effects of nearly the same magnitude).

114. JONATHAN RAUCH, THE CONSTITUTION OF KNOWLEDGE: A DEFENSE OF TRUTH 131 (2021). *See also* Zaruhi Hakobyan & Christos Koulovatianos, *Populism and Polarization in Social Media Without Fake News: The Vicious Circle of Biases, Beliefs and Network Homophily* 3 (Nat'l Res. U. Higher Sch. of Econ., Working Paper No. WP BRP 227/EC/2020, 2020), https://papers. ssrn.com/sol3/papers.cfm?abstract_id=3570384 ("Networks make fundamental biases be enhanced by peer-induced amplification factors and these biases lead to more network features that promote these biases, a vicious circle of populist trends."); Arthur Campbell et al., SOCIAL MEDIA AND POLARIZATION 19 (2019), https://papers.ssrn.com/sol3/papers.cfm?abstract_id=3419073 ("We show that either greater connectivity or greater homophily increase[s] the prevalence of niche-market content. . . . The same forces that promote the prevalence of niche-market content tend to also increase polarization."). "Homophily" is a measure of how likely an individual in a network is connected to someone with similar characteristics.

115. Edward L. Glaesar & Cass R. Sunstein, *Extremism and Social Learning*, 1 J. LEGAL ANALYSIS 263, 275 (2009).

116. Mark Scott & Laura Kayali, *What Happened When Humans Stopped Managing Social Media Content*, POLITICO (Oct. 21, 2020), https://www.politico.eu/article/facebook-content-moderation-automation/.

117. *Id.*

118. *Meet the Board*, OVERSIGHT BOARD, https://oversightboard.com/meet-the-board/ (last visited Mar. 21, 2022).

119. Jack M. Balkin, *How to Regulate (and Not Regulate) Social Media*, 1 J. FREE SPEECH L. 71, 81–82 (2021).

120. ROBERT C. POST, DEMOCRACY, EXPERTISE, AND ACADEMIC FREEDOM: A FIRST AMENDMENT JURISPRUDENCE FOR THE MODERN STATE 17 (2012) (tying "democratic competence" to the necessities for democratic self-government).

121. Yasmin Dawood, *Protecting Elections from Disinformation: A Multifaceted Public-Private Approach to Social Media and Democratic Speech*, 16 OHIO ST. TECH. L. J. 1, 7 (2020).

122. *See* Christopher A. Bail et al., *Exposure to Opposing Views on Social Media Can Increase Political Polarization*, 115 PROC. NAT'L ACAD. SCI. 9216, 9220 (2018) (finding that exposure to opposing viewpoints on Twitter resulted in *increased* polarization rather than the would-be expected decrease in polarization); *see also generally* JAMES T. HAMILTON, ALL THE NEWS THAT'S FIT TO SELL (2003) (noting empirical studies that demonstrate that media outlets cater political coverage to the "interests" of their target demographics, a shift away from providing exposure to opposing viewpoints that has arisen out of desires to attract more viewers); *id* at 6 ("News emerges not from individuals seeking to improve the functioning of democracy but from readers seeking diversion, reporters forging careers, and owners searching for profits.").

123. Dawn C. Nunziato, *The Marketplace of Ideas Online*, 94 NOTRE DAME L. REV. 1519, 1545 (2019) (describing the EU Code of Conduct regarding hate speech and social media platforms, and reform proposals).

124. Dawood, *Protecting Elections from Disinformation* at 27.

125. Persily, *Can Democracy Survive the Internet?* at 74; *accord* Dawood, *Protecting Elections from Disinformation* at 24 (citing Abby K. Wood & Ann M. Ravel, *Fool Me Once: Regulating "Fake News" and Other Online Advertising*, 91 S. CAL. L. REV. 1223, 1237, 1245 (2018)) ("There is a conflict of interest at work because online platforms are primarily motivated by a profit motive, rendering them unreliable as self-regulators due to the revenue streams generated by disinformation.").

126. *See* David Morar & Bruna Martins dos Santos, *The Push for Content Moderation Legislation Around the World*, BROOKINGS (Sept. 21, 2020), https://www.brookings.edu/blog/techt ank/2020/09/21/the-push-for-content-moderation-legislation-around-the-world/.

127. Mark S. Kende, *Social Media, the First Amendment, and Democratic Dysfunction in the Trump Era*, 68 DRAKE L. REV. 273, 276 (2020).

128. *See Case Decision 2021-001-FB-FBR*, OVERSIGHT BD. 1–2 (May 5, 2021), https://www.ove rsightboard.com/sr/decision/2021/001/pdf-english ("This was a fraudulent election, but we can't play into the hands of these people. We have to have peace. So go home. We love you. You're very special. You've seen what happens. You see the way others are treated that are so bad and so evil. I know how you feel. But go home and go home in peace.").

129. *Id.* at 2 (noting Facebook claimed the post violated "its Community Standard on Dangerous Individuals and Organizations").

130. *Id.* ("These are the things and events that happen when a sacred landslide election victory is so unceremoniously & viciously stripped away from great patriots who have been badly & unfairly treated for so long. Go home with love & in peace. Remember this day forever!").

131. *Id.* ("Facebook removed this post for violating its Community Standard on Dangerous Individuals and Organizations.").

132. *Id.*

133. *Id.*

134. Richard L. Hasen, *How to Keep the Rising Tide of Fake News from Drowning Our Democracy*, N. Y. TIMES (Mar. 9, 2022), https://www.nytimes.com/2022/03/07/opinion/cheap-speech-fake-news-democracy.html.

135. Brandenburg v. Ohio, 395 U.S. 444, 447 (1969).

136. PETA Deutschland v. Germany, App. No. 43481/09, ¶46 (Nov. 8, 2012), https://hudoc. echr.coe.int/eng?i=001-114273.

137. Scott & Kayali, *What Happened When Humans Stopped Managing Social Media Content* at 116; *see also* Billy Perrigo, *Brazil's Restrictive New Social Media Rules Could Be an Omen for the Future of the Internet*, TIME (Sept. 10, 2021), https://time.com/6096704/brazil-social-media-rules/ (discussing Brazil's social media regulation).

138. U.S. CONST. amend. I.

139. 47 U.S.C. § 230.

140. Nunziato, *The Marketplace of Ideas Online* at 1532 (describing the EU Code of Conduct re-garding hate speech and social media platforms).

141. *Id.* at 1533 (explaining the Network Enforcement Act, colloquially known as NetzDG).

142. *Id.* (internal quotations omitted) (quoting sections of the German Criminal Code referenced by the Network Enforcement Act).

143. *Id.* at 1535 (footnote omitted): ("In addition, critics claim that NetzDG has been enforced arbitrarily and in a politically biased manner, and that the law has had the counterproductive effect of shoring up support for those who have been censored.")

144. *Id.* (referring to Alternative fur Deutschland (AfD), a radical right party in Germany).

145. NetDG is Netzwerkdurchsetzungsgesetz (Network Enforcement Act), Dec. 12, 2017, BMJ, http://www.bmjv.de/SharedDocs/Gesetzgebungsverfahren/Dokumente/NetzDG_engl. pdf?__blob=publicationFile&v=2.

146. Adam Littlestone-Luria, Communications Revolution: Democratic Fragmentation, Content Moderation, and the Intractable Transformation of the Digital Public Sphere at 36 (unpublished manuscript on file with author) (citing Svea Windwehr & Jillian C. York, *Turkey's New Internet Law Is the Worst Version of Germany's NetzDG Yet*, EFF (July 30, 2020), https://www.eff.org/deeplinks/2020/07/turkeys-new-internet-law-worst-version-germa nys-netzdg-yet). ·

147. Shannon Bond & Bobby Allyn, *Russia Is Restricting Social Media. Here's What We Know*, NPR (Mar. 21, 2022), https://www.npr.org/2022/03/07/1085025672/russia-soc ial-media-ban.

148. Michael C. Bender & Georgia Wells, *How the Trump Social-Media Ban Paid Off for Trump, Platforms*, WALL ST. J. (Jan. 9, 2022), https://www.wsj.com/articles/how-the-trump-social-media-ban-paid-off-for-trump-platforms-11641729604.

149. Krakoff, *Big Tech Is Not Big Tobacco*.

150. EMILE DURKHEIM, THE ELEMENTARY FORMS OF RELIGIOUS LIFE (2001).

151. <IBT>Ezra Klein, WHY WE'RE POLARIZED 238 (2020)</IBT> (quoting David Roberts, *Donald Trump and the Rise of Tribal Epistemology*, VOX (May 19, 2017), https://www. vox.com/policy-and-politics/2017/3/22/14762030/donald-trump-tribal-epistemol ogy) (explaining tribal epistemology as only trusting information that is confirmed by or confirms the worldview of an elite or tribe).

152. *Id.* at XV.

153. Steve Charnovitz, *International Standards and the WTO* 11 (George Washington Univ. Law Sch. Pub. Law and Legal Theory, Working Paper No. 133, 2005), https://papers.ssrn.com/ sol3/papers.cfm?abstract_id=694346.

154. Margaret Blair et al., *The Roles of Standardization, Certification and Assurance Services in Global Commerce*, 4 COMP. RES. L & POL. ECON. 1, 26–31 (2008).

155. Adam Thierer, *Fact and Fiction in the Debate Over Video Game Regulation* 4 (Progress & Freedom Found. Progress on Point Paper No. 13.7, 2006), https://papers.ssrn.com/sol3/ papers.cfm?abstract_id=985585.

156. David M. Waguespack & Olav Sorenson, *The Ratings Game: Asymmetry in Classification*, 22 ORG. SCI. 541, 544 (2011).

157. Nunziato, *The Marketplace of Ideas Online* (describing the EU Code of Conduct regarding hate speech and social media platforms).

158. *Id.*

159. *Id.* at 1548 (noting that user-driven alterations to the feed "seem likely to entrench in-formation silos and filter bubbles"). *See also* CHRIS TENOVE ET AL., DIGITAL THREATS TO DEMOCRATIC ELECTIONS: HOW FOREIGN ACTORS USE DIGITAL TECHNIQUES TO UNDERMINE DEMOCRACY 27 (2018), https://papers.ssrn.com/sol3/papers.cfm?abst ract_id=3235819 ("More generally, those who purchase or create computational prop-aganda mechanisms can drown out contributions by other voices on social media platforms.").

160. Persily, *Can Democracy Survive the Internet?* at 74; *accord* Dawood, *Protecting Elections from Disinformation* at 24 ("There is a conflict of interest at work because online platforms are pri-marily motivated by a profit motive, rendering them unreliable as self-regulators due to the revenue streams generated by disinformation.").

161. Matteo Monti, *The New Populism and Fake News on the Internet: How Populism Along with Internet New Media Is Transforming the Fourth Estate* 8, 20 (Sant'Anna Legal Studies, Stals Research Paper 4/2018, 2018).

162. Kende, *Social Media, the First Amendment, and Democratic Dysfunction in the Trump Era; see also* Jack M. Balkin, Lecture, *Information Fiduciaries and the First Amendment*, 49 U.C. DAVIS L. REV. 1183, 1186–87 (2016); Jack M. Balkin & Jonathan Zittrain, *A Grand Bargain to Make Tech Companies Trustworthy*, THE ATLANTIC (Oct. 3, 2016), https://www.theatlantic.com/technology/archive/2016/10/information-fiduciary/502346/.

163. *Id.* (internal quotations omitted) (quoting sections of the German Criminal Code referenced by the Network Enforcement Act).

164. Jonathan Haidt, *Why the Past 10 Years of American Life Have Been Uniquely Stupid*, THE ATLANTIC (Apr. 11, 2022), https://www.theatlantic.com/magazine/archive/2022/05/social-media-democracy-trust-babel/629369/.

165. *Id.*

166. Steve Rathje et al., *Out-Group Animosity Drives Engagement on Social Media*, 118 PNAS 26 (2021), https://www.pnas.org/doi/10.1073/pnas.2024292118.

167. Renée DiResta, *The Supply of Disinformation Will Soon Be Infinite*, THE ATLANTIC (Sept. 20, 2020), https://www.theatlantic.com/ideas/archive/2020/09/future-propaganda-will-be-computer-generated/616400/.

168. Rathje, *Out-Group Animosity* at 5.

169. PEW RESCH. CTR., PARTISAN CONFLICT AND CONGRESSIONAL OUTREACH (2017).

170. Rathje, *Out-Group Animosity* at 7.

171. *Id.*

172. *Id.* at 2, 4–5, 7.

173. *See* ZEYNEP TUFEKCI, TWITTER AND TEAR GAS: THE POWER AND FRAGILITY OF NETWORKED PROTEST ix–xi (2017).

174. MARTIN GURRI, THE REVOLT OF THE PUBLIC AND THE CRISIS OF AUTHORITY IN THE NEW MILLENNIUM (2018).

175. JONATHAN RAUCH, THE CONSTITUTION OF KNOWLEDGE: A DEFENSE OF TRUTH (2021).

176. Jimmy Stamp, *Fact or Fiction? The Legend of the QWERTY Keyboard*, SMITHSONIAN MAGAZINE (May 3, 2013), https://www.smithsonianmag.com/arts-culture/fact-of-fiction-the-legend-of-the-qwerty-keyboard-49863249/.

177. BENJAMIN CONSTANT, THE LIBERTY OF THE ANCIENTS COMPARED WITH THAT OF THE MODERNS 6 (1819).

178. STEPHEN HOLMES, BENJAMIN CONSTANT AND THE MAKING OF MODERN LIBERALISM 33 (1984).

179. THE FEDERALIST NO. 10 (James Madison) (2012) ("The greater number of citizens and extent of territory which may be brought within the compass of republican than of democratic government . . . renders factious combinations less to be dreaded in the former than in the latter.").

180. *See generally* Robert D. Putnam, *Bowling Alone: The Collapse and Revival of American Community* (2001) (describing the disintegration of social structures in the United States).

181. James Fishkin, *Democracy When the People Are Thinking: Deliberation and Democratic Renewal*, 163 AM. PHIL. SOC'Y 1, 1, 4 (2019)

182. *Id.* at 10.

183. *What Is Deliberative Polling?*, STAN. CTR. FOR DELIBERATIVE DEMOCRACY, https://cdd.stanford.edu/what-is-deliberative-polling/ (last visited Jan. 29, 2022).

184. Hélène Landemore, *Democratic Reason, in* COLLECTIVE WISDOM: PRINCIPLES AND MECHANISMS 251, 251–53 (Hélène Landemore & Jon Elster, eds., 2012).

185. *Id.* at 265.

186. *See* Pablo Barberá, *Social Media, Echo Chambers, and Political Polarization, in* SOCIAL MEDIA AND DEMOCRACY: THE STATE OF THE FIELD, PROSPECTS FOR REFORM 35 (Nathaniel Persily & Joshua A. Tucker, eds., 2020) (noting empirical studies finding that "most" political exchanges on social media are between people with "similar ideas," though noting more "cross-cutting" interactions than expected).

187. *See* David M. Estlund, *Opinion Leaders, Independence, and Condorcet's Jury Theorem*, 36 THEORY AND DECISION 131, 138 (1994) (explaining that the "question of independence" in the jury theorem is "whether the several individuals' votes are independent events").

188. *See* Ville Satopää, Marat Salikhov, Philip Tetlock, & Barb Mellers, *Decomposing the Effects of Crowd-Wisdom Aggregators: The Bias-Information-Noise (BIN) Model* (Feb. 8, 2021), https://papers.ssrn.com/sol3/papers.cfm?abstract_id=3781405 (providing a bevy of citations confirming wisdom of the crowds and building models to aggregate predictions and opinions of many individuals).

189. Although, some suggest that sortition's strength shines not in its application as a governance model but in the more limited role of government oversight. *See* Samuel Bagg, *Sortition as Anti-Corruption: Popular Oversight Against Elite Capture*, AM. J. POL. SCI. (https://doi.org/ 10.1111/aips.12704) (manuscript at 1) (arguing that a lottery's power "lies in obstructing elite capture at critical junctures: a narrower task of oversight that creates fewer opportunities for elite manipulation").

190. HÉLÈNE LANDEMORE, OPEN DEMOCRACY: REINVENTING POPULAR RULE FOR THE TWENTY-FIRST CENTURY 11–13 (2020); *see also* Nathan Heller, *The Future of Democracy: Politics Without Politicians*, NEW YORKER (Feb. 19, 2020), https://www.newyorker.com/news/the-future-of-democracy/politics-without-politicians (summarizing Landemore's argument as akin to jury duty in that "every now and then, your number comes up, and you're obliged to do your civic duty—in this case, to take a seat on a legislative body. For a fixed period, it is your job to work with the other people in the unit to solve problems and direct the nation. When your term is up, you leave office and go back to your normal life and work."); Daniel Steinmetz-Jenkins, *Can "Lottocracy" Save Democracy from Itself?*, THE NATION (Sept. 1, 2021), https://www.thenation.com/article/politics/helene-landemore-open-democracy/.

191. D. Clark, *Share of Votes for CDU and SPD in German Elections 1953–2017*, STATISTA (Sept. 23, 2019), https://www.statista.com/statistics/1037985/cdu-and-spd-vote-share-by-elect ion/. To view the underlying French election data, see Manuel Álvarez-Rivera, *Election Resources on the Internet: Presidential and Legislative Elections in France*, ELECTION RES. (last visited Feb. 18, 2022), electionresources.org/fr/.

192. Jennifer McCoy & Benjamin Press, *What Happens When Democracies Become Perniciously Polarized?*, CARNEGIE ENDOWMENT FOR INT'L PEACE (Jan. 18, 2022), https://carneg ieendowment.org/2022/01/18/what-happens-when-democracies-become-perniciously-polarized-pub-86190.

193. *Id.*

194. SAMUEL ISSACHAROFF, PAMELA S. KARLAN, RICHARD H. PILDES, & NATHANIEL PERSILY, THE LAW OF DEMOCRACY: LEGAL STRUCTURE OF THE POLITICAL PROCESS 1210–13 (5th ed., 2016) (discussing Duverger's work on single-member, first-past-the-post systems); *see also* Pamela S. Karlan, *The New Countermajoritarian Difficulty*, 109 CALIF. L. REV. 2323, 2334–35 (2021) (noting the U.S. single-member, first-past-the-post system is one of the reasons "our political system may be incapable of reflecting the new majority").

195. Samuel Issacharoff & Pamela S. Karlan, *The Hydraulics of Campaign Finance Reform*, 77 TEX. L. REV. 1705 (1999).

196. RAYMOND J. LA RAJA & BRIAN F. SCHAFFNER, CAMPAIGN FINANCE AND POLITICAL POLARIZATION: WHEN PURISTS PREVAIL 5 (2015) ("The laws have institutionalized a 'candidate-centered' system of financing, which encourages candidates to reach out to non-party sources for funds.").

197. *Id.* at 9; *accord* Bruce A. Desmarais et al., *The Fates of Challengers in U.S. House Elections: The Role of Extended Party Networks in Supporting Candidates and Shaping Electoral Outcomes*, 59 AM. J. POL. SCI. 194, 196 (2015) ("Despite pursuing somewhat disconnected policies, political actors choose to create a long[-term] coalition that strives to stay together . . . to increase the likelihood that each will achieve their particular goals.").

198. LA RAJA & SCHAFFNER, CAMPAIGN FINANCE AND POLITICAL POLARIZATION at 11.

199. Natalie Andrews & Eliza Collins, *How the Capitol Riot Turned a Partisan Congress "Toxic,"* WALL ST. J. (Dec. 29, 2021), https://www.wsj.com/articles/how-the-capitol-riot-turned-a-partisan-congress-toxic-11640601010.

200. *Id.*

201. Jesse H. Rhodes et al., *Detecting and Understanding Donor Strategies in Midterm Elections*, 71 POL. RES. Q. 503, 503 (2018) (explaining that research suggests that for individual donors "making campaign contributions is a form of consumption . . . [with an] emphasi[s on] the

proximity of a donor's ideology to candidates to whom they contribute"); ZACHARY ALBERT
ET AL., CAMPAIGN FINANCE AND PRIMARY ELECTIONS 37 (2015), https://papers.ssrn.
com/sol3/papers.cfm?abstract_id=2909026 ([It appears that the most ideologically extreme candidates benefit from small donations ... [and] bring out passionate supporters.");
Richard H. Pildes, *Small-Donor-Based Campaign-Finance Reform and Political Polarization*,
YALE L. J. F. (2019) ("The ideological profile for individual donors is bimodal, with most
donors clumped at the 'very liberal' or 'very conservative' poles and many fewer donors
in the center, while the ideological profile of other Americans is not bimodal and features
strong centrist representation.").

202. LA RAJA & SCHAFFNER, CAMPAIGN FINANCE AND POLITICAL POLARIZATION at 51; *cf. id.*
at 110 ("Those who have access to money exercise influence because politicians naturally
depend upon them.").

203. *Id.* at 111.

204. Mike Norton & Richard H. Pildes, *How Outside Money Makes Governing More Difficult*, 19
ELECTION L. J. 486, 500 (2021).

205. *Id.* at 488 ("Although they do not directly control the legislative agenda, [interest group]
influence over members' campaign war chests provides ample ability to sow division within
the caucuses and affect choices regarding which potential bills get killed off.") (citing LAUREL
HARBRIDGE, IS BIPARTISANSHIP DEAD? POLICY AGREEMENT AND AGENDA SETTING IN THE
HOUSE OF REPRESENTATIVES (2015)).

206. Richard H. Pildes, *Focus on Fragmentation, Not Polarization: Re-Empower Party Leadership*,
in SOLUTIONS TO POLITICAL POLARIZATION IN AMERICA 146, 153 (Nathaniel Persily, ed.,
2015)) (explaining that current campaign finance laws have "'drained [parties] of a significant source of funding at the same time that powerful new incentives were created for donors
to send their money to nonparty entities,' emboldening ideological purists and weakening
party pragmatists").

207. LA RAJA & SCHAFFNER, CAMPAIGN FINANCE AND POLITICAL POLARIZATION at 104.

208. Frances McCall Rosenbluth & Ian Shapiro, *Empower Political Parties to Revive Democratic
Legitimacy*, AM. INTEREST (Oct. 2, 2018), https://www.the-american-interest.com/2018/
10/02/empower-political-parties-to-revive-democratic-accountability/.

209. Rucho v. Common Cause, 139 S. Ct. 2484 (2019) (holding claims of partisan gerrymandering
non-justiciable).

210. *See* Richard Pildes, Opinion, *How to Keep Extremists Out of Power*, N.Y. TIMES (Feb. 25,
2021), https://www.nytimes.com/2021/02/25/opinion/elections-politics-extremists.
html (arguing that the primary system contributes to "extreme" candidates by requiring
candidates to take up fringe positions to survive primaries); *see also* RAYMOND J. LA RAJA &
JONATHAN RAUCH, VOTERS NEED HELP: HOW PARTY INSIDERS CAN MAKE PRESIDENTIAL
PRIMARIES SAFER, FAIRER, AND MORE DEMOCRATIC 9 (2021), https://www.brookings.
edu/research/voters-need-help-how-party-insiders-can-make-presidential-primaries-safer-
fairer-and-more-democratic/#part3 ("When a lot of candidates are in the race, it is often
safest to woo purists—who are over-represented as primary voters—by making imprac-
tical promises or extreme appeals."); Nick Troiano, *Party Primaries Must Go*, THE ATLANTIC
(Mar. 30, 2021), https://www.theatlantic.com/ideas/archive/2021/03/party-primaries-
must-go/618428/ (noting that in 2020, only 10 percent of the electorate voted in primaries
and writing that "partisan primaries motivate legislators to keep in lockstep with a narrow
and extreme slice of the electorate").

211. Rosenbluth & Shapiro, *Empower Political Parties to Revive Democratic Legitimacy*.

212. *Id.*

213. *2020 Virginia Election Results*, N.Y. TIMES, https://www.nytimes.com/interactive/2020/11/
03/us/elections/results-virginia.html (last visited Dec. 27, 2021).

214. *Virginia Election Results*, N.Y. TIMES, https://www.nytimes.com/interactive/2021/11/02/
us/elections/results-virginia.html?action=click&pgtype=Article&state=default&module=
styln-elections-2020&region=TOP_BANNER&context=election_recirc (last visited Dec.
27, 2021).

215. Michael Ginsburg, *Lessons Learned: The Strategy and Rationale Behind the 2021 Convention
and Why It Worked: The Convention Process Positioned Glenn Youngkin to Define Himself as His*

Own Man, AM. SPECTATOR (Dec. 17, 2021), https://spectator.org/lessons-learned-the-strat egy-and-rationale-behind-the-2021-convention-and-why-it-worked/.

216. *Alaska Better Elections Implementation*, AL DIV. ELECTIONS, https://www.elections.alaska. gov/Core/RCV.php (last visited Mar. 21, 2022); *see also* Richard H. Pildes, *More Places Should Do What Alaska Did to Its Elections*, N.Y. TIMES (Feb 15. 2022), https://www.nyti mes.com/2022/02/15/opinion/alaska-elections-ranked-choice.html (discussing Alaska's top-four primary system and arguing for expansion to other states).

217. *Mayoral Election in Buffalo, New York (2021)*, BALLOTPEDIA, https://ballotpedia.org/Mayo ral_election_in_Buffalo,_New_York_(2021)#June_22_Democratic_primary_and_af termath (last visited Mar. 21, 2022); *see also* Luis Ferré-Sadurní, *How India Walton Pulled It Off in the Buffalo Mayoral Primary*, N.Y. TIMES (June 23, 2021), https://www.nytimes. com/2021/06/23/nyregion/india-walton-socialist-nyc-primary-buffalo.html (discussing Walton's victory in the low-turnout primary).

218. *Mayoral Election in Buffalo, New York (2021)*, *supra* note 204; *see also* Jesse McKinley, *India Walton Says She's Unlikely to Beat the Write-in Incumbent, Byron Brown, in the Buffalo Mayor's Race*, N.Y. TIMES (Nov. 3, 2021), https://www.nytimes.com/2021/11/03/nyregion/ byron-brown-buffalo-mayor.html (discussing Brown's dominant general election, write-in victory).

Epilogue

1. Robert Rubin & Samuel Issacharoff, *Fair Elections and a Strong Economy: Both Are at Risk*, THE HILL (Sept. 2, 2011), https://thehill.com/opinion/campaign/570535-fair-elections-and-a-str ong-economy-both-are-at-risk?rl=1.

2. *Id.*

3. Reid J. Epstein & Trip Gabriel, *As Michigan G.O.P. Plans Voting Limits, Top Corporations Fire a Warning Shot*, N.Y. TIMES (Apr. 13, 2021), https://www.nytimes.com/2021/04/13/us/polit ics/michigan-voting-rights-republicans.html.

4. *Michigan CEO Executive Chairman Joint Statement on Voting Rights*, SCRIBD (Apr. 13, 2021), https://www.scribd.com/document/502713561/Michigan-CEO-Executive-Chairman- Joint-Statement-on-Voting-Rights#from_embed?campaign=SkimbitLtd&ad_group= 88890X1542029X3453d03d388a92b35ebf388e289699e6&keyword=660149026&source= hp_affiliate&medium=affiliate (signed by executives at companies such as GM, Ford, and Quicken Loans).

5. Martin Reeves, Leesa Quinlan, Mathieu Lefévre, & Georg Kell, *How Business Leaders Can Reduce Polarization*, HARV. BUS. REV. (Oct. 8, 2021), https://hbr.org/2021/10/how-business- leaders-can-reduce-polarization (explaining that polarized consumer bases are not attractive to investors and business).

6. Andrew Edgecliffe-Johnson & Lauren Fedor, *US Companies Condemn Election Fraud "Falsehood" on January 6 Anniversary*, FIN. TIMES (Jan. 6, 2022), https://www.ft.com/content/ 712d9e1a-68dc-451e-a094-0d7db570dfd7.

7. TOM GINSBURG & AZIZ Z. HUQ, HOW TO SAVE A CONSTITUTIONAL DEMOCRACY 166–67 (2019) (discussing alliances in France, Denmark, and Finland between liberal and conserva- tive parties, seeking to prevent power grabs by would-be populist or authoritarian figures).

8. Kori Schake, *Putin Accidentally Revitalized the West's Liberal Order*, THE ATLANTIC (Mar. 1, 2022), https://www.theatlantic.com/international/archive/2022/02/vladimir-putin-ukra ine-invasion-liberal-order/622950/?utm_source=twitter&utm_medium=social&utm_c ampaign=share.

INDEX

For the benefit of digital users, indexed terms that span two pages (e.g., 52–53) may, on occasion, appear on only one of those pages.